The Bobwhite Q...

Classic Upland Tales

Edited by LAMAR UNDERWOOD

Foreword by
GENE HILL
Drawings
by DONALD SHOFFSTALL

THE LYONS PRESS
Guilford, Connecticut
An imprint of The Globe Pequot Press

Library of Congress Cataloging-in-Publication Data

The Bobwhite quail book : classic upland tales / edited by Lamar
Underwood ; foreword by Gene Hill ; drawings by Donald Shoffstall.
        p. cm.
Originally published: Clinton, N.J. : Amwell Press, 1980.
        ISBN 1-59228-419-1 (trade pbk)
1. Quail shooting. I. Underwood, Lamar.

SK325.Q2B6 2004
799.2'46273—dc22
                                        2004048913

CONTENTS

FOREWORD

OVER THE PAST few years I have spent enough time in various hunting camps with Lamar Underwood to have amassed about twelve-thousand dollars in gin rummy I.O.U.s. One of the reasons for my outstanding success is that Lamar spent so much time talking about the South and quail hunting that he forgot to knock when he should have, which is dangerous for anyone who plays a man with my legendary mathematical gifts.

But along with all this non-negotiable paper came several facts; among them the realization that Lamar is among the most passionate quail men I've ever met and that he has the most singular memory for what has been written on the subject of anyone I'll ever know. As you'll see, Lamar has an eye for word paintings that's most discerning, most literary and along with all that, a feel for the necessary salt of humor or humanity that makes him judge and jury, as far as I'm concerned, as to what a good quail story ought to be.

Lamar Underwood is about to take you along on the best quail hunts in our literary history. You'll see the good dogs, the bad and the indifferent. You'll smell the powder, feel the wind and sense the love and understanding we all have for this small brown bird. What we have here is an *appreciation* for a sport that transcends all the parts . . . giving us a whole of emotion that's very akin to a religion since men and dogs discovered what quail are here on earth for.

You'll find all your old favorites here and make some new friends as well. And if somewhere along the line you don't get an irresistible urge to reach down and pet a hunting buddy or walk over to the gun cabinet and swing your sweet-handling 20-bore or at least have a touch of bourbon and branch then you're not really a quail hunter.

When I finished this book I sat back, closed my eyes and had a sweet vision of a shambles of a hunting car pulling up in my driveway, imperiously honking for me to hurry along, and when I tucked a gun under my arm, called for Lady or Jess and ran out to climb aboard, there was Mr. Babcock, Mr. Ruark and Mr. Nash waiting to take me to dreamland. It was lovely.

I wish you, too, all joys of the hunt. And here they are in the proper time and the perfect places—set in the soft amber of forever . . . just waiting for you to come along.

GENE HILL
Robinwood Farm

INTRODUCTION

EVERY YEAR I tell myself things will be different, but I can never bring that to be.

Long before a certain winter dawn, with the headlights of my pickup truck making eerie splashes on the mossy beards that hang from the oaks along a narrow country lane, I will pull into a clearing and switch off the engine. Then, with even a promise of the dawn's glow still at least half an hour away and my heart already pounding like a kid's at Christmas, I sit amid the sounds of impatient whines and shufflings from the dog box, the tick of cooling metal from the engine, and the hoots of owls from farther down the swamp. Why, I ask myself, have I rushed up on the day in this unnecessary and zealous way? The coveys of bobwhite quail that loom in my thoughts will not be moving on this very cold morning until the sun is bright on the pines and warm on the grassy patches that have sheltered the nightly huddles of the birds. There will be no trails for the pointer dogs, Mack and Jumper, to work on for some time yet. I leave the question of impatience unanswered and reach for the thermos of coffee. The cup is warm in my hand, and a pleasant flush of warmth spreads through my body with each sip. I have come around to my day of days again. I am grateful that this is so, and I will use it all, every hour. I simply like beginning it this way.

I trace a mental map of this place I have chosen to hunt today, my mind touching visions of fields, woods edges, creek bottoms, timbered swamps. The coveys of bobwhites that range throughout these areas are old friends. But their ways are familiar only to a certain point of logic. Beyond what I know to be dependable patterns of movement based on feed, weather and terrain, there will be situations where my understanding of these things, and even the great noses of my dogs, will undoubtedly be no match for the vagaries of the habits of the birds. We will face perplexing failures and hope to unravel the problems with a bit of real and mental footwork.

Early in the season, failure to find a familiar covey touches off that nagging ache that perhaps something has happened to them. Then, to change the normal pattern of your hunt, to be rewarded by a point and know that you've still got that covey, that it has not gone out of the country, out of your life—that's the sweetest part of the day.

An explosion of impatient movement and whining from the dog box forces me to think about the puppy, Jumper, and the effect he will have on this day, this season. I have not had time to put in the pre-season work I had hoped for him. Whelped in the late summer of the year before, he had missed the hunting of his first year, except for some late-season romping. Now the time had come for him to begin the serious work that would turn his great potential into the talents of his effective sire, Mack.

Hunts with the old dog, I knew, would be a strong force in the molding of the youngster. If only the strength and eagerness did not turn into uncontrollable wildness. I had been pleased with our yard drills and the small amount of field practice I had seen, but I remembered well all those times in my life when I had failed to establish touch with other young dogs and ended up losing important areas of ability that should have been developed strongly. I felt what I had learned could help Jumper. Those earlier puppies had trained *me*.

The sun edged on up to burn red through the pines but still I lingered at the truck, walking about a bit, another cup of coffee feeling great against the bite of the cold. The day held the promise of fairness, with little wind. I took out the gun case, pulled the little 20-gauge double from its fleece-lined nest, and fondled the familiar lines and creases of its metal and the smooth, deep touch of the walnut stock and forearm. It came to my shoulder easily as I downed an imaginary right and left. Then I could wait no longer, and I shucked my jacket, really feeling cold but knowing my wool shirt would be sufficient as I walked into the warming morning. I picked up my shell vest and shrugged into its familiar, weighty heft. A separate thermos and the bulk of two sandwiches and an apple bulged through the canvas.

I stepped to the rear of the truck and fumbled with the latch on the dog box. Pandemonium ensued. Then there was a blurry rush of white as Mack and Jumper stormed out and began cavorting through the usual rituals of muscle-loosening excitement while I tried to keep them under some semblance of control with a voice that shattered the morning stillness.

We stepped out across the sandy lane and into a cathedral-like stand of enormous pines. Mack and Jumper raced across the broad, pine-needled expanse under the trees. Jays scolded from the branches and a flock of crows flapped away, complaining of our presence. I could hear squirrels crashing in the adjacent swamp. The morning was coming to life, but I expected no quail here. The ground beneath the pines was open and easy for walking, a good place for the dogs to settle down a bit during the few minutes it would take us to reach the tattered line of the corn and soybean field that I could see far ahead through the trees. Up there, in the field or in the cover alongside, I hoped to strike the season's first covey.

The puppy hit the edge of the field at something like a semi-gallop. He bounded over the fence and crashed away through the corn. The veteran Mack paid these antics no heed and worked down the fencerow and through the pines and gallberries in a smooth, easy lope that is his way of going. Jumper responded to my first disciplinary cry to "Hunt Close!" and we were a three-some again, the dogs flashing white in the sun as we slowly moved down the line of trees. "Any time now," I thought. "We must be very close."

But we went on for awhile, the sun warming on my shoulders, the dogs moving steadily. Had the covey flown to the corn? Many of the bevies throughout the range I was to hunt that day were not above that depressing tactic, but the covey I sought now had usually moved about on a predictable basis. No, I decided. Fifty yards more, then we'll bend back deeper into the pines and hunt back the other way. If we still don't nail them, I'll put both dogs in the corn and work all the way down the field. They're right here, somewhere. Mack went out of sight around a tallish clump of gallberries. I was about to whistle him back and begin our turn when I saw Jumper freeze solid, then go into a low crouch and start easing in Mack's direction. "Whoa!" I yelled, hurrying on.

Good old Mack. Somewhere up there he was locked up solid, and the young dog had him in sight and was going to back him.

Well, maybe he was—because now he was moving in that catlike crouch again. "Whoa, sir!" That stopped him and he stood as though carved from granite. Then, heart pounding, I had Mack in view, and he had 'em all right. Boy, he looked solid, head up into the wisp of a breeze, tail curving skyward. Slowing to a more reasonable and unexcited pace, I watched Jumper carefully, thinking: "You mess this up and I'll stomp you." Then thinking, "No I won't!" but hoping all the time that it was all going to work and wondering, for what seemed like the millionth time in my life, just why I could never see a covey point without nearly having a heart seizure. My hands seemed to shake and felt sweaty, and the gun had become some strange, unwieldy club.

Directly in front of Mack, an old blowndown pine sprawled in the frost-glistened grass. Scattered dead branches and clumps of brown needles carpeted the ground along the rotting carcass of the once mighty trunk. I came up to the dog. He did not move as I stepped past him. The rush of wings I expected failed to occur. Tension hung over the scene like a fog. Moving slightly to the side, I stepped around the log. A feathery explosion erupted in my face. The covey was away in a total, sudden rush. Brownish forms were hurtling through the pines, sickeningly fast, it seemed, as I sought to get the broad plane of the double pointed at one bird. Then I wasn't seeing the gun anymore, only the bird, only a blurry form that somehow had become so distinct that all the others were forgotten. As the gun jarred against my shoulder, the bird folded. I was trying to find another one but couldn't do it as he ducked behind a pine. Then I panicked and merely poked a shot in his direction as he curved back into view. He flew on strongly, and I watched them all go that way, 12 maybe 15 birds faraway in the pines now, setting their wings for the long glide into the cover along the creek.

Mack had my bird in his mouth and was trotting it to me, while Jumper needlessly vacuumed the area with his nose for other possibilities. I liked the way the smoking barrels smelled as I opened the double, then the tight snick as I closed it with fresh shells. Then I took the first quail of the year from Mack's chops. The season was on again!

As much as I love it, my bobwhite quail hunting lately has been under the considerable strain of change. Mister Bob, it seems to me, has become a sly fugitive, haunting dreary creek swamps and capable of mischievous disappearing acts. That once-obliging little fellow that walked from cover to feed, then picked its way leisurely through the corn or bean patch, now *flies* on such missions. A gentleman he is not, as my friend Gene Hill so aptly points out in one of the chapters ahead.

Two big changes in quail habitat have been reshaping the character of my favorite bird.

The modern agriculture combine is an efficient machine that helps put food on our tables. However, despite the claims of my farmer-cousin—"I can set that thing up so that a chicken walking along behind it would starve to death!"—the machine does leave some spillage. Breakfasting or dining bobwhites can literally feed in minutes, then melt back into some gloomy tangle, leaving little or no trail for a bird dog to pick up. The bird's favorite haunts, thanks to restrictions on burning and unlimited grazing, have become jungles of vines, high bushes, briers. Only Tarzan and his chimp could hunt them.

To cope, I've just about stopped thinking about open-field coveys. I keep my dogs in the woods or along the ragged edges of the fields. My odds of rendezvousing with a few coveys are considerably improved. Naturally, under such conditions my shooting average has dropped, but I get action.

After the *blam, blam* of the covey rise, I measure my chances of locating the singles carefully before committing the dogs to hunt in that direction. Another covey may be easier to find than coping with singles scattered in five acres of impenetrable cypress swamp. My blood pressure can fare nicely without the boost given by bumped birds whirring away unseen and my shouts at my dogs, also unseen, during thirty or so minutes spent floundering after singles. No, unless I like the setup, I'm off to find another covey.

The trick in hunting the swamp coveys is to accept the fact that you have to have close-working dogs and you must move slowly. I try to relax and pick my way through the tangles as best I can. My gun hand is bare, but I wear a glove on my left hand—not against the chill but to grasp and ward off vines and briers. When the covey goes, I'll fire through the brush at any glimpse of a bird. Sometimes it works.

Two, maybe three times a year, I get really lucky and run into wide-open covey rises, the kind outdoor artists paint, which keep you dreaming. In that dream, the dogs are standing like statues as you walk up. The birds are away against the wide blue sky, and two feathery puffs appear as the gun speaks. The retrieves are perfect.

Sometimes when I catch myself or my friends launching into a catalogue of complaints about the modern quail hunting condition, my mind slips back to boyhood days when my elders were voicing the same complaints. Even in those days of bountiful, obliging coveys and dogs that were super stars, things were seldom perfect.

And the memories that we treasure of our favorite game bird are cut from the same varied tapestry. They are mostly little moments of the richness of our encounters—hits and misses, the perplexing problems of locating certain coveys, heroic and interesting dog work along with aggravating and frustrating dog work, the fellowship of our friends, the smother-fried treasure that waits on the table as we lift our glasses high. We remember them all and, God willing, will build upon them to whatever extent we can.

If you feel that way about your quail shooting—regardless of how it might have slipped in quality—this book should be an enriching experience for you.

Over the years that I worked as editor-in-chief of *Sports Afield* and *Outdoor Life,* I became fascinated with all the literature of my favorite sport. In poking around among a lot of dusty pages, and in reviewing the works of contemporary writers, I built up an appreciation for certain authors and pieces. That's why I was so delighted when Jim Rikhoff asked me to put a quail book together. Now I have the opportunity to share with bobwhite aficionados everywhere all the great tales that have been such close and rewarding fireside companions over the years. Many were published in obscure, hard-to-find sources, and their existence will come as a pleasant surprise; others are better known. Together they form a picture of quail hunting and hunters that, hopefully, will draw you to these pages again and again.

Jim and I were in agreement at he beginning of the project: We did not want to do one of those "How to Be a Better Quail Hunter" type of book. There's plenty of how-to here, all right. And you may indeed come away a better quail hunter. That's just one of the rewards you'll bag from sharing the experiences and memories of the writers who have captured the drama and mysteries of days afield with America's greatest gamebird.

SHOFFSTALL

ACKNOWLEDGMENTS

FOR ARRANGEMENTS made with various authors, their representatives and publishers, where copyrighted material was permitted to be reprinted, and for the courtesy extended by them, the following acknowledgments are gratefully made:

Henry Holt and Company, New York, and *Field & Stream* Magazine, New York: "The Brave Quail" by Robert C. Ruark from *Field & Stream* and from *Field and Stream Treasury,* Henry Holt and Company; "You Separate the Men from Boys" by Robert C. Ruark from *Field & Stream* and *The Old Man and the Boy,* Henry Holt and Company.

E. P. Dutton, New York, and *Sports Afield* Magazine, New York: "My Respects to Mr. Bob" by Gene Hill, from *Sports Afield* and *Hill Country,* E. P. Dutton. Reprinted by permission of the author. Oxmoor House, Inc., Birmingham, Alabama, for: "What Is a Quail Hunter?" by Charley Dickey from the book *Charley Dickey's Bobwhite Quail Hunting.* Article originally appeared in *Field & Stream* Magazine and is reprinted by permission of the author.

Georgia Department of Natural Resources for: "The Bobwhite as an Individual" by Charles Elliott. Reprinted by permission.

Archibald Rutledge and *Sports Afield* Magazine, New York, for: "The Enemies of Quail" by Archibald Rutledge; also "Quail of the Kalmias," *The American Hunter.* Reprinted by permission.

Warren Page and *Field and Stream* Magazine, New York, for: "To Hit a Quail in the Tail" by Warren Page. Reprinted by permission of the author's estate.

Mrs. Alice Babcock and the estate of Havilah Babcock for: The following articles which originally appeared in *Tales of Quails 'n Such,* published in 1951 by Greenburg Publisher, New York: "How to Miss Birds," "Sometimes You Can't Find Them," "Slim Boggins' Mistake," "The Old Maid." Reprinted by permission. Winchester Press, New York, for: "The London Gun" by Robert Brister from *Moss, Mallards and Mules* by Robert Brister. Reprinted by permission. "The Sundown Covey" by Lamar Underwood from *Hunting Moments of Truth,* edited by Eric Peper and Jim Rikhoff, reprinted by permission of the author. "A Private Affair" by Colonel Harold P. Sheldon from *The Tranquillity Stories,* reprinted by permission.

Charles Scribner's Sons, New York, for: "Mollie," by Paul Hyde Bonner, from *The Glorious Mornings* by Paul Hyde Bonner. Reprinted by permission.

The estate of Nash Buckingham for: The following Nash Buckingham stories: "Bobwhite Blue! Bobwhite Gray!" and "Play House," from *De Shootinest Gent'man,* G. P. Putnam's Sons, New York; "Bobs of the Bayou Bank," from *Mark Right!,* G. P. Putnam's Sons, New York; "Carry Me Back," from *Hallowed Years,* The Stackpole Company, Harrisburg, Pennsylvania; "Pipeline 'Pottiges,'" from *De Shootinest Gent'man and Other Hunting Tales,* Thomas Nelson & Sons, New York. Reprinted by permission.

Field and Stream Magazine, New York, for: "The Mystery of Scent" by Ray P. Holland. Reprinted by permission.

Thomas Nelson & Sons, New York, for: "Jack" by Ray P. Holland from *Seven Grand Gun Dogs* by Ray P. Holland. Reprinted by permission.

James C. Rikhoff for "They Only Shoot Cockbirds in Carolina" from *The National Sporting Annual,* reprinted by permission of author.

Field and Stream Magazine and Doubleday & Company, Inc., New York, for: "Quail of the Eastern Sho'" by A. R. Beverley-Giddings, from *Field and Stream* and the *Field and Stream Reader,* Doubleday. Reprinted by permission.

Tom Kelly and *Outdoor Life* Magazine, New York, for: "The Home Covey" by Tom Kelly. Reprinted by permission of the author.

William Humphrey and William Morrow & Co., New York, for: "The Shell," originally published in *The Last Husband and Other Stories* by William Humphrey, published by William Morrow & Co. Reprinted by permission of the author.

G. P. Putnam, New York, for: "End of A Perfect Day" by Horace Lytle, from *Gun Dogs Afield,* 1942. Reprinted by permission.

Dial Press, New York, for: "The Biscuit Eater" by James Street, from *Short Stories,* 1945. Reprinted by permission.

A. A. Wyn, Incorporated, New York, for: "The Hunting Coat" by Paul Annixter, from *Brought to Cover,* by Paul Annixter. Reprinted by permission.

Lifestyle of the Upland King

THE BRAVE QUAIL

Robert C. Ruark

The publication of this piece in Field & Stream *in December,* 1951, *was of special significance in outdoor journalism. First, it brought to quail hunters everywhere the freshest, brightest profile of their favorite bird ever written. And, perhaps even more importantly, it marked Robert Ruark's professional turning point. Ruark had been a nationally known syndicated newspaper columnist when he had made his first safari to Africa in* 1950. *The experience changed his life. He began writing* Horn of the Hunter, *the magnificent book that captures all the action and emotions of that safari, and individual articles for* Field & Stream. *His relationship with* Field & Stream *that began with "The Brave Quail" led to the creation of the "Old Man and the Boy" series. (Those pieces have been collected in two hard-cover books published by Holt, Rinehart and Winston.) His love affair for Africa led to the novels* Something of Value *and* Uhuru *and to some of the hunting sections in his other two novels,* Poor No More *and* The Honey Badger. *All are excellent reads and I highly recommend them.*

In many ways, Ruark's life reminds me of Jack London. Both were bright, shooting stars, destined to be extinguished quickly. Ruark, who loved and lived life to the fullest, died of illness in 1965 *at the age of* 50. *But he left behind many precious gifts, including this, the one that started it all.*

LET'S SAY it's a nice crisp autumn day, with the sun warm and the breeze winy, and you are approaching a copse of brier and leveled timber on a high hill with pine trees growing on it. One of your dogs is cantering easily, nose proudly in air, with a cock to his ears that convinces you he knows where he is heading. The other dog is circling rapidly, nose to ground, and all of a sudden both hit happily on a strange sort of radar beam. The nose-in-the-air dog wriggles down close to the earth and performs a hula with his hips. The circling dog crowds into the act, and the contest is suddenly clear. One of those dogs will freeze, and may even lift his right, left, front or hind foot. His tail will either stick straight up or straight behind him like a baton. And it will not quiver.

Whichever dog to lose the contest will honor the winner by dropping and freezing.

The man walks up behind the dog. His face is white. He sweats. His hands are shaking. His heart is pounding a rumba-beat. He is carrying a shotgun, generally with a 26-to 28-inch barrel. The gauge of the gun is an index to the ability of the man to prove his manhood at that moment. If it is a 12-gauge, he is so-so at his business. If it is a 16, he is pretty good. If it's a 20-gauge he is excellent, and if it's a .410 he is bragging.

This man's mouth is cottony. At the very moment he feels like a bull-fighter awaiting a *toro bravo,* a big-game hunter preparing to meet an African buffalo's charge, a soldier verging on a desperate destruction of a machine-gun emplacement. His reflexes are cocked, and his reputation is at stake. Also, his stomach is full of squirrels.

He prods the hummocks with a foot, and possibly the dogs sneak ahead to freeze again. The man draws his breath sharply inward. He kicks again. Nothing happens. Again. Nothing. The dogs inch forward.

The man scuffs his boot. The lead dog switches his snout and points it downward. The man says the old cliché: *This is it.* He kicks, and the world erupts around him. The noise has something of the sound of an exploding land-mine, something of the rapid belch of an Oerlikon 20-millimeter. It is otherwise indescribable.

Small birds burst from the ground. They take off in all directions. They are traveling at more than 40 miles an hour, and they present a target as large as a big orange. If they are to be killed they must be killed before they have traveled 60 yards, and if the cover is heavy they may need to be shot within 20 yards. They may have to be shot from the hip, or off the biceps, or even off the nose.

First, though, the gunner must select a bird from the thundering mass of rocketing fowl, because the man who shoots into the brown takes home no meat. A split-second selection must be made. The quail comes into the eye, the gun goes under the eye, the trigger is pressed, and if the man is good the bird drops in a shower of feathers. If the man is very good, he then switches to another bird, which he selects from the speeding gang, and fires again. If he is very, *very* good, another bird drops.

Then the man turns around with his face split by a grin. He pats the dogs as they fetch the dead game. He lights a cigarette, and for a moment he is Belmonte, the bull-fighter. He is Dwight Eisenhower. He is Clark Gable. He is the late Frank Buck. He is David, standing over the prostrate form of Goliath. He is one hell of a big guy—to himself, if he is alone—to the others, if he is accompanied.

This is because, using the ancient Chinese invention of gunpowder, a great deal of luck and the skill of his dogs, he has just killed a couple of creatures that, while delicious to chew on, can be consumed in a couple of munches. He has just slain a little bird called a quail, bobwhite, or partridge, according to where he lives.

The American bobwhite quail has never been known to attack a man, even in defense of its young. Yet the dictionary lists a verb, "to quail," which means to curdle or coagulate. This curdling and coagulation occurs each fall, according to local game laws, when big brave men, armed with shotguns, step past a pointing dog and await the roaring rush of wings that signal the take-off of a little speckled brown bird that is prey to hawks, eagles, cats, foxes, rain, drought, high grass, low grass and man himself. Man—armed man—is scared stiff of the quail. He is easily as frightened as the *matador de toros* who faces the bull in the *corrida* on a sunny afternoon. After all, the *torero* will only be scared by a maximum of three bulls. Quail, on the other hand, get up in flocks.

Some twenty-five million quail die annually in this nation in order to prove that a man is superior to a bird. The quail breeds well; a couple of clutches will build a covey up to twenty-five. He sticks to his own ground. The "same" covey will inhabit the same acreage for years if sufficient seed birds are left to rear a family. As a child I shot the great-great-great-great-grandchildren of my first feathered friends in the four acres that comprised my own backyard. But he is not too long for this world unless he is rigidly protected. Weather, varmints, mankind and the auto have conspired to make him a potential candidate for extinction, except in areas where he is conserved by law and human consideration.

The quail has never been satisfactorily explained in terms of his relationship to man, his peculiar fascination *for* man, or the occasional nobility or fraud he inspires *in* man. He seems to have been created especially for his catalytic approach to the genus *Homo*, and comes off heavily best by comparison.

You may say, for a start, that as a result of association with quail all quail shooters are liars. They are also braggarts, when the opportunity allows, but they are self-apologists and ingrowing liars first. Quail shooters do not merely lie to other people. They lie first to themselves. I know this because I am a quail shooter, raised in the company of quail shooters.

By the same standard you will rarely find a dedicated quail shot who is not a pretty nice guy. He has to be a nice guy, because he is performing for the benefit of the dogs, himself and his companions, and all are expert in the detection of fraudulent behavior in the field. Lying afterward is permissible; ducking the basic conflict between bird and man is not. A man who comports himself shoddily in the presence of quail is stoned in the trade marts and derided in the taverns. Friendships have been broken when one friend detected an unpleasantness in his buddy's approach to quail.

Mr. Bernard M. Baruch, the millionaire elder statesman, is fond of saying that there are two things a man cannot abide being kidded about: his prowess with the ladies and his ability to shoot quail. Mr. Baruch is a fair expert on both matters, especially on the latter. He has been a passionate quail shooter for something like 65 years, and is, at 81, possibly the best senior quail assassin in the land.

Mr. Baruch shoots quail three months a year. For the past 50-odd he has shot them in the vicinity of Kingstree, South Carolina, where he has leased and maintained thousands of acres near-by his plantation, Hobcaw Barony. Shooting quail, to Mr. Baruch, is a grave ritual, and he claims that his longevity is largely due to the sport. It has kept him active long after his contemporaries have retired to the bath-chair.

The old gentleman takes his quail a touch more seriously than he used to regard the stock market, and his millions attest that he never approached the market on a frivolous basis. There is no levity about B. M. B. when the subject of quail comes up, although he can kid about the other shooting sports, and long ago gave up duck and turkey shooting.

Quail killing at Mr. Baruch's is regarded as the top shooting privilege in the nation today. General Omar Bradley shoots birds with Baruch, as do a gross of other citizens with recognizable handles. Mr. Baruch coddles his birds as other rich folk look after jewels.

The preservation of his quail is a local industry. His acres are constantly patrolled by a fleet of overseers, under the strong hand of a Mr. David McGill, who does not shoot quail himself. Cats, run wild, are exterminated. Bounties are paid on varmints. At the end of the season the woods are burnt free of underbrush, so that the little birds will not be trapped in the matted grasses. Poaching is more of a sin in that neighborhood than voting Republican. Clutches of eggs are lifted from the wet spots to higher ground.

I do believe Mr. Baruch would shoot a man who would shoot a sitting quail, and I am certain he would fire any friend who ever exceeded the South Carolina limit of 15 birds per day. He limits the number of birds to be killed in any one covey to three, on a given day. Although he shoots six days a week for three months every year, his birds are rarely shot over more than twice, or three times at most. In this way Mr. Baruch maintains a backlog of birds that is almost unknown in a country in which indiscriminate shooting is ruining the bobwhite.

Mr. Baruch does not approve of more than one gun per party, so that each hunter starts out with his own entourage. At the moment the old boy runs three rigs. They consist of Mr. McGill, who generally takes over B. M. B.'s personal safari, and two Negro boys, and two other sets of three men each.

Dave McGill rides a horse and handles the dogs. The two colored lads have separate functions—one marks down the dead birds and the other watches where the singles fly. They are usually mounted on mules.

Mr. Baruch rides a horse, as does his nurse, Elizabeth Navarro, who sometimes goes along with him. Miss Navarro is not a quail shot, yet. She shoots squirrels with a .22 rifle, but since she has acquired a little mansion of her own, close to the quail grounds, she is beginning to make noises like a quail *aficionada*.

It is a remarkable sight to see an 81-year-old man fork a horse, ride him three hours in an afternoon and alight as much as fifty times in that day, and still best most of his guests with the gun.

Mr. Baruch is 81, after all, and he is deaf as a post, and when he shoots he does not wear a hearing aid. Most quail shooting is based on the association of sound and movement. A bird roars up to your right, your left, or behind you, and you whirl and gun him down—or miss him, as the case may be. Anything that does not rise in front of Mr. Baruch he does not shoot at, because he must depend entirely on sight. This cuts off a good 60 per cent of his possible shots.

Yet the old gent consistently comes home with the best part of his limit, and will often bring in the full 15—more than the combined score of his best-shooting guest. His record of 15 birds in 17 shots he recently bettered by 15 birds in 13 shots, an amazing score for anybody, and utterly incredible for a four-score old man with no hearing to help him.

Fifty per cent is considered excellent in quail shooting A man who can average 30 per cent, for shells expended, is good. Sixty per cent is fantastic, except among pothunters, and 75 per cent is nearly unheard of. Getting a limit at all, even with the profusion of game that Baruch's grounds boast, is a signal for champagne at the big house.

Yet the senior statesman frequently kills *three* birds on a covey rise. He shoots a double-barreled 16-gauge. He likes to take a pot at the outriding cock bird as it roars aloft to signal the rest of the flock. Then he swiftly breaks the gun, ejects the spent cartridge, and blasts twice at the main herd as they jet themselves away. Often as not he is successful.

On the long ride back home Mr. Baruch does not talk atom bomb, world affairs, or finance. He talks quail. It is a peculiar fascination of bird-for-man that even rubs off on the help, who are not allowed to shoot. When a guest comes in after a good day, all hands beam. When a guest comes in after a sour day, all hands are silent and respectful, as at a wake. This is a time-hallowed treatment of the wing-shot. *Never cross a hunter when his timing is off* is ingrained in the tradition.

My friend Ely Wilson, a pleasant Negro gentleman who runs my hunt when I am lucky enough to go down to South Carolina, falls into a fit of desperation for hours if the dogs are not working well, or if I am in my usual state of firing much and dropping little. Ely would stay up all night to look for a bird that is known to be shot down but is difficult to find. On at least one occasion I have watched him search for an hour in a swamp looking for a crippled bird that the best retriever in the world, a nondescript and now deceased critter named Joe, had given up on. Ely finally found the cripple in a creek, and caught him with his hands. There is a lack of nobility in the man if he goes away and leaves a wounded quail. Ely is so good that on one occasion he finally found a highly rumpled corpse of a quail that General Bradley had shot two weeks before. The bird had lodged in a tree.

"I lost him once," Ely said, "but I just *knew* that bird was around here somewhere."

Not many hunters are lucky enough to indulge themselves under such luxe circumstances as the men who have made a hobby of creating their own game preserves, but the thrill of chasing the bobwhite is as great for the poor man as for the tasseled tycoon. Hundreds of thousands of quail shooters achieve the same sensation when the little brown bazooka takes off under their feet—a sort of delicious momentary terror followed by triumph or despair. The satisfaction of the autumn day, the working dog, the dramatic moment of point is as great for a small boy with a mongrel and a 10-dollar smokepole as for the well-heeled big shot with the hand-carved Purdey or Greener or Sauer shotgun.

Some people step into their backyards to shoot quail; others spend thousands of dollars annually for the same privilege. But they all share one defect of character; all quail shooters are abject liars. I know, for I have been lying steadily about quail and bird dogs since I was eight, and got physically sick from excitement when I killed my first one.

The quail shooter's mind works roughly like this:

They aren't making the same kind of cartridges any more, because when you point them at the bird the bird won't drop. Obviously something wrong with the powder.... The sun was in my eyes.... The damn bird flew around a branch just as I shot.

The dogs have lost their sense of smell.... The rabbit hounds ran up all the quail.... One of the other hunters was in the way, or I would have killed two.... It was getting too dark to shoot with safety.

All the birds got up wild, away ahead of the dogs.... I slipped and fell.... I had a headache and my timing was off.... When I was going good after the first two coveys, we couldn't find any more for an hour and I cooled off.

The safety on my gun jammed.... The little single dog won't backstand a point any more.... The woods were too thick.... The birds wouldn't hold to a point.

These are the things you tell yourself. You tell other people that you only used half as many shells as you really used, and then you say that you had to run down a couple of wounded birds and shoot some more.

You impugn the honor of the retrievers. You mention that you shot at least half a dozen you didn't bring home, but the dog's nose was off, or the bird fell in a swamp, or they are making the birds tougher now than they used to. Then you find that you are counting in the birds that you didn't collect with your full total. I have known men who could go to any bank and walk out with a colossal loan, on their face alone, to callously raise the total of their quail bag by 50 per cent a couple of days later, and for no reason except the salving of their ego. And remember, a quail is not a rhinoceros. It is less than a half pound of flesh and feathers.

The quail shot also lies about the dogs he has known. Such as my old Llewellin setter Frank, long gone to his fathers, result of hanging himself as he tried to hurdle a fence to get at something comely in the way of a gal-dog. Frank was an expert in the quail profession. Today I wouldn't believe myself under oath when I talk about old Frank of Tennessee.

Frank was a connoisseur of shooters. If you were going good, Frank would cooperate. That's to say, Frank would work. If you were shooting badly, Frank would go home. I missed thirteen straight shots one day, and finally, in desperation, took a crack at a bird that had roosted in a tree. This is unusual behavior for quail, and for me, too. I missed the bird in the tree.

Frank took one look at me and sneered. He went home, and refused to hunt for a week. I could take him out into the fields, but he would just sit and sneer.

Frank was what is known as a force-broken retriever. That means he didn't like to fetch things for the sheer love of it, but had been induced to retrieve by rigid training. Frank never so much as wet a bird, let alone crush one. He would come with the quail hanging limply from his lower lip, and he would rear up, put his paws on my chest, and nudge the bird inside my hunting jacket.

One day I was training a pointer puppy named Tom, who was fast as Jackie Robinson, and this adolescent upstart beat Frank to a point. Birds roared up. I shot and killed one. Held onto the old dog to give the youngster a sense of gratification in his work. Puppy found the dead bird and retrieved him faultlessly. I patted the puppy. Told him he was a fine, noble puppy. Old dog looked at me and glared.

Then the puppy found a couple of single birds. Shot again—I was going good that day—and another bird dropped. Again held the old dog to let the puppy strut his stuff, which he did. Old dog glared some more.

Then Frank, the old codger, found another single. Bird got up and I killed him. Frank went and got his own bird. He brought the bird to me and looked up. He said a variety of things, all profane, with his eyes.

Then he bit the bird in two pieces. He spat the bird out on the ground. Then he turned on his heel and stalked off. He didn't speak to me for a week afterward. This was a dog I have seen point a covey with a dead bird in his mouth. This was a dog that I have seen hold one bird in his mouth and press another, wounded bird onto the ground with his foot.

At least I believe I have. Us liars are never quite sure later.

This Frank, a setter, was the all-round best gun dog I ever saw, in general savvy, but he was not much better than Sam, a big young pointer operated by Mr. Henry Nelson of Kingstree, South Carolina, or the late Joe, owned by my friend Ely of the same community. It does not make too much difference about the breed. Joe was a hodgepodge of nothing much, but on his good days he could make a bum out of anything with Ch. in front of his handle. On one exceptional day when Joe found everything except Adolf Hitler, his boss got off the horse and briefly placed Joe in the saddle.

"This dog too good to have to walk between coveys," Ely said.

A couple of liars I know in Fort Lauderdale, Florida, claim to have hunted over a dog which would find a covey of birds, wait a reasonable time for the hunters to appear, and then back off to find the hunters and beckon them up to the birds. There was a story, too, about a dog so stanch that he was lost for years. They finally found his skeleton frozen into a point over a bevy of skeletonized quail, but that is a little rich for even a practicing quail-liar to believe. We all know bones fall apart.

Each man builds his bird dog in his own image, but the definition of a good dog, like the definition of a good man, is one who knows and *respects* the bobwhite. No sincere hunter will overshoot a covey, out of concern for next year's sport. No good dog will flush a covey of birds until the hunter is at his side. No good dog will encroach on the point of another. A smart dog knows more than any man about the likeliest spot to find his quarry. No good man or good dog is happy to leave a wounded bird unfound. No good man hogs the best shot, as no good dog is disrespectful of the rights of his hunting companion. Altogether the quail manages to bring out a great deal of fineness in both dogs and men.

Unfortunately the available quail are becoming less available for the average man with a gun. There were practically no posted lands when I was a nipper. Now nearly all populous game land is posted and protected, leased or owned by serious hunters. A hunter may no longer park his buggy by a strange peafield and expect to find a covey of birds unless he is friendly with the farmer or leases the land. The automobile, in the last 20-odd years, has contributed greatly to the come-down of the quail, because it has made him available to a vastly increased number of occasional hunters, many of whom are careless of conservation. There are people who will shoot a bevy down to its last survivor. Added to the other vermin, plus the occasional awful inroads of weather, the indiscriminate hunter has come close to ruining the free domain of the friendly bobwhite. The brave quail is also the frail quail, who loves to live near man, and has suffered some pretty awful consequences thereby. Just like man himself.

Protected, however, and shot with reverence and moderation, the quail still comprises the noblest American sport in the eyes of many men who have gone against grizzlies and rassled single-handed with mountain lions.

If there is a broad explanation for the fascination of quail shooting, it must be that no man can bet on just how good he'll be on any given day. The challenge of bird to man is permanent. You will catch a full night's sleep, find perfect shooting the next day, and miss everything that flies. You can get drunk as an owl, sit up all night, fly a plane from dawn until noon, and with a bellyful of butterflies kill all that rustles. My personal record of 15 out of 18 shots was set on a basis of no sleep at all for two nights, due to work and travel, with a splitting headache and hands that shook like maraca gourds. Recently I had 11 in the bag with 13 shots. We couldn't find bird No. 12, and this so upset my timing that it took me 22 shots to get the other four quail. And we literally chased the last one to death.

Apart from his courage and trickiness in the field, the bobwhite has the power of inspiring magnificent nostalgia in the evening, when the fire snaps and hisses and the bourbon melds gently with the branch-water. He tastes as good on the plate as he looks in the field, and no bird of paradise was ever handsomer to the hunter than this little brown gentleman's gentleman. He often ennobles the man who shoots him, a trick that has not yet been perfected by humans in relationship to each other.

MY RESPECTS TO MR. BOB

Gene Hill

When I was appointed editor of Sports Afield *in 1970, one of the first things I did was to seek out Gene Hill and urge him to write a column. I had admired his "Parting Shots" column in* Guns & Ammo *for some time, and I knew that getting him into* Sports Afield *would be a coup for our readers. Gene is basically shy with strangers, and when we met at a New York restaurant he seemed a little ill-at-ease. We ordered drinks, and I looked across the table and said, "You sure do write good." Well, that broke the mood, and we've been close friends ever since. Gene began writing "Tail Feathers" in* Sports Afield *and left the same time I did. His pieces in* Guns & Ammo, Sports Afield, *and* Field & Stream *have been collected in the books* Hunter's Fireside Book *and* Mostly Tail Feathers (*both Winchester Press*) *and* Hill Country (*Dutton*). *This piece from* Sports Afield *and* Hill Country *is prime, bonded Hill. I once called Gene "the best outdoor writer since Robert Ruark"* and I've never changed my mind. He makes us remember the precious old things, appreciate the good new ones, and treasure the company of our friends. Someone once asked me to define specifically the quality that I see in Gene's writing. After verbally stumbling around for a few moments, I finally came up with: "It is engaging and illuminating." I'll stick to that. So when you think of Harvard University, be kind. Kennedys and Galbraiths, yes. But Gene Hill and Nash Buckingham came out of there too.*

I'D LIKE FOR YOU to wander around with me while I mess with quail. I know it's kind of a funny way to put it, but quail days seem to be filled with a soft and very special music. The slow melody of a Southern afternoon itself, with Red or Billy Joe singing out "Slow there, Sally . . . Rip—stay put" . . . and, like a crackling brown burst of flame, the birds arise and flare, then drift like smoke back into the dark and deep and green.

If you know me, you know I'm a Yankee-born. But if you know me very well, you know I like the liquid sound of saying that a lot

---

* Publisher's Note: It's interesting to note that Hill has the same friends as the late Bob Ruark. He tells the same story about the skeleton dog and quail that Mr. Ruark relates in the preceeding chapter . . . or maybe Gene is just a good "researcher."

of Alabama-Georgia folk could call me kin. So, although it sounds a little strange, I feel pretty much at home, down South, and gunning quail.

No picture that I carry in my mind is more vivid than remembering my first-time, deep-Southern shoot and a pair of pointers, one lemon-ticked and the other with peanut-butter-colored spots, standing spine-high in broom grass between the shafts of shadow thrown by spindly pines. I felt strange and somewhat rude as I walked in behind the point and honor—I was a man walking into what was so much like a famous painting that I almost had to laugh.

But, if you're lucky, that's what a lot of quail hunting is—a series of lovely paintings that we walk into and out of all day long. If you sketched me in, you'd better have a trembling brush. Quail always have—and I'm afraid always will—scared the hell out of me. But I don't mind—after all, that's kind of why I'm there.

Anyone who's messed with quail has messed with some mighty strange dogs. Pointers and setters so pretty you could cry at the perfection of line that shapes their gallant heads, and scruffy droppers, or of even less visual lineage, with so many of the pretty ones worthless and so many of the others simply "not for sale."

I remember gunning in North Carolina, years ago, over a sort of plum-colored little dog that might have been setter and springer and pointer—and a little something else thrown in just for luck—but to the young man who owned her she was simply his bird dog. Even he didn't say she was anything else but "his dog." But he was a quail hunter, and as they say, "Papers don't pin down coveys." And that Queenie could do. It might be very fair to describe her as as good as she was homely. She did what she was supposed to do and expected to do, with no fanfare, no praise, no petting—almost no notice.

I was tempted once to mention that Queenie had done a really fine piece of work on a very touchy covey, but then, with a little thought for once, thought better of it and kept my mouth shut. It would have meant no more to the man who owned her than if I'd sat watching him plow half a field and then had gone over and praised his tractor.

Queenie. Have you ever hunted a season without working behind a dog called Queen? Can't be done. Nor can you miss a Jack, Lady, Jill, or Buck. And you're going to hunt those Jills and Bucks around the schoolhouse covey, the churchyard covey, and the cabin covey. I sometimes suspect that there are more "churchyard coveys" in Georgia than there ever were churchyards, but we all know that there are some things you don't get talking about, especially if you're a Yankee: Gettysburg, Baptists, and what the lemony-colored stuff is in the Mason jar. The side-traditions of quail hunting are a lot more than shotguns, dog flesh, and cream gravy.

I like all the traditions of quail hunting. Especially the stories; the kind that, if they aren't true, they ought to be. I don't know when they all started, but I'd bet that the oldest one is about the dog that was lost and finally, after a week or so of looking around and advertising for him, he was just given up and forgotten— until two years later, back in the same area, they found the skeleton of a pointer, and when they looked around a little more, the skeletons of eight quail. Now you'll hear that before they pass the Mason jar around the second time. Then'll come the ones about Old Preacher; he could count and would tap his paw on the ground for you to let you know how many birds there were in the covey. And standing behind these dogs might be Leroy—he's the man who carried an old model 97 Winchester hammer pump and could put down five quail on a big rise nine times out of ten. I guess that Old Jesse ought to only have hunted with Leroy, because he's the dog that wouldn't hunt with you if you missed three times running—just go back and sulk scornfully under the wagon.

They say you can't profit as much by other people's mistakes as you can by your own, but mine are universal enough to be passed on. It ought to be basic that you brag neither about your shooting ability nor about your dog's superlative qualities—before they have been demonstrated. Looking down the throat of a jar may make you feel like Narcissus staring into the spring—but resist, my friend, for I have sat in that seat, and it can be mighty uncomfortable the next day. Let somebody else shoot over the first point of the day—it's a lot easier on the nerves the second time the covey bomb goes off. Try to say something nice about your host's dog—if you hardly see him all afternoon, mention that you like the way he covers ground. If you've stepped on him and stumbled over him every so often, note how close he works in a nice clear voice. But don't get carried away like one friend of mine who gushed and praised and came close to lyric verse over one dog every time he went on point and retrieved a bird, until finally the exasperated owner said, "My God, man, that's what he's *s'posed* to do!" If you're lucky enough to have a good day behind your gun, give that the soft pedal; nothing was ever said truer than that the sun don't shine on the same dog's rear every day.

At the camp table there will be some green stuff that looks odd to the stranger. This is either collards or beet greens. Both very good. There's another green veg that tastes like library paste—that's okra. Most everything else is easily recognized—but a word of caution: You can find harder ways of starting a fight than to say the ham is too salty—that's the way it's done in some places, so just drink lots of water. Do not ever, unless you and your Daddy were born and raised in the county, touch one drop of the stuff in the jar filled with little red and green or yellow peppers; it's no worse than being kicked in the mouth by a mule, but no better either. Take my word for it—those peppers would raise a blister on a work glove . . . they're only there in case the local sheriff drops in and wants to feel mean all afternoon.

I consider myself sort of an authority on Southern cooking because I was raised on it. Everything is boiled or fried or both. Only biscuits, johnny cake, cornbread, and pies and cakes are baked. I could live, and have, on a diet composed in the main of cornbread, chitlins, and buttermilk. Grits and red-eye gravy is as good as anything that ever came out of France, as are ham hocks and blackeyed peas. Dixie cooking is like sour mash—when it's so-so it's still good, and when it's good it's ambrosia.

Sooner or later the good talk creeps in, and the men shuffle around and drag out the gun cases and barrels, and fore-ends are clicked into place. As much as I like the doubles, I know what a man can do with a pump gun. And I doubt if anything has brought down more birds than the fine-pointing, hump-backed Browning. But for much the same reasons that I'll sometimes gun wearing a necktie, I like the old side-by-sides. And if I were given a dream-come-true gun to haul up with me in the democrat wagon, I know just what I'd like; and, like a lot of good things, it's a victim of progress—or what they call old-fashioned. A real 16 would make me smile. And not too light—say about 6½ pounds, maybe a bit more. I've found out the hard way that light guns are sweet to carry, but as easy to stop in the swing as they are to start. Make it with 28-inch barrels so it would be smooth-flowing on crossing shots, and cylinder-bore in the first barrel and about 40 percent of choke in the second. It would have a straight-grip, English-style stock, a single trigger, and a splinter fore-end. I'd like it just a bit dressed up, the way I like to see a pretty girl. A gold disc with my initials in the stock and some classic floral etching on the receiver. I suppose I wouldn't do much better or worse with my dream 16 than I would with your 20 or 12, but I just happen to like it, for no better or worse reason than I like orange-ticked setters and liver-and-white pointers, old corduroy coats and soft felt hats. All put together, it's a rather shambling excuse for style— but it's me, for better or worse. But here we go. You with your favorite gun and me with mine, up behind a pair of dogs who have done their job and expect us to do ours.

My job seems to be to stand there and shake for a minute and then shoot just over one or two birds. At least on the first covey. Then I kind of calm down and scratch out the odd bird or so over the next few points.

I consider myself a pretty good duck shot, average or so on doves and grouse, but quail can do a number on me, more often than not. Now, I know how to gun quail as well as you do. You just remain calm, pick a bird out of the 23 that just unexpectedly exploded under your feet and headed low and fast over the 2½ yards that separated them from some pitch-black hole in the honeysuckle. Nothing to it. We've seen it done time and time again. Two shots, two trips for dogs, and on to the next covey. I won't bore you with a list of the things I can't do well, but getting applause from my compatriots on my behavior in such a situation is not a regular thing. I stand there and marvel, I stand there shocked, scared, bewildered, and stupefied. I watch a good part of the forest floor take to random wing and leave my safety on, change my mind six times, shoot twice into a solid mass of feathers, and watch them all disappear intact.

The first time or so the man handling the dogs comes over and shouts "Dead bird!" where there would be a dead bird if Annie Oakley were gunning. The dogs look at me as if they just saw me pick pennies out of the poor box—they know if and where something needs their attention, and I know they know. I tell old Red that I had a little trouble with the safety and let's move on to pick up the singles.

Now, I'm death on singles in any kind of open cover. Well, maybe not death exactly, but nobody has to look away all day and pretend they're not laughing. There are several things a quail can do that surprise me, a few things that amaze me, and one or two that render me as ineffective as a stone dog on a lawn. But, by and large, the odds are in my favor if I have to have birds for supper. A few quail are smarter than I am, but not all of them.

At least I've quit saying "Fly on with your heart shot out." I've quit staring at the empty and then putting it carefully in my pocket, remarking "I ought to send this one back to Remington." But I haven't quit smiling—I've just quit thinking that I ought to do better than I know how.

Anyway, since the average quail costs us about $30 a pound, not counting incidentals, travel, and excise tax, and the cook is having pork chops for dinner anyway, all I really have to worry about is staying on the good side of the dogs.

About the time of day when the sun sinks down to where it just pinks the scrub oaks and the owls start shooing you off, it's a natural instinct to swing toward the spot you like to save for last. One gunning friend called it his "sundown covey," and that says as much about it as has to be said. Yours may be by the trumpet vines and mine by what's left of a corncrib, but it always seems important to have this little evening rendezvous—to pause and give our best regards to Mr. Bob.

The music of the day comes to its sweetest end with that small whistle we have come to catch and carry with us in our ear and in our heart. With Old Jesse and Queenie, perked up and heading for the barn, at our heels and maybe a sliver of moon to silver the path, we might do well to stop once more, say we'd like to light our pipe—and hope that somewhere amidst the easy sounds of dusk we hear him one more time. Just to make sure that there will be something good waiting for us in our tomorrows.

WHAT IS A QUAIL HUNTER

Charley Dickey

As an editor, I have admired and appreciated Charley Dickey's words and photographs for a long time. He is part of that select stable of outdoor writers who can always be counted on to be thorough, accurate and interesting. His book Bobwhite Quail Hunting *(Oxmoor House), from which this piece is taken, is the best overall treatment of the sport ever published. "What Is a Quail Hunter?" originally appeared in Field & Stream as part of a "What Is A . . . . ." series. Charley says the entire project was inspired by Alan Beck's famous "What Is A Boy?" This piece has always been especially meaningful to me, but became even more so after I started attending the Grand National Quail Hunt in Enid, Oklahoma. One of the highlights of this annual invitational shoot is the reading of "What is a Quail Hunter?" In that banquet room filled with celebrities and just plain bird hunters, many an eye will be misty when Charley's poignant words are read aloud.*

BETWEEN A BOY'S FIRST SHOTGUN and a tottering old man we find a delightfully unpredictable creature called a quail hunter. Quail hunters come in assorted sizes, but all of them have the same creed: To enjoy every second of every minute of every hour of every hunting trip—and to violently protest when the sun sinks beneath the horizon and it gets too dark to hunt.

Quail hunters are found nearly everywhere—on steep ridges, bragging in offices, field trials, swamps, sporting good stores, conservation meetings, Sunday schools, back rooms and at board meetings. Mothers love them, young girls hate them, older brothers and sisters tolerate them, the boss envies them, and Heaven protects them. A quail hunter is Truth with dirt on its face, Beauty with a briar scratch on its finger, Wisdom with Nature as its God, and the Hope of the future with good-will toward man.

When you are busy, a quail hunter is thinking of pointers, setters and country roads. When you want him to make a good impression on a client, he may talk only of the triple he once bagged, the way Ole Spot honors a point, the spring bird hatch or the prospects of his newest pup.

A quail hunter is a composite—he is content with "rat" cheese and crackers for lunch at a country store but his ulcer has to be pampered with a special diet when he's home; he will drink from any old well without question; he has the energy of a hurricane when he starts hunting although in the office it tires him to walk to the pay window; he has the lungs of a dictator when he yells at the dogs although his secretary complains that he whispers all the time; he has the imagination of a scientist as he looks for coveys along each likely edge; he shows the audacity of a steel trap as he tramps through green briars oblivious of the pain in his thighs; he has the enthusiasm of a firecracker as he beats every brush pile, and when the dogs do go on point, he has forgotten to load his gun.

He likes dirty hunting pants, old guns, hunting knives, leaky boots, long weekends, all kinds of field dogs, back roads, wool shirts, abandoned farms and questionable companions who also are quail hunters. He is not much for social gatherings between Thanksgiving and March, stray cats, neckties, educational books, weekend company, barbers, people who post land, and clients who don't hunt. Without thought of race, creed or color, he likes people who hunt bobwhite quail three months a year and talk about it twelve.

Nobody else is so early to rise, or so late to supper—during the bird season. Nobody else gets so much fun out of chasing dogs, trampling honeysuckle, and getting mud on his feet. Nobody else suffers so silently with aching feet, twisted ankles and strained muscles. Nobody else can cram into one pocket a rusty knife, 17 No. 8 shells, an extra pack of smokes, a compass that doesn't work, six dog biscuits, change for lunch, a hunting license, waterproof matches, a crow call, a red handkerchief, last year's duck stamp, extra boot laces, a broken dog whistle, a snake-bite kit, and a bottle opener.

A quail hunter is a magical creature—you might get sore at his constant chatter about birds but you can't lock him out of your heart. You can assign him itineraries in the spring, but you know where he'll be in the fall. His sales chart will be as good as the next, but he'll get it there in his own sweet time. He may be the very one who sells the "rich old buzzard" who spends his winters quail hunting in Georgia.

You might as well give up—the quail hunter is a child of Nature with a hopeless one-track mind. He'll do his work with the best of them, but when December rolls around he's out in the field behind a young pup and an old veteran on the prowl for Mr. Bobwhite. He's earnest in his work but he's just a little more sincere when he's slow-trailing a jumpy covey.

And though you get sore at him in the winter, you know you'll always like him. There's something about him that rings true—he's almost too honest. He's a simple and kindly man who asks no more of life than that the birds fly fast, the dogs hold tight, and everything has a sporting chance to live or die.

TWO

Bobwhite Through the Year

THE PRINCE OF GAME BIRDS

Charlie Elliott

Among the many qualities I've always cherished in the works of Charlie El-liott, Outdoor Life's *longtime peripatetic Southeastern field editor, is his tremendous ability to share knowledge without being didactic. Charlie is the kind of writer and outdoorsman who knows that the best way to teach some-one to become a good quail hunter is* not *to say "do this" or "don't do that" but to give the student as much knowledge as possible about the* game *itself. And that's what this section is all about. As a Georgian who headed the state's fish and game department for many years, Charlie is uniquely quali-fied to write about quail. The following three selections from his book,* The Prince of Game Birds (*Georgia Department of Natural Resources*), *con-tain nuggets of wisdom on the bird's obvious and secret habits that every seri-ous quail hunter will find rewarding—both in reading and in the field. By the way, Charlie's book has a terrific introduction by America's most famous quail hunter. That fellow who jogs and has a daughter named Amy.*

THE BOBWHITE AS AN INDIVIDUAL

The first step in the management program for any game bird or animal is knowing all about the individual and about group habits of the species and how these relate to the general ecological characteristics of the territory in which it makes its home.

Bobwhite, whose scientific name is *Colinus virginianus*, is a dis-tinct species with several closely related subspecies and a number of cousins with different generic names that live in other parts of North America. Beautiful birds, most of these, and several are considered great game birds, but because of range, abundance, and habits, none compares with the bobwhite.

The range of *Colinus virginianus* is noted in Bent's *Life Histories of North American Gallinaceous Birds* (Dover Publications, 1963): "chiefly the eastern United States, ranging west to eastern Texas, eastern Colorado and the Dakotas . . . with introductions over the entire country." The bobwhite is native to Georgia and is found throughout the state.

To give a description that might fit all bobwhite quail would be as difficult as writing a description to fit every man. One quail

might be a dark red and the next so light a brown that you'd wonder whether they belonged to the same clan. One full-grown adult
might be as much as an ounce or two heavier than another. Apparently latitude does have some effect on the size of the birds;
those from the northern portions of quail range in the United
States are generally larger than southern specimens. The difference is apparent even between the mountain and coastal birds in
the Cracker state.

Without being technical about such things as scapulars, tail-
coverts, and axillars, the bobwhite can be described simply as a
plump bird that weighs close to six ounces and normally wears a
reddish-brown coat with a lighter colored vest, all accentuated
with both white and dark markings, and with a solid throat patch
and stripe that extends up over the eye from the bill to the nape of
the neck. In the male this patch and stripe are white; in the female more of the subdued golden brown. Study a quail closely
and you will be amazed at the variety of color patterns in its coat
and the precise way that parts of it are edged in black or white.
This coloration is not for beauty alone. As with most of Her creatures, Nature has so designed the bobwhite's plumage to camouflage the bird in its normal habitat. Crouching motionless or flattened against the ground, bob becomes a part of the landscape
and unless he moves, even the sharpest eye seldom detects him. It
is alleged that when the bird crouches to escape visual detection,
it may compress its feathers so tightly that little scent passes from
its body, and often many of its keen-nosed enemies are said to
drift on by without being aware of the bird's presence.

An adult bobwhite is amazingly fleet of foot as well as being a
very strong flier, as almost any quail hunter can attest. It runs so
fast that its legs are little more than a blur to the human eye. A
bird with a disabled wing can dodge so quickly through the brush
and grass tunnels that a man is hard put to corner and catch it
with his hands. But it's the stubby, rounded wings with powerful
breast muscles which help to give it status as a special game bird.
A bobwhite chick begins to develop its wing muscles the moment
it leaves its egg shell and, barring misfortune, retains flight capa-
bility as long as it lives. As far as we can learn, no one has ever
counted the number of wing beats per second when a bob roars

off the ground in front of a pointing dog, but the explosion of air it creates can stir the blood of the most veteran hunter. A mature adult hurtles away from danger at about 35 miles per hour and at times even faster. We know some experienced wing shots who swear that a bob can double that speed when he is in a real hurry.

Biologists, researchers, and game managers have devoted a lot of attention to the lifespan of quail. Knowing what happens to the birds at various ages is a necessary part of the plan to build sound game programs on any type of quail habitat. How long a bird lives and the age class composition of the population depend on both controllable and uncontrollable factors. But even those beyond man's power to regulate can be allowed for in our management programs.

Normally, hunting is not a major problem in maintaining an optimum bobwhite population. Researchers have found that the majority of quail from egg to adult die of natural causes such as predation and weather and that these losses are often compounded by habitat deficiencies. The more confined the territory, naturally, the more hunting does affect the average lifespan of the birds. A farmer with only two coveys on his place can shoot them down to the last bob or hen if he's got the stamina to stay after them long enough. But over a large area, hunting is not necessarily the decisive factor.

Quail in captivity have been known to live seven or eight years and a few are thought to have been around for as long as ten years. But that was under ideal conditions. In the wild it's far different. Here, a bird that is able to fly well and fend for itself and therefore might be considered full grown has a life expectancy of nine to twelve months.

Very few birds ever make adulthood. Studies by a number of biologists have indicated that only about one-third of all eggs laid by mother quail get as far as hatching into chicks. This is an astounding percentage until one considers the numbers of creatures that find quail eggs a tasty tidbit. This list is long and it ranges from rodents to snakes, opossums, crows, raccoons, jays, and a hundred others, even including the wild turkey, which will eat both eggs and baby chicks. In addition to these, the weather is a factor, spring rains having flooded out many a setting of quail eggs. Usually if a clutch is lost for any reason, the quail pair makes a second attempt to bring off a brood and if this also fails, it may try a third time. The number of eggs in the second and third nests are progressively fewer. The reproductive urge is strong and many a hunter can tell you of flushing half-grown birds in the opening days of quail season in November.

After the chick has pipped its way out of the shell with the sharp "tooth" on its beak (it sheds this tooth in two or three days), it enters one of the critical stages of its existence. The little quail comes out of its shell virtually on the run. As soon as their fluffy down is dry, and sometimes even before if the brood is disturbed or threatened, the chicks leave the nest with their parents.

For a couple of weeks until their wings develop enough to allow them to flush and fly for short distances, the chicks are most vulnerable to any number of dangers, including their natural predators, heavy rains, and even the hot sun, and they are brooded during this time by one or both parents.

As the weeks go by the flight range is extended, along with chances of survival, but with disease, parasites, and an abundance of ravenous creatures on the prowl, life for the young quail continues to be precarious. As one of the noted authorities points out, 70 to 80 percent of all bobwhites hatched out will not be alive at the end of the first year, which means about a three-quarters turnover in the quail population each season. An infinitesimal percentage of an age group continues to survive to the end of its third year. Years of quail research have shown that the same level of turnover occurs in both hunted and unhunted populations. What doesn't wind up in the bag is lost to natural causes. Most quail management programs are founded on this precept.

Those who have had close daily association with a number of individual bobwhites claim that each bird has traits of its own and by its looks and mannerisms may be recognized from the others. Years ago one of the plantation trainers told me about a bobwhite in one of his coveys that seemingly had found the secret of staying alive. The quail was marked by several white feathers in its wing so that it was easily identified. The trainer observed that whenever the covey was flushed, this special quail always managed to get up in such a position where it could fly toward or over the hunting wagon, and naturally no one ever shot at it. All of my hunting life I've seen quail pull this stunt, but never knew whether the same birds were going that route every time.

We have already noted that the Cooper's hawk and other winged predators are thought to be responsible for the trait which makes the bobwhite such a great game bird—that of freezing against the ground in front of the dogs, until the hunters walk up. The coveys generally do this; but where foxes and other such animals that prey on them are abundant, the birds may often get up well ahead of any four-legged animals, including bird dogs, fly off for a way, and then light in trees instead of coming back to earth. This is usually most annoying to trainers and game managers who generally shoot any such bird off the tree limb—"That'll l'arn th' little varmints not to light in trees." But apparently it's a fixed species defense mechanism for under certain circumstances, quail continue to seek the safety of the tree tops.

Those who know him well will tell you that bob is a bird whose mood of the moment may be reflected in his actions and in his voice. He doesn't have a topknot as such, but when angry or ready to battle for the lady of his choice, a rooster quail raises that tuft of feathers on top of his head until it almost looks like a topknot, and you seldom have to guess when he is aroused. Normally, however, bob is typically quiet, shy, and on the alert.

A quail's attitude or activity is often expressed in its voice. Who hasn't heard the ringing "bob-white! bob-bob-white!" in the spring and summer months? You can't want a more cheerful greeting to the world, and you feel that the bird is bursting with the joyfulness of the season and pouring its heart out to any who will listen. Most biologists, however, say it isn't so—that this song of the quail, like the songs of most birds, is not one of elation but a warning to all other male quail to stay out of his home territory.

While this is generally the recognized purpose of most bird songs, Stoddard thinks it is not entirely true of the bobwhite. His findings indicated that most of the "bobwhite" calls come from males that for one reason or another are unmated. During their quail studies, Stoddard and his associates found that even in areas where nests were concentrated, after all the unmated cock birds were trapped and removed, the "bobwhite" calls were no longer heard.

In addition to this familiar call in mating season, the bobwhite family uses a large number of other notes, most of them difficult to put in words or even print as music. But each series indicates some definite communication among members of a quail family. One of these most familiar to hunters if the "cur-lee" or "cur-lee-he" of birds of a covey that has been scattered. Sometimes this call, or a slight variation of it, is also used at the roosting site as the apparently spontaneous greeting of a new day, or as a "good morning" to other coveys in the vicinity, for they often call back and forth to one another at this special hour. Hunters often locate the general vicinity of a covey by listening to these morning calls.

Quail men list a variety of other notes by which the bobwhites talk with one another. With the exception of the sharp alarm and the distress calls, most are soft musical conversation apparently having to do with food and rearing a family. Often these convey a message that even the duller human ears can understand. Last spring I encountered a rooster that circled about twenty feet in front of me, making notes that told me he had a bevy of young chicks flattened out nearby and was warning them to stay where they were. Suddenly his instructions to his brood were interrupted by a sharp note of alarm. He flew straight up about four feet into the air and to the ground again ten feet farther on, as though he were jumping over a danger spot.

Curious, I walked over and found a big copperhead coiled in the grass. While the snake and I were terminating our brief relations, the bobwhite put on his broken wing act, whether for the benefit of the snake or me, I did not know. After I had dispatched this danger to the quail family I walked on, leaving the rooster to gather his brood and conduct it to safer quarters.

Many times while hunting I've heard mature quail run ahead of the dogs, all the while carrying on a discussion or argument among themselves as to the best procedure under the circumstances. Though I could not interpret the conversation, I felt I knew what the birds were talking about.

The prince of game birds enjoys the companionship of his kind and might be considered a sociable, chivalrous fellow for a large part of the year. He is attentive to his own family and he mingles affably with members of other coveys. But when winter blows past and the warmer days of spring come on, his personality undergoes a subtle change. Although it may be weeks before he'll take a mate, his antagonism grows toward all other cock birds, even those in his own covey, which by now may be made up of remnants of several coveys. The other males meet him with equal vigor, for they feel the same way. They puff out their feathers and frequently run at one another, but there is no actual combat. That comes later on when the birds begin to pair off for nesting season.

As mating time grows near, this belligerence increases and the cock birds begin to get into actual physical contact. Their actions are much the same as those of hostile barnyard roosters. They run at one another with heads lowered, each pecking at the other around the head and neck. This is a great show of hostility and it possibly helps to establish the pecking order, but seldom are there any serious consequences and almost no fatalities, though this has been known to happen when two cocks of equal determination meet in combat. Usually, however, the more aggressive bird makes his display and after a few rounds the lesser bird turns and runs. He is chased for a little way by the winner who then comes back to his hen—or hens if he has yet to make a choice. The hens then put on a little show of their own, with distended feathers and quivering wings, which makes the male go into an ecstatic courtship dance, after the manner of other gallinaceous birds.

Why two birds are attracted to one another would probably be as difficult to explalin as in humans; but assuming that quail in the wild are not vastly different from their hatchery breathren, we have evidence to indicate that this selection of mates must be agreeable to both birds. Back in the days when the state was in the quail-raising business on a large scale, the hatchery manager paired off the birds by placing one male and one female in each laying pen. The agreeable males would take almost any hen offered them, but not so the females. They'd jump on a cock bird they didn't like and make the feathers fly. Frequently, the manager had to rescue the poor bob more dead than alive. In many instances an aggressive hen would whip each male put into her pen until the right one came along. As a matter of interest, those fastidious females were usually the best layers at the quail hatchery.

Almost always the mated birds are a devoted couple. They stay together the remainder of the year and as a team rear their brood. They are attentive and conscientious parents throughout the life of the family.

Although some quail pairs start much earlier, the height of the nesting season is said by most students of the bobwhite to be through the months of May, June, July, and August. From the time the nest is started until the chicks hatch out usually requires a period of five to eight weeks, depending mainly on the number of eggs laid.

The bobwhite nest is not a complicated, interwoven structure as are the nests of many birds. Bob and his mate build on the ground. They scratch up a little saucer-like depression of earth, high on the sides, possibly to give it better drainage, and lay a mattress of grass, pine needles and similar material in the bottom. The sides of the nest are built up and these extended over into a roof, which hides the incubating bird and probably helps protect it from the elements.

For this home site quail like cover that is not too dense, so that they may move freely to and from the eggs. A large percentage of nests are bult in or close to the edge of overgrown fields. Whether or not both birds work at building, the nest is normally completed in a few days.

The hen usually lays one egg each morning until the set is complete. The average number of eggs from hundreds of nests observed by many researchers is 14 or 15, so that about two weeks may be required to complete this chore. The pair remains together, though when the hen comes to the nest each morning to make her deposit, the male might remain from a few to a dozen or more yards away, never accompanying her all the way to the nest. This apparently is done for the sake of safety.

When the clutch is complete, incubation may begin immediately, but certainly within a few days. One of Nature's miracles is that She has given each embryo a period of dormancy so that even though the first egg may be laid two weeks or longer before the last, none start to develop until the actual incubation begins and all generally hatch out within an hour or two of one another.

In a majority of instances the hen broods the eggs, but it is not unusual for the bob to assume this household duty, though the reason for this nobody knows but the quail. The parent that takes this job usually follows it to its completion. While the brooding bird is on the nest, the other remains quietly nearby, and the birds seldom communicate until one is ready to leave the nest for food, water, and a bit of relaxation, at which time they exchange barely audible words in their language and arrange a meeting place. They are together until time to return to the nest. If, during this period of incubation, one of the pair is killed and the eggs left intact, the other will usually take over and finish the job.

When hatching time rolls around; all of the chicks pip and squirm their way out of the shells, with the exception of some not strong enough to make it. They are as wet as if they had been dunked by the bills, but dry quickly into buff and brown balls of down and within a few hours of hatching are ready to leave the nest and make their way in their new world. Almost immediately the chicks are mobile and the family leaves the nest as soon as possible. The other parent joins them for this exodus. Still at too tender an age to face the rigors of weather, the chicks are brooded for a couple of weeks, especially through periods of hot sunshine, rain, and cold, and even after that they seek out shade in the middle of the day.

Unlike many nestlings of the bird class, young quail start out in life practically fending for themselves, instead of having to be parent-fed for a length of time. They subsist on a diet of soft-bodied insects, berries, and the tender parts of new leaves. It is instinctive for them to scratch to uncover some of their tidbits. For liquid they drink the morning dew as well as eat the juicy bugs, and they partake of a fine grit that helps to grind up the food in their gizzards.

These young are also very alert. At an alarm signal from either parent, they simply flatten out against the ground and disappear; and even a sharp-eyed varmint can pass within a few feet without seeing or smelling them. I've watched young quail happily trailing along with the family group and then, when the hen or her mate discovered me with a soft note of warning, suddenly the chicks I had been watching all along just weren't there anymore. I've even walked over to the spot where I saw them last, walking carefully not to step on one, and I've stood in one spot for minutes, searching every inch of ground around me, without ever seeing one chick though I knew a number of them were within my range of sight. Only on a couple of occasions have I spotted one of the young birds and though it lay only inches from the toe of my boot, it remained perfectly immobile, while I backed away very cautiously, praying that I wouldn't step on another.

Naturally while all this was going on, the parent birds were off to one side, pulling all manner of gyrations. They are superb actors, demonstrating broken wings, broken legs, or staggering as though they are very drunk on chinaberries. Although this particular two-legged predator was not fooled, for he has seen the act before, many predators are duped and go off in chase of the "wounded" bird, which somehow manages always to stay just out of reach.

Although it can fly at a much earlier age, in seven or eight weeks the young bird has developed flight feathers strong enough so that it can wing its way far enough to discourage any creature that thought it had an immediate meal. About this time, too, the growing quail also begin to roost with their parents in a tight circle for protection and warmth and possibly for companionship. The young birds have developed enough flight and body feathers for protection against rain and cold and are well on their way to maturity. Out of these materialize the coveys the hunter finds in the fall.

Coveys normally are made up of families, portions of families, bobs and hens that have been unsuccessful at nesting, and extra single birds that either went unmated or had been lost from their own coveys. This formation of the coveys often starts in late summer or early fall, and a bevy may be composed of several different age groups.

The bobwhite is a gregarious creature and apparently does not like to be alone. One can almost detect the alarm in the voice of a lone bob when he's lost and does not get an immediate answer to his loud, insistent "cur-loi-hee, cur-lee, cur-lee, cur-lee." Birds lost or separated from their own group do not hesitate to join other coveys; this interchange of individuals seems to be a continuous process from the time a brood hatches until the birds break up for nesting in the spring.

Where the birds were abundant on a large Southern plantation, I believe I've seen this change from one covey to another take place a number of times when we located single birds out of a flushed covey that had spread itself all over the flatwoods. A lone bird that got up wild, or that we had missed, would fly only a short distance before it came to earth again and often in following this single for a third try, we'd stumble into a brand new covey where the individual had gone down.

There is evidence that before a large group breaks up into smaller units, it may contain birds of several ages that have ranged together. One of the theories as to why several coveys may be formed out of a big flock is that too many birds cannot roost comfortably or safely together. Another is that for smaller units, food in sufficient quantities is less of a problem. On the other hand, it is true that where disease, predators, and hunting reduce the number in a bevy, the remnant often joins up with another to swell its ranks. A hunter who has located a covey regularly in or near one location is often surprised to discover that no matter how many birds he takes out of this covey, it never seems to diminish in size.

Last season we had two coveys on our back lot. One originally contained fifteen birds; the other twelve. We knew they were separate units for sometimes we flushed both within minutes or within a hundred feet or so of each other. We counted the birds in each many times when they came to where we broadcast scratch feed for other birds in our back yard. We never hunted these back yard coveys but know that house cats, a pair of foxes, and other varmints took their toll, for all fall and winter we watched both groups grow smaller. After mid-winter the two coveys got together and for the remainder of the season continued to operate as one.

It has been determined that each covey does have a definite range in which it feeds, though the boundaries of this range may not be well defined and several feeding areas may overlap. Stoddard's trapping and banding experiments over many years showed that the range of most coveys is within one-quarter to one-half mile, though individual birds—possibly with nomadic tendencies—sometimes cover many miles. The farthest a banded bird was known to have traveled in Georgia was seven miles, but reports from other states indicate even greater peregrinations. One Oklahoma bird was recaught 17 miles from where it had been banded, but this one was probably just looking for a tree.

Coveys do feed close together and on one plantation where birds were abundant, I've often seen two or three more coveys fly up when we shot into the one pointed by the dogs. Many times they all fly in the same direction and pitch down together in the same area. Whether, when they separate, each covey retains its identity with the same members has never, as far as we can learn, been determined. Possibly here, there may be some interchange of members.

One mystery to many hunters is why a covey they have found time and again in the same general location suddenly seems to disappear. This has happened to me a number of times and to other hunters I know, and we could find no evidence that the birds had been shot out by other parties or caught by predators. One logical explanation is that they had eaten themselves out of house and home and moved on to another location. Certain choice foods, as acorns and pine mast, are consumed by a number of animals and birds and when the current crop is gone, most will move their living quarters unless another source of food is available in the same location.

In addition to a bob's fondness for companionship, the mature quail covey remains together for several more basic reasons. Two of the most important of these are safety and comfort. Naturally the more eyes a covey has, the less chance there is of being surprised by a hawk, fox, or other predator, so that not only do the birds feed rather closely grouped during the day, but roost together as a unit at night.

Unlike most birds—even their big gallinaceous cousins the turkeys, which go to the tall trees to sleep—the quail is a ground roosting bird. Bobwhites have been known on occasion to spend the night in vines, thick-crowned trees, and in other locations above the ground, but this is unusual. Most coveys feed almost to the site where they will roost and then travel afoot to the selected spot. Where they have been unduly harassed by four-legged predators, they have been known to fly instead of walking to their roosting locations, possibly to avoid leaving a scent trail.

Roost sites vary from broomsedge fields and other grassy areas to low scattered vegetation and open woods; but heavy thickets, matted grass, and a dense copse of any kind are avoided, since such places might hinder a quick getaway if the covey is threatened during the hours of darkness.

Quail roost with their tails together and heads out, forming a neat little circle, in such a manner that they can take off instantly. The tightness of this circle depends on the weather. It is rather loosely formed when temperatures are mild, much more tightly so in cold periods. Usually no more than 12 or 15 birds roost together; they may split into two rings if the number of bobs and hens in a covey is too large for a single roost. This close circle in cold weather is for warmth. Long years ago, experiments in Pennsylvania's artificial weather machine, which could duplicate almost any type of weather, showed that at extremely cold temperatures the survival rate of quail was in direct proportion to the number of birds roosting together. However, our Cracker temperatures seldom go far below freezing or remain there long enough to affect our bobwhite populations.

The covey may use the same roosting place night after night, or change locations frequently, sometimes from one night to the next. It leaves piles of droppings that experienced hunters can read as to covey size and frequency of use, and many sportsmen will base how closely they hunt an area on the number of roosts and droppings they find.

HIS RANGE AND HABITAT

Whether you are a sportsman whose interest centers on quail only in the colder months, or a farmer and landowner who lives with bob and his family through all seasons, it is to your advantage as well as pleasure to be thoroughly acquainted with this handsome little prince of game birds. Such knowledge helps the hunter, both in the successful pursuit of game and in enjoying

himself whenever he is afield. It is vastly more valuable to the
man who owns the property where bob makes his home if the
owner is inclined to build up his quail crop for his own pleasure or
as a part of his farm income.

One must first know where this bird makes his home, why he
might prefer one field or stretch of woods over the one adjoining
it, and, as will be explained later in this volume, how the land
might be managed to create salubrious conditions for the bobwhite quail, without interfering with the normal operation of a
farm or the management of timberland.

We've noted that the growth of agriculture in the early history
of our country has been responsible for the expansion of the bobwhite's natural range. When the first permanent white settlers
came, bob and his family lived from Maine and Florida westward
to the upper Mississippi Valley and Texas. In much of this region
the bobwhite was not overly abundant, for the land was covered
with virgin expanses of trees that were more suitable for the deep
woods species of bird and animal life. In this far-flung forest,
quail coveys were found around natural open areas, timber stands
kept clear of underbrush by periodic fire, and lands cultivated by
the Indians.

Quail were more plentiful at the west and northwest limits of
their range, where the trees petered out and the prairie began,
and in some of the open edges bordering marshland. The birds
were said to be abundant on the open landward fringes of the
marsh along the Gulf of Mexico from Mississippi to Texas.

As the white man migrated westward, felling the forests and
opening the lands for agriculture on an increasing scale, the bobwhite prospered and extended its range. By the 1850s, some of the
birds had spilled over into southern Ontario and as far west as
South Dakota. The actual boundaries of the bobwhite's range
now span a territory which, within recorded history, is the most
extensive it has ever been. The bird ranges from eastern Massachusetts as far west as extreme western Wyoming, Colorado, and
New Mexico and southward far down into old Mexico. This
range includes all races of the true bobwhite. The bird has also
been introduced into a number of far Western states and terri-
tories, including Idaho, Washington, Oregon, and British Colum-

bia, where it has had some degree of success at becoming established. In more northern latitudes and at higher elevations the bird is hard put to survive because of extreme cold and lack of winter feed, so the areas of greatest abundance are possibly the Midwestern and Southern states, where the hunters, landowners, and game agencies consider it one of the most popular game birds and devote much attention to it.

The bobwhite is a common resident throughout Georgia and according to Dr. Thomas D. Burleigh, who was the leading authority on all reisdent and migrant Georgia birds, it is found in every one of the Cracker state counties. Its area of greatest abundance is thought to be south of the "fall line" that runs generally between Columbus and Augusta. In some areas of the piedmont, between the fall line and the mountainous regions of the state, where conditions are right the quail population is as high or higher than in many portions of the coastal plain and provides excellent shooting in season.

For several reasons not as much quail hunting is done in the mountain valleys and associated lower slopes. The valleys inhabited by humans are generally divided into small farms, few of which provide an expansive enough layout for a day's hunt. Occasionally a combination of contiguous farms can be worked out with the respective landowners, but most of the quail hunting in these locations is done by the owners themselves.

A sizeable percentage of the mountains around the valleys is owned by the U.S. Forest Service and other government agencies and most of this is too rugged to be attractive to the average urban quail hunter. These forested mountain slopes and ridges do contain birds, but not so abundantly as the lower levels. While hunting deer, grouse, or turkeys, I have blundered into bobwhite coveys so far from a field or open space that I knew they must live out their lives in the deep woods. There are times when I've watched a covey roar off a mountain slope and cross a deep, narrow valley to the other side, and feel at least slightly relieved that it was other game I was after and not quail.

We must admit that bobwhite hunting under these conditions is not as appealing as that in other places where the birds are more numerous and the terrain far less rugged. Although the birds are generally larger than those of the coastal plain and even parts of the piedmont, whoever brings home a "mess" of them is more than likely to have earned it. These quail in their deep woods setting have several times put me to wondering just how many types of habitat quail might thrive in. Throughout the overall range of the bird, which extends from semi-tropics to almost sub-boreal, there must be thousands of combinations of conditions that will support the bobwhite, so it is not out of order to suggest that this is a very adaptable bird.

As every game man knows, however, any environment that will support quail must include adequate food, water, and cover. Although water is least likely to be a problem of management, no one of these requirements is more important than the other two, any more than there would be one most important leg on a three-legged stool. Eliminate one and any quail program is well on its way toward collapse. Each is dependent on the other.

To say that a bobwhite's diet is varied is an understatement. This bird will eat anything of nutritional value that it can swallow and that is not poisonous or otherwise harmful. In his six-year quail investigation, Herbert Stoddard and his associates found over only a two-county area in south Georgia and north Florida more than one thousand different seeds, insects, and other food items on the quail menu.

Like most birds, the quail is a hardy eater. All birds have a high rate of metabolism, which involves the digestion and assimilation of food and disposal of waste material. Food is converted into energy and warmth, and because of their rapid metabolism many smaller birds must feed constantly during the daylight hours to sustain body requirements. It is said that some of the song birds are capable of consuming almost as much food in a single day as they themselves weigh.

Some orders of birds possess storage places for this food, so that it does not have to pass through the body as soon as it is swallowed, but may be held back and used as needed. In a quail this storage place has been described as a membranous, expandable little sac located at the lower portion of the esophagus and known as the crop or craw. Here the food is stored and held until the body calls for it, at which time it moves on down to the gizzard, where the thick muscular walls grind it up and pass it along the digestive tract.

The bobwhite's ability to store food has an influence on its feeding habits. As a rule, depending on weather conditions, a quail covey devotes itself to finding food a couple of times each day. One of these feeding periods is in the morning some time after the birds come off the roost. The crops are empty—or nearly so—then and must be filled again. The feeding is rather leisurely; the birds spread out, talking back and forth in low tones and always with an eye out for danger. Near the middle of the day, if the weather is extremely dry or there has been little or no dew, the covey may go to water. Ordinarily they find a dusting place where they take a "bath" to help control the lice or mites and clean their feathers. Apparently these siesta hours are among their most enjoyable of the day.

Normally the birds go back to feeding in the middle of the afternoon and sometimes later and feed until almost dark. Their crops full again, they go to the roost and all night the food is passed from its storage place into the gizzard as needed. The several rounds of droppings during the night indicate that the metabolic processes have continued. By morning the birds are ready to feed again.

All wild creatures seem to have built-in barometers and the bobwhite is no exception. The birds sense unusual weather conditions ahead and prepare themselves by storing as much food as possible in their crops. The most positive indication I've ever had of this was once when I hunted bobwhites with Stoddard on his Sherwood Plantation. The day was perfect for quail shooting— not a cloud in the sky, scenting conditions good, dogs working beautifully, the birds flying strong, and my gunning eye reasonably well on target.

Late that afternoon, just before we called in our dogs for the day, Stoddard asked me, "Have you noticed anything peculiar about these quail?"

"They appear to be especially fat, but strong fliers," I guessed.

"Feel the crops in every one of these birds," he replied. "They are so tight they seem almost ready to pop open. Bad weather of some kind is on the way."

That night the clouds moved in, the temperature went down, and for several hours this Deep South region experienced one of its rare heavy snowfalls, after which the red mark plummeted to the bottom of the thermometer for two or three of the coldest days Sherwood and the surrounding plantations had ever experienced—and not even the weather people had predicted it.

Naturally what a quail eats depends on the season of the year. Its diet may lean more heavily to seeds in the fall and winter and to fruits and insects in the warmer months. The most bountiful period in a bobwhite's life is the autumn harvest season when Nature's larder is at its fullest for all creatures. At this time the migrant birds are beginning to come south for the winter and there is competition for the harvest bounty. The leanest period is in late winter and early spring when the supply of seeds runs low and the crops of new vegetation and insects have not yet appeared.

Vegetable matter forms the bulk of a quail's diet over a 12-month period. One of his wild food preferences is the beggarweed, which occurs over most of the state and grows seeds that continue to cling tenaciously to the stalk and furnish food through the lean months. The seeds of many kinds of grasses and weeds are choice items of diet. In those years of bumper pine mast, bob and his family wax fat on the nutritious seeds of several pine species, though he has much competition from other birds and rodents in the harvest of this bonanza. In fall and winter, acorns are on his preferred list. The smaller varieties of live oak and water oak are more easily handled—acorns up to one-half inch in diameter have been found in his crop—but often he feeds behind such creatures as squirrels, bluejays, turkeys, hogs, and other eaters of large acorns, which leave particles and fragments of the oak mast when they feed. The list of seeds and nuts in the bob's diet is long.

In the warmer months, fruits and berries form a substantial part of bobwhite's fare. Since his preferred feeding range is within a few inches of the ground, he usually devotes himself to those low-growing plants, though he may jump for such fruits as blackberries and grapes, just as he does for some of the bush seeds. He has also been known occasionally to fly into trees for higher growing fruits and berries.

The quantity of insects a quail consumes depends largely on the time of year. When the warm days of spring begin to bring out the beetles, weevils, plant lice, aphids, grasshoppers, and other insects, these become a convenient source of supply. The hen especially needs this rich protein before and during egg-laying time and the chicks start out in life feeding on insects.

Since the first settlers came to cut down the forests and open up the country for gardens and crops, the bobwhite has been known as a special friend of the farmer because of the large quantities of both insects and noxious weed seeds it consumes. Those who make studies of such things have come up with some astonomical figures on the number of mosquitoes, potato bugs, weevils, and such that make up a quail's fare. One of the more conservative estimates is that one bird is capable of eating between 50,000 and 75,000 insects a season, depending on location and the need for this special type of protein. Other estimates not so conservative run the bug fare as high as "568 mosquitoes in two hours . . . 5,000 plant lice in a day . . . 1,532 insects in a day, 1,000 of which were grasshoppers . . ." and so on.

Even with this voracious appetite, bob doesn't swallow everything that comes his way. He avoids certain insects as the spiny caterpillar, which might injure his insides, and some seeds as those of coffeeweed, which have flinty, sharp edges and under certain circumstances may be poisonous.

Around areas of cultivation, the bobwhite fares even better than where he has to depend on native foods. At certain locations in the state, he may help complete the harvesting of peanuts, corn, grain, and other crops where there has been some loss in gathering by mechanical means. The machinery leaves a small percentage in the field and many times the livestock is turned in on this. Fragments left by hogs and other animals make good foraging for the birds. On many farms, crops are planted especially to feed the quail and help tide them over late winter when native foods are scarce. Chief among these are small peas of several varieties, planted in one-quarter to one-half-acre plots scattered through the quail woods, and grain planted in the firebreaks and occasionally along the back roads. The game men feel that this is better than artificial feeding, though sometimes grain or cracked corn may be scattered during periods of critical food shortage. All of this will be discussed more fully in later chapters.

Possibly the biggest boon for the state's quail population was the introduction into Georgia in the mid 1940s of bicolor lespedeza. With the help of federal money from Pittman-Robertson funds (excise taxes on guns and shells), Georgia led the way in this program, furnishing thousands of bicolor plants and hundreds of pounds of seed to farmers and landowners all over the state, for border plantings around fields and along hedgerows. Bicolor grown in the Cracker state also went to the other Southeastern states so that they could start programs of their own. This species of lespedeza proved to be one of the most important bobwhite foods ever introduced into the South. From the time the seeds are ripe, quail gather in and around the strips and patches to feed. Like the beggarweed, the seeds stay on the stalks over the winter and through the less productive weeks of the year.

To date, the only fault the biologists have found with this plant is its aggressiveness. Under certain conditions and situations, it may spread and practically take over an area, to the detriment of the native plants bobwhite also uses for food and cover.

Whatever his choice of food and whenever he feeds, bobwhite avoids the broadly open areas where he might be easy game for such predators as the Cooper's and sharp-shinned hawks. He prefers to do his dining around or close to cover, where he can duck out of sight if danger presents itself. We have seen many coveys in practically denuded fields, but most of them were near enough to the edge for a quick getaway to denser cover.

The thickets, copses, high weeds, grass, and open woods belong in this bird's life. They are at least a part of his protection from the creatures that find him a tasty meal or morsel. I have watched birds that were raised on wire and held in pens before being put out in an open field. When they got up in front of the pointed dogs and guns, they seldom flew any way except toward the nearest thicket; and if they escaped the shot patterns, they went to cover if their rearing-pen wings would let them fly that far. It is instinct with quail not to remain in the open, too far away from protective vegetation.

Describing ideal quail habitat would be difficult because they adjust themselves to many combinations of trees, shrubs, weeds, grasses, and other low-growing vegetation. Every quail land manager knows that for the normal daily activities through which the quail feeds, dusts, siestas, and roosts, it is likely to avoid those places of growth so dense that it finds running or flushing difficult, or that provide cover for the creatures that prey on it.

The type of site bob prefers is one where the forest trees do not grow too thick, so that patches of sunlight can create an understory of scattered clumps of brush in and around them, and a semi-open blanket of ground cover which runs from ankle deep to about knee high. This provides his food and allows him to move freely about, on the ground or in the air. When a quail range is allowed to become too thick, the birds usually move on to a less overgrown location.

The quail wants no part of dense clumps or thickets in the normal routine of his daily affairs, but he may use one to escape or hide. We've seen quail, after feeding covey was flushed, bury themselves so deep in matted grass that after a dog pointed one, it literally had to be pushed out of the grass by the foot of a hunter before it would fly. However, this behavior is not common; usually the flushed birds land where they may move freely on the ground or in the air.

I occasionally hunt with a friend who operates a commercial shooting preserve devoted exclusively to quail. He owns and leases several thousand acres and manages these intensively for the bobwhite. His 12-month program includes prescribed burning of his range, planting food patches, and other techniques that will give him the maximum number of birds for his customers.

In his treatment of the land he leaves untouched a variety of escape routes for his quail. Two of his wild coveys live around a narrow branch head about one-half mile long. On one side of the head is a big cultivated field, with a 100-foot wide strip of rough between it and the head. This strip has low cover, is semi-open with brush clumps and a variety of plants that furnish feed for the birds. The branch head is bordered on the other side by an old field with a couple of brush-choked ditches draining into it. The narrow spit of swamp is wooded but open enough to provide for scattered tangles of honeysuckle, green briars, and head-high thickets of blackberries along the more open edges. A hunter can penetrate the place only with great difficulty.

When either of these coveys living on the edges are flushed they make straight for this swamp. It's possible for man and dog to sweat through the jungle and they may find an occasional single bird there, but getting a shot at one is something else again. The birds run through tangles and get up on the other side, either out of range or in a place so thick that only a whir of wings will tell a hunter one has gone. Needless to say, those coveys are never shot out in a season.

Another couple of coveys on that place find refuge in a stretch of marsh bordered by an open stand of hardwoods. The ground cover in the woods is low and reasonably sparse—a perfect home for the birds, with plenty of wild feed, plus a couple of planted patches. The coveys range all around the marsh, which is chocked on the edge with thickets of gallberry bushes and fairly open in the middle. The marsh pond seems perennially too deep for hunting boots but has many scattered high grass tussocks. The disturbed coveys usually go to those. Only once did I wade into the place to flush a couple of birds and with wet, cold feet the remainder of the day, decided the effort was far greater than the rewards.

Quail use these safety areas adjoining their range. There is scarcely a hunting territory anywhere that does not have its "swamp covey"—birds that live in more open surroundings along the border of a creek or river jungle into which they can dive at any threat of danger. Almost any old-time quail hunter will tell you, "You'd better get what birds you want out of that bunch on the covey rise. That's the only crack you'll get at them." The typical swamp in which they seek refuge is thick enough with brush, brambles, vines, or cane to impede the progress of a man, but open enough close to the ground so that the birds can travel afoot through it. And there are occasional open areas from which they may launch themselves into the air.

Then there are those coveys that live alongside a large creek or river. Their safety lies in flying across the stream to the other side, where only their winged predators can follow with ease. They are as likely to be found on one bank as the other of this natural barrier.

One covey I've known for years inhabits a wide bench above a steep bank that drops off to the rim of a wide river. Instead of making a long flight across the stream, the birds pitch down to the almost vertical hillside along the river. A man with a gun can follow them, using caution to keep from falling into the water, but if he flushes a single, he has to hold on with one hand and try to shoot with the other. Birds flushed a second time often leave the hillside and fly across the river to the far shore.

Other safety areas are the long, thick hedgerows separating fields. These are usually left—especially on managed lands—to grow up into a rough of sedge, briars, and clumps of small trees, but open enough at ground level so that the birds can run through them from one end to the other, or cross the strip and fly out on the side that presents the least danger.

One fact stressed by the biologists is that the quail is a weak scratcher and picks his food from the ground and off plants rather than digging for it. Optimum conditions mean that not only must standing vegetation be kept open, but mulch on the surface of the ground must also be maintained in a reasonably thin condition, so that the bird can find food items.

Anyone striving to create good quail range is careful to work for open stands of woodland which provide more food and the kind of low cover the bobwhite quail prefers.

WHY QUAIL POPULATIONS FLUCTUATE

No population of living creatures remains constant. The number of individuals that occupy any given area varies from season to season and year to year. The abundance of certain species in a locality often increases or decreases too slowly to be noticed by the casual observer; but sometimes changes in population are sudden and disastrous. The rate of fluctuation may depend on one—but usually more than one—factor. Proper management is one way to keep population change from being drastic and harmful.

The biologists feel that habitat changes are the most important cause of shifts in bobwhite populations. Habitat includes both food and cover. The impact of the environment on quail numbers can be range-wide and can extend over a long period of time. An example is the rise and fall of quail with the conversion of extensive forest lands to primitive and then advanced farmsteads in our country; the sequence went from unbroken tree cover to small planted patches, to larger and larger fields and finally to intensive cultivation and expanding improved pasture.

On a local basis and for shorter periods, some fluctuations in quail numbers are quite noticeable and tend to adjust naturally, without man's intervention. Where conditions are favorable, the annual low point in population is in the spring before the new broods begin to appear. The trend from that point is upward through the summer and early fall as production continues and while the cover remains good and the food supply adequate. In late fall and winter, natural and other causes begin to take their toll and the number of birds decreases. The point is that although this fluctuation goes on season after season, where the habitat remains stable the number of birds remains approximately the same from year to year. Where there are major changes in the environment, the population curve may go upward or downward over a period of years.

Factors other than habitat influence quail population changes. Weather is one that plays an important part in the life of a bobwhite. In Georgia it is not as severe as in some of the more northern portions of the quail's range, where extreme temperatures and heavy snowfalls in the winter are the rule rather than the exception. In his volume *Birds of Massachusetts and Other New England States* (Commonwealth of Massachusetts, 1925), William Howe Forbush says that

"A hard winter will not destroy all the New England bobwhites, though it may kill off all the northern outposts and 90 percent of the others ... The greatest danger faced by bobwhites in winter is a hard crust on the surface after a heavy fall of snow. When heavy snow comes, the bevy gathers in its usual circle on the ground near some thicket or under some sheltering branch, and soon is covered deep by fast falling snow. If then rain comes, followed by freezing cold, a crust which they cannot break forms above the birds. Imprisoned thus under the snow, they may be able to move about a little and get some food from the ground, but if the crust does not thaw they must eventually starve, and during severe winters large numbers sometimes perish in this way."

Fortunately, Georgia is seldom plagued with such extreme conditions. Our coldest weather usually comes to the mountains and is of short duration. One winter some years ago, a heavy snowfall visited the upper piedmont for more than a week with almost two feet of snow. This was followed by plummeting temperatures; and several days later a game survey was made to determine the damage. The biologists found that in a number of places where the quail were able to travel on crusted snow, they were eating seeds which normally would have been out of reach. The biologists picked up a few dead birds with empty crops, but whether they were victims of starvation or the quick, intense drop in temperature was not known. This sudden chilling factor is a known killer of animal life.

Possibly the Cracker state's most severe weather problem in connection with quail is excessive rain during the nesting season. Stoddard estimated that about 30 percent of nest desertions and failures was because of the elements. Nests built in low places during dry weather are often flooded out by thunderstorms, or by long rainy periods in which the ground becomes saturated and an area that is normally dry holds enough surplus water to either cover the eggs or so saturate the nest that the hen abandons it.

The chicks fare somewhat better. Brooded, led to higher ground, and otherwise cared for by the parent birds, they usually escape the heavy rains and flooding. Those that do drown are thought to have strayed away from the brood to be caught in ditches and other low places, or their downy bodies may become so saturated they cannot escape the creatures that prey on them. Unnatural wetting may cause malfunctions of the body, resulting in weakness followed by disease. Cold, wet weather is especially bad for chicks. There is little evidence that the mature quail is affected one way or another by the heaviest of downpours or storms.

Another weather condition that affects a clutch of eggs is intense heat, which sometimes starts the eggs incubating before the hen is ready. This may make the hatching period of the separate eggs so spread out that the parent birds will depart the nest with a partial brood leaving the remainder to die in the shell or to become victims of the first passing predator.

Hail, especially the large pellets, is a third weather feature that occasionally will break up a nest or even strike down a mature bird. There is little evidence that it causes any appreciable widespread destruction, though severe damage has been known to occur from local storms.

Naturally, hunting takes its toll of the bobwhite clan, but it is only one of a number of factors in the rise and fall of quail populations in any given area. Compared to loss from natural causes, the harvest of birds by gun adds up to only a modest percentage of those that initially hatch out. Almost any experienced quail manager will tell you that whether the coveys are shot or not, about the same number of birds live on a place year after year. The population remains only as high as the range will support, whether the crop of birds is harvested by man or nature.

Some of the old-time quail hunters insist that "if you don't shoot a covey down to less than six birds, there'll always be a covey in that same place next year." There's a color of truth in this. But the number of birds that should be left in a covey for natural propagation the next season depends on many things, not the least of which are losses to such variables as unusual weather, predation, and possibly disease.

Most game managers, especially those who have the responsibility of providing an abundance of birds and good shooting year after year on the larger plantations, agree that the percentage of birds taken in a single season should not apply to the individual coveys, but to the population as a whole. Most are familiar enough with their territory and with the number of birds in the various segments of it to make a fairly accurate estimate of the population and on this they base their recommendations for the total allowable kill each season.

Estimates by the experts for this harvest vary. It runs between 25 and 50 percent or more; and here again the prime factors, such as abundance of food, suitable range, and predation are involved. Some of the larger estates undershoot their birds and one manager assured us that more birds die each year of old age than fall before a gun. Stoddard felt that it was reasonable to allow 25 to 30 percent to be taken from the overall population of a given territory, though in saturated ranges this percentage might go higher.

The plantation concept is thought to apply as well to the smaller landowner. The average farmer who is also a bird hunter knows approximately how many coveys he has on his property and he keeps up with the number of birds in each. Many make a practice of not shooting into a covey rise that contains less than five or six birds, since they "want to leave some for seed."

Crippling losses are a factor that must be taken into consideration. Various estimates have been made on the percentage of birds that fly on with shot in them or die later in some copse or covert and be picked up by a scavenger. As far as we know, no definite method of accurately gauging loss of cripples has been worked out and there have been estimates only.

Responsible quail hunters make every effort to locate and retrieve a crippled bird. Often one flutters down with a wing tip broken and hits the ground running. It may dive into the nearest thick clump of grass, or sprint for cover some distance away, or duck into a stump hole or gopher hole for safety. How many of these "crips" recover no one knows.

Many birds that are hit in vital places as they fly away show no sign of being rocked by the shot pattern and many remain airborne for long distances before they fall to the ground. At times we've watched birds we had no idea were wounded fly almost out of sight, then suddenly collapse in mid-air as though they'd run into an invisible wall; and we've had our dogs retrieve a dead bird when we thought we'd made a clean miss. There is no way to determine which wounded birds that get away will survive or be picked up by predators, though the percentages favor the latter. For management purposes the estimated number of unretrieved cripples should be reckoned as a part of the total kill. The consensus from managers and others is that the birds shot and then lost runs around 20 percent of the bag.

Predators are thought by some to account for the greatest fluctuations in bobwhite populations. Others claim that in the light of recent findings on the subject, the less said about predators the better, and that as far as the bobwhite is concerned, predators as a whole have little influence on the number of birds any area is capable of supporting. Both with agencies and with individuals who manage quail lands, the subject of predators is a controversial one, capable of generating long and sometimes heated discussions.

Regardless of what any game man thinks about the role of creatures that influence a quail crop, all will admit that many forms of wildlife do relish a tasty dish of quail, as well as their eggs and young. In a later chapter, we will discuss more fully the interrelationship of predators and quail in regard to management, but a few words at this point on the effect of predators on quail populations are in order, since disagreement is so widespread.

The mortality rate from egg to a year old bird is so high that one wonders why the bobwhite has not already gone the way of many other vanished species. Biologists agree that among the factors contributing to this heavy toll is predation; yet, as contradictory as it may seem, predators are necessary for the survival of some species. This apparent contradiction lies at the heart of the controversy surrounding predation and the quail. Biologists have learned that a prey animal that has nothing to hold it in check simply multiplies itself out of living space and then there is a massive die-off from stress, starvation, and disease. This has happened with a number of species.

This could happen to the bobwhite if in any given area all the creatures that prey on the bird were removed. Fortunately, the elimination of all types of predators is impractical if not impossible. In the case of the bobwhite, many of the creatures that feed on him also feed on one another and some degree of balance is maintained.

In the past one of the problems of predator control was that too often the elimination of a species was the goal, bringing on unforeseen and unfortunate consequences. In the early days of the Southern plantation, many managers concentrated on the destruction of all "varmints" that were supposed to prey on mature quail. The "harmful" species included hawks, owls, foxes, bobcats, minks, and weasels. Unfortunately, this left their natural prey, the rodents, to multiply and the result was a destructive backlash that practically wiped out the quail in several locations. The rodent population zoomed and over-ran nests and eggs, so that a successfully hatched and reared brood of quail was a rarity. Red-tailed, red-shouldered, and marsh hawks are eaters of snakes and of the young of such creatures as opossums as well as rats and

mice. The great horned owl, whose diet was found to include almost no quail, was arch nemesis of the skunk and possibly its only
control in the region. When these hawks and owls were wiped out,
the creatures on which they preyed became a sizeable adverse
factor in quail-breeding season.

Over a period of years, after dire results in some instances,
predator elimination was gradually modified to a predator control program in an effort to keep the quail and varmints in balance. Emphasis was shifted from the killing of each and every
hawk and owl, once the value of these in rodent control was recognized, and care was taken in curbing the numbers of such known
egg-eaters as skunks, opossums, and raccoons, and also known de-
stroyers of both eggs and young birds, as foxes, cats, and some of
the snakes.

A few of the large landowners kept hounds, and both fox and
'coon hunting became one of the rituals of plantation life. Some
owners paid a small bounty to their employees on evidence that
one of the predators on their list had been eleminated, and this
went on over a period of years, but always with an eye toward
leaving enough of the varmints to help control the rodents and
other small creatures that threatened the quail crop.

In recent years, however, we have learned a great deal more
about wild predators and their relation to the sudden decline or
rise of quail populations, and now have federal and state laws to
protect such species as the hawks and owls. On the whole, these
species may be of much more value than harm to the bobwhite
family.

Domestic animals with predatory tendencies are something else
again; they are a problem statewide to most wildlife species. Cats
and dogs that live with rural families are often allowed to range
free and they take their toll of most smaller mammals and birds
and their young. Feral housecats are common over most of the
state. Tender-hearted owners of unwanted kittens often drive to
some spot out in the country and drop the little animals, hoping
they can make their own way. Some make it, some don't. Those
that survive do so by learning to live off the land, as their original
ancestors did for thousands of generations, by predation. Many
quail hunters we know will shoot any housecat that his dogs jump
or put up a tree, if it's far enough from a rural residence.

Feral dogs create the same problem. Those shifting for them-selves often join together in packs that prey on domestic stock as well as wildlife and while usually they are not a severe menace to quail, they are a factor.

There is no way of determining the overall extent of harm or good done by all the creatures that prey on quail. But the positive consequences of predation are often overlooked. Not only do the bob's predators help control each other, they serve the quail in other ways. For example, we know that old and diseased birds are more likely to be the victims and there may be occasions when se-rious outbreaks of disease among quail are curtailed by the elimi-nation of infected birds by their predators. Then too, many of these animals are scavengers that pick up birds which have died of one cause or another.

The bobwhite is subject to many parasites and diseases that plague the gallinaceous clan. Although these afflictions are likely to be the dread of every man who attempts to raise quail in wire pens under crowded conditions, no evidence has been found that either disease or parasites have been responsible for serious fluc-tuations in wild quail numbers.

The lice, mites, chiggers, and ticks found on quail seem to do little more than cause the birds annoyance, especially in long rainy spells. In normal drier periods, when bob may enjoy the luxury of his daily dust bath, he is able to discourage these pests; and he can keep himself cleansed of the more tenacious ones by picking them off with his bill.

The diseases that may cause appreciable loss of birds confined in hatcheries include coccidiosis. It has caused many a hatchery man to wring his hands in despair when an epidemic among his young chicks has killed off a sizeable percentage of the brood. Al-though this disease occurs in mature birds, it is less often fatal. Coccidia have been found in wild birds, but appear to have far less effect on the free-ranging coveys than on hatchery birds. Thus far, no one has presented evidence that this disease is responsible for appreciable mortality among either young or old wild birds, possibly because the wild chicks cover much ground during the time they hunt for food and seldom remain in contact with drop-pings of other quail, as hatchery birds may often do.

Because parasites and diseases seem to be relatively minor factors in the fluctuations of wild populations, they are seldom included in quail management plans.

"Pesticide" and "insecticide" have become familiar words in our language. These man-concocted treatments have allowed the growth of more abundant farm crops by the destruction of noxious insects and plant diseases that attack crops from seed to harvest. Over the years, more and stronger poisons have been developed until the kinds and combinations of kinds make up the hundreds of different formulations put on the market. Some of these substances were chlorinated hydrocarbons that did not deteriorate but remained in the food chain, and biologists began to suspect that they were a factor affecting animal life above the insect level. Most intimately associated, they said, were the birds that ate the poisoned insects, and then the animals or birds that ate the birds that fed on the insects. In some places, they claimed, many of the avian species began to disappear, or those that hung grimly on laid eggs with shells so thin that the clutch was either broken in the nest or failed to hatch. They cited such species as the osprey, a fish-eating hawk, whose ranks were being considerably thinned from damage by these persistent hydrocarbon poisons that got into the stream, lake, and ocean environments and contaminated the organisms on which the fish lived. Others declared that the pesticides were not as dangerous as claimed and are used in quantities so minute that the lethal impact does not go to any appreciable extent above the insect level in the food chain ladder.

For two decades the controversy between these two schools of thought has grown instead of diminishing.

Although some studies have been made, there are not many published reports on just how severely the pesticides have affected the quail population. In her book *Silent Spring*, which came out in 1962, Rachel Carson, one of the first scientists to take up the banner against chlorinated hydrocarbon and organo-phosphate insecticides, points out that in two study areas in the Southern states where quail were abundant, the wholesale distribution of poison to control fire ants resulted in the loss of all quail, and most of the other song birds as well. All of the dead quail examined contained enough of the poison to have caused death.

In his book *The Bobwhite Quail,* Walter Rosene lists two plantations in South Carolina where the number of adult birds declined, along with a marked decrease in the number of juveniles during years when insecticides were used on crops, and bounced back after those seasons in which the crops were not treated.

Our observations have not been scientific, but over a number of years since the pesticide controversy developed, we have hunted on both large plantations and small farms where seed were treated and crops sprayed with insect-killing chemicals without being aware of any decline in the number of coveys. Who can say the bobwhites would not have been more numerous if the toxic sprays had not been used?

For a decade, on one of these properties where quail management is the first consideration with all farming operations subjugated to it, the seeds and crops have been treated to protect them from insects and disease. The quail shooting there must be as excellent as that found anywhere; birds have remained more than plentiful over many years. There may be reasons for this which have nothing to do with insecticides, since less than one-fourth of the farm is in cultivation and all the remainder is under a quail management program. The birds can range and nest in large areas unaffected by the chemicals and it may be that the expansion in natural areas offsets any loss from eating poisoned bugs around the fields.

Both pen and field studies have been and are being made on many of the widely used pesticides. Some of the earlier forms were found deadly and the use of them banned. All those toxic to wildlife are now required to carry that information on the label. These studies are a never-ending job, for new pesticides continue to flood the market. Although some of the most dangerous compounds have been ruled out, each must be tested for its toxic effects.

It all adds up to a grave problem for both the ecologist and agriculturist, not only for the sake of wildlife, but for the very survival of the human race as well.

THE ENEMIES OF QUAIL

Archibald Rutledge

Archibald Rutledge's name is synonymous with great hunting stories and nature pieces set in his beloved South Carolina low-country. His famous plantation, Hampton, where he spent his boyhood then lived on for 36 years following his retirement from teaching in 1937, was a perfect setting for his work. His experiences and observations in the field produced marvelous nature books, poems (he was a Poet Laureate of South Carolina), and the two grand collections of hunting stories, Hunter's Choice *and* An American Hunter. *This look into the darker side of the bobwhite's lifestyle was one of his last before illness forced him to put aside his pen for the final time. It appeared in* Sports Afield *in 1965 and has never before been anthologized.*

WHILE NOT THE LARGEST, and in some respects inferior to a lordly bird like the ruffed grouse, the bobwhite quail stands first in the hearts of America's hunters. When farming was less mechanical than it now is, quail probably were more numerous, and extended over a wider range. Nevertheless, the bobwhite has shown the steel in its nature by meeting the challenge of modern farming and multiplying.

This beautiful, and I might say perfect game bird, naturally has its enemies, as every other creature has. Of these, I suppose we must include man, for except in sanctuaries the quail is hunted wherever he is found. Yet it is a strange biological fact that man's invasion of the covey may well have a beneficial effect.

In Dr. Axel Munthe's famous book *The Story of San Michele* he described the plague in Florence. The feature that impressed him most was the utter abandonment with which people threw themselves into one another's arms when men and women were dying on doorsteps, in the streets, even in theatres. The reason was plain. Nature was saying: "The race is dying. Increase and multiply and replenish the earth."

The same principle works in time of war or any other disaster. People rush into each other's arms as they would never do in any ordinary time. Nature impels them to do so. And so it certainly is with quail. If you have a covey of standard size—12 to 16 birds—

and don't hunt them, or permit them to be hunted, there is a good chance that none of them will ever mate and nest. The following year you may have the very same covey. But if you shoot into them, break them up, scatter them—then the old biological urge takes hold of them. They, too, feel that the race is in danger; and as soon as the mating season comes, they will pair off and rear new broods. Quite often a pair of quail will raise two successive broods, and occasionally three.

But it is not of man as an enemy of quail that I would write. Many men protect them; others, by planting the crops on which these birds love to feed, keep them in safe country. I know a good many farmers who deliberately let a fencerow grow up in weeds, briars and bushes, so that quail will be afforded protection, especially in time of snow. Of the men who hunt quail, all true sportsmen will always leave at least six or seven birds in a covey. I have been invited to a hunt on quail preserves where there was a rule that no hunter should kill more than two quail out of one covey.

This did not seem to me a sensible rule, for no consideration was given to the size of the covey. One might have 20 birds and another might have six.

As a rule, I should be in favor of leaving more than six or seven birds in any one covey; because in hunting these birds, it is not possible when they are in flight to recognize the sex. The sex, of course, can easily be distinguished if the birds are on the ground. The cocks look a little larger, and have so much more white about the head. But in the melee of a covey's rise, all the birds look alike.

Disregarding man, who is often a good friend to the quail, let us consider its natural, and therefore inveterate, enemies. Of these, strange as it may seem, I would put the house cat first. A cat is one of those animals that has a dual nature. You look at Tabby lying on your hearth, and you might consider her the most gentle and harmless of creatures. But late in the afternoon her wild nature awakes. She will slip out of the house and prowl your garden. If a field is near, she will go there as a nocturnal huntress, giving her sinister attention to anything she can catch—especially birds of all kinds, and rabbits. Of the birds, quail are perhaps the favorite quarry.

However well fed your tame cat may be, and however much of

a homebody it may appear, a few moments outdoors, especially if a garden, field or wood lot be near, will transform it into a regular wildcat. And it is amazing how far such a supposedly tame creature will travel. I have seen many a "tame" cat more than a mile from where it belongs, stalking game. I have seen several of my own cats in this dual role, and as a lover of quail their behavior set me against the whole race of cats—at least in rural or semirural areas. While living in a fair-sized village, on several occasions I have been shocked to see my old house cat bring in a quail.

Some cats, of course, go wild, taking permanently to the woods and fields; and these, wholly dependent on their own efforts for their food, develop a sinister cunning, and become the very worst predators of all.

It may seem strange that I do not put the true wild-cats—the bobcat and lynx—ahead of the ordinary tame cat as a dread enemy of quail. But the truth is that the wildcat is a creature of the deep woods, and rarely goes into fields, though he may travel old roads and trails. But his natural haunt is a thicket, his den a deep hole under a stump or in the cavity beneath the roots of a hurricane-thrown tree.

On the other hand, except in the rarest of exceptions, quail will not roost in the woods. They seek out a dry marsh, a stubble field or a big area of grass. In fact, at twilight I have seen a covey rise from the edge of a patch of woods and fly far out over a favorable field. If quail especially like a certain roosting place, they may frequent it night after night. They never roost on the same spot, but in the same general area. I have found as many as 15 "roosts" within a space of half an acre.

It might be supposed that game birds, such as quail, pheasants and wild turkeys, all of which nest on the ground, would fall easy prey to predators during the nesting season. But wise nature intervenes. She makes at least three provisions against such a disaster. First, whether designedly or not, she fills the woods and fields with a confusing myriad of scents and fragrances. I have seen one of my fine old bird dogs, working upwind in a path, pass within six feet of a setting quail without noticing a thing. Under those conditions in the autumn or winter, he would have winded that quail 20 or 30 feet away.

] 65 [

Again, if a ground-nesting bird becomes suspicious that she may be followed by her scent to her nest (and this is especially true of the wild turkey, the scent of which is almost as strong as that of a deer), the mother bird will fly to and from her nesting site. It is a touching thing to see a prospective mother so protect her eggs.

In the third place, I have heard it said (but I cannot prove this except by conjecture based on observation) that in the spring and summer, a ground-nesting mother bird gives out less scent than usual, or else has the power to hold in the scent by compressing the feathers close to the body. Whether this is really done, or can be done, I am unable to say; but certainly neither hounds nor bird dogs appear able to scent game birds or animals in the spring and summer as they do in the autumn and the winter. Moreover, if dogs could work as well in hot weather as in the regular hunting seasons, the consequent destruction of game birds would surely become almost immediately apparent.

If, as I think, the common house cat is the worst enemy the quail has, the second, probably because he is so widely distributed, is the opossum. As soon as dusk falls, he begins to travel; and he forages all night. A possum has a good nose, and for his size he is very strong. He is especially fond of eggs of all kinds; and birds that nest on the ground are in constant peril from him. He will not only destroy the eggs but will kill the nesting mother. I once had a tame turkey hen killed on her nest by an opossum. I was sure of his identity, for I caught him in a trap beside the turkey he had killed. Then, too, I had seen his tracks.

A possum covers so much ground, and is so adept at getting over and under fences and through dense cover, that I consider him one of our worst predators, utterly worthless, and a constant and evil enemy of quail.

About 60 miles north of where I live there is one of the greatest quail countries of North America. Many millionaires from the North rent thousands of acres there to enjoy the sport. I personally have never seen so many quail anywhere. On a brief hunt one winter's afternoon I put up 12 coveys.

But a few years ago this concentration of birds caused a gathering of their enemies, especially of foxes. Year by year the quail decreased in numbers. This decrease was attributed to the foxes, which seemed to abound everywhere.

So serious did the situation become that the renters of several large properties talked with me seriously of giving up the sport. About that time an epidemic of hydrophobia assailed the foxes. Highly infectious, this disease is nearly always fatal. In that district, foxes were almost exterminated.

Within a single year, men who rented large quail areas told me that the birds had suddenly increased at least 100 per cent; and they did not hesitate to attribute this upsurge in the number of quail to the disappearance of the foxes.

I confess that until this time I had not considered the fox as an outstanding enemy of quail. He is, of course, carnivorous, feeding on birds, rabbits, mice, rats, squirrels; and occasionally raiding a chicken yard. But because he is primarily a creature of the woods, I had often thought of him as harder on the ruffed grouse and the wild turkey, which are birds of the woods, than on quail, which are essentially birds of the field. Quail will take refuge in woods, and will dust themselves in sand along the sunny edges of thickets and wood lots, but they feed and they roost in fields. Of course, under cover of night, foxes traverse fields, and come close to farmhouses and buildings, where they might well encounter quail, and I do not think they would pass a quail by. But I do not think a fox specializes in quail; and in the delicate balance of nature, he probably, by feeding on predators, does as much good as harm.

Whether the foxes that died of hydrophobia because of the great numbers of quail in their habitat had therefore become regular feeders on these fine birds, I have never been able to determine.

In fields where quail nest are usually found skunks, rats and mice. All these will destroy quail eggs; but fortunately, as soon as one clutch of eggs is destroyed, the mother quail, turning around in the grass until the place becomes a nest, will begin to lay again.

And it should be remembered that little quail, like little grouse and wild turkeys and other game birds that nest on the ground, are precocial. That is, they belong to that group of birds that are "ready to go" as soon as they are hatched. They do not seem to have a fledging stage, an awkward age. As soon as they hatch, they almost immediately leave the nest; in fact, I have seen baby quail running around when they were so young that snowy fragments of eggshell were still sticking to their backs! And when they are barely out of the nest, at a single note of alarm from the mother, with swift intelligence every one will hide. Once when a mother was giving her warning cry, I picked up one of her babies. It cuddled down between two of my fingers, and hid there!

While he might not pass by a nest full of eggs, I have never considered the raccoon a real enemy of the quail. He is a dweller in the woods; and as a rule, he haunts the edges of ponds and marshes. He loves fish, frogs, shellfish; at times he feeds on acorns, but he is rarely found at any distance from the water.

There are certain hawks that are enemies of quail; but the bobwhite is so swift to take cover that I do not believe that many are taken by these marauders. I have seen coveys and single birds attacked by the pigeon hawk, the Cooper's, the marsh and the red-shouldered. I once watched a marsh hawk vainly beating his wings on top of a briar patch, in the dusky safety of which a covey was securely hiding.

In my experience, there is only one condition which makes a hawk a distinct and constant menace to quail. That is when deep snow blankets the ground. In these times, strange to say, their assailer is a *buteo*, one of the milder-mannered hawks such as the red-shouldered or the red-tailed. Many of these stay in cold and snowy countries during the winter, whereas the fierce *accipters,* of which the Cooper's is typical, are more common in my section of the South.

I suppose the swift and devastating duck hawk would pursue a quail; but he is more inclined to pursue larger game such as the ruffed grouse and the wild duck. However, once over a desolate sea marsh I watched one pursue a Wilson's snipe. By his dazzling speed and his expert dodging, the snipe escaped. It may be added that in open country few birds, whatever their swiftness, ever escape this superb marauder.

I mention the notorious menace of a *buteo* to a covey of quail. I have watched it often with deep misgiving; and on occasion have brought my rifle into play against this aerial corsair.

When a deep snow comes, with perhaps a glaze on it, a covey of quail will try to outlast the cold and exposure by harboring along a bushy and briared fencerow. Of course, with so glaring a background, they are easily seen, particularly from the air. A big hawk, of one of the species that is reputed to be mild-mannered, will locate the covey. Then he will take up his watch on a leafless tree nearby. Day by day this same hawk will kill and eat at least one quail. I have often known such a predator, at such a time favorable to him, to destroy the greater part of a covey of quail, and at times to take the last bird. When I knew what was going on, I would correct the situation by creeping up on the marauder through the snow-covered woods with my small but quite effective high-powered rifle.

I know that professional ornithologists may tell you that these big *buteo* hawks are harmless to game. But I know what I have seen; I know also that these powerful and hungry hawks have not read the books that declare that they will not harm any game species.

As he is of wide distribution, merciless nature and wise in a minatory way, I believe that the great horned owl is a constant and dreadful enemy of the bobwhite. The only rift in the cloud is that this grim tiger of the wildwoods is comparatively rare. It is unusual for more than a pair to inhabit a certain stretch of woodland. They love woods that are lonely and wild, and timber that looks primeval.

It may be that his smaller cousin the barred owl will take an occasional quail, but he is nothing like the menace to this fine bird that the great horned owl is.

The great horned owl nests in the winter, while the coveys of quail are still intact. Once, beneath a nest of such an owl, in the fork of a giant oak, I found the remains of at least 11 quail, and these had been freshly killed. A hunter once told me that he had come on one of these fierce predators eating a wild turkey. I do not know if he killed this great game bird, but he was quite capable of doing so.

For many years in the wild mountains of southern Pennsylvania, I used to hunt that lordly bird the ruffed grouse. Like other game birds they had their favorite haunts. There was one place in particular, full of greenbriars, wild grapes and a few old apple trees of a deserted orchard where I had, until this certain year, been able to find grouse—not one or two, but 12 or 15. But this year they had vanished.

I revisited the place several times, but never saw a sign of a grouse. I did, however, find where two had been killed. Some of the feathers of these grouse were rolled in a ball—a typical owl manner of regurgitating indigestible matter. I also discovered that two great horned owls had taken up their residence in that little swampy valley. Before I left there, I managed to make way with these two marauders, whose lives were one long career of murder.

The following season the grouse returned to their loved little retreat. I believe that when horned owls move into a locality, most birds move out.

A last enemy of quail I shall mention is found only in the southeastern part of our country. This is the lordly diamond-back rattlesnake, growing to an extreme length of nine feet. He is a persistent feeder on quail, usually the mature birds, which he captures by scent at night. I once opened one of these huge serpents whose body appeared bulgy. It contained three undigested quail.

The timber rattler and other forms of this species have a much wider range, but I doubt if they molest quail to any degree, if at all. But the lethal diamond-back is a dangerous foe. Other snakes destroy quail by eating their eggs: among these are the black snake, the chicken snake and the corn snake.

The quail, like the white-tailed deer, takes kindly to civilization. In this respect they are the opposite of the ruffed grouse and the wild turkey. These are true lovers of the wilderness.

If you have a rural or semirural residence that might harbor quail, or a farm, or a regular quail preserve, if you love the bobwhite as I do, you must keep his enemies under control—the housecat, the opossum, the fox, certain of the predatory hawks, all egg-eating snakes, the great horned owl and the diamond-back rattlesnake. These last two are not likely to be found near you unless you live, as I do, in the heart of the wilderness—which can be both frightening and beautiful.

THREE

The Gun and the Game

SHOFFSTALL

TO HIT A QUAIL IN THE TAIL

Warren Page

When Warren Page passed away two years ago, those of us who knew him personally realized that we had lost a unique, interesting and generous friend. In many ways, Warren was bigger than life itself. Extremely intelligent, he was one of the greatest conversationalists I've ever known, interested in almost any subject you cared to bring up and blessed with the gift of the patience to listen. *I've always thought his writings reflected that sense of sharing. This piece from his shooting department at* Field & Stream *is typical of Page at his best, avoiding the pitfalls that trip lesser gun writers—colorless language and unchecked worship of cumbersome technological phrases. Despite his advice, our search for the perfect quail gun must remain infinite. Otherwise we lose the best excuse we have for those horrendous misses.*

THE THEATER was jammed, as well it might be since "Annie Get Your Gun" had been wowing Broadway for months. As Annie, the backwoods sharpshootress, musical comedy star Ethel Merman was belting out, inimitably, a ditty of love's lament. She was plucking the heartstrings of the audience with the line, "You can hit a quail in the tail, but you can't get a man with a gun."* But in that audience, I suspect that at least one shooting-minded male other than myself was moved to cogitate not on Annie's frustrations of *amour,* but on the equally painful frustrations of shooting at, and missing, the lively-winged quail.

Annie, so the story went, had shot quail for market with a rifle, taking them on the wing with a rifle, head shots at that. But that was a bit of Rodgers & Hammerstein fiction. Most of us have a tough time bagging quail even with a scattergun, and we hit a lot more in the posterior than we do elsewhere. If we bag a bird with a pair of shells, on the average, we do better than the average.

Which is reason for serious consideration of a problem. How to hit quail, and with what? The second half of that major query is a lot easier than the first, thank heaven.

* Copyright by Rodgers & Hammerstein.

Quail have been brought to bag with goose loads of 2's. Such a mixture is not recommended though it did suffice one Oklahoma morning when we found a running covey on our way to goose blinds on the South Canadian. Quail have also been grassed with dust shot, 11's and 12's, back when such piddling pellets were loaded. The right prescription lies somewhere between, and it's a prescription that has to be suited to the epidemic. Close-sitting bobwhites on the one hand, and marathon experts like the top-knotted blue or scaled quail on the other, need quite different treatment.

As far as shot size goes, the classic dosage for these southeastern states where the bobwhite is king, where the birds lie close to the dog and have learned to dive into brush with only two whirs and a zip, calls for 9's or 8's in the early season, later 7½'s, at least in the second barrel, as the season wears on and the birds get tougher, smarter. Figure on skeet loads, or the shells now put up as target loads, there being no need for big shot doses for 20-25-yard shooting. For the kind of classical quail hunting artists paint pictures about, I for one would figure to get along nicely with 8's and let it go at that, thank you.

But quail hunting as she is isn't always so classical and cir-cumstances alter cases. Certain adventures and misadventures in Texas last January come to mind. The Lone Star State, at least in its west central section, in the 1958-59 season had more quail than anybody save the really big liars could remember, scads of quail. Two fine hatching seasons in succession with enough rain for good weed cover meant that by late fall of '58 there were bunches of birds fairly keeping the ground alive under the mesquites. On Bus Wharton's Waggoner Ranch outside Vernon, which incidentally harbors more lesser Canada geese than I'd ever seen in one clot before, there were jillions.

But two peculiarities. In the first place, this same land area had been scourged by even greater numbers of cotton rats. They'd eaten the grass cover down until in much of the acreage the birds were running around naked. And I mean running around, be-cause for whatever reason the top-knotted scaled quail locally called blues, bigger birds than the Texas-Mexican bobwhite and many times better as sprinters had mixed in with the bobwhite coveys and were busily teaching them to run. Run my foot—gallop!

Couple this with dry weather so the dogs had trouble scenting properly and you have quail shooting of a sort unknown down in Georgia. Not one bird in forty would hold. When the birds did fly, they flew far out. And a footrace across Texas is a long footrace!

First morning down there I started with my little 20-bore Browning fitted with a pair of barrels marked skeet both top and bottom, tubes that actually shoot a solid improved cylinder, had my shell pocket stuffed with 8's. Previously this had been a most effective quail combination but it was a bum deal under the circumstances, and by noon the game pocket in my jacket was emptier than it should have been. After lunch, even though I had slowed down considerably on the footracing, these old gams not being what they were, a switch to a pair of modified and full tubes and a box of 7½'s, big one-ounce doses, brought better results. I even tried a few of the Federal 3-inch firecrackers in the second barrel. These latter are pheasant loads, really. But the flushes were coming out beyond the thirty-yard mark, which means birds hit at thirty-five, forty and beyond, nigh onto twice the range of the classical quail shot.

Improved cylinder or skeet patterns, regardless of the gun, are as open as broken windows out around forty yards. They have to be, because the gross spread of the pattern is some sixty-five inches or better, with no more than half the pellets in the center half. Thin out that scatter by using those charge weights, 1⅛ in a twelve, ⅞ in in a twenty, which are normally considered proper for improved cylinder shooting, and you don't have a forty-yard kill likely on anything, certainly not on quail. Hoisting up the pellet count by going to the heavier loads isn't going to save the day, though it helps. For that extraordinary situation then, one combining thin cover, running birds, an almost impossible scenting problem for the dogs, long flushes, we needed a combination of choke and charge weight which is certainly not the ordinary prescription for quail.

But was it such an extraordinary situation? Anywhere east of the Mississippi and south of Maryland, yes, it probably was. But not so in the south*western* part of these United States, not so in the areas where the quail, whether the ornithologists call them scaled, valley, California quail or what have you, are likely to wear top-knots and can surely out-spring Dave Sime, let alone us fat and forty types. These characters call for more shot, perhaps a size larger shot, and a tigher choke than does the more gentlemanly bobwhite of the Southeast.

Undoubtedly more 12-gauge guns are fired at quail than any other bore, and this is reasonable enough since there are more 12-gauge guns around. The 12-bore single-barrel should be choked skeet or improved cylinder for the tighter-sitting eastern birds and their brushier habitat, two-barrelled guns no closer than improved and modified. A few gunners use the same full-choked barrels they fire at waterfowl. This is downright sinful when hunting behind dogs for southeastern bobwhite, not only because the birds are ruined for the pot but also because they're missed too easily with the full-choke spread, less than two feet at the 20-yard mark. The tightest boring is excusable only when the running birds of the west combine with poor cover, no place even to pause, or the gun is in the hands of some lead-foot who probably won't get close enough to flush the runners anyway. Modified makes better sense on the topknotted western runners.

But for my own choice, be it a double, pump, or selfloader, the quail gun is a twenty. It is somehow the inevitable gauge for quail. Light to be easy on the carrying arm, quick on the point because in the brush country where he's really sporting the quail demands fast gunhandling. If the birds are running or flushing wild I'd usually rather beef up the 20-gauge shot charge weight by changing shells or go to a somewhat tighter choke but still in a 20-bore barrel, than to adopt the 12-gauge gun. The .410 is the expert's gun and yet he is helpless with it on flushes at range; the 28 comes closer especially in recent Federal loadings; but the twenty is, for my money, the gun for quail.

Of all our upland gunning save possibly the pursuit of woodcock, quail shooting is the most heavily clothed in tradition. Hence for it the classic two-barreled gun has always seemed most correct. Again classically, for bobwhites we repeat that the first barrel should be bored no tighter than improved cylinder, the second tighter by one degree of choke. A gun throwing 45 per cent first barrel with a 55 per cent second is probably ideal in Eastern covers though there are some quick gun handlers who prefer both tubes open. But since the only first-quality side-by-side in recent years on the U.S. list, the Winchester 21, has gone into custom-only status at a very heavy price, and the "hundred dollar" U.S. guns are no marvels of grade and elegance though solidly made for the money, it would appear that the quail hunter who wants a light 20 has the choice of paying a stiff charge for a used Parker, L. C. Smith, or Winchester, or buying one of the inexpensive non-ejector guns we do still make in this country, the Marlin 90 O-U, Fox Model B-ST, Noble Model 420 or Stevens Model 311. However, we do now have a batch of imports that aren't too rough on the pocketbook of a saving man. Browning, Dakin, Continental, Firearms International, Stoeger have been in hot competition since the war with both vertical and horizontal doubles. Over-unders have been brought in to offer at least token competition with the long-proven Browning Superposed and the representatives of the other four firms named have chased all over Europe for guns to fill the blanks in American side-by-side manufacture. Their activities have brought on to the market doubles selling for about one and a half C-notes that carry single triggers, automatic ejectors. The Stoeger model tagged the Zephyr Pinehurst fits those specifications, is a 6-pound twenty, sells for $150, as only one example. Dakin has doubles by other Spanish builders in the same general price category, FI likewise, and Continental is in there pitching with a variety of grades of Belgian-built guns a shade higher in price. Importer Galef has some deals cooking with Beretta for ejector models. Or if our saving man can keep his piggy bank uncracked until it holds from two-fifty to three hundred he's ready to buy a Browning Superposed in either Standard or Lightning weights, or can choose from any of a dozen engraved horizontal doubles from overseas. The importers have been making hay because of the great gap in our double-gun manufacture.

Not that quail-hunting tradition is so strong that the man without a light 20 double or the wherewithal to get one has to go hide in a corner. At a rough guess, about ninety per cent of the people who live in the quail states and shoot over their own dogs wave pumps and autoloaders, with the hand-operated corn-shellers ahead.

Which is fine and dandy because we now have some properly lightweight 20-bore guns on these actions. Without ribbed barrels, flossy wood, or muzzle gadgets, standard guns like the latest Model 12 Winchester and 870 Remington pump, semi-autos like the 11-48 and 58 Remington types, or the Stevens 77, which weigh about 6½ pounds in 20-gauge size. Perhaps not ideally light but not too heavy for long carrying either. The latest Browning semi-auto, even with a 28-inch barrel hefts under 6½ on my scales. As a twenty the Ithaca Model 37 pump runs only six pounds, and Stoeger's Franchi self-loader shades even that by ten.

And while we think of it, there's at least one twelve-bore on the self-loading list that truly is as light as a twenty—the two-shotter Browning calls the Twenty-weight Double-Auto. The one I have weighs six pounds five ounces when loaded. Makes a right nice quail gun, providing you're not so hard-headed as to take advantage of its .729 bore and stuff in high-recoil loads. Stick to target loads, 1⅛ oz. of shot, in deference to the gun's weight.

There's no sense here in wrestling with the list of conventional 12-bore possibilities because there are too many and there'd be no changing you to a twenty if you're a convinced twelve-gauge man anyway. Suffice it to say that for quail a twelve should be as light and as fast as feasible and the barrel should be no more than 26 inches long. Unless you plan to do some pole-vaulting with it, that is.

Essentially, the one prime requisite of a personalized quail gun is handling speed anyway. The scattergun for pheasants can be twice as slow to start and swing because the bird gets up so much slower and is shot more often in open fields. Only the ruffed grouse, in my opinion, beats the quail in demanding a gun that is sprightly in the hands.

Not that the quail flies so cussed fast. He doesn't, really, proba-bly at no time getting up to the straightaway speed of an old cock pheasant scaling downwind. But he buzzes off right quick and very noisily. He probably leaves you flat-footed when he does it and he will time and again dive into handy cover almost as quickly. You'd better get on him, right now.

One of the minor failings of the beginning quail shooter who is confronted by a covey rise in moderately open cover, is to interpret the need for handling speed in a quail gun as a demand for instantaneous shooting, before the birds are opened out into full flight. Reasonable enough, considering what happens to the nerves of the hardiest among us when twenty bobwhites let go at once. Actually, when a covey does come up in a burst, leaving only that one tail-end Charlie to tantalize us after we've blown both barrels, it is sound technique to pick out the one bird and go after him firmly and decidedly even if a bit more slowly. You can't hit the whole covey anyway, and you'll be a lot deadlier on the one bird, or even on two that happen to cluster or cross, with a pattern properly opened out at twenty to twenty-five yards than you will be at half that range. You have to be faster than on slow-rising pheasants, but not as fast as a covey explosion makes you think. The gun still needs to be a quick gun, however, because the quail who flies dead straight, requiring no quick correction of swing, is a dumb quail.

It is also my personal conviction that a great many quail are missed by overleading. Bobwhite, for example, makes a horrendous fuss when he gets up, has those wings going so fast and is relatively so small in body as compared to most other upland birds, that we figure he's going faster and is further away than he really is. In a covey rise if the center of the bunch breaks straight away from the gun they need very little deflection. It's the birds that break off sharply right or left, or the birds that are flushed by one gunner and cross diagonally ahead of the other that call for any significant amount of deflection. The second gun does have to swing well ahead in that situation, admittedly, but I still feel that there's a tendency to over-estimate bobwhite leads.

The running breeds of quail are the ones that call for considerable daylight between beak and gun muzzle. If you have to sprint them into the air, the yardage out to the flushing point is further stretched by your having to skid to a halt, untangle your feet, and then get the gun going, during all of which time Mr. Topknot is steaming off. Shot pellets from quail loads take more than twice as long to travel forty yards as they do twenty, .1415 seconds as opposed to .0612 if you want to be technical about it, and the angles of flush seem to run wider on the running breeds of quail. And if you're operating on the sprinters by boxing them, with one gun cutting around ahead so that the bunch flushes somewhere between the guns, the sky is the limit on ranges and angles so that the needed leads build up, though they're never as long as the forward allowance we must use.

But the one greatest reason for missing quail is not a matter of gun-swing or lead. Rather is it one of target selection. If a dog points a pheasant and you or the pooch busts the bird out there is no debate as to what to shoot at. The only cause for hesitation is the cock-or-hen question. You have only one possible target. But let from six or sixteen quail churn into the air and any normal human being such as you or I is momentarily confused. He starts going after one bird, decides another is a better chance, has dreams about bagging a double, flubs around indecisively and ends up in a desperation wham at the poorest target of the bunch. Far better is it to pick *one* bird, on the edge, focus only on him, even if he isn't the closest to you. Get *him* down and then worry about picking off a second. It is only the real skilled quail shot, the chap who has been hunting them all his life, who can every time instinctively select the choicest and easiest *pair* from a covey. And the gink who claims he deliberately held fire until a pair lined up or crossed so he could take both with the one pattern is likely to be more a skilled bar room liar than a really skilled quail shot. Pick one out of a covey and stay with him.

The quail is a great game bird, probably more sheer fun to gun than any other. He's petering out in many sections where plowing clean to the fence robs him of cover; much of his best range is private controlled even in the traditional bobwhite states, where the pen-stocked preserves like Dick Hawes' Briar Creek establishment today offer non-residents the best shooting. But he'll always be with us one way or another, thank heaven, daring us to get on him with that quick-barrelled twenty.

HOW TO MISS BIRDS

Havilah Babcock

Okay, here comes Havilah Babcock. About time, you say, and I certainly agree with you. His name is synonymous with good quail stories. The late South Carolina English professor has written so many captivating pieces that selecting some for this book caused considerable hand-wringing on my part: No matter what I choose, I'm bound to leave out some reader's favorite. Hopefully, though, you'll agree with me that the four I've included in this book are among his very best. Whether he was writing on quail, or tick bites, or turning catalpa worms inside-out to catch bluegills, Babcock had a flair for sprightly writing that few can match. I've always wondered what he was like in person, since I never had a chance to meet him. I'm sure we would have hit it off, missing birds and trying to find some of those ghost-like swamp coveys. This piece from Tales of Quail 'n Such *is the first of four we're presenting. For a full course of Babcock you can check out his books. Most have been reissued by Holt, Rinehart and Winston and include, along with the aforementioned,* My Health is Better in November, Jaybirds Go to Hell on Fridays, I Don't Want to Shoot an Elephant, *and* The Education of Pretty Boy.*

IN CASE you haven't heard, I had a missing streak during the past quail season, a streak that made all others in my long and graceless career look puny by comparison. If you didn't hear about it you were in the minority, because I asked everybody and his Uncle John for advice. I finally recovered from my historic slump, but the remedy was so drastic and unorthodox that it should be recommended only in last-ditch cases.

"Just how bad is your slump?" asked the first friend to whom I repaired for counsel.

"Well, I couldn't hit a taurine in the poopdeck with a horticultural implement," I said, or words to that effect with a minor syntactical substitution here and there. "During the past week I shot 35 times and got 7 birds. A dozen beautifully pointed coveys I missed with both barrels, and in the wide open. The 7 birds I did get were unannounced singles that I accidentally knocked up in the thickets. That's the most insulting thing about my slump."

"Right much of a come-down for you," he clucked sympathetically. "Last time we hunted together you clipped 9 out of 10."

"Now don't go harking back to used-to-be's! That's like reminding a fellow with lumbago how good his back felt before he got it."

"Very well. Suppose we get down to brass tacks," he suggested with a professional air. "Are you using the same gun?"

"Same gun."

"Same shells?"

"Same shells. Also same birds," I added as a bitter afterthought.

"Then you must be doing something different," he announced with the finality of a great diagnostician putting his finger on the pathological spot.

"The invincibility of your logic touches me deeply," I said. And I picked up my slump and left. I hoped the touch of old-world courtliness with which I bowed myself out did not go unobserved.

The next day I heard about another gunwise acquaintance. And a very thorough workman he proved to be. Meticulously he measured me from forelock to fetlock and back again, methodically jotting his discoveries in a little book. He measured my hands, my arms, my neck, my shoulders. Even my cubit, which I had never had measured before. And all with an air of professional preoccupation. A doctor would have charged me 25 bucks for such a going-over. Many a jaybird has been classified 1A on less.

With equal thoroughness he addressed his mathematical inquiries to my gun. This fellow would make a crack foreman of a coroner's jury, I thought. Having satisfied himself about the gun, he directed his researches toward my torso again. Arranging me before a large mirror, he said:

"Now aim the gun at your forehead and pull both triggers."

"Won't one trigger be enough?" I asked, demurring a bit. "That left barrel—"

During this suicidal scene he stood behind me, with head cocked like an art connoisseur on the verge of a great discovery. Having never practiced shooting at myself, I am afraid I didn't score too high on this part of the quiz, evincing no doubt a cowardly tendency to flinch. But a generous and perceptive gent he was.

"Well, old man," he beamed, "I have discovered your trouble."

"You have?"

"Precisely. Too much drop."

"Too much drop?"

"Your gun has too much drop for a middling-short neck like yours," he amplified.

"Then what I need is another gun with—"

"My dear fellow," he waxed benevolent, "why incur such needless expense? You see, I happen to be something of a gunsmith, with a little workshop here in my own home. If you'll just leave your gun with me a few days—"

A strange hunger crept into the fellow's eyes. It was a sort of chop-licking gleam somewhere between that of a corporation lawyer sensing a fat fee, and a Bluebeard about to seduce his 15th blonde. With maybe a dash of Oh-Grandmother-what-makes-your-ears-so-big thrown in. I thanked him for his altruism and promised to leave the gun with him later, but I knew I was telling the biggest lie in history.

Funny thing about amateur gunsmiths. Fine people they are the world over—good neighbors who will lend you the very paste off their toothbrushes, upstanding Rotarians with here and there a deacon thrown in, good solid folks who vote the straight ticket and all that. In short, you can trust an amateur gunsmith with your lawnmower, your mandolin, and your wife's shoe-trees. *But never with your gun.*

"Might as well face the facts," I said on my way home. "Looks like I need a new gun. Or a new neck. But I'll give them both another trial before I decide anything. So my neck is middling-short is it?" I had always assumed, without giving the matter too much thought I admit, that it was more or less standard. What rules do you go by in classifying necks anyway, I wondered.

The next day was a dismal repetition of the others. Again I ignominiously missed eight pointed birds in the wide open, and bagged two unannounced swampers that went rocketing through the tupelos. Surely, I said, there ought to be somebody—. And there apparently was. A policeman tipped me off to a man across the river who Really Knew Guns. From A to Z. So across the river I hied myself.

Quite a ballistician and collector this fellow proved to be. He had more guns than Carter had oats. And I soon saw that he meant to outdo all his rivals in thoroughness of approach. Sundry parts of my anatomy were minutely measured, unguessed reflexes pried into, and my personal habits given a judicial airing. Again I stood before a mirror and shot myself nicely between the eyes. I had gotten used to committing suicide by this time and hope I acquitted myself better.

"Ah!" the man who Really Knew Guns finally announced, clucking like old Archimedes when he first discovered something else besides water in his bathtub. "We have hit the nail on the head!"

"On the head?" I repeated, for hope springeth eternal in the breast of the slumper.

"Beyond peradventure, my friend. Your gun hasn't got enough drop. You have a middling-long neck, you know, and with insufficient drop you would naturally—"

"Then the thing for me to do—"

"Is to leave your gun with me a few days. You see, I happen to be something of a gunsmith, and we have here in our own little home—"

Oh Grandmother, what makes your *eyes* so big! Come into my parlor, said the spider to the fly. With profuse thanks I picked up my gun, my slump, my neck and left.

"Damn!" I said on the way home. My neck was too short last night, and too long tonight. Versatile cuss, at least. I couldn't think of any use I had put it to overnight that might have stetched it. I had always gotten along with my neck O.K. In fact, it had been the only part of me that hadn't ever had anything wrong with it. In a general way I suppose I was proud of it, although the matter had never been brought specifically to my attention. Now I was becoming neck-conscious. Anyway I was glad that I had been re-classified. Going around with a sub-standard neck is not the best thing for a man's morale.

A few days later I had an idea that approached brilliance. Maybe my trouble wasn't physical after all. Maybe it was a psychosis, a neurosis or some junk like that. My next door neighbor was a professor of psychology. In fact, the old codger had written a book or two. Besides, he wouldn't have the face to charge me anything. My lawnmower had been over there going on four months.

The professor listened with his best bedside manner, fondling his Phi Beta Kappa key the while. When my tale was told, he said:

"The psychology of the slump is quite intriguing. As I was saying to Professor Jenks only yesterday, my ping pong has undergone a most inexplicable decline during the past fortnight. Psychologically it is most interesting, but—"

"To get back to guns," I brought him back to earth.

"To be sure. Offhand, I'd say you merely have an inferiority complex."

That sounded plausible enough, especially the inferior part. About the complex I wasn't so sure.

"What can I do about this complex?" I pursued.

"Don't worry. Those things cure themselves, sooner or later. When you start hitting birds again, I dare say your complex will disappear. Now about my ping pong slump—"

"Maybe you are trying too hard," I said, and pushed my lawnmower back home.

During the next week I hunted nearly every day, absorbed advice like a sponge, and missed everything that got up in front of me. Except, of course, a few wild shenanigans that bounced up unexpectedly. You may wonder how I found time to do so much finding and missing. Well, hang it, they were mostly the same birds! It's surprising how a few coveys will last if you just shoot *at* them.

One night I sidled up to a soda counter for another bromo to assuage my miseries. There sat a fat bus driver licking a banana split.

"Hear your shooting is off," he opined.

"Yeah. I hear the same thing," I concurred.

"Maybe you got my old trouble. Had to give up hunting on account of it."

"What was that?" I dully wondered.

"Bifocals."

"Bifocals?" I perked up a bit.

"Yeah. Think right good now. Which part do you shoot through, your uppers or your lowers?"

After the fashion of bifocalers the world over, I bobbed my head up and down, picking out imaginary targets in the drugstore.

"Well," I answered, "when a bird leaves the ground I'm looking through my upper field of vision, which is correct."

"Okey doke. Now when that same bird rises into your shooting zone—?"

I flushed a bird from a case of cod liver oil on the floor and watched it ladder up the shelves, finally clearing a bottle of Lydia E. Pinkham's in the far corner.

"Great balls of fire!" I said. "Do you mean to tell me—"

"Exactly. Unless a man's got a didapper neck, he'll wear himself plumb out a-watching birds zigzag from his uppers to his lowers thataway. Yessir, them bifocals will sure Gawd ruin a man's shooting."

The sweet plausibleness of the idea overcame me, and my spirits soared into the empyrean. I had been knocking at the doors of experts in vain, yet this observing man-of-the-people had infallibly diagnosed my trouble. A tide of brotherly love welled up in me and I set the bus driver up to two more banana splits. I came home and aimed my gun all over the place to confirm the great discovery. Then I took Alice out and treated her to a four-buck lobster dinner. Life was suddenly sweet again.

The next day I had a pair of old-fashioned single-lenses made, using only my distance prescription. Now I could really see all over the world! Then I promised birds all over the neighborhood and jumped into my car. Those saucy covies that I had lulled into security were headed for a rude awakening!

But I came home that night feeling two grades lower than a corporal's orderly. My wonderful glasses made no difference whatever. I still missed shots a left-handed boy could have bagged with a set of dominos. I was beginning to rue the largess of that second banana split, and that Maine lobster I had squandered on Alice.

"By the way," remarked Alice, who is usually about two days late in her inspirations, "weren't those bifocals you discarded the same ones you shot so well with last season?"

"Aw, go to hell," I invited.

But she wouldn't even do that.

Now some of you will wonder how a man of my apparent intelligence could be such a sucker for advice. But a drowning man grabs at a straw. There are only three kinds of people who will believe absolutely anything you tell them: slumpers, boarding-school girls just turned 16, and voters on election day. Surely there must be somebody in the crowd who has had a kindred experience and can conjure up a little fellow-feeling!

I had now absorbed so much advice, both oral and written, that my shooting had become quite a ceremony. Also something of a memory test, since I had so many tips, admonitions, and scraps of advice to rehearse before slipping the safety catch. Whenever a dog pointed, I began automatically to check off the do's and don't's on my list. It was quite a memorandum that I had accumulated.

Having gone through my rehearsal with great fidelity and punctiliousness, I would step victoriously forward and miss with both barrels. The ordeal was then over, except for the post mortems, which usually lasted until the dogs pointed again. I had become such a fatalist that I missed before I shot, and found myself almost wishing that I didn't have to shoot at all. Heck, I said, I'd better quit before I become a darned blinker!

While all this slumping was taking place I hunted alone for two reasons: first, because my disgrace was bad enough without an audience; and secondly, because Dr. Jim Havers, my hunting companion for 20 years, was away during the first three weeks of the season. When Jim did get back I was so dejected that a proposed two-day hunt in the birdy low-country left me unmoved.

"Take somebody along who can shoot," I said, magnanimous in my grief. "Leave me alone with my miseries."

Never a loquacious fellow at best, Jim said nothing, just kept packing my things in his car. Two hours later Fleet and Tobey were pointing in a low-country peafield, and Jim beckoned me alongside.

"Wait until I get fixed," I pleaded.

Straightway I went into a rehearsal of the do's and don't's I had accumulated, anxiously ransacking my memory for additional scraps of advice that might save the day. I even shadow-boxed with my gun a few times to make sure of my timing and coordination. Then I stepped up and missed 18 birds with both barrels. It was quite a feat.

Jim didn't say anything because he was a gentleman. I didn't say anything because I didn't have anything to say. Like the boy the calf ran over. As I trudged along the uselessness of life hit me afresh, and I felt terribly alone in he world. After a while Jim lit his pipe and casually opened up.

"Tell me," he said, "have you been getting any advice about this slump? Talked with anybody, or read any books about shooting?"

"I've talked to everybody who would listen, and listened to everybody who would talk," I reassured him. "And I've read three books on shooting, including a piece I wrote myself some ten years ago. Thought it was pretty good too," I shamelessly admitted.

"In other words, you've become a walking encyclopedia on shooting, haven't you?"

Our dogs next pointed at the edge of a cypress pond, where the shooting would be fast and tricky. The covey, having been trailed a hundred yards, had scuttled under a brushpile, around which our dogs were expectantly frozen.

"Wait," I interrupted, "until I get fix—"

Suddenly Jim Havers ran amock. With a yell like that of an Indian brave being bereft of his family jewels, he bounded forward and came crashing down atop the brushpile. The birds underneath took off as if the Devil had a mortgage on their tails and went swooshing through the treetops. It was the best close-up of jet-propulsion I had ever seen.

"Of all the damned fool things! I told you I wasn't ready!" I exploded.

"You're not going to be hereafter either. I'll see to that. Now pick up your two birds, you shingle-butted idiot!" grinned Jim, unscrambling himself from the brushpile.

"You mean I got a double? Why, I don't even remember—"

"That's why you got them. I didn't even shoot," he said, breaking his gun as evidence.

"But what prompted you to do a fool thing like that?"

"Everybody gets into a slump now and then—except the fellow who stays in one," he explained. "The best thing to do with a slump is to let it alone, if it's an honest-to-goodness slump. It will cure itself sooner or later. But you, being a superior sort of idiot, decided to hurry yours up. The result was an overdose of advice. When a man has been doing something reasonably well, it doesn't pay him to become too analytical about how he does it. You've just been thinking too much before you shot."

"Could that be the reason I miss the easy, deliberate shots and get those that catch me offguard?" I asked hopefully.

"Exactly. Now quit thinking and go to shooting. To make sure you do, I'm going to jump slam-bang onto every bird that's pointed this morning."

He did just that, the butt-headed and benevolent cuss, and I shot as in my palmiest pre-slump days. By noon his jumping antics were no longer necessary. I mentally did the jumping myself, walking up briskly and shooting fast, *before I had time to think.*

By nightfall we both had a jacketful of birds, and as we cruised slowly homeward we agreed that this old world, in spite of the ills that beset it, was still a pretty good place for two half-cracked birdhunters to be in.

"You know," Jim philosophized between puffs, "sometimes thinking is the worst thing a man can do."

SHOPFSTALL

THE LONDON GUN

Bob Brister

Bob Brister has spent most of his life in the Southwest, but as shooting edi-tor of Field & Stream *he has had the opportunity to pursue his favorite sports around the world. He's a champion shot, fascinated with the mysteries of getting more out of the smoothbore. "The London Gun," from his super collection of stories* Moss, Mallards and Mules *(Winchester Press), provides a glimpse at some of the fast company he keeps.*

THE SO-OBVIOUSLY BRITISH GENTLEMAN with the muttonchop sideburns was standing militarily beside a white column of ante-bellum elegance, looking very much as if he, not Harry Winthrop, had inherited the mansion and the old Spanish land grants to that general vicinity of South Texas.

Nick Dyer smiled into his mug of cold beer and decided the limeys are still the world's coolest con men.

Winthrop was standing beside the Englishman, greeting guests and looking somewhat stooped by comparison, smiling with satis-faction that the hunting party of this house guest, none other than Mr. Lawrence Payne of London, had already been such a success.

The lunch had turned out particularly well, even for corn-fed steer buried in the ground and cooked slowly, Mexican style, for two days. And the right people had come.

"Ah think it's just marvelous," Mrs. Winthrop was saying, but she never got to say what because Jimmy Callahan, who owned the local sporting goods store, broke in to ask about fine European shotguns.

"I know the so-called London gun is supposedly the best in the world, but really, I mean if a guy can't afford to pay four thou-sand and wait a couple of years for delivery, what do you think about some of the top-grade Italian guns, like the Beretta or the Perazzi? Aren't they very similar in balance and design?"

"Yeah," said Mike Crawford, his best customer, "and far as that goes, I've heard AYA in Spain can duplicate a Purdey, piece for piece, and for about a fourth the price. Far as that goes, you can buy a Japanese copy of a Browning for three hundred bucks that'll shoot just as far and last about as long as any of us will ever live."

"Oohhh?" breathed Lawrence Payne.

"That's right," said Crawford, "so what's really the difference with a London gun when it just comes to shooting?"

A Japanese or a Belgian might have been backed to the wall, Nick thought, but the Englishman stood straighter and taller.

"Aye suppose one of those little Japanese cars, or perhaps a lover from the Fiji Islands, might be, shall we say, serviceable," he smiled condescendingly, "but one would scarcely care to discuss them at length with others."

"Well stated, Mr. Payne," Winthrop smiled. "In a little while perhaps we'll show them the difference."

Nick drove Mike and Jimmy over to the pasture to be hunted, and filled them in on the arrangement he'd made with Winthrop the night before.

"I laid him a case of scotch that you guys can outshoot the knickers off that stuff-shirted limey."

"Dunno so much about that," Jimmy said suspiciously. "He was talking about lock time, whatever that is, and static balance and hammer fall. Hell, we don't know that much about shotguns."

"You know how to kill quail with 'em," Nick grinned, "and that's the bet."

Harry Winthrop kept a kennel of the finest pointers in South Texas, and for the special occasion he'd brought along his professional trainer to handle them. It was Butler Griffin, in fact, and the two young pointers he was grooming for the field trials which seemed to interest the Englishman the most.

"Are they as, uh, staunch as our setters?" Payne questioned, obviously concerned that one of the pups might jump up on his freshly pressed knickers. "They do seem a bit, uh, boisterous."

Butler had trouble keeping a straight face.

"They're right boisterous, for sure," he said, "but right good at findin' birds in cockleburs and cactus. Setter's a fine dog, sir, but not for this country. It's too hot and too rough."

They had put down the dogs to run off a little steam before they went into the hunting pasture, and Butler watched with interest as the Englishman took from Winthrop's car a black, leather-covered wooden case with many decals and travel stickers on it. With precisioned care he released the catches and opened it and the others gathered around to see. Therein, cradled in red velvet as if lying in state, rested a delicately beautiful double with classic straight-grip English stock, intricate scroll engraving on detachable sidelocks, and two sets of barrels nestled into their fitted compartments. Mr. Lawrence Payne made the most of the moment, joining the action to the barrels carefully and delicately, snapping the slender splinter of a forend into place with one tiny, perfectly meshing click.

"You're not going to shoot a 12-gauge at quail, are you?" Mike blurted.

"Oh, yes," Payne replied, "but you see our upland load for the 12-bore is essentially the same as your 20-bore loading. Perhaps, say by American standards, it could be considered an overbored 20-gauge."

He held up a fat, short little shell two and one-half inches long. "Our upland guns are chambered for the very light load, and of course they are rather lightweight weapons. Would you like to feel this one, sir?"

Mike accepted the graceful double as carefully as a bachelor taking a baby, felt its incredibly featherlight heft and balance, but realized the stock was so long, and so high, that when he put the gun up it hung under his shirt sleeve and the barrels seemed to be pointing for the sky.

"Man, I'd shoot three feet high with this thing," he grinned.

"Perhaps not," the Englishman said. "You see we believe in a sight picture which reveals a good deal of the barrel. Great aid to pointing out a target at an angle. By regulating the impacts of the barrels, this particular gun was made to shoot quite low, in fact. It could scarcely be used effectively on driven grouse or pheasant, but I suppose it will suffice for your quail over dogs."

"I see," said Nick. "And do you change guns for every different bird?"

The Englishman looked at him coolly. "Almost any gun can be made to perform satisfactorily on any game if the shooter is sufficiently accustomed to it. But under certain conditions it is more comfortable to shoot a gun bored for a particular type of target, and the incoming target such as driven grouse is easiest met with a gun which shoots relatively high, making it unnecessary to blot out the approaching target to establish the necessary lead in front."

Butler had cut himself a chew of tobacco, eyes squinting in amusement. "What happens," he asked, "if a pair of birds jump and one goes straight away and the other comes hookin' back over your head? Be pretty hard to carry two guns for that, wouldn't it?"

The Englishman snapped his heels together, threw the double to his shoulder at an imaginary going-away bird, and then dropped the gun from his shoulder, whirled with knickered legs crossed awkwardly one over each other, and mounted it again.

"That is the manner in which it is done, in driven grouse shooting," he said. "The first shot is taken as the birds approach, and then the turn is made for the second; one in front and one behind."

Butler shook his head, having trouble keeping from laughing, and Nick realized for the first time the Englishman had begun to redden slightly at the temples.

"Sir, I noticed that you took the gun from your shoulder, then remounted it to simulate the second shot. Is that also established procedure?"

"Indeed, and quite necessarily so for smoothness of swing. The tracking of the target, the swing, and the shot are all accomplished in one movement culminated by the shot at the instant the gun butt touches the shoulder. This eliminates the common American fault of stopping the swing. Thus, after one shot is made, the gun butt is dropped slightly to permit the restart of the cycle."

"I'd think a man would have to cycle pretty quick to get on two of those quail in a thicket," Butler observed. "Let's go see if we can find us a few."

The lemon-and-white dog was tearing over the pasture at breakneck speed. He whipped through a patch of cactus, then whirled in midair and came skidding down sidewise, nose and tail taut as if stretched by some invisible wire.

"Aye say," mused the Englishman, visibly impressed. "Devilishly stylish."

"Fair," said Butler.

The black-and-white dog was honoring the point and they walked past him three abreast. The birds obviously were nailed in a patch of brush at the edge of the timber.

Mike was on the left, Jimmy on the right, and the Englishman was coming up straight behind the dog when the covey exploded, the most of the birds going past Jimmy.

He nailed two, missed the third shot, and Mike powdered a sleeper that came up behind him. The Englishman did not fire.

"What were you waiting for?" Harry Winthrop fumed.

"Rather dislike potting another man's bird," Lawrence Payne said starchily, glancing at Jimmy, who had blasted the lone quail that jumped ahead of the Englishman.

The singles had fanned out into tall grass well away from the woods, and the black-and-white dog was already down.

"Shall we take turn about?" Payne asked. "Or take them as we may?"

"Since there's a bet on, sir, I'd suggest you just fire at will," Nick said quickly.

"Very well."

They walked in on the singles, this time the Englishman dropping back and working his way to the far left, away from the dog. A quail fluttered up out of the grass and there was an instantaneous report as it folded in a shower of feathers two feet from the nose of the dog.

"Sorry about firing so near the animal, old man," Payne apologized to Butler, "but since there is a bet of sorts, you know."

Butler rubbed his eyes and tried to remember when he'd seen a bird hit that hard, that fast.

They were walking over to the lemon dog, which had come down at the edge of the fencerow, when two birds flushed wild behind them. Nick ducked to the ground, heard two loads of shot go over his head, and saw the Englishman standing there in the awkward, cross-legged stance, blowing the smoke out of his barrels.

"Grassed them both, Aye believe," Lawrence Payne said stiffly to Butler. "Afraid Aye failed to center the second bird, if you'd care to send the dogs for him first."

Nick felt his face flushing in the sun as Harry nudged him and laughed in his ear. "You want to press the bet, young man?"

Mike and Jimmy began missing shots they'd normally kill, trying to shoot too quickly, and the Englishman seemed to need only to point his magic double in the general direction and the birds would fall. Once, as a bird towered and banked overhead, a diamondback rattled in a prickly pear patch beside the Englishman's left foot, and he killed the quail and then, calmly, the snake.

"Rotten sound," he observed.

When Butler halted the hunt to let the dogs water and rest in a little creek, Jimmy and Mike sat disgustedly down on the bridge and the Englishman stood looking into the distance, unwilling to risk dirtying the bottom of the knickers on the boards.

"What is your business back in England?" Nick asked.

Lawrence Payne glanced at Harry, received a nod, and smiled broadly for the first time.

"Actually, Aye suppose my title should be stated as vice president, but my principal function with the company is senior shooting instructor at our grounds just outside of London."

"What company?"

"Oohh, thought you knew, Holland and Holland. Make guns, you know."

"Now," said Nick, slumping to the ground against a tree, "I know."

On the way back they passed the ruins of a tenant farmer's shack with a trashpile and an ancient automobile rusting in the grass behind it, and Jimmy walked up beside Payne and fell into step.

"I'm just curious," he said, "but would you mind shooting that gun just one time at that old car door over there? We'd like to see what kind of pattern that thing really throws."

The Englishman drew himself up and glanced at the rusty old Ford. "Oh, Aye suppose so," he said, restraining a smile. "But it does seem something of a shame. Couldn't we perhaps locate a slightly later model, old chap?"

SHOFFSTALL

SLIM BOGGINS' MISTAKE

Havilah Babcock

This is another Havilah Babcock gem, from Tales of Quail 'n Such. *Poor Slim Boggins—he never has a chance against one of the meanest tricks I've ever seen pulled on a man. Enjoy the piece, friend, but a word of caution goes with it: Try to get it out of your mind before you walk in to your next covey rise!*

A BIG COVEY exploded from the brown fern and went corkscrewing through the tree-tops. Only a jumping-jack could have drawn bead on those pettifogging politicians. I got one bird and thanked providence for its kindly intercession.

"How did you come out?" I turned to my companion.

"Short and simple are the annals of the poor," he answered, glancing wryly at the interlacing tree-tops. "When I zigged, they zagged. And vice versa. There are too many bones in the human body for that sort of shooting. Even my head got in my way."

Then as we stood by, explaining our misses to each other's entire satisfaction, a fat cock lifted leisurely from the fern and loafed tantalizingly away through the only opening in the thicket. We looked ruefully at our empty guns.

"Could have knocked him down with a second-hand washboard," was Cliff's unhappy comment. "Third time that's happened this morning. Hereafter I'm going to save a shell for the sleeper, so help me Hannah!"

I have never figured out the psychology of the sleeper, that saucy jackanapes who gets up belatedly and flies provokingly low and straight away while the gunner stands like a simpleton with an empty gravel-shooter. Is his tardy take-off due to wariness or to unwariness? Is he a dastardly fellow who deliberately lets his compatriots take the rap? Is he a slow-coach and addle-pated dunce who requires an extra interval to think things out? Or is he the Phi Beta Kappa of the class who figures thus to disadvantage the gunner?

That morning I was shooting indifferently because of the sleepless night I had spent. Regularly, for a quarter of a century, inability to sleep the night before has made a wreck of me on Thanksgiving, the traditional opening day for quail in South Carolina. I doubt that I have slept twenty-five winks in twenty-five years during that particular night.

I count everything that can jump a fence or go through a gap, and wear out every sleep-inducing device known. "I could be bounded in a nutshell and count myself a king of infinite space were it not that I had bad dreams," I quote Shakespeare, who was something of a hunter himself.

"Tomorrow is an important day," I spend the night reminding myself. "If I don't get some sleep, I'll feel like the wreck of the Hesperus and shoot worse than a constipated owl with a crooked shotgun." Maybe I make it too important. I'm a bird hunter, not a psychologist. Finally, I deliver an ultimatum to my uncooperative body: "Now, damn your hide, you can sleep or stay awake just as you like, but you are going to catch the devil tomorrow and you needn't expect any sympathy from me. So if I were you—"

You'd think an old codger like me would have too much gumption to behave like this. But if you are a born bird hunter and had rather hunt birds than do anything else on this slightly flattened and somewhat cock-eyed globe, you might discover in your heart a modicum of sympathy.

For twenty-five years I have hunted with the same companion, which must establish some sort of record for mutual tolerance! Now, there are both advantages and disadvantages in having the same side-kick so long. We know the idiosyncrasies of our dogs, which enhances the pleasure of the hunt. We also know the idiosyncrasies of each other, which *sometimes* enhances the pleasure of the hunt.

During twenty-five years of companionship any two men will accumulate a fund of experiences to talk about, but long association tends to reduce the necessity of conversation. We know each other so well that we don't have to talk. A monosyllable may effect a meeting of minds, a meaningful glance may recall some experience memorable to both. Even a wide grin becomes an adequate reminder.

But such intimate companionship makes bragging next to impossible. How can you embroider some past exploit with glowing details if your audience was there when it happened? It's like gilding the lily in the presence of your mother-in-law, like having an extra conscience always following you around.

"No man is a hero to his valet," remarked Carlyle. And seldom to his hunting companion. When I inventory my deficiencies as a side-kick, I realize that only a great and magnanimous gentleman would put up with me for twenty-five years. But calling Cliff a gentleman doesn't keep him from bossing me around at times.

"Havilah!" his voice boomed through the flatwoods. "Why don't you quit wool-gathering and look after your dog?"

Fleet, my sedate little setter, was trailing in a patch of beggar's-lice near a cornfield. Cliff's slim-legged pointer raced in, verified Fleet's discovery, and seconded the motion. But neither was dead yet. Every quail dog has some mannerism that advertises the proximity of game and tells the discerning owner how the quest is progressing.

I never cock a gun over Fleet, however imminent things look, until her merry tail stiffens and curls at the tip. Cliff never slips the safety over Carrie until her right hind foot is lifted gingerly from the ground. The beggar's-lice was seven feet tall and seed showered down as we passed through.

"Why do people import food for birds when this native beggar's-lice is unbeatable? There's enough food here for ten coveys," remarked Cliff.

"True," I replied. "But in a few weeks it will be plowed under. After all, that's the greatest single enemy of quail—the plow."

At the far end of the patch both dogs dropped dead, a big bevy hurtled up, and we downed three birds on the rise. One of the secrets of bird hunting is marking the flight of a decamping covey, an art at which Cliff is especially adept. But this time we both saw it: fully twenty birds deploying beautifully in the broomstraw 350 yards away.

"Lovely! Lovely!" rhapsodized Cliff. "The enchanted dream of every bird hunter. Your masterpieces of art, your fabled beauties of the boudoir, your deathless symphonies—what can hold a candle to a picture like this?"

"First one like that I've seen for quite a spell," I admitted, "except on a patent-medicine calendar."

"Button up your shootin' britches and shake a leg," Cliff relapsed into English. "Let's go down and take up collection before they start socializin' and get together."

We did. And that's one of the things I like about quail shooting in the Carolina low country: You can usually see where your birds go down. That is, approximately where. I don't mean you can saunter nonchalantly down and spit on their tails, and I'm not guaranteeing you can hit them when you get there. That's a horse of another complexion.

But the gunner's vision is often unobstructed for a quarter of a mile, and he gets at least a general idea as to the line of flight. He doesn't have to tramp over half a county to exhaust the possibilities, as he must often do in broken terrain where singles shooting is little more than a process of elimination: you just look everywhere they *could* have flown.

This flat country is also friendly to my aging legs. Indeed, my old underpinnings have a deep affection for the gentle terrain of this half-forgotten kingdom. But how they do argue and upbraid me when they have to propel my *corpus delicti* up and down the red hills of my native Virginia, as they do ten days every season! Yes, mine is definitely a flat-country species of leg.

I like the low-country too because it is unfenced—one of the few unenclosed and unspoiled provinces left on the map. It is said that barbed-wire did more to tame the Wild West than did the six-guns of the United States marshals, but I don't want anything tamed. Don't fence me in! On the sprawling plantations I can walk or ride the livelong day without encountering a single fence. Yes, sir, I've hunted bobwhite over a fair segment of his range, and I'll take mine in the South Carolina low-country every time.

"By the way," I asked after we had pocketed enough singles from the beggar's-lice bevy, "where was Timrod while the other dogs were trailing back there? I completely forgot the pup."

"Timrod was excusin' himself from the proceedings," laughed Cliff. "He stalked stiff-legged forty yards behind the other dogs, with his ears pricked up and an awfully worried look on his face. He figured something was going to pop, and he didn't want to be caught with his suspenders down."

Carrie is Cliff's dog, and Fleet is mine, but Timrod, a six-month-old setter pup, is *our* dog. We had taught him the backyard rudiments before the season opened, but this was his first day in school, his maiden voyage afield. Nearly every season we have a stripling coming along, not only as an eventual replacement, but for the pleasure of watching a youngster discover himself. We have a theory too that teaching a up his a-b-c's keeps a hunter's heart young.

A mighty hunter is Timrod, and the world is full of wonderful things to be pointed. During the morning he must have pointed a full twenty times, stretching out on everything from stink sparrows to terrapins. And at noon he wound up in a blaze of glory by dropping as dead as chiseled granite on a yoke of oxen plowing in a field.

Not only have I hunted for twenty-five years with the same companion, but over the same territory, and in many instances the identical coveys themselves. Indeed, it would not be inaccurate to say that I have been shooting at the same birds for a quarter of a century! Successive generations have brought me both pleasure and embarrassment. Bob is a durable fellow and a great begetter of his kind. And he is a stable freeholder who sticks to the old homestead as long as it remains congenial to his tenancy.

Down through the years many of these coveys have earned pet names for themseles, such as Lazy Mule, Barking Dog, Foolish Virgins, Mother-in-Law, Po' Chance and Handshake. Years ago—it must have been in the late 'twenties—Cliff and I each downed three birds with a single shot and spent the rest of the afternoon admiring each other. It was an epic event, one enshrined in the memory of two men who are no longer spring chickens. Thus the covey we still call Handshake won a niche in our affections.

There are practical advantages in hunting the same territory and the same coveys year after year. We have learned the flight habits of many families, and how to dispose ourselves to best advantage before a rise. We have learned their range, their probable feeding ground and their sanctuaries, because we have read their diaries from season to season. We know when and where to hunt a particular covey. Such information can be a very present help in time of need.

It was in the Po' Chance country that we found ourselves on Thanksgiving afternoon, and here we ran into one Slim Boggins, a neighborhood character famed for his shooting prowess and not in the least averse to demonstrating it.

"Have you gents ever heard of a fellow who can drap fo' birds on a rise?" he pushed his cap back and asked.

We didn't think we had. With an occasional fluke shot maybe, but certainly not with any measure of consistency. Was there such a fellow?

"You air talkin' to him now. Slim Boggins by name. My ole she-bitch is trailin' yonder. Come on over and I'll give y'all a demonstratin'."

Striding loose-jointedly behind his dog, he kicked up a covey and neatly dropped four birds on a simultaneous flush. Furthermore, he made it look easy, almost inevitable, in fact.

"That air is what I mean, gents. And I ain't usin' no fancy autymatic neither. Jes' this here ole flippity-flop pump gun. Shucks, 'tain't nothin'," he discounted.

I looked at Cliff and Cliff looked at me, and we conveyed a lot without saying anything. This cocky, self-contained and unbookish fellow, this gangling son of the swamp, was the nearest thing to a natural shot we had ever seen. And the ancient pump which he fondled was as nerveless and supple-jointed as its owner. Never tell me that a repeater can't compete with an automatic in speed!

"Two birds fromped down in that broomstraw yonder. Come on over and I'll give you gents another demonstratin'," our uninvited guest announced.

A few minutes later the gaunt "ole she-bitch" pointed and her gangling master beckoned to us. "Now I'll th'ow this ole gun on the ground till the birds get up. Then I'll grab her and politely drap 'em both."

Two birds hurtled away toward a pine thicket. Slim swooped down, retrieved his gun and dropped them both. And they were as dead as a quarter past four when they hit.

" 'Tain't nothin'," he manfully deprecated. "Also shoots 'em from the hip. If you gents want a free sample—"

Cliff and I were impressed by this backwoods paragon. We

were also scared. If this "demonstratin' " kept up, there would be precious few birds left in Po' Chance. This two-legged epidemic that called himself Slim Boggins had to be curbed in some way.

With his usual resourcefulness, Cliff launched the attack. A flank attack it proved to be, and its very simplicity at first baffled me.

"Most wonderful shooting we have ever seen, and we are indebted to you for the exhibition," Cliff laid the groundwork. "It probably won't improve our shooting any, but may I ask you one question?"

"Shore, shore. Anything to oblige," expansively offered our Mr. Boggins.

"Do you practice monocular or binocular shooting?"

"Says how much?" Slim blinked.

"Do you shoot with one eye closed, or with both open?" Cliff pursued.

"Aw, that. Funny thing, I ain't never noticed. Never crossed my mind till you brung it up. Funny, ain't it? Tell you what, I'll take notice and let you gents know. It mout help y'all some. That's me, Slim Boggins."

Fleet had a single at the base of a cypress stump. I raised my gun, but Cliff shook his head. The bird flew as straight as a martin to its gourd. Slim raised his gun and confidently banged away. Then he banged again, but the bird reached the haven of the swamp untouched. A frown of perplexity gathered on Slim's face, but it was quickly dissipated.

"Shucks. Had my left eye closed that time. That ain't the way I been doing it. I shoot with both eyes open. It's come to me now. Show you gents next time," he quickly reassured himself.

A few minutes later Carrie froze at the edge of a peapatch. Two birds got up and sauntered straight down main street. Slim pumped away four times, but nary a feather did he cut. Stock-still he stood, enveloped in an awful silence. The shadow of amazed disbelief crept over his face. Picking up an empty cartridge, he absently fingered it, then shook his head as if to dispel a grisly vision.

"Great balls of fire! I helt both eyes open that time. That must not be the way I do it either!"

An awful doubt had insinuated itself into the soul of Slim Boggins. He eyed his dog distrustfully and regarded his faithful old pump with new-found suspicion, as if the wife of his bosom had unaccountably betrayed him.

"Jes' happened to think," he explained limply. "Got fo' cows to milk when I get home. If you gents will excuse me—" And he sloped off across the field.

That's the last we saw of Slim Boggins. But not the last we heard. A hundred yards away he must have stepped into a single, because we heard a rapid succession of shots and then, "Great balls of fire!" Three hundred yards away another fusillade rent the air, and the word "fire!" resounded through the hushed flatwoods and died away in the swamp.

"Cliff, the devil's going to get you for sure!" I said. "For a trick like that, your carcass should be hanged, quartered and dried on a 'simmen bush. Besides, there's a constitutional amendment about cruel and unusual punishments."

"I haven't done a thing, not a blessed thing!" Cliff protested with a twinkle discernible at fifty feet. "Our Mister Boggins just made the mistake of thinking. He shot well because he shot unconsciously, in a manner of speaking. He was not handicapped by a college education. But he made the mistake of thinking, and that's sometimes fatal. Now let that teach you a lesson, son," he admonished with a solemn chuckle.

"Well, our friend will recover in time, but chances are he won't insist on demonstrating to us again," I said. "And these Po' Chance birds will give you the thanks of the republic. They've had enough for one day. We have only an hour or so before dark. Let's amble over to the Mother-in-Law covey and see how they fared this summer."

It was in the Mother-in-Law country that Timrod won his spurs. These birds are great gadabouts, and it was nearing nightfall before Carrie and Fleet found their names on the society page. Then they trailed across a bog, through a field of wild partridge-peas, and into an uncultivated strip fingering out from the swamp. These both dogs came to a peremptory halt.

But we instantly lowered our guns and looked at each other for swift confirmation. There, slightly ahead of the other dogs, was little Timrod on point. He had intercepted the homeward-bound covey and pinned it down in the brown cinnamon fern, under whose friendly canopy Bob so loves to doze. And there stood Timrod, with both eyes resolutely shut, rigid as a bisque figurine.

"I'll just be damned!" breathed Cliff. "Do you see what I see?"

"Shut up! Ain't you got no manners?" I grinned back.

As we eased forward Timrod covertly opened his eyes and glanced at Carrie, his guardian and preceptor. Her right hind foot delicately scorned the ground. Carefully Timrod lifted his foot to conform. Carrie's muzzle angled sharply to the left. Timrod, who had been manfully pointing the whole world more or less, shifted his muzzle to match. Then he sort of looked over his glasses at us and ventured: "Is this something like it, *mister?*"

Lowering his gun, Cliff nodded to me and lifted one finger. I shot once at the scudding bevy, and we held the other dogs while Timrod proudly retrieved the bird. Then we danced a jig around the newest member of our family, playfully pommeled him in the fern and called him "old horse." The starry-eyed Timrod pranced around and yipped his great pleasure. "Come on, let's find some more!" he barked.

"We've got a dog in the family now," Cliff said. "When you get home, write that down in your diary."

And I did. I wrote: "On this day Timrod, a pup of whom I have high hopes, graduated from the first grade and received his diploma."

It was nightfall now, and the hunt was over. Another Thanksgiving had come and gone. It had been a pleasant but somewhat arduous day, and as I climbed gratefully into the car I fervently sighed: "May the Lord be thanked for putting a night between every two days!"

FOUR

Hunting Around

THE WARWICK WOODLANDS

Frank Forester

His real name was Henry William Herbert, but the byline that he placed on America's first pure sporting works was Frank Forester. He produced volumes of outdoor books, of which three have been given special prominence by being reprinted in various new editions over the years (including Derrydale). These are The Deerstalkers *(1843),* My Shooting Box *(1848), and* The Warwick Woodlands *(1850). This excerpt from* The Warwick Woodlands *has been one of my favorite pieces for many years. For me, its charm is something that can be experienced again and again. I love the way the hunt begins: The sense of the gathering unfolding; the laughter, food and drink; the camaraderie provided by the enormous presence of Tom Draw, Harry Archer and the ubiquitous servant Tim. The action in the field includes a great deal of woodcock and grouse shooting, as well as quail, a diversion I trust you will not mind in our quail book. I don't really like to read the didactic how-to pieces that seem so popular with many outdoor magazines today, but whenever I do stumble through one on quail I'm always amused when some new self-proclaimed expert warns us not to follow the single birds too quickly after a covey rise. Well, Forester passed on that tip in* The Warwick Woodlands *in 1850, but he does it with wit and elan, as you shall see.*

Day the Second

Much as I had heard of Tom Draw, I was I must confess, taken altogether aback when I, for the first time, set eyes upon him. I had heard Harry Archer talk of him fifty times as a crack shot; as a top sawyer at a long day's fag; as the man of all others he would choose as his mate, if he were to shoot a match, two against two—what then was my astonishment at beholding this worthy, as he reared himself slowly from his recumbent position? It is true, I had heard his sobriquet, "Fat Tom," but, Heaven and Earth! Such a mass of beef and brandy as stood before me, I had never even dreamt of. About five feet six inches at the very utmost in the perpendicular, by six or—"by'r lady"—nearer seven in circumference, weighing, at the least computation, two hundred and fifty pounds, with a broad jolly face, its every feature—well-formed and handsome, rather than otherwise—mantling with an expression of the most perfect excellence of heart and temper, and overshadowed by a vast mass of brown hair, sprinkled pretty well with gray! Down he plumped from the counter with a thud that made the whole floor shake, and with a hand outstretched, that might have done for a Goliath, out he strode to meet us.

"Why, hulloa! hulloa! Mr. Archer," shaking his hand till I thought he would have dragged the arm clean out of the socket—"How be you, boy? How be you?"

"Right well, Tom, can't you see? Why confound you, you've grown twenty pound heavier since July!—but here, I'm losing all my manners!—this is Frank Forester, whom you have heard me talk about so often! He dropped down here out of the moon, Tom, I believe! at least I thought about as much of seeing the man in the moon, as of meeting *him* in this wooden country—but here he is, as you see, come all the way to take a look at the natives. And so, you see, as you're about the greatest curiosity I know of in these parts, I brought him straight up here to take a peep! Look at him, Frank—look at him well! Now, did you ever see, in all your life, so extraordinary an old devil?—and yet, Frank, which no man could possibly believe, the old fat animal has some good points about him—he can walk *some!* shoot, as he says, *first best!* and drink—good Lord, how he can drink!"

"And that reminds me," exclaimed Tom, who with a ludicrous mixture of pleasure, bashfulness, and mock anger, had been listening to what he evidently deemed a high encomium; "that *we* hav'nt drinked yet; have you quit drink, Archer, since I was to York? What'll you take, Mr. Forester? Gin? yes, I have got some prime gin! You never sent me up them groceries though, Archer; well, then, here's luck! What, Yorkshire, is that you? I should ha' thought now, Archer, you'd have cleared that lazy Injun out afore this time!"

"Whoy, measter Draa—what 'na loike's that kind o'talk?—coom coom now, where'll Ay tak t' things tull?"

"Put Mr. Forester's box in the bed-room off the parlor—mine up stairs, as usual," cried Archer. "Look sharp and get the traps out. Now, Tom, I suppose you have got no supper for us?"

"Cooper, Cooper! you snooping little devil," yelled Tom, addressing his second hope, a fine dark-eyed, bright-looking lad of ten or twelve years; "Don't you see Mr. Archer's come?—away with you and light the parlor fire, look smart now, or I'll cure you! Supper—you're always eat! eat! eat! or, drink! drink!—*drunk!* Yes! supper; we've got pork! and chickens——"

"Oh! d—n your pork," said I, "salt as the ocean I suppose!" "And double d—n your chickens," chimed in Harry, "old superannuated cocks which must be caught *now*, and then beheaded, and then soused into hot water to fetch off the feathers; and save you lazy devils the trouble of picking them. No, no, Tom! get us some fresh meat for to-morrow; and for tonight let us have some hot potatoes, and some bread and butter, and we'll find beef; eh, Frank? and now look sharp, for we must be up in good time to-morrow, and, to be so, we must to bed betimes. And now, Tom, are there any cock?"

"Cock! yes, I guess there be, and quail, too, pretty plenty! quite a smart chance of them, and not a shot fired among them this fall, any how!"

"Well, which way must we beat to-morrow? I calculate to shoot three days with you here; and, on Wednesday night, when we get in, to hitch up and drive into Sullivan, and see if we can't get a deer or two! You'll go, Tom?"

"Well, well, we'll see any how; but for to-morrow, why, I guess we must beat the 'Squire's swamp-hole first; there's ten or twelve cock there, I know; I see them there myself last Sunday; and then acrost them buck-wheat stubbles, and the big bog meadow, there's a *drove* of quail there; two or three bevys got in one, I reckon; leastwise I counted thirty-three last Friday was a week; and through Seer's big swamp, over to the great spring!"

"How *is* Seer's swamp? too wet, I fancy," Archer interposed, "at least I noticed, from the mountain, that all the leaves were changed in it, and that the maples were quite bare."

"Pretty fair, pretty fair, I guess," replied stout Tom, "I harnt been there myself though, but Jem was down with the hounds arter an old fox t'other day, and sure enough *he said* the cock kept flopping up quite thick afore him; but then the critter *will* lie, Harry; he *will* lie like thunder, you know; but somehow I concaits there be cock there too; and then, as I was saying, we'll stop at the great spring and get a bite of summat, and then beat Hell-hole; you'll have sport there for sartin! What dogs have you got with you, Harry?"

"Your old friends, *Shot* and *Chase*, and a couple of spaniels for thick covert!"

"Now, gentlemen, your suppers are all ready."

"Come, Tom," cried Archer; "you must take a bite with us— Tim, bring us in three bottles of champagne, and lots of ice, do you hear?"

And the next moment we found ourselves installed in a snug parlor, decorated with a dozen sporting prints, a blazing hickory fire snapping and sputtering and roaring in a huge Franklin stove; our luggage safely stowed in various corners, and Archer's double gun-case propped on two chairs below the window.

An old-fashioned round table, covered with clean white linen of domestic manufacture, displayed the noble round of beef which we had brought up with us, flanked by a platter of magnificent potatoes, pouring forth volumes of dense steam through the cracks in their dusky skins; a lordly dish of butter, that might have pleased the appetite of Sisera; while eggs and ham, and pies of apple, mince-meat, cranberry, and custard, occupied every vacant space, save where two ponderous pitchers, mantling with ale and cider, and two respectable square bottles, labelled "Old Rum" and "Brandy—1817," relieved the prospect. Before we had sat down, Timothy entered, bearing a horse bucket filled to the brim with ice, from whence protruded the long necks and split corks of three champagne bottles.

"Now, Tim," said Archer, "get your own supper, when you've finished with the cattle; feed the dogs well to-night; and then to bed. And hark you, call me at five in the morning; we shall want you to carry the game-bag and the drinkables; take care of yourself, Tim, and good night!"

"No need to tell him that," cried Tom, "he's something like yourself; *I tell* you, Archer, if Tim ever dies of thirst, it must be where there is nothing wet, but water!"

"Now hark to the old scoundrel, Frank," said Archer, "hark to him pray, and if he doesn't out-eat both of us, and out-drink any-thing you ever saw, may I miss my first bird to-morrow—that's all! Give me a slice of beef, Frank; that old Goth would cut it an inch thick, if I let him touch it; out with a cork, Tom! Here's to our sport to-morrow!"

"Uh; that goes good!" replied Tom, with an oath, which, by the apparent gusto of the speaker, seemed to betoken that the wine had tickled his palate—"that goes good! that's different from the darned red trash you left up here last time."

"And of which you have *left* none, I'll be bound," answered Archer, laughing; "my best Latour, Frank, which the old infidel calls trash."

"It's all below, every bottle of it," answered Tom: "I wouldn't use such rot-gut stuff, no, not for vinegar. 'Taint half so good as that red sherry you had up here oncet; that was poor weak stuff, too, but it did well to make milk punch of; it did well instead of milk."

"Now, Frank," said Archer, "you won't believe me, *that I know;* but it's true, all the same. A year ago, this autumn, I brought up five gallons of exceedingly stout, rather fiery, young, brown sherry—draught wine, you know!—and what did Tom do here, but mix it, half and half, with brandy, nutmeg, and sugar, and drink it for milk punch!"

"I did *so,* by the eternal," replied Tom, bolting a huge lump of beef, in order to enable himself to answer—"I did *so,* and good milk punch it made, too, but it was too weak! Come, Mr. Forester, we harn't drinked yet, and I'm kind o' gittin dry!"

And now the mirth waxed fast and furious—the champagne speedily was finished, the supper things cleared off, hot water and Starke's Ferintosh succeeded, cheroots were lighted, we drew closer in about the fire, and, during the circulation of two tum-blers—for to this did Harry limit us, having the prospect of un-steady hands and aching heads before him for the morrow—never did I hear more genuine and real humor, than went round our merry trio.

Tom Draw, especially, though all his jokes were not such alto-gether as I can venture to insert in my chaste paragraphs, and though at times his oaths were too extravagantly rich to brook repetition, shone forth resplendent. No longer did I wonder at what I had before deemed Harry Archer's strange hallucination; Tom Draw *is* a decided genius—rough as a pine knot in his native woods—but full of mirth, of shrewdness, of keen mother wit, of hard horse sense, and last, not least, of the most genuine milk of human kindness. He is a rough block; but, as Harry says, there is solid timber under the uncouth bark enough to make five hundred men, as men go now-a-days *in cities!*

At ten o'clock, thanks to the excellent precautions of my friend Harry, we were all snugly berthed, before the whiskey, which had well justified the high praise I had heard lavished on it, had made any serious inroads on our understanding, but not before we had laid in a *quantum* to ensure a good night's rest.

Bright and early was I on foot the next day, but before I had half dressed myself I was assured, by the clatter of the breakfast things, that Archer had again stolen a march upon me; and the next moment my bed-room door, driven open by the thick boot of that worthy, gave me a full view of his person—arrayed in a stout fustian jacket—with half a dozen pockets in full view, and Heaven only knows how many more lying *perdu* in the broad skirts. Knee-breeches of the same material, with laced half-boots and leather leggins, set off his stout calf and well turned ankles.

"Up! up! Frank," he exclaimed, "it is a morning of ten thousand; there has been quite a heavy dew, and by the time we are afoot it will be well evaporated; and then the scent will lie, I promise you! make haste, I tell you, breakfast is ready!"

Stimulated by his hurrying voice, I soon completed my toilet, and entering the parlor found Harry busily employed in stirring to and fro a pound of powder on one heated dinner plate, while a second was undergoing the process of preparation on the hearth-stone under a glowing pile of hickory ashes.

At the side-table, covered with guns, dog-whips, nipple-wrenches, and the like, Tim, rigged like his master, in half boots and leggins, but with a short roundabout of velveteen, in place of the full-skirted jacket, was filling our shot-pouches by aid of a ca-pacious funnel, more used, as its odor betokened, to facilitate the passage of gin or Jamaica spirits than of so sober a material as cold lead.

At the same moment entered mine host, togged for the field in a huge pair of cow-hide boots, reaching almost to the knee, into the tops of which were tucked the lower ends of a pair of trowsers, containing yards enough of buffalo-cloth to have eked out the main-sail of a North River sloop; a waistcoat and single-breasted jacket of the same material, with a fur cap, completed his attire; but in his hand he bore a large decanter filled with a pale yellowish liquor, embalming a dense mass of fine and worm-like threads, not very different in appearance from the best vermicelli.

"Come, boys, come—here's your bitters," he exclaimed; and, as if to set the example, filled a big tumbler to the brim, gulped it down as if it had been water, smacked his lips, and incontinently tendered it to Archer, who, to my great amazement, filled himself likewise a more moderate draught, and quaffed it without hesitation.

"That's good, Tom," he said, pausing after the first sip; "that's the best I ever tasted here; how old's that?"

"Five years!" Tom replied: "five years last fall! Daddy Tom made it out of my own best apples—take a horn, Mr. Forester," he added, turning to me—"It's *first best* cider sperits—better a darned sight than that Scotch stuff you make such an etarnal fuss about, toting it up here every time, as if we'd nothing fit to drink in the country!"

And to my sorrow I did taste—old apple whiskey, with Lord knows how much snake-root soaked in it for five years! They may talk about gall being bitter; but, by all that's wonderful, there was enough of the *amari aliquid* in this *fonte*, to me by no means of *leporum*, to have given an extra touch of bitterness to all the gall beneath the canopy; and with my mouth puckered up, till it was like anything on earth but a mouth, I set the glass down on the table; and for the next five minutes could do nothing but shake my head to and fro like a Chinese mandarin, amidst the loud and prolonged roars of laughter that burst like thunder claps from the huge jaws of Thomas Draw, and the subdued and half respectful cachinnations of Tim Matlock.

By the time I had got a little better, the black tea was ready, and with thick cream, hot buckwheat cakes, beautiful honey, and—as a stand by—the still venerable round, we made out a very tolerable meal.

This done, with due deliberation Archer supplied his several pockets with their accustomed load—the clean-punched wads in this—in that the Westley Richards' caps—here a pound horn of powder—there a shot-pouch on Syke's lever principle, with double mouth-piece—in another, screw-driver, nipple-wrench, and the spare cones; and, to make up the tale, dog-whip, dram-bottle, and silk handkerchief in the sixth and last.

"Nothing like method in this world," said Harry, clapping his low-crowned broad-brimmed mohair cap upon his head; "take my word for it. Now, Tim, what have you got in the bag!"

"A bottle of champagne, sur," answered Tim, who was now employed slinging a huge fustian game-bag, with a net-work front, over his right shoulder, to counterbalance two full shot-belts which were already thrown across the other—"a bottle of champagne, sur—a cold roast chicken—t' Cheshire cheese—and t' pilot biscuits. Is your dram-bottle filled wi' t' whiskey, please sur?"

"Aye, aye, Tim. Now let loose the dogs—carry a pair of couples and a leash along with you; and mind you, gentlemen, Tim carries shot for all hands; and luncheon—but each one finds his own powder, caps, etc.; and any one who wants a dram, carries his own—the devil a-one of you gets a sup out of my bottle, or a charge out of my flask! That's right, old Trojan, isn't it?" with a good slap on Tom's broad shoulder.

"Shot! Shot—why Shot! don't you know me, old dog?" cried Tom, as the two setters bounded into the room, joyful at their release—"good dog! good Chase!" feeding them with great lumps of beef.

"Avast! there Tom—have done with that," cried Harry; "you'll have the dogs so full that they can't run."

"Why, how'd you like to hunt all day without your breakfast—hey?"

"Here, lads! here, lads! wh-e-ew!" and followed by his setters, with his gun under his arm, away went Harry; and catching up our pieces likewise, we followed, nothing loth, Tim bringing up the rear with the two spaniels fretting in their couples, and a huge black thorn cudgel, which he had brought, as he informed me, "all t' way from bonny Cawoods."

It was as beautiful a morning as ever lighted sportsmen to their labors. The dew, exhaled already from the long grass, still glittered here and there upon the shrubs and trees, though a soft fresh south-western breeze was shaking it thence momently in bright and rustling showers; the sun, but newly risen, and as yet partially enveloped in the thin gauze-like mists so frequent at that season, was casting shadows, seemingly endless, from every object that intercepted his low rays, and chequering the whole landscape with that play of light and shade, which is the loveliest accessory to a lovely scene; and lovely was the scene, indeed, as e'er was looked upon by painter's or by poet's eye—how then should humble prose do justice to it?

Seated upon the first slope of a gentle hill, midway of the great valley heretofore described, the village looked due south, toward the chains of mountains, which we had crossed on the preceding evening, and which in that direction bounded the landscape. These ridges, cultivated half-way up their swelling sides, which lay mapped out before our eyes in all the various beauty of orchards, yellow stubbles, and rich pastures dotted with sleek and comely cattle, were rendered yet more lovely and romantic, by here and there a woody gorge, or rocky chasm, channelling their smooth flanks, and carrying down their tributary rills, to swell the main stream at their base. Toward these we took our way by the same road which we had followed in an opposite direction on the previous night—but for a short space only—for having crossed the stream, by the same bridge which we had passed on entering the village, Tom Draw pulled down a set of bars to the left, and strode out manfully into the stubble.

"Hold up, good lads!—whe-ew—whewt!" and away went the setters through the moist stubble, heads up and sterns down, like fox-hounds on a breast-high scent, yet under the most perfect discipline; for at the very first note of Harry's whistle, even when racing at the top of their pace, they would turn simultaneously, alter their course, cross each other at right angles, and quarter the whole field, leaving no foot of ground unbeaten.

No game, however, in this instance, rewarded their exertions; and on we went across a meadow, and two other stubbles, with the like result. But now we crossed a gentle hill, and, at its base, came on a level tract, containing at the most ten acres of marsh land, overgrown with high coarse grass and flags. Beyond this, on the right, was a steep rocky hillock, covered with tall and thrifty timber of some thirty years' growth, but wholly free from under-wood. Along the left-hand fence ran a thick belt of underwood, sumach and birch, with a few young oak trees interspersed; but in the middle of the swampy level, covering at most some five or six acres, was a dense circular thicket composed of every sort of thorny bush and shrub, matted with cat-briers and wild-vines, and overshadowed by a clump of tall and leafy ashes, which had not as yet lost one atom of their foliage, although the underwood beneath them was quite sere and leafless.

"Now then," cried Harry, "this is the 'Squire's swamp-hole!' Now for a dozen cock! hey, Tom! Here, couple up the setters, Tim; and let the spaniels loose. Now Flash! now Dan! down charge, you little villains!" and the well broke brutes dropped on the instant. "How must we beat this cursed hole?"

"You must go through the very thick of it, concarn you!" exclaimed Tom; "at your old work already, hey? trying to shirk at first!"

"Don't swear so! you old reprobate! I know my place, depend on it," cried Archer; "but what to do with the rest of you!—there's the rub!"

"Not a bit of it," cried Tom—"here, Yorkshire—Ducklegs—here, what's your name—get away you with those big dogs—atwixt the swamp hole, and the brush there by the fence, and look out that you mark every bird to an inch! You, Mr. Forester, go in there, under that butter-nut; you'll find a blind track there, right through the brush—keep that 'twixt Tim and Mr. Archer; and keep your eyes skinned, do! there'll be a cock up before you're ten yards in. Archer, you'll go right through, and I'll——"

"You'll keep well forward on the right—and mind that no bird crosses to the hill; we never get them, if they once get over. All right! In with you now! Steady, Flash! steady! hie up, Dan!" and in a moment Harry was out of sight among the brush-wood, though his progress might be traced by the continual crackling of the thick underwood.

Scarce had I passed the butter-nut, when, even as Tom had

said, up flapped a woodcock scarcely ten yards before me, in the open path, and rising heavily to clear the branches of a tall thorn bush, showed me his full black eye, and tawny breast, as fair a shot as could be fancied.

"Mark!" halloaed Harry to my right, his quick ear having caught the flap of the bird's wing, as he rose. "Mark cock—Frank!"

Well—steadily enough, as I thought, I pitched my gun up! covered my bird fairly! pulled!—the trigger gave not to my finger. I tried the other. Devil's in it, I had forgot to cock my gun! and ere I could retrieve my error, the bird had topped the bush, and dodged out of sight, and off—"Mark! mark!—Tim!" I shouted.

"Ey! ey! sur—Ay see's um!"

"Why, how's that, Frank?" cried Harry. "Couldn't you get a shot?"

"Forgot to cock my gun!" I cried; but at the self-same moment the quick sharp yelping of the spaniels came on my ear. "Steady, Flash! steady, sir! Mark!" But close upon the word came the full round report of Harry's gun. "Mark! again!" shouted Harry, and again his own piece sent its loud ringing voice abroad. "Mark! now a third! mark, Frank!"

And as he spoke I caught the quick rush of his wing, and saw him dart across a space, a few yards to my right. I felt my hand shake; I had not pulled a trigger in ten months, but in a second's space I rallied. There was an opening just before me between a stumpy thick thorn-bush which had saved the last bird and a dwarf cedar; it was not two yards over; he glanced across it; he was gone, just as my barrel sent its charge into the splintered branches.

"Beautiful!" shouted Harry, who, looking through a cross glade, saw the bird fall, which I could not. "Beautiful shot, Frank! Do all your work like that, and we'll get twenty couple before night!"

"Have I killed him!" answered I, half doubting if he were not quizzing me.

"Killed him? of course you have; doubled him up completely! But look sharp! there are more birds before me! I can hardly keep the dogs down, now! There! there goes one—clean out of shot of

me, though! Mark! mark, Tom! Gad, how the fat dog's running!"
he continued. "He sees him! Ten to one he gets him! There he
goes—bang! A long shot, and killed clean!"

"Ready!" cried I. "I'm ready, Archer!"

"Bag your bird, then. He lies under that dock leaf, at the foot of
yon red maple! That's it; you've got him. Steady now, till Tom
gets loaded!"

"What did you do? asked I. "You fired twice, I think!"

"Killed two!" he answered. "Ready, now!" and on he went,
smashing away the boughs before him, while ever and anon I
heard his cheery voice, calling or whistling to his dogs, or rousing
up the tenants of some thickets into which even he could not force
his way; and I, creeping, as best I might, among the tangled
brush, now plunging half thigh deep in holes full of tenacious
mire, now blundering over the moss-covered stubs, pressed
forward, fancying every instant that the rustling of the briers
against my jacket was the flip-flap of a rising woodcock. Suddenly, after bursting through a mass of thorns and wild-vine,
which was in truth almost impassable, I came upon a little grassy
spot quite clear of trees, and covered with the tenderest verdure,
through which a narrow rill stole silently; and as I set my first foot
on it, up jumped, with his beautiful variegated back all reddened
by the sunbeams, a fine and full-fed woodcock, with the peculiar
twitter which he utters when surprised. He had not gone ten
yards, however, before my gun was at my shoulder and the trigger
drawn; before I heard the crack I saw him cringe; and, as the
white smoke drifted off to leeward, he fell heavily, completely rid-
dled by the shot, into the brake before me; while at the same moment, whir-r-r! up sprung a bevy of twenty quail, at least, startling me for the moment by the thick whirring of their wings, and
skirring over the underwood right toward Archer. "Mark, quail!"
I shouted, and, recovering instantly my nerves, fired my one remaining barrel after the last bird! It was a long shot, yet I struck
him fairly, and he rose instantly right upward, towering high!
high! into the clear blue sky, and soaring still, till his life left him
in the air, and he fell like a stone, plump downward!

"Mark him! Tim!"

"Ey! ey! sur. He's a de-ad un, that's a sure thing!"

At my shot all the bevy rose a little, yet altered not their course the least, wheeling across the thicket directly round the front of Archer, whose whereabouts I knew, though I could neither see nor hear him. So high did they fly that I could observe them clearly, every bird well defined against the sunny heavens. I watched them eagerly. Suddenly one turned over; a cloud of feathers streamed off down the wind; and then, before the sound of the first shot had reached my ears, a second pitched a few yards upward, and, after a heavy flutter, followed its hapless comrade.

Turned by the fall of the two leading birds, the bevy again wheeled, still rising higher, and now flying very fast; so that, as I saw by the direction which they took, they would probably give Draw a chance of getting in both barrels. And so indeed it was; for, as before, long ere I caught the booming echoes of his heavy gun, I saw two birds keeled over, and, almost at the same instant, the cheery shout of Tim announced to me that he had bagged my towered bird! After a little pause, again we started, and, hailing one another now and then, gradually forced our way through brake and brier toward the outward verge of the dense covert. Before we met again, however, I had the luck to pick up a third woodcock, and as I heard another double shot from Archer, and two single bangs from Draw, I judged that my companions had not been less successful than myself. At last, emerging from the thicket, we all converged, as to a common point, toward Tim; who, with his game-bag on the ground, with its capacious mouth wide open to receive our game, sat on a stump with the two setters at a charge beside him.

"What do we score?" cried I, as we drew near; "what do we score?"

"I have four woodcocks, and a brace of quail," said Harry.

"And I, two cock and a brace," cried Tom, "and missed another cock; but he's down in the meadow here, behind that 'ere stump alder!"

"And I, three woodcock and one quail!" I chimed in, naught abashed.

"And Ay'se marked doon three woodcock—two more beside yon big un, that measter Draa made siccan a bungle of—and all t' quail—every feather on um—doon i' t' bog meadow yonner—

ooh! but we'se make grand sport o't!" interposed Tim, now busily employed stringing bird after bird up by the head, with loops and buttons in the game-bag!

"Well done then, all!" said Harry. "Nine timber-doodles and five quail, and only one shot missed! That's not bad shooting, considering what a hole it is to shoot in. Gentlemen, here's your health," and filling himself out a fair sized wine-glass-full of Ferintosh, into the silver cup of his dram-bottle, he tossed it off; and then poured out a similar libation for Tim Matlock. Tom and myself, nothing loth, obeyed the hint, and sipped our modi-cums of distilled waters out of our private flasks.

"Now, then," cried Archer, "let us pick up these scattering birds. Tom Draw, you can get yours without a dog! And now, Tim, where are yours?"

"T' first lies oop yonner in yon boonch of brachens, ahint t' big scarlet maple; and t' other—"

"Well! I'll go to the first. You take Mr. Forester to the other, and when we have bagged all three, we'll meet at the bog meadow fence, and then hie at the bevy!"

This job was soon done, for Draw and Harry bagged their birds cleverly at the first rise; and although mine got off at first without a shot, by dodging round a birch tree straight in Tim's face, and flew back slap toward the thicket, yet he pitched in its outer skirt, and as he jumped up wild I cut him down with a broken pinion and a shot through his bill at fifty yards, and Chase retrieved him well.

"Cleverly stopped, indeed!" Frank halloaed; "and by no means an easy shot! and so our work's clean done for this place, at the least!"

"The boy *can* shoot *some*," observed Tom Draw, who loved to bother Timothy; "the boy *can* shoot *some,* though he *doos* come from Yorkshire!"

"Gad! and Ay wush Ay'd no but gotten thee i' Yorkshire, measter Draa!" responded Tim.

"Why! what if you had got me there?"

"What? Whoy, Ay'd clap thee iv a cage, and hug thee round t' feasts and fairs loike; and shew thee to t' folks at so mooch a head. Ay'se sure Ay'd mak a fortune o' t!"

"He has you there, Tom! Ha! ha! ha!" laughed Archer. "Tim's

down upon you there, by George! Now, Frank, do fancy Tom Draw in a cage at Borough-bridge or Catterick fair! Lord! how the folks would pay to look at him! Fancy the sign board too! The Great American Man-Mammoth! Ha! ha! ha! But come, we must not stay here talking nonsense, or we shall do no good. Show me, Tim, where are the quail!"

"Doon i' t' bog meadow yonner! joost i' t' slack,* see thee, there!" pointing with the stout black-thorn; "amang yon bits o' bushes!"

"Very well—that's it; now let go the setters; take Flash and Dan along with you, and cut across the country as straight as you can go to the spring head, where we lunched last year; that day, you know, Tom, when McTavish frightened the bull out of the meadow, under the pin-oak tree. Well! put the champagne into the spring to cool, and rest yourself there till we come; we shan't be long behind you."

Away went Tim, stopping from time to time to mark our progress, and over the fence into the bog meadow we proceeded; a rascally piece of broken tussocky ground, with black mud knee-deep between the hags, all covered with long grass. The third step I took, over I went upon my nose, but luckily avoided shoving my gun-barrels into the filthy mire.

"Steady, Frank, steady! I'm ashamed of you!" said Harry; "so hot and so impetuous; and your gun too at the full cock; that's the reason, man, why you missed firing at your first bird, this morning. I never cock either barrel till I see my bird; and, if a bevy rises, only one at a time. The birds will lie like stones here; and we cannot walk too slow. Steady, Shot, have a care, sir!"

Never, in all my life, did I see any thing more perfect than the style in which the setters drew those bogs. There was no more of racing, no more of impetuous dash; it seemed as if they knew the birds were close before them. At a slow trot, their sterns whipping their flanks at every step, they threaded the high tussocks. See! the red dog straightens his neck, and snuffs the air.

"Look to! look to, Frank! they are close before old Chase!"

* Slack—Yorkshire. Anglice, *Moist hollow.*

Now he draws on again, crouching close to the earth. "Toho! Shot!" Now he stands! no! no! not yet—at least he is not certain! He turns his head to catch his master's eye! Now his stern moves a little; he draws on again.

There! he is sure now! what a picture—his black full eye intently glaring, though he cannot see any thing in that thick mass of herbage; his nostril wide expanded, his lips slavering from intense excitement; his whole form motionless, and sharply drawn, and rigid, even to the straight stern and lifted foot, as a block wrought to mimic life by some skilful sculptor's chisel; and, scarce ten yards behind, his liver-colored comrade backs him—as firm, as stationary, as immovable, but in his attitude, how different! Chase feels the hot scent steaming up under his very nostril; feels it in every nerve, and quivers with anxiety to dash on his prey, even while perfectly restrained and steady. Shot, on the contrary, though a few minutes since he too was drawing, knows nothing of himself, perceives no indication of the game's near presence, although improved by discipline, his instinct tells him that his mate has found them. Hence the same rigid form, still tail, and constrained attitude, but in his face—for dogs *have* faces—there is none of that tense energy, that evident anxiety; there is no frown upon his brow, no glare in his mild open eye, no slaver on his lip!

"Come up, Tom; come up, Frank, they are all here; we must get in six barrels; they will not move; come up, I say!"

And on we came, deliberately prompt, and ready. Now we were all in line: Harry the centre man, I on the right, and Tom on the left hand. The attitude of Archer was superb; his legs set a little way apart, as firm as if they had been rooted in the soil; his form drawn back a little, and his head erect, with his eye fixed upon the dogs; his gun held in both hands, across his person, the muzzle slightly elevated, his left grasping the trigger guard; the thumb of the right resting upon the hammer, and the fore-finger on the trigger of the left hand barrel; but, as he had said, neither cocked. "Fall back, Tom, if you please, five yards or so," he said, as coolly as if he were unconcerned, "and you come forward, Frank, as many; I want to drive them to the left, into those low red bushes; that will do: now then, I'll flush them; never mind me, boys, I'll reserve my fire."

And, as he spoke, he moved a yard or two in front of us, and under his very feet, positively startling me by their noisy flutter, up sprang the gallant bevy: fifteen or sixteen well grown birds, crowding and jostling one against the other. Tom Draw's gun, as I well believe, was at his shoulder when they rose; at least his first shot was discharged before they had flown half a rood, and of course harmlessly: the charge must have been driven through them like a single ball; his second barrel instantly succeeded, and down came two birds, caught in the act of crossing. I am myself a quick shot, *too* quick if anything, yet my first barrel was exploded a moment after Tom Draw's second; the other followed, and I had the satisfaction of bringing both my birds down handsomely; then up went Harry's piece—the bevy being now twenty or twenty-five yards distant—cocking it as it rose, he pulled the trigger almost before it touched his shoulder, so rapid was the movement; and, though he lowered the stock a little to cock the second barrel, a moment scarcely passed between the two reports, and almost on the instant two quail were fluttering out their lives among the bog grass.

Dropping his butt, without a word, or even a glance to the dogs, he quietly went on to load; nor indeed was it needed: at the first shot they dropped into the grass, and there they lay as motionless as if they had been dead, with their heads crouched between their paws; nor did they stir thence till the tick of the gunlocks announced that we again were ready. Then lifting up their heads, and rising on their fore-feet, they sat half erect, eagerly waiting for the signal:

"Hold up, good lads!" and on they drew, and in an instant pointed on two several birds. "Fetch!" and each brought his burthen to our feet; six birds were bagged at that rise, and thus before eleven o'clock we had picked up a dozen cock, and within one of the same number of fine quail, with only two shots missed. The poor remainder of the bevy had dropped, singly, and scattered, in the red bushes, whither we instantly pursued them, and where we got six more, making a total of seventeen birds bagged out of a bevy, twenty strong at first.

One towered bird of Harry's, certainly killed dead, we could not with all our efforts bring to bag; one bird Tom Draw missed clean, and the remaining one we could not find again; another dram of whiskey, and into Seer's great swamp we started: a large piece of woodland, with every kind of lying. At one end it was open, with soft black loamy soil, covered with docks and colts-foot leaves under the shade of large but leafless willows, and here we picked up a good many scattered woodcock; afterward we got into the heavy thicket with much tangled grass, wherein we flushed a bevy, but they all took to tree, and we made very little of them; and here Tom Draw began to slow and labor; the covert was too thick, the bottom too deep and unsteady for him.

Archer perceiving this, sent him at once to the outside; and three times, as we went along, ourselves moving nothing, we heard the round reports of his large calibre. "A bird at every shot, I'd stake my life," said Harry "he never misses cross shots in the open;" at the same instant a tremendous rush of wings burst from the heaviest thicket: "Mark! partridge! partridge!" and as I caught a glimpse of a dozen large birds fluttering up, one close upon the other, and darting away as straight and nearly as fast as bullets, through the dense branches of a cedar brake, I saw the flashes of both Harry's barrels, almost simultaneously discharged, and at the same time over went the objects of his aim; but ere I could get up my gun the rest were out of sight. "You must shoot, Frank, like lightning, to kill these beggars; they are the ruffed grouse, though they call them partridge here: see! are they not fine fellows?"

Another hour's beating, in which we still kept picking up, from time to time, some scattering birds, brought us to the spring head, where we found Tim with luncheon ready, and our fat friend reposing at his side, with two more grouse, and a rabbit which he had bagged along the covert's edge. Cool was the Star champagne; and capital was the cold fowl and Cheshire cheese; and most delicious was the repose that followed, enlivened with gay wit and free good humor, soothed by the fragrance of the exquisite cheroots, moistened by the last drops of the Ferintosh qualified by the crystal waters of the spring. After an hour's rest, we counted up our spoil; four ruffed grouse, nineteen woodcocks, with ten brace and a half of quail beside the bunny, made up our score—done comfortably in four hours.

"Now we have finished for to-day with quail," said Archer, "but we'll get full ten couple more of woodcock; come, let us be stirring; hang up your game-bag in the tree, and tie the setters to the fence; I want you in with me to beat, Tim; you two chaps must both keep the outside—you all the time, Tom; you, Frank, till you get to that tall thunder-shivered ash tree; turn in there, and follow up the margin of a wide slank you will see; but be careful, the mud is very deep, and dangerous in places; now then, here goes!"

And in he went, jumping a narrow streamlet into a point of thicket, through which he drove by main force. Scarce had he got six yards into the brake, before both spaniels quested; and, to my no small wonder, the jungle seemed alive with woodcock; eight or nine, at the least, flapped up at once, and skimmed along the tongue of coppice toward the high wood, which ran along the valley, as I learned afterward, for full three miles in length—while four or five more wheeled off to the sides, giving myself and Draw fair shots, by which we did not fail to profit; but I confess it was with absolute astonishment that I saw two of those turned over, which flew inward, killed by the marvellously quick and unerring aim of Archer, where a less thorough sportsman would have been quite unable to discharge a gun at all, so dense was the tangled jungle. Throughout the whole length of the skirt of coppice, a hundred and fifty yards, I should suppose at the utmost, the birds kept rising as it were incessantly—thirty-five, or, I think, nearly forty, being flushed in less than twenty minutes, although comparatively few were killed, partly from the difficulty of the ground, and partly from their getting up by fours and fives at once. Into the high wood, however, at the last we drove them; and there, till daylight failed us, we did our work like men. By the cold light of the full moon we wended homeward, rejoicing in the possession of twenty-six couple and a half of cock, twelve brace of quail—we found another bevy on our way home and bagged three birds almost by moonlight—five ruffed grouse, and a rabbit. Before our wet clothes were well changed, supper was ready, and a good blow-out was followed by sound slumbers and sweet dreams, fairly earned by nine hours of incessant walking.

THE MORNING'S SPORT

It was not yet broad daylight when Harry Archer, who had, as was usual with him on his sporting tour, arisen with the lark, was sitting in the little parlor I have before described, close to the chimney corner, where a bright lively fire was already burning, and spreading a warm cheerful glow through the apartment.

The large round table, drawn up close to the hearth, was covered with a clean though coarse white cloth, and laid for breakfast, with two cups and saucers, flanked by as many plates and egg-cups, although as yet no further preparations for the morning meal, except the presence of a huge home-made loaf and a large roll of rich golden-hued butter, had been made by the neat-handed Phillis of the country inn. Two candles were lighted, for though the day had broken, the sun was not yet high enough to cast his rays into that deep and rock-walled valley, and by their light Archer was busy with the game-bag, the front of which he had finished netting on the previous night.

Frank Forester had not as yet made his appearance; and still, while the gigantic copper kettle bubbled and steamed away upon the hearth, discoursing eloquent music, and servant after servant bustled in, one with a cold quail-pie, another with a quart jug of cream, and fresh eggs ready to be boiled by the fastidious epicures in person, he steadily worked on, housewife and saddler's silk, and wax and scissors ready to his hand; and when at last the door flew open, and the delinquent comrade entered, he flung his finished job upon the chair, and gathered up his implements with

"Now, Frank, let's lose no time, but get our breakfasts. Halloa! Tim, bring the rockingham and the tea-chest; do you hear?"

"Well, Harry, so you've done the game-bag," exclaimed the other, as he lifted it up and eyed it somewhat superciliously— "Well, it is a good one certainly; but you are the queerest fellow I ever met, to give yourself unnecessary trouble. Here you have been three days about this bag, hard all; and when it's done, it is not half as good a one as you can buy at Cooper's for a dollar, with all this new-fangled machinery of loops and buttons, and I don't know what."

"And you, Master Frank," retorted Harry, nothing daunted, "to be a good shot and a good sportsman—which, with some few exceptions, I must confess you are—are the most culpably and wilfully careless about your appointments I ever met. I don't call a man half a sportsman, who has not every thing he wants at hand for an emergency, at half a minute's notice. Now it so happens that you cannot get, in New York at all, anything like a decent game-bag—a little fancy-worked French or German jigmaree machine you can get anywhere, I grant, that will do well enough for a fellow to carry on his shoulders, who goes out *robingunning,* but nothing for your man to carry, wherein to keep your birds cool, fresh, and unmutilated. Now, these loops and buttons, at which you laugh, will make the difference of a week at least in the bird's keeping, if every hour or so you empty your pockets— wherein I take it for granted you put your birds as fast as you bag them—smooth down their plumage gently, stretch their legs out, and hang them by the heads, running the button down close to the neck of each. In this way this bag, which is, as you see, half a yard long, by a quarter and a half a quarter deep, made double, one bag of fustian, with a net front, which makes two pockets— will carry fifty-one quail or woodcock, no one of them pressing upon, or interfering with, another, and it would carry sixty-eight if I had put another row of loops in the inner bag; which I did not, that I might have the bottom vacant to carry a few spare articles, such as a bag of Westley Richards' caps, and a couple of dozen of Ely's cartridges."

"Oh! that's all very well," said Frank, "but who the deuce can be at the bore of it?"

"Why be at the bore of shooting at all, for that matter?" replied Harry—"I, for one, think that if a thing is worth doing at all, it is worth doing *well*—and I can't bear to kill a hundred or a hundred and fifty birds, as our party almost always do out here, and then be obliged to throw them away, just for want of a little care. Why, I was shooting summer cock one July day two years ago—there had been heavy rain in the early morning, and the grass and bushes were very wet—Jem Blake was with me, and we had great sport, and he laughed at me like the deuce for taking my birds out of my pocket at the end of every hour's sport, and making Timothy smooth them down carefully, and bag them all after my fashion. Egad I had the laugh though, when we got home at night!"

"How so," asked Frank, "in what way had you the laugh?"

"Simply in this—a good many of the birds were very hard shot, as is always the case in summer shooting, and all of them got more or less wet, as did the pockets of Jem's shooting jacket, wherein he persisted in carrying his birds all day—the end was, that when we got home at night, it having been a close, hot, steamy day, he had not one bird which was not more or less tainted*—and, as you know of course, when taint has once begun, nothing can check it."

"Ay! ay! well that indeed's a reason; if you can't buy such a bag, especially!"

"Well, you cannot then, I can tell you! and I'm glad you're convinced for once; and here comes breakfast—so now let us to work, that we may get on our ground as early as may be. For quail you cannot be too early; for if you don't find them, while they are rambling on their feeding ground, it is a great chance if you find them at all."

"But, after all, you can only use up one or two bevies or so; and, that done, you *must* hunt for them in the basking time of day, after all's done and said," replied Frank, who seemed to have got up somewhat paradoxically given that morning.

"Not at all, Frank, not at all," answered Harry—"that is if you know your ground; and know it to be well stocked; and have a good marker with you."

"Oh! this is something new of yours—some strange device fantastical—let's have it, pray."

"Certainly you shall; you shall have it *now* in precept, and in an hour or two in practice. You see those stubbles on the hill—in those seven or eight fields there are, or at least should be, some five bevies; there is good covert, good *easy* covert all about, and we can mark our birds down easily; now, when I find one bevy, I shall get as many barrels into it as I can, mark it down as correctly as possible, and then go and look for another."

"What! and not follow it up? Now, Harry, that's mere stuff; wait till the scent's gone cold, and till the dogs can't find them? 'Gad, that's clever, any way!"

---

* This is a fact—thirty birds were thrown away at night, which had been killed that same day.

"Exactly the reverse, friend Frank; exactly the reverse. If you follow up a bevy, of *quail* mark you, on the instant, it's ten to one almost that you don't spring them. If, on the contrary, you wait for half an hour, you are sure of them. How it is, I cannot precisely tell you. I have sometimes thought that quail have the power of holding in their scent, whether purposely or naturally—from the effect of fear perhaps contracting the pores, and hindering the escape of the effluvia—I know not, but I am far from being convinced even now that it is not so. A very good sportsman, and true friend of mine, insists upon it that birds give out no scent except from the feet, and that, consequently, if they squat without running they cannot be found. I do not, however, believe the theory, and hold it to be disproved by the fact that dead birds do give out scent. I have generally observed that there is no difficulty in retrieving dead quail, but that, wounded, they are constantly lost. But, be that as it may, the birds pitch down, each into the best bit of covert he can find, and squat there like so many stones, leaving no trail or taint upon the grass or bushes, and being of course proportionally hard to find; in half an hour they will begin, if not disturbed, to call and travel, and you can hunt them up, without the slightest trouble. If you have a very large tract of country to beat, and birds are very scarce, of course, it would not answer to pass on; nor ever, even if they are plentiful, in wild or windy weather, or in large open woods; but where you have a fair ground, lots of birds and fine weather, I would always beat on in a circuit, for the reason I have given you. In the first place, every bevy you flush flies from its feeding to its basking ground, so that you get over all the first early, and *know* where to look afterward; instead of killing off one bevy, and then going blundering on, at blind guess work, and finding nothing. In the second place, you have a chance of driving two or three bevies into one brake, and of getting sport proportionate; and in the third place, as I have told you, you are much surer of finding marked birds after an hour's lapse, than on the moment."

"I will do you the justice to say," Forester replied, "that you always make a tolerably good fight in support of your opinions; and so you have done now, but I want to hear something more about this matter of holding scent—facts! facts! and let me judge for myself."

"Well, Frank, give me a bit more of that pie in the mean time, and I will tell you the strongest case in point I ever witnessed. I was shooting near Stamford, in Connecticut, three years ago, with C—— K——, and another friend; we had three as good dogs out, as ever had a trigger drawn over them. My little imported yellow and white setter, Chase, after which this old rascal is called— which Mike Sandford considered the best-nosed dog he had ever broken—a capital young pointer dog of K——'s, which has since turned out, as I hear, superlative, and P——'s old and stanch setter Count. It was the middle of a fine autumn day, and the scenting was very uncommonly good. One of our beaters flushed a bevy of quail very wide of us, and they came over our heads down a steep hillside, and all lighted in a small circular hollow, without a bit of underbrush or even grass, full of tall thrifty oak trees, of perhaps twenty-five years' growth. They were not much out of gun-shot, and we all three distinctly saw them light; and I observed them flap and fold their wings as they settled. We walked straight to the spot, and beat it five or six times over, not one of our dogs ever drawing, and not one bird rising. We could not make it out; my friends thought they had treed, and laughed at me when I expressed my belief that they were still before us, under our very noses. The ground was covered only by a deep bed of sere decaying oak leaves. Well, we went on, and beat all round the neighborhood within a quarter of a mile, and did not find a bird, when lo! at the end of perhaps half an hour, we heard them calling—followed the cry back to that very hollow; the instant we entered it, all the three dogs made game, drawing upon three several birds, roaded them up, and pointed steady, and we had half an hour's good sport, and we were *all* convinced that the birds had been there *all* the time. I have seen many instances of the same kind, and more particularly with wing-tipped birds, but none I think so tangible as this!"

"Well, I am not a convert, Harry; but, as the Chancellor said, I doubt."

"And that I consider not a little, from such a positive wretch as you are; but come, we have done breakfast, and it's broad daylight. Come, Timothy, on with the bag and belts; he breakfasted before we had got up, and gave the dogs a bite."

"Which dogs do you take, Harry; and do you use cartridge?"

"Oh! the setters for the morning; they are the only fellows for the stubble; we should be all day with the cockers; even setters, as we *must* break them here for wood shooting, have not enough of speed or dash for the open. Cartridges? yes! I shall use a loose charge in my right, and a *blue* cartridge in my left; later in the season I use a *blue* in my right and a *red* in my left. It just makes the difference between killing with both, or with one barrel. The *blue* kills all of twenty, and the *red* all of thirty-five yards further than loose shot; and they kill *clean!*"

"Yet many good sportsmen dislike them," Frank replied; "they say they ball!"

"They do not *now*, if you load with them properly; formerly they would do so at times, but that defect is now rectified—with the *blue* and *red* cartridges at least—the *green*, which are only fit for wild-fowl, or deer-shooting, will do so sometimes, but very rarely; and they will execute surprisingly. For a bad or uncertain rifle-shot, the *green* cartridge, with SG shot is the thing—twelve good-sized slugs, propelled with force enough to go through an inch plank, at eighty yards, within a compass of three feet—but no wad must be used, either upon the cartridge or between that and the powder; the small end must be inserted downward, and the cartridge must be chosen so that the wad at the top shall fit the gun, the case being two sizes less than the calibre. With these directions no man need make a mistake; and, if he can cover a bird fairly, and is cool enough not to fire within twenty yards, he will never complain of cartridges, after a single trial. Remember, too, that *vice versa* to the rule of a loose charge, the *heavier* you load with powder, the *closer* will your cartridge carry. The men who do not like cartridges are—you may rely upon it—of the class which prefers scattering guns. I always use them, except in July shooting, and I shall even put a few *red* in my pockets, in case the wind should get up in the afternoon. Besides which, I always take along two buckshot cartridges, in case of *happening,* as Timothy would say, on some big varmint. I have four pockets in my shooting waistcoat, each stitched off into four compartments—each of which holds, *erect,* one cartridge—you cannot carry them loose in your pocket, as they are very apt to break. Another advantage of this is, that in no way can you carry shot with so little inconvenience, as to weight; besides which, you load one third quicker, and your gun *never* leads!"

"Well! I believe I will take some to-day—but don't you wait for the Commodore?"

"No! He drives up, as I told you, from Nyack, where he lands from his yacht, and will be here at twelve o'clock to luncheon; if he had been coming for the morning shooting, he would have been here ere this. By that time we shall have bagged twenty-five or thirty quail, and a ruffed grouse or two; besides driving two or three bevies down into the meadows and the alder bushes by the stream, which are quite full of woodcock. After luncheon, with the Commodore's aid, we will pick up these stragglers, and all the timber-doodles!"

In another moment the setters were unchained, and came careening, at the top of their speed, into the breakfast room, where Harry stood before the fire, loading his double gun, while Timothy was buttoning on his left leggin. Frank, meanwhile, had taken up his gun, and quietly sneaked out of the door, two flat irregular reports explaining, half a moment after, the purport of his absence.

"Well, now, Frank, that *is*"—expostulated Harry—"that *is* just the most snobbish thing I ever saw you do; ain't you ashamed of yourself now, you genuine cockney!"

"Not a bit—my gun has not been used these three months, and something *might* have got into the chamber!"

"Something *might not,* if when you cleaned it last you had laid a wad in the centre of a bit of greased rag three inches square and rammed it about an inch down the barrel, leaving the ends of the linen hanging out. And by running your rod down you could have ascertained the fact, without unnecessarily fouling your piece. A gun has no right ever to miss fire *now;* and never *does,* if you use Westley Richards' caps, and diamond gunpowder—putting the caps on the *last thing*—which has the further advantage of being much the safer plan, and seeing that the powder is up to the cones before you do so. If it is not so, let your hammer down, and give a smart tap to the under side of the breech, holding it uppermost, and you will never need a picker; or at least almost never.

Remember, too, that the best picker in the world is a strong needle headed with sealing wax. And now that you have finished loading, and I lecturing, just jump over the fence to your right; and that footpath will bring us to the stepping stones across the Ramapo. By Jove, but we shall have a lovely morning."

He did so, and away they went, with the dogs following steadily at the heel, crossed the small river dry-shod, climbed up the wooded bank by dint of hand and foot, and reached the broad brown corn stubble. Harry, however, did not wave his dogs to the right-hand and left, but calling them in, quietly plodded along the headland, and climbed another fence, and crossed a buckwheat stubble, still without beating or disturbing any ground, and then another field full of long bents and ragwort, an old deserted pasture, and Frank began to grumble, but just then a pair of bars gave access to a wide fifty acre lot, which had been wheat, the stubble standing still knee deep, and yielding a rare covert.

"Now we are at the far end of our beat, and we have got the wind too in the dogs' noses, Master Frank—and so hold up, good lads," said Harry. And off the setters shot like lightning, crossing and quartering their ground superbly.

"There! there! well done, old Chase—a dead stiff point already, and Shot backing him as steady as a rail. Step up, Frank, step up quietly, and let us keep the hill of them."

They came up close, quite close to the stanch dog, and then, but not till then, he feathered and drew on, and Shot came crawling up till his nose was but a few inches in the rear of Chase's, whose point he never thought of taking from him. Now they are both upon the game. See how they frown and slaver, the birds are close below their noses.

Whirr—r—r! "There they go—a glorious bevy!" exclaimed Harry, as he cocked his right barrel and cut down the old cock bird, which had risen rather to his right hand, with his loose charge—"blaze away, Frank!" Bang—bang!—and two more birds came fluttering down, and then he pitched his gun up to his eye again and sent the cartridge after the now distant bevy, and to Frank's admiration a fourth bird was keeled over most beautifully, and clean killed, while crossing to the right, at forty-six yards, as they paced it afterward.

"Now mark! mark, Timothy—mark, Frank!" And shading their eyes from the level sunbeams, the three stood gazing steadily after the rapid bevy. They cross the pasture, skim very low over the brush fence of the cornfield—they disappear behind it—they are down! no! no! not yet—they are just skirting the summit of the topped maize stalks—now they are down indeed, just by that old ruined hovel, where the cat-briers and sumach have over-spread its cellar and foundation with thick underwood. And all the while the sturdy dogs are crouching at their feet unmoving.

"Will you not follow those, Harry?" Forester inquired—"there are at least sixteen of them!"

"Not I," said Archer, "not I, indeed, till I have beat this field—I expect to put up another bevy among those little crags there in the corner, where the red cedars grow—and if we do, they will strike down the fence of the buckwheat stubble—that stubble we must make good, and the rye beside it, and drive, if possible, all that we find before us to the corn field. Don't be impatient, and you'll see in time that I am in the right."

No more words were now wasted; the four birds were bagged without trouble, and the sportsmen being in the open, were handed over on the spot to Tim; who stroked their freckled breasts, and beautifully mottled wing-coverts and backs, with a caressing touch, as though he loved them; and finally, in true Jack Ketch style, tucked them up severally by the neck. Archer was not mistaken in his prognostics—another bevy had run into the dwarf cedars from the stubble at the sound of the firing, and were roaded up in right good style, first one dog, and then the other, leading; but without any jealousy or haste.

They had, however, run so far, that they had got wild, and, as there was no bottom covert on the crags, had traversed them quite over to the open, on the far side—and, just as Archer was in the act of warning Forester to hurry softly round and head them, they flushed at thirty yards, and had flown some five more before they were in sight, the feathery evergreens for a while cutting off the view—the dogs stood dead at the sound of their wings. Then, as they came in sight, Harry discharged both barrels very quickly—the loose shot first, which evidently took effect, for one bird cowered and seemed about to fall, but gathered wing again, and went on for the present—the cartridge, which went next, although the bevy had flown ten yards further, did its work clean, and stopped its bird. Frank fired but once, and killed, using his cartridge first, and thinking it in vain to fire the loose shot. The remaining birds skimmed down the hill, and lighted in the thick bushy hedge-row, as Archer had foreseen.

"So much for Ely!" exclaimed Harry—"had we both used two of them, we should have bagged four then. As it is, I have killed one which we shall not get; a thing that I most particularly hate."

"That bird will rise again," said Frank.

"*Never!*" replied the other, "he has one, if not two, shot in him, well forward—if I am not much mistaken, before the wing—he is dead now! but let us on. These we must follow, for they are on our line; you keep this side the fence, and I will cross it with the dogs—come with me, Timothy."

In a few minutes more there was a dead point at the hedgerow. "Look to, Frank!"

"Ay! ay! Poke them out, Tim;" then followed sundry bumps and threshings of the briers, and out with a noisy flutter burst two birds under Forester's nose. Bang! bang!

"The first shot too quick, altogether," muttered Archer; "Ay, he has missed one; mark it, Tim—there he goes down in the corn, by jingo—you've got that bird, Frank! That's well! Hold up, Shot"—another point within five yards. "Look out again, Frank."

But this time vainly did Tim poke, and thrash, and peer into the bushes—yet still Shot stood, stiff as a marble statue—then Chase drew up and snuffed about, and pushed his head and forelegs into the matted briers, and thereupon a muzzling noise ensued, and forthwith out he came, mouthing a dead bird, warm still, and bleeding from the neck and breast.

"Frank, he has got my bird—and shot, just as I told you, through the neck and near the great wing joint—good dog! good dog!"

"The devil!"

"Yes, the devil! but look out man, here is yet one more point;" and this time ten or twelve birds flushed upon Archer's side; he slew, as usual, his brace, and as they crossed, at long distance, Frank knocked down one more—the rest flew to the corn-field.

In the middle of the buckwheat they flushed another, and, in the rye, another bevy, both of which crossed the stream, and settled down among the alders. They reached the corn-field, and picked up their birds there, quite as fast as Frank himself desired—three ruffed grouse they had bagged, and four rabbits, in a small dingle full of thorns, before they reached the corn; and just as the tin horns were sounding for noon and dinner from many a neighboring farm, they bagged their thirty-fourth quail. At the same moment, the rattle of a distant wagon on the hard road, and a loud cheer replying to the last shot, announced the Commodore who pulled up at the tavern door just as they crossed the stepping-stones, having made a right good morning's work, with a dead certainty of better sport in the afternoon, since they had marked two untouched bevies, thirty-five birds at least, beside some ten or twelve more stragglers into the alder brakes, which Harry knew to hold—moreover, thirty woodcock, as he said, at the fewest.

"Well! Harry," exclaimed Frank, as he set down his gun, and sat down to the table, "I must for once knock under—your *practice* has borne out your *precepts.*

THE QUAIL

"Certainly this is a very lovely country," exclaimed the Commodore suddenly, as he gazed with a quiet eye, puffing his cigar the while, over the beautiful vale, with the clear expanse of Wickham's Pond in the middle foreground, and the wild hoary mountains framing the rich landscape in the distance.

"Truly, you may say that," replied Harry; "I have travelled over a large part of the world, and for its own peculiar style of loveliness, I must say that I never have seen any thing to match with the vale of Warwick. I would give much, very much, to own a few acres, and a snug cottage here, in which I might pass the rest of my days, far aloof from the

Fumum et opes strepitumque Romae."

"Then, why the h—l don't you own a few acres?" put in ancient Tom; "I'd be right glad to know, and gladder yit to have you up here, Archer."

"I would indeed, Tom," answered Harry; "I'm not joking at all; but there are never any small places to be bought hereabout; and, as for large ones, your land is so confounded good, that a fellow must be a nabob to think of buying."

"Well, how would Jem Burt's place suit you, Archer?" asked the fat man. "You knows it—jist a mile and a half 'tother side Warwick, by the crick side? I guess it will have to be sold anyhow next April; leastways the old man's dead, and the heirs want the estate settled up like."

"Suit me!" cried Harry, "by George! it's just the thing, if I recollect it rightly. But how much land is there?"

"Twenty acres, I guess—not over twenty-five, no how."

"And the house?"

"Well, that wants fixin' some; and the bridge over the crick's putty bad, too, it will want putty nigh a new one. Why, the house is a story and a half like; and it's jist an entry stret through the middle, and a parlor on one side on't, and a kitchen on the t'other; and a chamber behind both on 'em."

"What can it be bought for, Tom?"

"I guess three thousand dollars; twenty-five hundred, maybe. It will go cheap, I reckon; I don't hear tell o' no one lookin' at it."

"What will it cost me more to *fix* it, think you?"

"Well, you see, Archer, the land's ben most darned badly done by, this last three years, since old 'squire's ben so low; and the bridge, that'll take a smart sum; and the fences is putty much gone to rack; I guess it'll take hard on to a thousand more to fix it up right, like you'd like to have it, without doin' nothin' at the house."

"And fifteen hundred more for that and the stables. I wish to heaven I had known this yesterday; or rather before I came up hither," said Harry.

"Why so?" asked the Commodore.

"Why, as the deuce would have it, I told my broker to invest six thousand, that I have got loose, in a good mortgage, if he could find one, for five years; and I have got no stocks that I can sell out; all that I have but this, is on good bond and mortgage, in Boston, and little enough of it, too."

"Well, if that's all," said Forester, "we can run down tomorrow, and you will be in time to stop him."

"That's true, too," answered Harry, pondering. "Are you sure it can be bought, Tom?"

"I guess so," was the response.

"That means, I suppose, that you're perfectly certain of it. Why the devil can't you speak English?"

"English!" exclaimed Frank; "Good Lord! why don't you ask him why he can't speak Greek? English! Lord! Lord! Lord! Tom Draw and English!"

"I'll jist tell Archer what he warnts to know, and then see you, my dear little critter, if I doosn't English you some!" replied the old man, waxing wroth. "Well, Archer, to tell heaven's truth, now, I doos *know* it; but it's an *etarnal* all-fired shame of me to be tellin' it, bein' as how I knows it in the way of business like. It's got to be selled by *vandoo** in April.

"Then, by Jove! I will buy it," said Harry; "and down I'll go to-morrow. But that need not take you away, boys; you can stay and finish out the week here, and go home in the Ianthe; Tom will send you down to Nyack."

"Sartain," responded Tom; "but now I'm most darned glad I told you that, Archer. I meant to a told you on't afore, but it clean slipped out of my head; but all's right, now. Hark! hark! don't you hear, boys? The quails hasn't all got together yit—better luck! Hush, A——, and you'll hear them callin'—whew-wheet! whew-wheet! whe-whe-whe;" and the old Turk began to call most scientifically; and in ten minutes the birds were answering him from all quarters, through the circular space of Bog-meadow, and through the thorny brake beyond it, and some from a large rag-wort field further yet.

"How is this, Frank—did they scatter so much when they dropped?" asked Harry.

"Yes; part of them 'lighted in the little bank on this edge, by the spring, you know; and some, a dozen or so, right in the middle

---

* *Vendue.* Why the French word for a public auction has been adopted throughout the Northern and Eastern States, as applied to a Sheriff's sale, deponent saith not.

of the bog, by the single hickory; and five or six went into the swamp, and a few over it."

"That's it! that's it! and they've been running to try to get together," said the Commodore.

"But was too skeart to call, till we'd quit shootin'!" said Tom. "But come, boys, let's be stirrin', else they'll git together like; they keeps drawin', drawin', into one place now, I can hear."

No sooner said than done; we were all on foot in an instant, and ten minutes brought us to the edge of the first thicket; and here was the truth of Harry's precepts tested by practice in a moment; for they had not yet entered the thin bushes, on which now the red leaves hung few and sere, before old Shot threw his nose high into the air, straightened his neck and his stern, and struck out at a high trot; the other setter evidently knowing what he meant, though as yet he had not caught the wind of them. In a moment they both stood steady; and, almost at the same instant, Tom Draw's Dash, and A——'s Grouse, came to the point, all on different birds, in a bit of very open ground, covered with wintergreen about knee deep, and interspersed with only a few scattered bushes.

Whir-r-r-r—up they got all at once! what a jostle—what a hubbub! Bang! bang! crack! bang! crack! bang! Four barrels exploded in an instant, almost simultaneously; and two sharp unmeaning cracks announced that, by some means or other, Frank Forester's gun had missed fire with both barrels.

"What the deuce is the matter, boys!" cried Harry, laughing, as he threw up his gun, after the hubbub had subsided, and dropped two birds—the only two that fell, for all that waste of shot and powder.

"What the deuce ails you?" he repeated, no one replying, and all hands looking bashful and crest-fallen. "Are you all drunk? or what is the matter? I ask merely for information."

"Upon my life! I believe *I am!*" said Frank Forester. "For I have not loaded my gun at all, since I killed those two last snipe. And, when we got up from luncheon, I put on the caps just as if all was right—but all is right now," he added, for he had repaired his fault, and loaded, before A——or fat Tom had done staring, each in the other's face, in blank astonishment.

"Step up to Grouse, then," said Archer, who had never taken his eye off the old brown pointer, while he was loading as fast as he could. "He has got a bird, close under his nose; and it will get up, and steal away directly. That's a trick they will play very often."

"He haint got no bird," said Tom, sulkily. And Frank paused doubtful.

"Step up, I tell you, Frank," said Harry, "the old Turk's savage; that's all."

And Frank did step up, close to the dog's nose; and sent his foot through the grass close under it. Still the dog stood perfectly stiff; but no bird rose.

"I told you there warn't no quails there;" growled Tom.

"And I tell you there are!" answered Archer, more sharply than he often spoke to his old ally; for in truth, he was annoyed at his obstinate pertinacity.

"What do you say, Commodore? Is Grouse lying? Kick that tussock—kick it hard, Frank."

"Not he," replied A——; "I'll bet fifty to one, there's a bird there."

"It's devilish odd, then, that he won't get up!" said Frank.

Whack! whack! and he gave the hard tussock two kicks with his heavy boot, that fairly made it shake. Nothing stirred. Grouse still kept his point, but seemed half inclined to dash in. Whack! a third kick that absolutely loosened the tough hassock from the ground, and then, whirr-r, from within six inches of the spot where all three blows had been delivered, up got the bird, in a desperate hurry; and in quite as desperate a hurry Forester covered it—covered it before it was six yards off! His finger was on the trigger, when Harry quietly said, "Steady, Frank!" and the word acted like magic.

He took the gun quite down from his shoulder, nodded to his friend, brought it up again, and turned the bird over very handsomely, at twenty yards, or a little further.

"Beautifully done, indeed, Frank" said Harry. "So much for coolness!"

"What do you say to that, Tom?" said the Commodore, laughing.

But there was no laugh in Tom; he only muttered a savage growl, and an awful imprecation; and Harry's quick glance warned A—— not to plague the old Trojan further.

All this passed in a moment; and then was seen one of those singular things that will at times happen; but with regard to quail only, so far as I have ever seen or heard tell. For as Forester was putting down the card upon the powder in the barrel which he had just fired, a second bird rose, almost from the identical spot whence the first had been so difficultly flushed, and went off in the same direction. But not in the least was Frank flurried now. He dropped his ramrod quietly upon the grass, brought up his piece deliberately to his eye, and killed his bird again.

"Excellent—excellent! Frank," said Harry again. "I never saw two prettier shots in all my life. Nor did I ever see birds lie harder."

During all this time, amidst all the kicking of tussocks, threshing of bog-grass, and banging of guns, and, worst of all, bouncing up of fresh birds, from the instant when they dropped at the first shot, neither one of Harry's dogs, nor Tom's little Dash, had budged from their own charge. Now, however, they got up quickly, and soon retrieved all the dead birds.

"Now, then, we will divide into two parties," said Harry. "Frank, you go with Tom; and you come with me, Commodore. It will never do to have you two jealous fellows together, you wont kill a bird all day," he added, in a lower voice. "That is the worst of old Tom, when he gets jealous he's the very devil. Frank is the only fellow that can get along with him at all. He puts *me* out of temper, and if we both got angry, it would be very disagreeable. For, though he is the very best fellow in the world, when he is in a rage he is untameable. I cannot think what has put him out, now; for he has shot very well to-day. It is only when he gets behind-hand, that he is usually jealous in his shooting; but he has got the deuce into him now."

By this time the two parties were perhaps forty yards apart, when Dash came to a point again. Up got a single bird, the old cock, and flew directly away from Tom, across Frank's face; but not for that did the old chap pause. Up went his cannon to his shoulder, there was a flash and a roar, and the quail, which was literally not twelve feet from him, disappeared as if it had been resolved into thin air. The whole of Tom's concentrated charge had struck the bird endwise, as it flew from him; and, except the extreme tips of his wings and one foot, no part of him could be found.

"The devil!" cried Harry, "that is too bad!"

"Never mind," said the Commodore, "Frank will manage him."

As he spoke a second bird got up, and crossed Forester in the same manner, Draw doing precisely as he had done before; but, this time, missing the quail clear, which Forester turned over.

"Load quick! and step up to that fellow. He will run, I think!" said Archer.

"Ay! ay!" responded Frank, and, having rammed down his charge like lightning, moved forward, before he had put the cap on the barrel he had fired.

Just as he took the cap out of his pocket between his finger and thumb, a second quail rose. As cool and self-possessed as it is possible to conceive, Frank cocked the left hand barrel with his little finger, still holding the cap between his forefinger and thumb, and actually contrived to bring up the gun, some how or other,* and to kill the bird, pulling the trigger with his middle finger.

At the report a third quail sprang, close under his feet; and, still unshaken, he capped the right hand barrel, fired, and the bird towered!

"Mark! mark! Tom—ma-ark Timothy!" shouted Harry and A—— in a breath.

"That bird is as dead as Hannibal now!" added Archer, as, having spun up three hundred feet into the air, and flown twice as many hundred yards, it turned over, and fell plumb, like a stone, through the clear atmosphere.

"Ayse gotten that chap marked doon roight, ayse warrant un!" shouted Timothy from the hill side, where with some trouble, he

---

* If I had not seen the whole of this scene with my eyes, and had I not witnesses of the fact, I would scarce dare to relate it. From the cutting the first bird to atoms, all is strictly true.

was holding in the obstreperous spaniels. "He's doon in a roight laine atwixt 't muckle gray stean and yon hoigh ashen tree."

"Did you ever see such admirable shooting, though?" asked A——, in a low voice. "I did not know Forester shot like that."

"Sometimes he does. When he's cool. He is not certain; that is his only fault. One day he is the coolest man I ever saw in a field, and the next the most impetuous; but when he *is* cool, he shoots splendidly. As you say, A——, I never saw anything better done in my life. It was the perfection of coolness and quickness combined."

"I cannot conceive how it *was* done at all. How he brought up and fired that first barrel with a cap between his thumb and forefinger! Why, I could not fire a gun so, in cold blood!"

"Nor could he, probably. Deliberate promptitude is the thing! Well, Tom, what do you think of that? Wasn't that pretty shooting?"

"It was so, pretty shootin'," responded the fat man, quite delighted out of his crusty mood. "I guess the darned little critter's got three barrels to his gun somehow; leastwise it seems to me, I swon, 'at he fired her off three times without loadin'!" I guess I'll quit tryin' to shoot agin Frank, to-day."

"I told you so!" said Harry to the Commodore, with a low laugh, and then added aloud—"I think you may as well, Tom—for I don't believe the fellow will miss another bird to-day."

And in truth, strange to say, it fell out, in reality, nearly as Archer had spoken in jest. The whole party shot exceedingly well. The four birds, which Tom and the Commodore had missed at the first start, were found again in an old ragwort field, and brought to bay; and of the twenty-three quail which Forester had marked down into the bog meadow, not one bird escaped, and of that bevy not one bird did Frank miss, killing twelve, all of them double shots, to his own share, and beating Archer in a canter.

But that sterling sportsman cared not a stiver; too many times by far had he had the field, too sure was he of doing the same many a time again, to dislike being beaten once. Besides this, he was always the least jealous shot in the world, for a very quick one; and, in this instance, he was perhaps better pleased to see his friend "go in and win," than he would have been to do the like himself.

Exactly at two o'clock, by A——'s repeater, the last bird was bagged; making twenty-seven quail, forty-nine snipe, two ruffed grouse, and one woodcock, bagged in about five hours.

"So far, this is the very best day's sport I ever saw," said Archer; "and two things I have seen which I never saw before; a whole bevy of quail killed without the escape of one bird, and a whole bevy killed entirely by double shots, except the odd bird. You, A——, have killed three double shots—I have killed three—Tom Draw one double shot, and the odd bird; and Master Frank there, confound him, six double shots running—the cleverest thing I ever heard of, and, in Forester's case, the best shooting possible. I have missed one bird, you two, and Tom three."

"But Tom beant a goin' to miss no more birds, I can tell you, boy. Tom's drinked agin, and feels kind o' righter than he did— kind o' *first best!* You'd best all drink boys—the spring's handy, close by here; and after we gits down acrost the road into the big swamp, and Hell-Hole, there arn't a drop o' water fit to drink, till we gits way down to Aunt Sally's big spring-hole, jest to home."

"I second the motion," said Harry; "and then let us be quick, for the day is wearing away, and we have got a long beat yet before us. I wish it were a sure one. But it is not. Once in three or four years we get a grand day's sport in the big swamp; but for one good day we have ten bad ones. However, we are sure to find a dozen birds or so in Hell-Hole; and a bevy of quail in the Captain's swamp, shan't we, Tom?"

"Yes, if we gits so far; but somehow or other I rather guess we'll find quite a smart chance o' cock. Captain Reed was down there a' Satterday, and he saw heaps on 'em."

"That's no sure sign. They move very quickly now. Here to-day and there to-morrow," said Archer. "In the large woods especially. In the small places there are plenty of sure finds."

"There harn't been nothing of frosts yet keen enough to stir them," said Tom. "I guess we'll find them. And there harn't been a gun shot off this three weeks there. Hoel's wife's ben down sick all the fall, and Halbert's gun busted in the critter's hand."

"Ah! did it hurt him?"

"Hurt him some—skeart him considerable, though. I guess he's quit shootin' pretty much. But come—here we be, boys, I'll keep along the outside, where the walkin's good. You git next me, and Archer next with the dogs, and A—— inside of all. Keep right close to the cedars, A——; all the birds 'at you flushes will come stret out this aways. They never flies into the cedar swamp. Archer, how does the ground look?"

"I never saw it look so well, Tom. There is not near so much water as usual, and yet the bottom is all quite moist and soft."

"Then we'll get cock for sartain."

"By George!" cried A——, "the ground is like a honey-comb, with their borings; and as white in places with their droppings, as if there had been a snow fall!"

"Are they fresh droppings, A——?"

"Mark! Ah! Grouse! Grouse! for shame. There he is down. Do you see him, Harry?"

"Ay! ay! Did Grouse flush him?"

"Deliberately, at fifty yards off. I must lick him."

"Pray do; and that mercifully."

"And that soundly," suggested Frank, as an improvement.

"Soundly *is* mercifully," said Harry, "because one good flogging settles the business; whereas twenty slight ones only harass a dog, and do nothing in the way of correction or prevention."

"True, oh king!" said Frank, laughing. "Now let us go on; for, as the bellowing of that brute is over, I suppose 'chastisement has hidden her head.' "

And on they did go; and sweet shooting they had of it; all the way down to the thick deep spot, known by the pleasing sobriquet of Hell-Hole.

The birds were scattered everywhere throughout the swamp, so excellent was the condition of the ground; scattered so much, that, in no instance did two rise at once; but one kept flapping up after another, large and lazy, at every few paces; and the sportsmen scored them fast, although scarcely aware how fast they were killing them. At length, when they reached the old creek-side, and the deep black mud-holes, and the tangled vines and leafy alders, there was, as usual, a quick, sharp, and decisive rally. Before the dogs were thrown into it, Frank was sent forward to the extreme point, and the Commodore out into the open field, on the opposite side from that occupied by fat Tom.

On the signal of a whistle, from each of the party, Harry drove into the brake with the spaniels, the setters being now consigned to the care of Timothy; and in a moment, his loud "Hie cock! Hie cock! Pur-r-r—Hie cock! good dogs!" was succeeded by the shrill yelping of the cockers, the flap of the fast rising birds, and the continuous rattling of shots.

In twenty minutes the work was done; and it was well that it was done; for, within a quarter of an hour afterwards, it was too dark to shoot at all.

In that last twenty minutes twenty-two cock were actually brought to bag, by the eight barrels; twenty-eight had been picked up, one by one, as they came down the long swamp, and one Harry had killed in the morning. When Timothy met them, with the horses, at the big oak tree, half an hour afterward—for he had gone off across the fields, as hard as he could foot it to the farm, as soon as he had received the setters—it was quite dark; and the friends had counted their game out regularly, and hung it up *secundum artem* in the loops of the new game bag.

It was a huge day's sport—a day's sport to talk about for years afterward—Tom Draw does talk about it now!

Fifty-one woodcock, forty-nine English snipe, twenty-seven quail, and a brace of ruffed grouse. A hundred and twenty-nine head in all, on unpreserved ground, and in very wild walking. It is to be feared it will never be done any more in the vale of Warwick. For this, alas! was ten years ago.

When they reached Tom's it was decided that they should all return home on the morrow; that Harry should attend to the procuring his purchase money; and Tom to the cheapening of the purchase.

In addition to this, the old boy swore, by all his patron saints, that he would come down in spring, and have a touch at the snipe he had heard Archer tell on at Pine Brook.

A capital supper followed; and of course lots of good liquor, and the toast, to which the last cup was quaffed, was

LONG LIFE TO HARRY ARCHER, AND LUCK TO HIS SHOOTING BOX, to which Frank Forester added

"I wish he may get it."

And so that party ended; all of its members hoping to enjoy many more like it, and that very speedily.

SHOFFSTALL

SOMETIMES YOU CAN'T FIND THEM

Havilah Babcock

Havilah Babcock once wrote: "Birds, like gold, are where you find them. They can be a lot of other places too." Now that's the truth, if I ever heard it. In this piece from My Health Is Better in November *Babcock reminds us of the tiresome hours and hard miles we must sometimes face to find a bunch of birds. You know how it goes: All day long you check on the whereabouts of coveys that normally are as obliging as old friends in their presence. Nobody home! Finally, just before dark, Old Belle pins a big bevy. You hurry forward, trying to eat up the two hundred yards with a brisk gait. But the puppy Joe gets there first, of course. "Whoa, Joe! Whoa, you son-of-a-biscuit!" You watch the vague forms of twenty-odd birds disappear into the maw of the darkening swamp. You've been there, haven't you, Friend?*

I HAVE READ—and written—articles on how to shoot quail, but what I want to know is how to *find* them. For you and I have learned, ofttimes to our chagrin, that birds can be very plentiful and yet unfindable. Two men may hunt precisely the same territory under identical weather conditions. One finds birds aplenty, the other finds precious few. Now I want to know why. Is there a sort of technique to locating birds, a technique based on an intimate acquaintance with their haunts and habits?

I had much rather read than write about this subject, but apparently few writers have had the rashness to tackle it. What I don't know about it would fill a book. On the other hand, what I do know often takes the sag out of my bag and adds immeasurably to the pleasure of the hunt.

With the hope of starting a friendly feud with other hunters who are more competent to testify, I venture to set down a few things I've picked up, often at the cost of embarrassment or long and bootless tramps afield, during the twenty-five years I have been cultivating the acquaintance of Bob White.

Are there a few rules that might be followed with reasonable prospect of success? Well, yes. But I am not guaranteeing that Bob and his bevy will always conform to the rules. There are non-conformists, precedent-breakers, and plain damn fools among birds as among us who hunt them.

To find birds you've got to go where they are. Not where they ought to be. Not where you'd like them to be. Not where they would be easy to shoot. You've got to go where they are at that particular time of the day, that particular stage of the season, and during that particular kind of weather. You've got to know your quarry as a ward-heeler knows his constituency.

There are times when a wise man refraineth from hunting, when he stayeth at home and regaleth his spouse. For instance, it is useless to start hunting early on a cold, brittle, and heavily-frosted morning. Birds are loth to leave the roost, and who can blame them? They may be caught in bed as late as ten o'clock on such mornings. And they seem to emit little scent when huddled together in such a compact and inert mass.

Dogs may overrun them entirely, or get too close before detecting their presence. So if the morning is of the aforementioned sort—benumbingly cold and heavily-frosted—you may lie in the bed an hour or two longer with impunity. Or you may doze about the kitchen stove and give your pancreatic juices a chance to act on your breakfast, with the assurance of forefeiting little thereby.

All you've missed is a fruitless tramp and a sniffy head cold. And a pair of half-frozen ears so sensitive that when a recalcitrant branch snaps back and clips one, well, I've seen it fetch tears to the eyes of manly and upstanding citizens. Be as sensible as the birds you're hunting and stay in bed. Some mornings are preordained for sleeping anyway.

But if, regardless of the precepts of philosophy, the admonitions of your wife, and the dictates of common sense you must start early, be sure to hunt the sunny exposures first, and continually caution your dogs lest they overrun a laggard covey.

If the morning is warm and sunny, you've got to get up betimes to beat Bob. He and his fussy fellows are hustling for breakfast almost at the crack o' day. Indeed, I have found them afield almost too early for good shooting in such weather.

Another excellent time for the quail-hunter to stay indoors is right after a heavy downpour or earth-drenching fog, when the weeds and fields are dripping-wet. Unlike the mourning dove,

Bob White has a marked aversion to getting wet. He is not a good Baptist. In such weather, birds will ensconce themselves under overhanging banks, under fallen logs, brush-piles, honeysuckle-thickets, or wherever a dry covert may be found. Certainly they will stir abroad as little as possible, and will feed only when desperate. And they may remain holed-up for days in such weather.

So when the outlook is on the sodden side, bow to the inevitable and stay at home. It is a fine time to reinstate yourself in the good graces of your wife by looking after the household odds-and-ends that you, as a well-meaning householder, have been meaning ever-so-long to look after. Every hunter ought to have a rainy day agenda to fall back on.

I have never found quail-hunting especially good in very windy weather either. A moderate, prevailing wind is unobjectionable. In fact, I like it. Birds circulate freely, and their scent is disseminated so that the dogs find them easily. But if the day is gusty and blustery, with high capricious winds, birds will move about precious little. They are apt to be on the leeward side of things, or holed-up in unfindable places.

And you will get little shooting if you do chance upon them, because a boisterous wind makes them jittery and hair-triggered. They nervously double their guard, as if realizing that the commotion about them renders them more vulnerable to attack. Certainly they are over-tense, flush easily, and fly unpredictably. So if you have that kind of weather, stay at home and play checkers with your grandchildren. And tell them about your prowess at school in the olden days. If they are young enough, they will believe your fireside epics. If you tell them often enough, you'll believe them yourself.

Hunting in extremely dry weather is vexatious business too, as I verified afresh during a recent season. South Carolina and Virginia suffered a prolonged drought that seared all vegetation and left the ground as dry as powder. Under such conditions, you can come amazingly close to birds and miss them altogether, regardless of how sharp your dogs are, or how closely you hunt. Your dogs can pass within a few feet, not yards, of a skulking covey without detecting its presence at all, yet the singles will almost unfailingly flush wild, and you get few decent shots.

On the opening day, I backtracked a few steps to retrieve a handkerchief and stepped into twenty birds, although four good dogs had just passed unsuspectingly within twenty feet of the spot. Birds were capricious, and dogs well-nigh helpless in the bone-dry and dust-laden fields. We had to step on a covey, and pray that singles would hold until we got there. Surely a man can't rightfully censure his dogs for overrunning birds under such conditions. We finally got a respectable bag by using a pair of rampaging young buckaroos to run them up, and a pair of gingerly-footed old ladies to gum-shoe the singles.

The only suggestion I can offer for drought-hunting is to *stay close to your dogs* and be ready for all sorts of unguessable antics on the part of the birds. Does this jibe with your dry-weather experience?

Another time when the wise man refraineth from hunting is during the middle hours of the day. From around twelve to three, I should say. During that period birds are not moving.

They might have sneaked off to their regular watering place, for a covey follows a schedule in this respect. They might be wallowing and dusting under a fallen log, or beside a rotting sawdust pile. Or they might be drowsing and preening themselves in some sunny spot. Wherever they are and whatever they are doing, they are not likely to be anywhere that will do you and me any good. It's big recess for them. Take a hint and follow suit.

Stretch out in a sunny spot yourself and leisurely eat the snack your thoughtful dame has prepared, giving a morsel now and then to the faithful dog at your feet. Then relax, speculate on life and its imponderables, and doze for an hour or two. Thanks to him who first invented sleep. This is the only sensible thing to do. Don't squander your energies fretting and fuming. Save yourself and your dogs.

To thresh feverishly about during this lull is a waste of effort you will rue during the choice afternoon hours yet to come. How often do our over-anxious fellows fret themselves and their dogs into exhaustion during the dead noon-hours, only to pay for it by lack of smartness and precision later when birds are on the move. So rest, weary wayfarer, and peradventure do a little cat-napping.

You will wake refreshed and ready for whatever lieth ahead. And brother, you will live longer too.

Thus far we have been talking mostly about when *not* to hunt. What are the best hunting hours of the day? It varies somewhat with weather, feeding habits, and other local factors. Some hunters prefer the morning hours, others the late afternoon hours. Some say birds feed more actively in the forenoon, having accumulated an overnight appetite. Others insist that they feed more briskly in the afternoon, in anticipation of an overnight fast. Every hunter is entitled to whatever opinion his own experience justifies. What is your preference?

The poet Browning has the peregrinating Pippa wax lyrical about the glories of early morn. "Morning's at seven" she sings. But not for bird-hunters. I'll take the last two hours before dark myself. This is the peak of the day. If undisturbed, birds have worked their way far afield, leaving a leisurely, meandering trail that can be easily picked up. They are apt to be far enough from base to allow good singles-shooting too. Intent on their feeding, they hold well. The air is mellow and resonant the last two hours, the dogs have gotten their second-wind and second-nose too, and likely enough a springiness has crept into the hunter's gait.

Birds are reluctant to leave the fields. They have become separated, are feeding in segments here and there, and there is no concerted action toward leaving. I have seen covies fly straight into the setting sun, and so have you. Pretty, isn't it? Indeed, they often feed so late that they fly to roost.

The last thirty minutes are the best of all. How often have I wearily trudged the fields the livelong day and reached late afternoon with my pockets empty and my hopes a-dragging at my heels,—to have the whole day redeemed by the last fifteen minutes before dark. How it compensates for a luckless day, and sweetens up the hunt, to have a big bevy nicely scattered then! Where is the bird-hunter who has not had a bootless day redeemed in such fashion?

To take advantage of the last precious minutes, you've got to stay afield as late as the birds do, regardless of a houseful of guests, the sanguine promises you've made the missus, or the overdraft bank notice at home. To heck with everybody and everything when birds are feeding and fish are biting. Stay late and lie like a dog if necessary.

In laying out the day's hunt, I always save my best territory until late afternoon. One who prefers the morning hours will prudently do likewise. To "mess up" good territory by hunting it at the wrong time bespeaks the over-eager amateur or the arrant bungler. The number of birds you get depends upon the judgment you exercise rather than the strenuosity with which you hunt.

Birds are astute weather-forecasters. Nature has endowed them, in common with many other animals, with a strange prescience. They carry barometers in their heads. So did man, until he took to carrying one in his pocket. There are no superfluities in nature. And weather, of course, markedly affects bird-behavior.

Have you ever noticed how dormant and inactive birds are, and how perfunctorily they feed, before the advent of a warm spell? And conversely, how active they are, and how protractedly and ravenously they feed before the advent of harsh weather? Especially before a heavy snowfall?

For years I have hunted quail in the foothills of Virginia, a section subject to rather heavy snowfalls. Again and again I have observed that on the day preceding a snowstorm, birds feed briskly and remain in the fields late, as if taking time by the forelock, as if in anticipation of an enforced fast. You have surely observed this same phenomenon.

I do not mean to imply that a good bird-hunter must be a weather prognosticator. But any observing hunter *can* arrive at a few deductions about the weather and bird-behavior, and enhance both his bag and his pleasure thereby. Such deductions, if based on the experience of a practical hunter in his own locality, should be fairly workable.

But all of us know that the behavior of birds may vary from day to day without any pronounced or even perceptible change of weather. There are times when quail are unaccountably inactive and listless, when they feed almost none, and are mysteriously unfindable even in the best territory.

There are also times when, equally without apparent reference to weather, they are extremely active. There are days too, when without any discoverable cause, they are excitable and jittery, flushing at the least provocation and often ahead of the dogs. Evidently there are subtle weather changes which, although unremarked by us, affect birds profoundly.

But one may encounter traits in the most commonplace animal that will baffle the most discerning student. Nobody can safely dogmatize about the conduct of anything. Shucks, we don't know how we ourselves are going to behave until the time comes, and then our conduct is often neither logical nor explicable. So we can guess with Bob White, but we can't out-guess him, and it is this element of the unpredictable that makes the game worth the candle.

Have you ever noticed the similarity in the behavior of quail and chickens? If you want to know whether conditions are propitious for a quail hunt, go into the backyard and consult your barred rocks and leghorns. If they are spiritedly scratching around for ration points, quail are probably doing the same thing. If they are disposed to remain inside, or stand droopily and lackadaisically around, stay at home and eat your chickens, for birds are probably not abroad. But please note that I said probably. I am too old a sinner to guarantee anything.

Some fishermen have the notion that they can likewise gauge the disposition of fish by glancing at their goldfish pools. Is there any substance to this notion? I have no evidence to offer, but it does seem plausible.

Regardless of the weather and Bob's frame of mind, luck favors the hunter who knows his dog and keeps up with him. He has got to know the mental make-up of his dog, his virtues and his limitations, his habits and his mannerisms. What the dog can do and what he can't do, what he will do and won't do. Otherwise, strangers are hunting together.

An alert hunter therefore keeps an eye continually on his dog, regardless of how good he is. No dog is infallible. The best will sometimes overrun, misjudge, or miscue in some way. That's why they have field trials. Even if your dog were infallible, you'd have to reckon with the unpredictableness of the quarry. The man who stays in close will get many a shot during the day that he otherwise wouldn't get, and you can lay to that.

] 163 [

I like to stay well up in front where I can command a view of operations, where I can instantly detect signs of game-making and field-faults in my dogs, where I can follow the flight of the covey that flushes wild, and where I can get some idea as to the whereabouts of a dog lost on point. Nothing is so pleasure-marring and time-consuming as looking for a lost dog when you haven't the vaguest idea where to look.

I dislike horseback hunting because I'm not on the spot when the unscheduled happens. I believe a man can get more birds by keeping up with an indifferent dog than by lagging negligently behind a good one. So, especially if you're in broken territory where your view is often obstructed, stay with your dogs, and I don't care how good your dogs are.

Now, will you stick *your* neck out a little?

YOU SEPARATE THE MEN FROM THE BOYS

Robert C. Ruark

Because of his "Old Man and the Boy" series in Field & Stream, *Robert Ruark was able to shuck his syndicated newspaper chores and devote himself full-time to his novels and outdoor pieces. For us as readers, the series meant hours of enjoyment of some of the warmest, richest stories ever written about hunting and fishing. They're all collected in the two books,* The Old Man and the Boy *and* The Old Man's Boy Grows Older (*Holt, Rinehart, and Winston*). *This piece, from the first book, is one of my favorites. Rereading it fills me with a sense of sadness that the opportunities for a young man to make such a hunt today, hunting alone under the difficult conditions, are depressingly hard to find.*

I DON'T KNOW why they didn't take February right out of the calendar, instead of monkeying around with it and making leap years out of it, because it is the worst-weathered of all the months, being halfway between winter and spring, with all the bad habits of both. I mean cold and rain and a little snow and a lot of wind and just natural nasty.

The trouble with February is that January's gone and March is coming next, and March is the most useless month of all, since there is nothing you can do in March except sniffle and wish the wind would quit blowing. All the hunting's over and generally it's too early to fish. There's still a long way to go until school's out, and "There ain't any wonder," the Old Man said, "that they told Caesar to beware the Ides of March." I didn't ask the Old Man what an Ide was. I was afraid he'd tell me.

But we aren't talking about March. The subject is February, and there's one thing you can do in February better than any other time of the year. That is shoot quail. For a long time I didn't believe it, but the Old Man always insisted that February was the best quail month of all.

I remember one day it was drizzling that slow, cold, nasty, steady sizzle-sozzle that is so cold it burns like fire and turns your ears into ice blocks and makes your nose run steady. The sky was a dark putty, and you could see the icicles hanging on the window frames and on the roof of the porch. The Old Man was sitting in front of a fire that was drawing so strong that she whistled as the flames sucked up the chimney, and occasionally he would cut loose and spit in the fire. It sounded like a blacksmith tempering a horseshoe. *Hissss!*

The Old Man stuck out his foot and nudged a log that had almost burned through. It dropped in a shower of red coal to the bottom of the hearth and shot fresh slashes of flame up through the topmost chunks. The Old Man looked at me.

"There is always one way to separate the men from the boys," he said. "That is to watch and see if a feller'll do a thing the hard way, when all the other fellers are sitting around grumbling and quarreling that it can't be done." He cut loose another amber stream at the fire and looked at me with his head cocked sidewise, like a smart old dog. "Most people quit doing things as soon as the wire edge has worn off and it ain't fashionable or comfortable any more. That makes it the beauty part for a few individualists. Soon as the clerks run to cover, the big people got the field to themselves."

I didn't say anything. I knew the old buzzard pretty well by now. He was as tricky as a pet coon. All I had to do was make one peep, and he'd have me hooked. It'd be something he wanted me to do that he didn't want to do himself. Such as going to the store in the rain for some new eating tobacco, or going out for more wood, or having to report on Shakespeare, or something.

"You take quail," the Old Man went on. "When the season opens around Thanksgiving, every damfool and his brother is out in the woods, blam-blamming around and trampling all over each other. The birds are wild, and the dogs are nervous, and they crowd the birds and run over coveys they ought to sneak up on. The ground is dry, and the birds run instead of holding. There practically ain't no such thing as good single-bird shooting, because the bobwhites take off and land as a covey, instead of scattering.

"Then along comes Christmas and New Year's, and the part-time quail hunter is tired of bird shooting, and it's too cold and too rainy, and he has to clean his guns ever' time he comes in to keep the rust off; so he ties up the dogs and forgets hunting until next year. This leaves the woods free of the city slickers and the ribbon clerks and the fashionable shooters. By this time the birds are steadied down and the dogs have had a lot of practice, and they've steadied down too. The young birds have been shot over and have grown their heavy feathers, and the young dogs have figured out that if they find birds the man will shoot some and they will bring them to the man, and that everybody—the dogs, the man, and the birds—is in business together. It ain't a game any more, like running rabbits. It's men's work."

I gave up. He had me nailed. "I'll go get my gun," I said. "You can drive me out and sit by the stove in Cox's Store while I catch pneumonia. That is, if the dogs will go out in this weather."

"They'll go out," the Old Man told me. "The dogs are professionals. They ain't part-time sports like some people I know. Go get 'em, and you better wear those oilskin pants and the oilskin jacket. The woods'll be sopping."

Man, I reckon I'm never going to forget that particular day. I sure was glad I wasn't a fish, because those woods were wetter than a well, with the little droplets clinging onto the low bush, the gallberries, and the broom grass, and the trees dripping steady. There wasn't a steady rain. It just sort of seeped down, half drizzle and half fog. My hands on the gun barrels were so cold that my fingers practically stuck to the steel. Rain collected on the gun sight and ran down the little streamway between the barrels. The dogs looked as miserable as any wet dog always looks, sort of like a land-borne otter.

Rain is miserable anywhere, but I expect there's nothing quite so cheerless as a wet wood in February. The sawdust piles have been soaked stiff and hard and dark brown. The green of the trees all turns black in the wet, so that you don't get any color contrasts, and the plowed ground is a dirty, ugly gray. The few shocks of corn that still stand are spotted and shriveled, and the sad little heads of cotton hanging onto the dead stalks look like orphans lost in a big city. But the good Lord put feathers and fur on birds and animals to keep them dry and warm, and life goes right on. Except that the Old Man is right, as he nearly always is. Wet woods make birds a heap easier to find, because the birds don't move around very much, and you can spot exactly where they're apt to be. And a dog's nose works dandy in the wet, just as a car runs better on a rainy night, when you get richer combustion.

I hadn't been out of the Liz for five minutes when Sandy, the covey dog, disappeared into a little copse of pine saplings halfway between a peafield and a broom-grassed stretch that led to a big swamp. Old Frank, the single-bird expert, went to have a look and then came back to give me the word. He jerked his head in the direction of the pine trees, impatient as a traffic cop who wants a car to move on, and then he dived into the bush with his tail assembly shaking like a hula dancer.

Maybe I have mentioned that I don't shoot very well except when I'm by myself or with the Old Man, because I'm not self-conscious in front of him and don't have to worry about shooting too fast or competing for birds. But when I'm by myself it seems as if it's almost impossible to shoot bad, because you shoot in any direction—backward, sideways, or whatever—without worrying about blowing somebody's head off.

I knew what old Sandy would be doing when I stepped into the dark, dripping grove. He would have suggested to the birds that they move to the outer edge of the pine thicket, so that they would have a nice clear field of soggy broom grass to fly over on their way to the swamp. I was pretty well trained by now. The dogs had been working on me for a couple of years, and the Old Man said he was surprised, that sometimes I showed as much bird sense as a half-trained puppy, and there was hope that I might grow up to where the dogs needn't be ashamed of me.

Sandy had herded the covey to the edge of the thicket, sure enough, and old Frank had come up on his right flank, inside the thicket, and was protecting the right wing. All I had to do was show a little common intelligence and walk along the left wing, outside the thicket, and when I came abreast of Sandy's nose Frank would run in from the right and Sandy would charge straight ahead and the birds would flush, leaving both me and the birds in the open. Then all I had to do was shoot some.

It was an enormous great covey—about twenty or twenty-five birds in it. Either it was two shot-over coveys that had got together, or one that had been missed entirely; I reckoned it was the latter. When Frank roared in from the right and old Sandy broke point and jumped into the birds, they got up in a cloud and fanned perfectly past me, giving me the best shot there is—a three-quarter straightaway where you lead just a little and let the shot string out behind your chosen bird.

This was jackpot day. Lots of times I had killed two birds with one shot, which is always an accident. You pick one out and aim at him, and the shot string knocks off another. I held on one of the front-flying cocks and pulled, and the whole doggone sky fell down. I stood there with my mouth open, just watching the rest of the birds sideslip into the edge of the swamp, and didn't bother to shoot the left barrel.

The dogs started to fetch—even Sandy, who doesn't care much about it as a steady job, because he reckons any damfool dog can pick up a dead bird and fill his mouth full of loose feathers. But they were interested in this job, because by the time they finished collecting the enemy I had six birds in my coat with one shot. The answer, of course, was very simple. Just as I pulled on the cock bird some of his relatives executed a cavalry maneuver and did a flank on him, and I simply fired right down the line, raking the face of the flank.

Sandy brought the last bird and spat him out on the ground and looked over at old Frank and sort of winked. *Lookit the kid,* Sandy was saying. *By the time he get home, he'll think he did it on purpose. This time next year it'll be twelve birds when he tells it.* Frank laughed and nodded agreement.

We hunted through the sopping woods, and everywhere a covey of birds was supposed to be, a covey of birds was. I couldn't miss anything that day. I had to use two barrels on one single, was all, and I got that extra barrel back again a little later. It was just one of those days when all the birds got up right, pasted flat within an inch of the dog's nose before they rose. The singles clung to the ground like limpets, and you literally had to kick them up. Birds fly slower when they're waterlogged, and it was pretty near murder.

The extra barrel I got back, to make the score perfect for the day, was a present from Frank. I shot into the last covey and had fourteen birds in the coat with a double on the rise. Frank fetched both birds and then disappeared into the big, spooky black swamp into which the rest of the covey had flown.

A year ago I would have thought he was acting like an idiot, but, as I said, the dogs had trained me pretty good, and Frank, of all dogs, was no covey chaser. I reckoned that I had hit another bird and wounded him without knowing it, and that Frank had seen a leg drop, or something. I sat down on a stump and let the rain punish my face, and old Sandy sat down by me and shrugged his shoulders as an adult will when he cannot control a child. *If that damfool dog wants to go drown himself in that swamp on a wild-goose chase,* Sandy said with his shrug, *let him. Not for me, bud. There are too many birds around.*

Frank was gone for nearly half an hour. When he came back, he was wetter than a drowned rat, but he had a live bird in his mouth. He had evidently chased the runner for half a mile. I cracked the fugitive's neck and shoved him in my coat and went back to the store to collect the Old Man. He laughed out loud when we came into the bright warmth of Mr. Cox's potbellied stove. We must have been a sight—wet dogs, wet boy, wet coat full of bedraggled birds.

The Old Man is real clever. "How many shells?" he asked.

"Nine."

"How many birds?"

"Fifteen," I said, with pardonable pride.

"Don't tell me how it happened right now," the Old Man said. "I want to get you out of those wet clothes, and I reckon I'll need a little spot of nerve medicine to make me strong enough to listen to the bragging. But tell me one thing: was I right about February bird shooting?"

"Yessir," I said. "But then you ain't generally very wrong about anything in the woods."

"That," the Old Man declared, as we walked out into the rain and climbed into the Liz, "is a very sage observation from one so young, and I am highly flattered. If it'll make you feel any better, I made all my mistakes when I was young, which is the difference today between an old man and a boy. Youth is for making mistakes, and old age is for impressing the young with your knowledge. My Lord, it's an awful day, isn't it?"

"It's a beautiful day," I said.

THEY ONLY SHOOT COCKBIRDS
IN CAROLINA

Jim Rikhoff

Jim Rikhoff can miss quail as well as the next man; but he can write about quail better than most, and that's why I'm especially happy to have this piece for The Bobwhite Quail Book. *They say that the late Bob Maytag used to amaze everybody down at his Sedgefields Plantation in Alabama by consistently dropping two cockbirds on covey rises. With a .410! Now I happen to know Jimmy well enough—having watched him miss birds in the United States, Canada, Mexico and Africa—to know that any aspirations he has along those lines of smoothbore performance are going to have to be shelved sooner or later. By the way, the perceptive reader will have noticed the character "Ely" back in our first story, Robert Ruark's "The Brave Quail." Yep, it's the same fellow. Obviously, the quality of his hunting "gent'men" has slipped over the years. For a full course of bonded Rikhoff see his book* Mixed Bag *(Amwell Press). Or you can take him in smaller doses in his column every month on the last page of* The American Rifleman.

SOMEONE ONCE SAID there are only two kinds of Southerners— those whose world revolved around "birds" and those poor unfortunates who know, or worse, care nothing about bobwhite quail. Needless to say, very little good can be said about the latter class of citizen, so we'll promptly dismiss them from any further consideration.

As it happens, the Visiting Sport was privileged to enjoy the hospitality of one of South Carolina's finest traditional sporting plantations for several hunts in the mid-1970s. It seems his good friend, Joe Hudson, at that time Chairman of the state's Wildlife and Marine Resources Commission, held a hunting lease on about 14,000 of the 20,000 acres that used to comprise the Little Hobcaw Plantation outside Kingstree. Those of us old enough to remember Bob Ruark's fine stories on Carolina quail hunting in *Field and Stream* in the 1950s, might recall that Little Hobcaw was the home of Bernard Baruch, the famed financier and consultant to presidents who avidly hunted quail right up until the year before his death a decade ago when he was well into his nineties.

Joe's lease was on that part of the old plantation that was

owned by Sonny McGill, whose father, David, had been Mr. Baruch's caretaker and whose son, Jot, helped take care of the lease, horses, dogs and other important matters for the Commissioner. Actually, the whole menage was really sort of run by Jack McGill, Sonny's cousin. If the familial relationships sound complicated, well, they are, but that's the way it was. Added to all the McGills were two extraordinary gentlemen in their own right— "Son," who was expert in cooking a fine Carolina barbecued pig and, most celebrated, one Ely Wilson, who was Mr. Baruch's trusted right hand man. Ely was also immortalized by Ruark in some of his magazine pieces.

Mr. Wilson, as they say, was and is a "piece of work." Of undetermined age, Ely can still march out with the best of them in the quail fields. He sports an old British Colonial-type pith helmet, proudly bearing a badge that plainly states to all that he is the "Chief Guide" and he means it. In his younger days, when Mr. Baruch brought the famed and wealthy to Little Hobcaw, Ely grew accustomed to the likes of Winston Churchill and such celebrities. There are very few situations and almost no personalities that are going to make much of an impression on him these days. Water seeks its own level and Ely, who had been known to share an occasional brandy and soda with the late British prime minister, knew exactly what sort of level impressed him. On a scale from one to ten, the Visiting Sport hung somewhere around the middle and was happy for that.

After meeting Commissioner Hudson in Spartanburg, the Sport and his companion, John Rhea, then of Alexandria, Virginia, and a noted figure in his own world of big game and conservation, headed for the King's Tree Inn, where they planned to headquarter during the two days they had to hunt quail. They inquired of the Commissioner just what was the custom of the country in regard to the next day's hunt. Neither had hunted quail in South Carolina before.

"Well," said Mr. Joe, as he was repectfully addressed by many of the locals, "Huntin' birds here is just like anyplace else down South where people have been followin' fine pointin' dogs and carryin' nice doubleguns after God's most splendid game bird for generations!" That sounded like the routine might entail more decorum and ritual than the two visitors were used to so they pressed for further details from their leader.

"We'll be on horses, you know, and the dogs—Runt and Freddie—Freddie's been ailin', don't know how he'll do," he mused, his voice trailing off a bit as he pondered Freddie's disability, but then brightening, "but don't worry, we'll have dogs enough and horses, not to speak of lots of bird ground to cover."

"While there'll be three of us out, only two guns will be down and forward for each covey point. The singles we'll handle as they come," he continued, viewing the guest guns over his glass. "I don't suppose I have to tell you gentlemen that you only shoot at the birds on your side of the covey rise. You don't shoot another man's birds," he sniffed.

"Yessir, Mr. Joe," the visitors were quick to pick up local custom.

"Also, be careful of your shootin' angles. Watch your swing and don't shoot at low flyin' birds. We don't want you shootin' each other or one of the dogs . . . especially the dogs," he added as a quiet afterthought. We got up to proceed to the dining room.

"Oh yes, one more thing and to me, as Commissioner, it's a very important consideration. Now, John, you're from Texas and live in Virginia, so you probably are familiar with our peculiar custom about quail shootin' here in South Carolina, but our friend here from the North," he shuddered slightly as the word escaped his lips, "may not know that we only shoot cockbirds in Carolina. Most important. Only cockbirds, covey-rise or singles, it makes no difference."

"You've got to be kidding," the Yankee said, momentarily forgetting his place. "How can you tell, for Pete's sake!"

"When one has shot as many quail as we have, you know," the Commissioner stated in a manner that brooked no further discussion of the matter and led the way to dinner, which ran its usual course when those three gathered together. They dined well, but not necessarily wisely.

The next morning found the group somewhat chastened, but none-the-less eager for the day's hunt. With a minimum of delay and confusion, the hunters made their appointed rendezvous with the McGills and Ely. Son had been left in charge of preparing the barbecue at "The Lake," an old cabin that served as headquarters for post-hunting celebration. Three horses were led out or, rather, it should be noted, two horses and a raggedy, non-descript pony with an evil eye and deceptively benign manner. The Commissioner indicated that the smaller animal was to be the Visiting Sport's mount. In short order, a somewhat bizarre band of horsemen meandered off toward the first field.

"Put the dogs down!" the Commissioner commanded, somehow resembling Don Quixote, with the Visiting Sport on his diminutive steed, an obvious Sancho Panza trailing in the rear. The two pointers, Runt and the ailing Freddie, freed from restraint, immediately did what all good bird dogs do, ran around in circles for a few moments and then went on "Kennel point." When they had finished that important preliminary, they then settled down to working the first field in good fashion, both quartering back and forth, using the wind and searching the obvious coverts for their adversary, the Bobwhite bird that was the focus of the day's attention.

It seemed only a matter of minutes until the dogs started making game; their eagerness making a smooth transition to alert attention, slowed approach and, after a final careful stalk, a rigid point, Runt in front and Freddie backing, like two twin canine monuments. Runt's nose twitched while Freddie's eyes rolled back toward the dismounting hunters like twin beacons beckoning the promised land.

"Here, you two go forward. No, don't argue. Y'all are guests," the Commissioner directed, "that's right—go right up—not too close to the dogs, you don't want to make them gun shy. Move right in now!" The visiting guns did, the covey burst, expected but, as always, still a nerve-shattering surprise; four shots sounded and, lo and behold, two birds fell, one on each side of the rise.

"Fetch 'em up," Ely called, "That's it, that's it, boy, bring him heah—now, Runt, over theah—hunt daid, hunt daid—that's it, good boy, good boy—bring 'em heah," he took the bird from Runt's mouth, carefully examined it and slowly shook his head in sorrow.

"Mr. Joe, we got a problem heah. One of these birds is a hen," his baleful glance left no doubt where the guilt lay.

"A hen! A hen you say!" the Commissioner recoiled in horror, "Cain't have no hen in our bag! Did you shoot that hen?" he turned accusingly to the Visiting Sport.

"It's possible," that unfortunate admitted, "Nobody's perfect."

"AFTER I TOLD YOU WE ONLY SHOOT COCKBIRDS IN CAROLINA!" the Commissioner's normally calm demeanor had vanished in the face of such ignominy. "We cain't have this. Nosirree, sir, we cain't have this. What would people say, back in Columbia, talkin' at the Club and such—there goes the Commissioner, brings Yankees down here to shoot our henbirds. Nosir, cain't have that."

"I'm terribly sorry. It will never happen again—," the culprit mumbled.

"You bet it ain't gonna happen again, sir. You're gonna take a lesson right now on Number One," he held up an official finger, "game identification and Number Two," another impressive digit joined the first in a sort of "V" for Victory sign that vaguely stirred old memories in Ely's soul, "you are going to watch two gentlemen shoot quail for the rest of the morning. Maybe, just maybe, if you are real attentive and sufficiently repentant, we might let you walk over one of our dog's points this afternoon. Come on, John, let's hunt up some of those singles."

It took Runt about ten seconds flat to find one of the singles. The Commissioner walked smartly forward, the bird flushed and, simultaneous to the shot, the bird fell to be quickly retrieved and delivered to Ely.

"Nice bird, yessir, nice big cockbird," the emphasis was on the last word and the point was taken by all. The Commissioner was already walking over to Freddie who was solid still on another point in a clump of trees bordering the field. Almost as the gunner pulled up by the dog, the bird flushed. The Commissioner's arm and gun rose as one in a graceful sweep, overtook the darting flash of feathers and, just as the barrel covered the prey and the others waited for the shot, Mr. Joe dropped his gun and reflexively broke the action.

"Henbird," he flatly stated.

"Wait til a covey rise," a small voice was heard to murmur.

The Commissioner turned as if to acknowledge the remark with a fitting rejoinder but, on apparent second thought, merely smiled in a somewhat cryptic fashion and walked over toward John Rhea, who was carrying two singles he had taken while the others were watching the Commissioner. Yes, the Sport noted with some shock, they were both cocks.

The shooting party mounted and proceeded on to the next covey, which the dogs found farther down the old soybean field. If Runt's nose was any indicator—and there was ample evidence to trust in that canine early warning system—the second batch of birds were pinned down in a patch of brush just off the cultivated ground. Without a word being said, but everything fully understood, John and the Commissioner quickly dismounted, unsheathed their doubleguns from their scabbards and hurried forward, one on each side of the dogs. The Visiting Sport remained mounted, his eyes seemingly downcast, but a sharp witness would have noted that swift glances were surreptitiously shot toward the anticipated action. There was no such person about, however; Ely, for his part, was studiously ignoring the Sport's presence as if some of his disgrace might be catching.

"Blam! Blam!" and a second later, two more "blams!" matched the first pair. As if on cue, four birds tumbled from the air, one bouncing as it hit a tree limb and fell to the ground. All of the birds had fallen in heavy cover and it took Runt and Freddie some time before the last bird was found and retrieved. The Sport remained silent and motionless on his pony. It was as if he knew his fate. Even before Ely came out of the brush with the last bird that Freddie had finally found, the Sport knew that there would be no forbidden fruit in Ely's mahogany hand. The birds had read the script, all right, and performed on cue. Life seemed particularly hard that day. Four more cockbirds joined their fallen brethren.

"Well, now, Mr. Yankee Smarty-Pants, what was that about waitin' for a covey rise," the Commissioner was not known to be overly generous in victory. "As I recall, you have often remarked that it is not so much that one succeeds, but one's best friend fails! I think that a most apt quote, indeed, to cover this heah situation. Shall we proceed? Now, watch close, you hear!" Since Mr. Joe followed Mr. Baruch's sage counsel and tried not to take more than three or, at most, four birds from a single covey in any given day, they mounted and proceeded to another field across the hedgerow on their right.

There is nothing to be gained by bearing further witness to the Visiting Sport's humiliation, chagrin and downright frustration. There was to be no end to his suffering that morning. Two hours and seven coveys later, the Commissioner halted the group, looked at his watch and innocently inquired of Ely how many birds—cockbirds, that is—they had in the saddlebags.

"Hm, Mr. Joe, we got thirty cockbirds and," he added with some distress, "*that* one henbird. Shore wish we could lose her somewhere."

"No, Ely, that simply won't do. Bad as it is to shoot one of our little ladies," the Commissioner's eyes rolled Heavenward and the Sport swore he heard a small choke in the other's voice, "it's worse to leave a dead bird to waste. We got to take her in. We'll just sort of keep this quiet for now. After all, thirty cockbirds for two guns is a limit and that ain't all bad for a fine Carolina morning. Too bad some folks can't play the game right," he sighed as if the thought was too much to bear.

The Commissioner led the way back to the barn where the McGills had left some lunch. While Mr. Joe, John and Ely chattered back and forth as successful hunters are wont to do after a good morning, the Visiting Sport was visibly distressed; so much so, that the Commissioner—after all, a Southern gentleman first, last and always—was sufficiently touched by the abject sight before him that he softened his previous stand.

"Now, old friend, I take it by your silence—a silence, I might add, most appreciated by John and me, who are so used to your raucous repartee on most occasions—well, your silence tells me you have indeed profited from your little experience this morning."

"I guess so," the Sport quietly answered.

"Consequently, although John and I have *our* limits, we are going to go out again this afternoon just so you have a chance to take some righteous cockbirds and rejoin the ranks of us gentlemen sportsmen!" Mr. Joe fairly beamed in the magnitude of his benevolence. Ely was heard to make a negative clucking sound in the background.

The three friends lingered over lunch until the warmth of the midday sun cooled a bit and both dogs and birds could be expected to move with more enthusiasm. Then, once more, the girths were tightened on the horses, the guns slid into their scabbards, the dogs roused from noontime naps. Runt and Freddie, after a few yawns and stretches, were soon trotting along with the horses, waiting to be cast out ahead. They knew their business, but weren't quite as eager as earlier in the day.

They did not have long to wait. Freddie, making a long slow quarter to the left, soon began winding that old familiar scent that set his tail to wagging. It was all business now as he carefully moved upwind until he glided into a point, head high and tail rigid. Runt, who had been doing his own thing over more to the right, but also had kept tabs on his partner's activities out of the corner of his eye, swung over and drifted into a very pretty backing point. It was, as they say, the "classic" Carolina quail scene. If A. B. Frost or David Maass were painting the scene, they would probably call it "The Twilight Covey" or some such. The Commissioner indicated that the Sport would have the honor of addressing this situation all by himself. With more than the usual ration of mixed emotions that accompany any walk into a pointed covey, the Sport moved toward the dogs. He did not appear overly anxious for the experience. He came abreast of Freddie and nothing happened!

"Touch his head," Ely said. That signal released the dog and he carefully minced forward, eyes darting and nose wrinkling, until he stopped as if transfixed by death itself. No doubt this time ... them birds is THERE! The Sport barely had time to place his feet solid when the covey—maybe twenty-five birds or more—flushed all around him. His heart pounding and the blood rushing, the Sport somehow kept his last few wits about him and didn't snap shoot into the covey. It would have been so easy. There were, after all, so many birds. But he remembered the oldest and best quail shooting advice there is: Pick one bird, follow it and drop it before you start thinking of the second and never, never, just shoot at the whole covey, or you'll end up with a pocketful of air. The birds were in the thicket when he shot and, joy of joys, he saw two birds come tumbling down! A crossing double! He held his second shot. Quit while you're ahead. No point in taking a chance. He turned to the others and his grin said it all. How about that for a spectacular comeback! The others smiled in gentle fashion but said nothing. Ely, meantime, had followed the dogs into the covert. It didn't take long to find the birds. They had fallen practically side-by-side.

"Well, Ely," the Commissioner asked, "What do we have here?"

"Good news and bad news, suh," Ely replied, his disgust evident.

"He got two all right, but one of 'ems a hen! Mr. Joe, what would Mr. Baruch say!" He shook his head, despondent at the image conjured by his remark.

"That's it." There was no shouting this time, simply a note of deceptive calm in the finality of his statement. "Pick up the dogs, Ely, we're headin' home. Sorry, John."

"That's all right, Joe, heck, *we* got our limit this morning anyway," and then, speaking to no one in particular, "I don't know why he always has to embarrass me wherever we go!"

"Come on . . . Haven't you guys carried this thing far enough? Have mercy on the old fella!" the Sport pleaded. The Commissioner turned to him with an ice-cold stare.

"Mercy, you say. Hmph, highly unlikely. How can a hen-killin' Yankee expect merciful consideration from a man descended from the hero who pulled the lanyard of the first cannon fired at Fort Sumter?" On his signal, the rest of the party, dogs and all, turned and headed back to the barn. The Sport had no choice but to follow. They had come in one car.

While things relaxed considerably around the superb barbecue at "The Lake" that evening and even the Sport was allowed to join in the good times, there was a certain strained silence when the subject of the last hunt the next morning was opened. As the evening progressed, the Sport found himself fascinated by the various hounds giving tongue in the woods surrounding the cabin. Some of the boys were running coonhounds that night and there were still a couple of deerhounds loose that hadn't been gathered up after the day's drives earlier. The Sport was the last to retire that evening.

The next morning the Sport decided that he would not accompany the last quail hunt of the trip. Enough was enough. He would rather spend the morning in his bed, contemplating his many sins and planning a little revenge, than continue as the butt of the Commissioner's little game. He had carefully checked the South Carolina Game Laws and there was no mention of cockbirds only. Just fifteen quail per day. After a faint-hearted attempt to rouse him, John Rhea and the Commissionr departed for a special hunt that had been arranged at a neighboring plantation where, it was said, the quail were packed like blackbirds in an unharvested field. The Sport brooded and waited, waited and brooded, until about noon he heard their car pull in front of his room. He lost no time in greeting the returning hunters. And how did the day go? Oh, very well, thank you. Get many birds? Enough. Like how enough. Our limit. All cockbirds, I suppose. The Commissioner silently led the Sport to the back of the stationwagon, opened the door and pointed.

There, lined up like so many helmeted troopers on parade were thirty cockbirds, their distinctive white heads glistening in the midday sun.

Epilogue

A few months later, Commissioner Hudson and John Rhea, their "Liberty Passes" validated for a New York visit, were enjoying refreshments and some old-fashioned story-telling while surrounded by admirers at the Leash Club, an establishment devoted to followers of the field sports. Mr. Hudson was regaling the audience with tales of Ely's exploits back in the days of Mr. Baruch, Winston Churchill, General Bradley, Bob Ruark and other notables.

"Oh, yes," he recalled, "Mr. Baruch hunted right up to the end, well into his nineties. 'Course, he was deaf as a stone and his eyes and legs were porely, but he kept huntin' birds. They—the McGills and Ely—rigged up his wagon so there was a platform he could stand on to shoot. They'd get him up close enough to the covey point so he could get off a shot when Ely'd flush the birds out. He was a fine gun in his day and they hated to see him miss at the end so they took care of him."

"What do you mean—took care of him?" the Sport was suddenly very interested.

"Why, my boy," the Commissioner blinked his eyes in innocence, "Ely always carried a freshly-killed bird in his coat. If Mr. Baruch missed, which he did some toward the last, why Ely would just go out in the brush—chantin' 'daid . . . daid'—while the dogs poked around and then, by golly, ol' Ely would bend down after a little bit more and pop up, saying 'Here it is, Mr. Baruch, *nice big cockbird!*' "

"Oh, yes, that reminds me of one more thing. Remember that last hunt John and I had at Kingstree, when we went to that special place. We never did take you around, maybe because we would have had to go by an ol' farm house I know there, the one that has a sign out front that says they have 'Quail for Sale—Live or Dressed!' As I recall, they had a special price if you bought two-dozen or more, even if they were all cockbirds." The Commissioner leaned back and, looking around him, asked, "Now, did I ever tell you boys why we only shoot cockbirds in Carolina?"

QUAIL OF THE EASTERN SHO'

A. R. Beverley-Giddings

For me, as both an editor and reader, one of the most important qualities in a story that attempts to embody the senses of places and experiences shared is the feeling that makes me say to myself: "Hey. I want to be there, doing that!" This piece by A. R. Beverley-Giddings is a gem in that regard. It originally appeared in Field & Stream *in 1933 and was later collected in the anthology,* The Field & Stream Reader, *published by Doubleday in 1946. The book, not to be confused with the* Field & Stream Treasury *published in the 1950's, is out of print and is one of the toughest "oldies" to get your hands on. The* Reader, *I can tell you, is just as good, or better, than the excellent* Treasury, *although it does not have the section of color plates of old covers and advertisements that helps make the* Treasury *so lively. The author and his friend have a great hunt in this story. So will you, reading it.*

FOR THE LAST DECADE I have kept a journal of my sporting days afield. Appropriately checked in red crayon are my red-letter days. They have titles such as these: The Day of the Cherry-Red Buck; The Day of the Ten Thousand Woodcock, when a norther breathed idly over Louisiana and it seemed that every clump of underbrush harbored a bird; The Day of the Brown Pelican, which tells of swarming canvas-backs rather than a pelican; The Lazy Day, a tale of snipe. And lastly, I find this unromantic title: The Day of the Puncture, which fortunately refers to a tire and not to anyone's person.

I was somewhat astonished to notice lately, while checking through this well-worn field journal, that with very few exceptions these red-letter days were the result of accident. I don't mean the luck which so largely governs the gunnerman's success or nonsuccess, but rather that rarely was one of these bright days planned in detail. They came about, almost without exception, through sheer accident.

Certainly, this was the case with the Day of the Puncture. We had taken a house on the Eastern Shore of Maryland for the summer and autumn. When the open season arrived, I soon exhausted the shooting in my neighborhood, though I may have been a little over-generous in the amount of seed stock I left behind, as one of my neighbors rather derisively informed me. But better to err on this side than on the other, even if one's game record remain anything but flattering.

Our part of the Sho' was a trifle too near certain large cities to be really prolific in game. A jaunt farther afield was indicated. I had heard that there was very good quail shooting in some of the lower counties; so I decided to venture forth more or less aimlessly and see what I could find.

I set out early one brisk November morning in a small car with my young Irish setter and an overnight bag which might or might not prove useful. If I found good shooting and the opportunity offered, I would stay over night and shoot the next day; if not, I would drive back the same night. By nine o'clock I was about sixty miles due south—and running short of gasoline.

I pulled up at a cross-roads store. While the proprietor attended to my wants I engaged one of the loiterers in conversation. I learned that there were "right smart quail" in that vicinity and received certain vague instructions as to their haunts. But the proprietor himself proved more explicit. About three miles down I would come upon a dirt cross-road. I was to turn right, go on another three miles and inquire for one Garvin.

There was no cross-road three miles down. But I had passed one a mile back, and a little reconnaissance showed there was another a mile farther on. I flipped a coin to determine which one I should take. The farther road won. So I turned to the right and proceeded leisurely through a flat, well-wooded region, interspersed with farms, swamps and patches of marsh, that looked birdy—looked a great deal, in fact, like some of South Carolina's finest quail country.

Dutifully I stopped when I had proceeded along this road for three miles and gazed around for some signs of Mr. Garvin. There wasn't a house in sight. I went on. In a few minutes I came upon a very small hamlet. There I was embarrassed by a wealth of Garvins. Half the village owned to the name, and I never did discover just which Garvin I had been originally directed to. They offered me almost every sort of shooting save the variety I wanted, and I did not escape these hospitable folk until I had promised that I would return some other time and have a duck shoot with them.

One suggested that I take a certain narrow road out of the village which ran due south for a few miles and then turned to parallel a river. All the rivers along the Sho' are tidal and may be anywhere from a few hundred feet to several miles in width. There were some fine large farms along this particular river, I learned, which held plenty of quail, and the farmers were a kindly, generous lot. One in particular my informant recommended—Joe Sprague, who was a great gunner and had some fine dogs. The rest of the Garvins concurred in this opinion. I thanked them and drove on.

Soon I came upon the river road and turned right, as I had been directed. Through the bare trees I began to catch glimpses of pleasant farmhouses, and now and again the sunlight flashed back to me from water that must have been the river. There is a certain charm to the Eastern Shore that I have never encountered elsewhere: the charm of gentle water stealing in and out between forested banks, or laving the foot of a wheatfield, or shimmering against a verdant lawn. There is that heart-tugging charm of abundance, of peace, of a people who live happily and well.

And now for a space the thick forest closed in upon the road. I saw squirrels in the trees and a cottontail on the bank of a ditch. Once a covey of quail crossed the road before me. I was sorely tempted to follow them into the fenced land, but restrained my impulse, though I saw no trespass signs.

Quite suddenly I came out on a cornfield, and it must have been right at the point where the woods ended and the field began that I picked up the staple. I noticed, before I became aware of the puncture, that the fence had recently been repaired here. Part of a bale of wire lay along the side of the road; a rotted post had been replaced with a stout new one of locust. I went on perhaps two hundred yards before I noticed the bumping of my front wheel. I stopped, got out and gave vent to the usual strong expressions of disgust which an occasion of this kind brings forth.

"Puncture, eh?"

I looked around. A little bird-like man with a soiled white nautical cap stuck jauntily on his head was leaning on a gate and surveying me with interest.

"Yes," I replied disgustedly, "a staple. Both prongs are in to the hilt."

"A staple," the little man repeated. He sighed, opened the broad gate, came out, looked at the tire. "Daw-gone!" he went on in a minute. "Thet's too bad. My fault. I must have dropped that danged staple in the road while I was fixin' the fence up above. Drive yore car in through the gate, an' I'll have William fix 'er. Hope you ain't in a hurry."

"Your name isn't Joe Sprague by any chance?" I asked him.

"Nope. Sprague lives five miles further down. My name's Harris. Better pull thet staple out fust before you drive the car in. Ain't no sense in makin' more holes. Got a pair of pliers?"

We removed the staple from the tire, and I drove through the gateway.

"You was lookin' for Joe?" he asked when I again got out of the car.

I explained my reason for seeking Joe Sprague.

"Shucks!" the little old man said. "If thet's all you want, I got plenty of it right here. Yes, sir! More quail on this place than Joe ever had on his. Come on up to the house."

We walked along an avenue of maple and linden to a fine old house that looked out across a broad, placid river. Well out from the shore were two duck blinds set up on piles and looking like brush heaps; closer in, a stake marked a private oyster bed. To the right of the house was a small orchard of pear, peach and apple trees, the fruit long gathered. A wheatfield, showing traces of green through the sere stubble, rolled away to the right. On the other hand was the cornfield I had just passed, its large neat shucks still standing. A score of tame white geese were disporting themselves on the river's shore; I heard the gabble of ducks, tame also, from a reed-fringed inlet that cut into the wheatfield. There were cows and chickens in the barnyard; a flock of sheep was busy with the grass along the margin of the driveway.

Such opulence in these lean days was heartening. I said something to this effect.

"Yes, sir," the little man replied; "it's right comfortable here.

All the fish, oysters an' crabs we want without no more work or cost than goin' out an' gettin' 'em. Lots of game in season; ducks, geese, snipe, woodcock an' birds." Bob-whites are generally given the proud title of "birds" below the Mason and Dixon line. "I have my own fruit, berries, corn, wheat, vegetables, poultry, mutton, lamb, pork, ham, bacon an' milk. Don't see much hard cash, but then I don't need much of thet.

"Inherited this place from my sister," he went on a minute or two later. "She married right well, bein' a mighty purty gal. Her husband was a jedge. Didn't get on with him perticler well myself. I didn't have style enough for him." He stopped to laugh softly. "I wasn't so welcome round here once, though sister didn't fall in with his high notions. And now I own the place. Daw-gone it, he wouldn't like thet!" He went off into another peal of gurgling laughter.

"Come inside," he added, when his mirth had subsided. "I'll send William down for your stuff."

"But I couldn't impose on you like this!" I protested. He cut me short with a brisk: "Shucks! I been achin' to do some bird huntin', an' I hate to go alone. Besides," he grinned, "I owe you somethin' for thet puncture. Come on in."

I followed him inside. Black William, loitering in the kitchen, where his cheery, buxom, brown-skinned wife presided, was sent to change the tire and fetch the dog and duffel. The little man then led me to a small room most attractively paneled in pine. There was a small fire burning on the hearth, for the morning was nippy. A Chesapeake dog got up from a rug in front of the fire, stretched leisurely and walked toward us with a friendly wag of his tail. We sank into great leather armchairs which were well worn from much friendly sitting.

I noticed a gun rack hanging on the wall just above my head.

"The jedge's guns," the little man informed me. "Good weapons, them. Take 'em down if you want."

There were four of them—hammerless, double-barrel ejectors. The topmost one was a heavy 10-bore; the second, a fine 12-bore made by one of the best American gunmakers; the third, an exceedingly light and handy 16 by an English gunmaker; the fourth, another 16 with longer barrels.

"Ol' Betsy Ann," the little man said as I lifted the big 10-bore down. "A shootin' fool. I used her this mawnin' on black duck. She's a mite heavy for me, though; ain't so young as I was. I ginerally use the 12-bore below her."

"What do you use on quail?" I asked.

From a corner he brought me a gun—a 20-bore pump with a 25-inch barrel, a length which would indicate that an amputation had been performed on it at some time or other. It was a deadly brush gun, a type favored by many guides I knew and had shot with. And rarely had I seen this kind of gun in the hands of an indifferent shot. My own double had bowed to its efficiency on more than one occasion. I glanced up quickly to find the little man's eyes upon me, and noticed for the first time how keen and brightly blue they were. At least, I told myself, I would not start out under-estimating his shooting prowess, nor be inveigled into counting shot against shot.

But he had a good word for my own light double. "Handsome," he said, as he took it from my hands a quarter of an hour later. "Balance jest right—jest where she should be. Short barrels, too; no need for long ones on birds. Mighty purty gun."

When I glanced at my watch, I found, to my astonishment, that the time was eleven-fifteen.

"Achin' to get out, ain't you?" the little man flung at me amiably. "Know jest how you feel. But they ain't no use goin' now before two or two-thutty. Set back an' make yourself comfortable."

It was after two when we left the house, accompanied by the little man's staid and dignified English setter and my own rollicking young red setter.

"Ain't never seen one of them dawgs thet was any good," the little man said, casting a dark eye at the Irishman. "Purty dawg to look at; purty dawg to have around; good pet dawg. But when it comes to finin' birds, them dawgs ain't natcherly there."

I explained that one of the best dogs I had ever shot behind was an imported Irish setter; that for years now I had used English setters and pointers and had found them quite satisfactory, but that nevertheless I was casting around in an endeavor to pick up a really good red dog again. This young dog was from famous parents; I expected something from him. Maybe not this year, but certainly the following one.

The little man heard me through patiently and then remarked: "I ain't much on pedigreed dawgs. The jedge had a pair the last year he was alive—blue Beltons, they was. Mighty good-lookin' pair, too. But they wasn't much on birds. I figgered that them dawgs was used to open-land gunnin'. They was just no 'count at all in the bush an' marsh. No, sir; I ain't what you might call per-ticler about pedigrees. If a dawg can't find birds for me, I don't want him—even if he has a pedigree as long as a duke's."

This being an unprofitable argument, I abandoned it, knowing well that my young dog would disgrace himself a dozen times be-fore the afternoon was over.

In a few minutes we reached a small peafield. A hundred yards in front of us was a stretch of woodland curving away to the west. The little man waved a hand at it.

"Want to explain the lay of the land to you now," he said, halting. "That there belt of trees is only a few hundred feet wide. It's shaped like a horseshoe, and it runs all the way around a hun-dred-acre marsh. A narrow crick runs through the middle of the marsh an' jines the river over there to the south. On the outside of the horseshoe there's fields, all the way round, some cultivated, some grown to weeds, some pasture. The birds feed in the fields an' in some of the clearings in the woods. When they flush, they go, sure as shootin', to the thick woods or the marsh. The marsh ain't very wet save near the crick, an' the birds ginerally don't go thet far out. There's a full dozen coveys around the entire horse-shoe, an' I ain't shot into any of 'em this year yet. I'm goin' to turn the dawg loose. There's a good covey right in this corner of the field ginerally. . . . Hey, you, Dick! Hunt birds!"

I released the red dog. He wasted a few minutes in exuberant leaping and barking, then started out full tilt through the woods, ignoring my shouts. Dick meanwhile had come upon a hot scent. Carefully, surely, the wise old dog unraveled the trail and finally came to a stanch stand in a little point of high grass along one edge of the peafield.

The little man shook his head. "Too durn close to the woods," he said. "Why, they ain't got ten feet to go. Wouldn't be surprised if they ain't roaded into the woods already. Daw-gone, there is nothing to do but flush 'em an' see."

The birds got up as the little man had predicted—right among the trees. I had a dim view of fleeting brown forms hurtling down dusky vistas of woods, and though I shot I had no hope of bagging my bird. Nor did I. But the little man was shouting: "Dead bird, Dick. Dead bird! Fetch!" He had not missed.

"That covey went to the marsh," he said with satisfaction as he took the plump cock bird from Dick. "Thet'll be more open shootin' which will help you get yore hand in. Might as well cut straight through here."

We came out, a few minutes later, on the edge of the marsh. As the little man had said, it was roughly horseshoe-shaped, though I had never seen a horseshoe quite so elongated, and entirely surrounded by a forested ridge which attained a maximum height of perhaps fifteen feet above the marsh. From my elevated position I could see the sluggish creek winding between its reed-grown banks. It widened into a small lagoon near the river, and wild ducks were bobbing on its surface there.

The red dog came bounding like a buck through the brush. I sent him on to hunt singles along the edge of the woods. To me it seemed far more likely that the birds were on this fringe rather than in the marsh. He seemed to show some interest, and I was congratulating myself on my keenness when the little man shouted and I saw Dick on point a full hundred feet out from the bank. The little man grinned at the look of astonishment on my face.

"They is sea-goin', these birds," he said as I drew near, and his grin widened. "I figger thet in another gineration or two they'll have web feet. Take the shot, Cap'n."

I moved forward. The bird flushed, headed straight for the woods. It was an easy shot, and down he came. At the report another bird flushed a few paces to the right. He, too, proved an easy target. The little man nodded his approval of the right and left.

"Yore dawg has somethin' on the bank," he said suddenly. "Woodcock, mebbe. Better see."

I hurried to the fringe of the woods and came up behind my

setter. He turned an uneasy glance on me that said woodcock plain as day. I flushed the bird, and it started boldly and foolishly across the marsh for the opposite bank. The little man was right in my line of fire. I dared not shoot. But he was watching. He took the 'cock as it passed him a few yards to his left and flung me a grinning "Thanks!"

He walked toward me. "Ther's eight or nine birds still in the marsh," he informed me. "We'll take one or two more an' then go on to the next covey. Hey, you Dick! Hunt birds!"

But Dick had no need of this admonition. He was diligently nosing among the marsh hummocks, pausing now and again to lift his head and try the wind. The red dog had come out from the bank and was working between Dick and the woods. It was a new experience for him, this hunting quail in a marsh. He registered deep disgust and open unbelief. It was to be expected that he would blunder on a single and send it up while we were still out of range. But his astonishment was so pronounced, so ludicrous, that I let him off with a very light scolding. He settled down then. Evidently there were quail in this marsh, he decided, and this being so he had better watch his step.

Dick had another bird. The little man generously beckoned to me, but I refused. He took the shot and got his bird. Dick started to retrieve the quail, went forward a few yards, and froze again.

"Another one," the little man called. "Come and take it."

I walked up to the dog. The bird did not flush. I went ahead an additional two steps. Still no sign of the bird. I took another cautious step forward and kicked at a reedy tussock. The bird flushed behind me, I swung around quickly, lost my balance, stumbled. The little man shot and missed.

"Out-thought us," I remarked. "He deserved to get away."

But a little farther on I got a bird that flushed in front of me. Then we decided to go on to a new covey.

We went back through the belt of woods to the pasture that lay beyond. Behind us the peafield, in front a cornfield separated from the pasture by a rail fence heavily overgrown with briers, bushes and weeds. Near this fence a big hawk was flying low. His behavior was peculiar; he seemed to be patrolling a stretch not more than fifty feet long. Every now and then he would dart savagely toward the ground in the immediate vicinity of the fence and then, without quite touching the ground, sweep upward again. The little man swore roundly.

"He has a covey pinned in them briers," he said. "Let's see if we can get close enough for a shot at him. You circle across an' come down the fence; I'll go in the woods an' come up toward you. Have you any large shot?"

I had—two shells containing No. 4's. I broke the gun, slipped in the 4's and made a wide circle toward the fence. When I reached the tangled growth which marked it, I found a paralleling ditch. It was heavily overgrown with briers and offered good cover for a stalk.

Carefully I worked my way along, keeping my head down, crouching, stopping frequently. In a minute or two I heard a shot and then the beat of heavy wings directly over me as the hawk flared wildly. He was well within range. At my shot he came down end over end. The little man yelled jubilantly.

I crashed through the briers to retrieve my kill and flushed the covey. The birds whirred away toward the woods. I saw the little man turn and follow their flight with his eyes. In front of me the hawk lay on his back. As I reached him his curved talons relaxed, his legs slowly straightened out. He was dead. I paused a moment to admire this graceless, wicked rascal, dignified even in death, but the little man came up and with a hearty cuss word kicked him into the briers.

"Thet covey didn't go far into the woods," he told me. "They're just inside the edge an' pretty well bunched. Let's get 'em."

It was from this covey that I took the largest quail I have ever seen in my life, or expect to see.

The birds were, as the little man had said, just within the edge of the woods. Dick soon came upon them and flashed into a point. I was very near him at the time; the little man was not far behind. Together we moved forward to take the flush. Four birds got up. I got one; the little man took another, making a beautiful shot on a wild bird that rocketed toward the tree-tops. Dick retrieved his master's bird. I found mine without assistance—a hen bird so large that it brought a shout of astonishment from me.

Most of my quail shooting had been done in the deep South—

in Louisiana, Mississippi, Florida and South Carolina—where the birds were, as a rule, a good deal smaller than the quail of Maryland and Virginia. All the quail we had shot on this particular day were fine large specimens; each one had brought forth comment from me. But this hen bird was truly as large as a squab chicken—a whopper, a prize. I handed it to the little man.

"Ain't seen many thet size," he admitted.

We dumped our bags together on the ground. The big hen was at least a third larger than the largest of the rest. I have kicked myself a dozen times since that I did not have that bird mounted, or at least authentically weighed.

The sweetly mellow autumnal afternoon drew on. By the time the sun was poised just above the hazy horizon, the little man had his limit of ten. I had nine—enough, I said, particularly as I had taken, in addition, two snipe, two doves and a woodcock. But he was particularly insistent that I fill out my bag. We turned homeward, cutting across the fields, leaving more than half of the marsh coveys undisturbed. There were other coveys scattered about the farm. The little man had one of these in mind to round out my day.

Half the sun was below the horizon when the red dog began making game in a peafield. He carried a high head, this setter, and a merry flag. Even the little man found joy in watching him. Head up-flung, he advanced half the length of the field treading as though on eggs, then stopped abruptly, froze. He had the covey pinned on the edge of the field. It was a pretty exhibition, and I was very proud as I walked toward him.

Then, to my dismay, he pounced. The birds roared aloft but within long range. I shifted my finger to the rear trigger and held for a lively cock bird speeding away in the fading light. Fortune favored me; he dropped to the report. I voiced my satisfaction. Fine sport, the limit—a perfect afternoon!

"Well, sir," the little man said cheerfully as Dick retrieved the bird, "we had a good afternoon. Let's shoot some ducks in the mawnin'."

BOBS OF THE BAYOU BANK

Nash Buckingham

What does one say when introducing the Chairman of the Board, the "Main Man" of outdoor literature? Nash Buckingham's works are so magnificent, constitute such an engaging portrait of what hunting was like during the halcyon years of waterfowl and upland bird populations, that they will never be equalled. First of all, the chances of swinging a smoothbore on the numbers of birds Buckingham shot are non-existent. Secondly, few writers have possessed his ability to "tell it like it is." George Bird Evans, in his superb portrait of Nash in his book, The Best of Nash Buckingham *(Winchester Press), describes Buckingham's unique strengths: ". . . for when he writes of his feeling for a dog, his response to mallards caught by shafts of early morning sunlight, he is living it again . . . Nash wrote with a sense of image because he was there to see it—lines like: 'The Big Hatchie . . . fans into a sheet of greenish black enamel . . . switching to lump amber when heavy thunderstorms scour the seamed faces of the basin's red headlands'; and describing a pointer striking scent, . . . 'when he went particularly* fragrant *as Horace used to put it'; and . . . 'Down from the northwest with the wind on its tail, swept a lone black duck, like a gale-pushed ace of spades on its way to somewhere.' His descriptions of predawn the countless times he witnessed it, of 'shavings of snow' beginning to fall, of a 'saw-edged north wind (that) fragiled our ears,' put the reader there. Each of us with years on his gun has been in these places, each knows he can't go back except in the way Nash takes him back. Even in writing technical detail, Nash makes you participate through his quality of experience. Whether he writes about the courageous performance of a dog in a field trial, of thousands of ducks and geese he saw and shot, of countless covey rises in old sedge fields, part of his genius lies in making his reader believe that it was so. These pieces are so much a part of the man who wrote them it is difficult to decide whether he was more a shooting man or a writer. For me, he was both, and at top pitch. Legendary in his skill with a shotgun, he was innately a raconteur, and what came out was shooting literature." Well, that's why we've felt obliged to put five Buckingham pieces into* The Bobwhite Quail Book. *This first selection is from the book* Mark Right!, *which George Bird Evans ranks second only to* De Shootinest Gent'man *as Nash's best book. I hope the story becomes one of your favorites, too.*

A RAW JANUARY MORNING! She-Who-Presides peers past Ollie's bulky shoulder into the ice chest. Deep concern mantles her countenance. She keeps repeating, "Are you certain, Ollie? Are you positive?"

And old Ollie moans, "Naw'm, Miss Irma, I ain' pos'tive, but I sho' is sho' dey ain' but fo' quails in hyar, sho' as de worl'—dey ain't but fo' lef', honey." And, at the same dramatic instant, out in the dog's run, Joe and Black Boy try out several canine barbershop chords.

Ollie straightens and faces me accusingly: "An' you, Mistah Boss, you done et three o' dem quails yo'se'f! You knows you done it, too. Now what you gwi' say 'bout dat?"

"Well," I defend myself, "what did you cook 'em for, to admire?"

At such attempted wisecracking, She-Who-Presides promptly gets her dander up and turns on the heat.

"In that case, Rip," she fires at me, "you can just hustle your lazy self and your dog Snyder out of my house and bring home a dozen birds or not come back for another twenty years. The girls at the Duplicate Bridge Club's meeting are expecting quail because—Well, because I promised. And besides, any man who deliberately wolfs down three of his hard-working wife's birds—" Stage business of dabbing at the eyes with a silly little wad of cambric.

My own eyes have been taking stock, out of doors. Two days' downpour have the region soggy. A pretty greeting, to be literally foraged out of the house like this! Ostentatiously I turn backstairward in time to overhear Ollie snicker, "He mek out lak he don't wanna go, but he do, honey, he do."

Since she happens to know so much, I hand her some instructions. "Give Joe and Black Boy their feed right away, then, and leave the kennel gate open." And, as a parting shot to Madame, "For my breakfast, my good woman, I demand grits fried in red ham gravy and poached eggs on anchovy toast. Exactly that, or I'll call off the deal, defy you, and ring the police."

A brisk fifteen minutes! Boots heavily vaselined in anticipation of gummy going. Breakfast satisfactory. "It is now," concludes Madame, "exactly seven forty-five. I am to drive you over to Arkansas, deposit you on Decker Bayou near the duck club, and return to the same spot by five o'clock? Remember," she bargains, "I 'suspect' company for dinner at seven this evening!"

"If it's birds you want," I come back at her, "less talk and more action!"

Seeing me thrust two cans of their iron rations and my own paper sack of cold victuals into my suspender pouch, is a signal to Black Boy and Joe. Ensues no end of high bouncing, rumpus in general, and back-of-the-neck licking as the car, with Madame at the wheel, heads westward. An exchange of looks between the two dogs says, more plainly than words, "What a break!"

A shade past nine o'clock, Madame rolls the car into a plantation road and about-faces for the unloading. Scarce needing invitation to "scram," Joe and his brace-mate stand not upon the order of their going. In two wags of a sheep's tail they jump the roadside gully and highball Decker Bayou's bank. I wave good-by to homeward-bound Madame. I'll get those birds for her or bust a hamstring.

Two minutes later I am in hot pursuit of the dogs, now quartering furiously a corn patch to my right. I slow down to watch maneuvers! A proper morning to make haste slowly. I hang to the cattle-stamped bank path for firmer footing.

Two hundred yards farther along, I catch unmistakable glimpses of a well-bunched bevy of quail, out over mid-stream of the bayou, and flashing toward me. I can scarce believe my eyes. Something has undoubtedly flushed them below, a straying cur or strolling sharecropper. To my chagrin, instead of pitching our way, they hold past and suddenly whip into the west bank's tall tangle. Black Boy, Joe, and I meet in a pocket where the heavy woods take in. Companions at heel through the brushy path, I finally emerge amid rolling wastes of corn and stripped cotton stalks. Now I realize what is really in store as to footing. Dump two days' rain into alluvial East Arkansas and jump in after it, if you don't believe me. I noticed—few and far between, however—scattered cotton-pickers braving even this direful weather to glean a few pounds "extry" of fleecy staple. They are sticking to the ridges, at that. It is, I tell myself, a silly business at my age, this pulling one's lungs and spare parts out of place trying for a quail limit in behalf of a lot of bridge-frolicking damsels. I should have stalled for time this morning, until the clubhouse road dried. I thought fondly of easier and drier hunting ahorseback.

Birds, I opine, will have taken to deep ditches and thicket. Needle, and haystack hunting! The dogs can take just so much of this sledding and no more. A pretty kettle of fish! Altogether, as the old Indian used to grunt, "too damn much howdy-do!" I strive mentally to clothe myself in Crusader's garb—Field of the Cloth of Gold, chain mail, two-handed sword and mace—Sir Lancelot out to do himself high honor for Cause and Fair Lady. But I lurch through ten inches of green water and almost topple! Sir Lancelot needing skid chains in a welter of gumbo instead of gore.

Fair Lady, my eye! I decide to regain the footpath and stick to it as much as possible. Reluctantly, but relentlessly, it comes to me that I am not definitely slowing up, but unquestionably slipping. Why, five years ago this would have been like shooting fish in a barrel! And just then, ahead and directly in the path himself, Black Boy suddenly sticks his nasal indicator skyward, caves in his spine a trifle, and pussyfoots into a classic point. Joe sights the deal and stiffens by the rule book.

Just before I take that inevitable one step too many which is parent to the shot, I compose myself to make hay while the sun shines. "These fellows," I reason, "will hop directly against this head wind and whip sharply back the way I've come. Well, let 'em—but a couple will stay behind."

How now, hounds, and have at ye! Fully fifteen winter-plumaged streaks buzz from the slope 'twixt Joe and the water. Easy pickings! Halfway through the webbed grasstops I select a cock bird and pin ahead of his spotted cheeks. Now!

Oh! you, too, gentle reader, must sometime have yanked, and grown livid, at a gun that wouldn't shoot. I even try all over again, in a frenzy. And at a fat laggard, too, coming out of the ditch slowly.

Black Boy and Joe almost turn a back-flip and stand aghast! I bawl out the cypresstops! Summon High Heaven and Fate to witness that there is no justice! Oh! for a long, gray beard to pluck out, hair by hair!

Now, rage pretty well spent, I investigate, fully prepared to kick myself for falling like a sap for the ancient, uncocked-gun gag. At that, I've fallen for such things before. And worse still, even forgotten to load! I open and close the gun. I work the safety slide. No "pushee," no "pullee," no "shootee!" I begin methodical examination. I fingerprint the selective single-trigger shift—possibly a clue and indictment there. I shift and reshift the mechanism and actually box the weapon's jaws. Now try to cock it! Eureka! The slide catches! Now try to snap it. Saints be praised, she clicks. But only the left tube. The starboard chamber and safety are definitely out of commission. I slip a shell into the left barrel, turn its muzzle into a cotton row and let go. "W-h-a-a-a-m!" Well, better half a loaf than none. But, cheerio, dogs! The hunt will go forward on one cylinder. If, as Adage has it, the stern chase is a long one, here's a fine chance to check up on the Old Man. Forward—dogs!

Mazes of cornfield. Mud enough to supply the muckrakers and -slingers of the world. Joe and Black Boy, wet as rats and plastered to their ears, stand nobly to the going. We pass the Caldwell home and pause for a breather on the wagon bridge spanning Decker. It might be better, I conjecture, to push more deeply north—across the "Mud Line" railroad to what proved extra-fruitful covey ground last winter. But keeping my appointment at five with Madame might be another story in case I strayed too far. So—let's be on our way, dogs!

Now, I bargain with myself, for some sure-enough soupy plowing. Lake bank, new ground, and "first bottom" corn. I "sojer" along the ridges awhile, Blacky and Joe prowling denser cover.

Unexpectedly, at the extreme tip of a coffee-bean belt, Joe lams into a point labeled "birds!" Up behind him and the backing Black Boy I pant, fingering the safety catch to be sure my one and only load is available. The covey rise is accommodatingly scattered. One plump masculine member of a nine- or ten-bird outfit turns head over heels. Feathers at last! Black Fellow makes the retrieve while I mark down singles. Two drop ahead into some thick, open pasture grass. The rest split and apparently dive into the lake's backwater. Pretty nearly "home free," those chaps. My canine companions, bidden sharply to "hunt close," soon pin those two nearest hiders-out. How I now long for that missing second shot!

"Fellow," I whisper to myself, "there's a long, long trail acomin' to you this day." But one shot must suffice, and does, for the first bob off the ground. Better so, as giving more time to watch his running mate's landing place. If I find him, I'll need a duck boat, however. A hundred yard's mushing, and out of a brush pile whirs a surprise. A fine cock bird of a fellow who makes a final mistake by not getting a great oak tree between us.

A half-mile more of fruitless gouging. Distant plantation bells sound the "Ring In." Coming high noon. Over the lake bank's slope and across the fields toward Decker, a darky's wide log cabin with hospitable "dog trot" attracts my attention. If I can make it that far, we'll sound mess call and maybe do a bit of bunk fatigue. Black Boy and Joe, spotting my change of course, instantly lope toward inevitable skirmish with a yapping outpour of five and hound-puppy keynoters.

A neat old colored woman answers my hail and smilingly accepts what amounts to my own invitation to enter and eat my snack by her fireside. My dogs, having by now toothed the "eggbusters" into cover beneath the cabin, first remove mud from their own hides by rolling in the woodpile chips, and then open negotiations for "chow." Three or four gulps each, and that show is over.

Meanwhile, the good old soul whose spotless kitchen I have invaded welcomes me as only her fast-fading race can when caring for their "white folks." She and her "old man" are identified as "Williamson darkies." "Yaas, suh, Cap'n, us bin wid Mistah Frank er long, long time—nev' wuz no finah man den him." To which finest of living epitaphs I add a mental "Amen, Aunty!"

She has been bustling about over something. Almost like fog wisps, coffee fragrance spreads from a purring stove. About now, "Uncle," her man, clumps in for his own noontime bait of greens, fat meat, and corn dodger. That's what I've been pot-and-pan sniffing. I wonder whether my appetite might stand a nominal amount of such addition to my own provender. "Uncle" and "Aunty," I learn, upon inquiry, are members of the same Fraternal Order and Sewing Circle Burial Society as our colored folks down at the clubhouse. Such identification via the "grapevine" firmly establishes my position in the household. Urged to tableside, I now admit that greens, tender hog jowl, and strong coffee go hand-to-mouth with a chicken salad sandwich and slice of coconut cake.

My black goodman graciously accepts a two-bit donation to the Fraternal Order and departs for an afternoon round with his wood wagon and jugheads. I readjust the rocker for foot space and bid Aunty awaken me upon the tick of two. Stillness. Peace. Comfort. Through drowsy mist I note the wary house puss reoccupying her abandoned stove corner. Across the dog trot I see wood ashes whirling up the chimney's throat. The mud isn't deep here—any more.

"Boss," laughs Aunty, "de clock done jes' struck two—das de orders, ain't it?"

We repair to the dog trot and sound "Inspection." Joe and Black Boy come running. The best route, I surmise, is to circle what was once a two-covey stretch down toward Sherman's field. Failing a find, then to recross Decker on the highway bridge and take a chance on starting all over again where we took off this morning. Nine birds behind schedule and three hours to go. Another two bits for Aunty's sewing circle, and the shoot is definitely afoot again. But Sherman's is utterly barren. That route's two bunches must be hanging back in the lake-bank woods.

The bayou path again! My own hobnailed boot tracks, half-dried out by the wind! Joe has decided on another whack at the corn. Why not. It has peas for a flooring. But Black Boy, with maybe some sort of hunch tickling his long, square nose, begins a crafty workout of Decker's fringed slope. And, all at once, putting on the brakes to avoid even a side slip through the greasy silt, he halts barely outside a brambled morass. I give the underfooting a rustle. Into the clear darts a single! But only to crumple just as he almost gained a bend in the trail. Bird in mouth on the return trip, Black Boy freezes into an aside! 'Attaboy, Black Fellow! Up again, down again. Thence, along a hundred and fifty yards, Black Boy potters into pantherish points. Doing himself proud this trip! Three additional quail for the bridge addicts.

Joe, attracted by the firing, has cut short his cast and dashed in to offer his services. But Black Boy's blood is up. It is his own private deal, Black Boy is telling the world! Practically waved aside, Joe takes a chance and drops in behind, to rework the ground. Something tells me to look backward, and, sure enough, the setter has trailed a bob to the very water's edge. It flushes a straight-away course across the bayou. And foolishly through an open space on the bank top, I cut him down too soon. Never mind if it is nine straight, there he floats a good twenty feet offshore in extremely deep, cold water.

At the shot, and just as I open the gun and start downhill through dense cover to investigate, another bird catapults toward freedom. Caught helpless, I watch him depart and, by chance, look down to resume reloading. No! I'm not dreaming! Just off my booted left foot, the coiled mass of it undulating into attack, ugly head switching to the roll of a darting, forked tongue, is a thick, six-foot snake. The fingered shell drops tubeward; the bore closes gently; muzzles twist cautiously past my left knee. W-h-a-m! Loam and snake innards spout into the bushes. The serpent head vanishes. Caught him just right.

Looking ahead, I discover that fate and a keen nose have thrown another single right down Black Boy's alley. Good fellow, you held to that snake shot, too. About now, Joe comes rolling into the picture and spots the curved Black Boy. He checks instantly and seems to say: "Well, he's probably landed the gentleman okay, or he wouldn't take the trouble to twist his spine out of shape like that." Boy's victim is sacked. Ten straight! Then I remember number nine, the cock bird floating offshore back yonder in Decker. He must be salvaged at all cost. That snake business all but drove him out of my mind. I retrace the path and reconnoiter fruitlessly for a makeshift bateau or raft. Wood-chopping comes to ear from the heavy copse. Three colored brothers at leisurely fuel gathering. Negotiations for loan of an ax, with the inevitable two bits in dual role of retainer and collateral, are successful.

I locate two thirty-foot second growth luckily almost overhanging Decker. I fell their trunks out over the stream toward the quail. The mass, caught from above by clinging withes of rattan, descends reluctantly, but I finally manage to pull the two main stems down until a sort of crude suspension bridge dangles across the soil-stained water. Ticklish business. I cut a long, light reaching pole and mount the tree bases for this semi-tightrope act. Now for the symphony orchestra to render "Deep River."

With a vine in one fist, for balance and life line in case of a give-away and ducking, and my "fetcher" in the other, I ease offshore. Fifteen feet from the bank I wish I hadn't come. My weight sags both treetops beneath the surface. I am ankle deep myself. Viny cables are taut as bowstrings. If even a tiny strand pops somewhere, I'll topple off anyhow, in sheer fright. Snakes and tightrope walking! My wispy ruler extends, gropes for Bob, and twitches him back, inch by inch. Guilding as I retreat, my nerve finally gives way four feet from shore. One despairing leap. Hooray! Bob is quickly raked ashore! Over more quickly than I figured!

My colored ax owner, apparently vastly relieved at having caught up with his implement, appears. Does he, by any chance, know the whereabouts of a covey of birds around here any which away?

My query meets intense deliberation, then, "Yaas, suh, Boss. Does you-all see dat 'ar leanin' tree wid mistletoe in de top, p'intin' to'ds dat shotgun house on de levee banquette away across't de fiel' yonder?" The various objectives are finally oriented. "Well, Boss-man, whin you-all 'rives nyarbouts to de leanin' tree, dar bees 'bout er fo'-acre patch o' sorghum an' ol' tall clumpy grass. Well, suh, I bin noticin' er pertickler big hover o' pott'idges whut mos' inginally visits right in dar."

With my first move, off scud Joe and Black Boy toward yon leanin' tree. For the first time I realize that our journeying has awakened dormant tendons in even my pretty well hike-hardened underpinning. Two hundred yards of mucky slogging. A small voice whispers, "You have ten birds. With what she has at home, that'll be enough for the party. Why not quit?"

Another fifty yards of punishment! If I stop I'll fall down sure as shooting. "What," shouts Old Man High Resolve, "fixing to fold up with the goal in sight, eh? You'd disappoint the Madame, would you? After all her trouble driving you over here? And your eating three of her birds?"

Hopping a lateral ditch, I roll heavily over its low levee. Reclining among the weeds, trying half-heartedly to see if there is mud in my gun tubes, I wonder if I'd best yield to common sense and sleep right here tonight. "This morning," I sneer at myself cynically, "you gabbed to yourself about Sir Lancelot. A great break for you the fair dames can't clap eyes on you now! Sir Lancelot! Sir Stick-in-the-Mud!"

Groggily I stumble through a belt of towering weed stalks and out into what must be the sorghum patch and clumpy grass. Joe and Black Boy, ignorant of my downfall of a moment ago, are combing the opening's outer rim. Twenty yards out into the clearing a dozen or more bobs, scattered feeding, set the stalks about me abuzz. Desperately I shove at the safety! Pin onto an almost overhead darter! Realize that, fairly struck, it will be blown to bits; I steady and whip off ahead of a cock skimming the weed tops. Down he hurtles! I almost fall over backwards trying to keep an eye on three singles splitting off toward the highway.

"Fellows," I tell the dogs, "as the situation stands, we are one bob shy of Madame's order. Without said bob, her luncheon may degenerate into a washout. Somewhere in yon gumbo stew are three adult quail! Are with me, boys?" Tail-wagging and knee-rubbing. Black Boy maintains a head of steam sufficient to attempt face licking! So, together, we mush a quarter mile of breast-high cotton stuck in glue.

Not one chance in a hundred, I tell myself. Those three bobs, I figure, darted over the hedge and whirled for the big woods, common-sense thing for today's smart birds. I begin a desperate struggle down the home stretch. Somewhere ahead my game dogs are at work. The cotton lowers and thins. There they are, Joe and Black Boy. They galvanize! Well ahead, off to their right, three birds, whose trail they have just struck, flush wild and wing across my line of fire. Old "One Shot" aims a wavering wallop. The captain slithers below the stalk tops! My dogs wheel!

I might as well admit it, we all break shot! What a race for the spot where that cock fellow disappeared! Too tired to aid my trailers, I give out the "Wanted—Dead or Alive" yell. I hastily bend down some cover, sink atop it, and lend loud vocal aid to the chase. Five minutes pass. Oh, joy! Oh, rapture! Bird in mouth, and with Black Boy trailing unenviously, up trots Joe!

We reel to the highway. In a "borrow pit," I slosh the mud from my boots and person. At the cabin I make application for fireside chair space. Joe and Black Boy are rubbed down with a tow sack and check in at the very andirons. Nobody minds. Colored folks after my own heart. Before long, She-Who-Presides will be sounding her recall. Well, I have her dozen birds, and here I am. Pretty soft—this armchair by the open fireplace. Her dozen bobs all safely sacked, too. Good old Joe and Black Boy!

My colored hostess shakes my shoulder gently. "Boss," she apologizes, "dar's a 'moble bin settin' down dar by de bridge fer ten minutes, blowin' de hawn—an'—an'—de white lady whut's in it sont dis hyar boy t'ask wuz dey a white gemman bin seed roun' hyar wid a gun an' two ol' big huntin' dawgs."

"Aunty," I reply, easing stiffly into my pack while clucking up the dogs and feeling for the customary two bits, "I've been asleep, haven't I?"

And she, honest black countenance agrin, answers my query with one of her own: "Boss, whin you sleeps, you show-Gawd does do some snorin', don't you?"

PIPELINE "POTTIGES"

Nash Buckingham

*This story demonstrates Nash Buckingham's remarkable staying power and
ability to capture the modern hunting scene as powerfully as he had portrayed
quail shooting at the beginning of the century. It was published in* The
American Field *in 1959 when Nash was 79 years old and was later collected in the anthology* De Shootinest Gent'man and Other Hunting
Tales, *published by Thomas Nelson & Sons, New York. (Not to be confused with the original* De Shootinest Gent'man.) *The story's mixture of
observations on today's quail shooting and reminiscences of the halcyon years
make it a must for* The Bobwhite Quail Book.

JOHN BAILEY BRAKED his mud-tractioned truck with its boat and
motor racks, storage bin, compartment for four bird dogs and tar-
paulin for emergency camping. He pointed into an open field
below us and east of the highway. Distant woods formed a jagged
skyline. We were en route from Grenada, Mississippi, north
through the Torrence and old Bryant Station area to John's
farm-lodge and shooting leases about four miles south of Coffeyville.

Said John: "See those four wide concrete stair steps sitting in
the open pasture over yonder? Well, they're all that's left of the
Dailey plantation home where you stayed in January, nineteen
eleven, and found thirty-three bevies of birds one day and
twenty-eight the next—walking." Staring into foreshadowing
dusk I could hardly realize the changes demanded by progress in
forty-eight years. That's why they are excavating for Pharaohs
and building missile nose-cones at the same time.

"When Grenada Lake's impoundment is carrying a full load of
water," continued John, "it it eight to ten feet deep where we are
sitting and a good way from the dam. Water comes to within half
a mile of the lodge. As the uppage ebbs and exposes it, thousands
of fishermen launch their boats from this old highway. Automobile bumpers tough from here to the dam. See those woods over
yonder? During duck season I bagged several limits of mallards in
some pools the far rise left behind in them."

John resumed our way. I caught a flash back of that 1911 bird hunt John mentioned. He was but four years old at the time and I was thirty-one.

At Mister Bill Dailey's, John Bourne, Brodie Finley and I had wagoned ourselves and four crackerjack bird dogs from Grenada to Mr. Bill's manor and found so many quail in its vicinity that sometimes I have doubted it myself. Those rolling, pine-clad and sequestered creek bottoms with natural partridge foods and cropped coverts were chockful of zooming bobwhites. And Mr. Bill guarded 'em—plenty—although he wasn't much of a hunter himself. We walked because it was too cold to ride. But the worst was over and the ground was just beginning to exhale moisture as sunlight flashed against it. Two little colored boys, "Parched Corn" and "Puddin'," packed lunches and extra shells. The provender provided by our genial host—turkey, pork hams, vegetables galore, hot biscuits, cream gravy, milk and pies—literally groaned the boards. The old home, with its completely encircling upper veranda, had no central heating. So the yardboy left extra pine knots and we took turns refueling and diving back under the blankets of the huge mahogany four-posters. I don't recall state game laws in those days but we had county licenses and the bag limit was, as I recall, twenty-five birds a day.

While a portion of the Torrence area which we hunted in the long ago is now at times covered by Grenada Lake water, the fact remains that naturally glorious quail country supported by the efforts of thoughtful landowners actually held the line meanwhile against overshooting and quail bootlegging, until Mississippi's highly competent Game Commission got going in the thirties. Under co-operative game management and educational programs going hand in hand with sound public relations, Mississippi's "public thinking" had made colossal strides even in these days of automatically increasing populations and outdoor pressures. Much less, when, within a hundred miles south of Memphis, Tennessee, the four impoundments of Arkabula, Sardis, Enid and Grenada provide, when full, in the vicintiy of 185,000 acres of water affording superb game fishing, duck shooting, no end of recreational facilities and, throughout surrounding fringes and forests, excellent deer hunting. A boon to natives and the sportsmen of surrounding states the great lakes country of north Mississippi is a vast credit to its progenitors in Congress and the federated sportsmen of the Magnolia State. I reflected, riding along with John, that today's bag limit of eight quail is not only fair enough but a conservative miracle due to the safeguard action of Americans still with the will to hunt. Our out of doors and its assets of soils, water, forest and wildlife resources is our sole remaining "share-the-wealth." That lost—all lost. We had best be careful—and hard.

By now we had turned off the old highway, climbed a winding eminence to a forested plateau facing eastward toward what John termed "Baskerville Mountain." Off through the gloaming flashed distant farm buildings. At the lodge's cheerful settlement we were greeted by dogs' shrillings and welcomings from the helpers. A cavern of bright logs. Walls burdened with oils and etchings of dogs and scenes familiar to John from forty years' roaming of hills and dales. Portraits and enlarged photographs of his greatest dogs on point recalled thrilling moments.

Long known to lovely Catherine Bailey as "meat and potatoes men," picture John and me "setting over" country fried steak, vegetable delectables and apple pie that curls toes and sends glances to rafters. Then John's diaries, dating back to first outings are studied; while we retrace steps leading to the time when the off-mainline railway of some twenty-five miles was built, beginning 1925, from Bryant Station and the Illinois Central eastward to what became the town of Bruce, Mississippi. It wound through the Scuna River Valley, now a tributary of Grenada Lake. I was then looking over the area for a township-size tract for a quail management experiment by the Western Cartridge Company of East Alton, Illinois; now Olin Mathieson Chemical Corporation. John's stack of diaries, over a foot high, probably hold more studies and experiments with Nature's proceedings and have done more to stabilize his prodigious memory of farming and its cultures than college courses encompass today. An entry gives us pause—"November 22nd, 1934. Nash Buckingham and I hunted together; had a wonderful long tramping hunt and discovered during lunchtime that he was double my age—54 to 27." That year, too, was when John became active management of his farm and several thousand acres of surrounding lands for the Webber Brothers, of Detroit, who bought the lodge from the late W. B. Marshon of Saginaw, Michigan.

It's "befo' daylight" when a light tap on his door brings an old bird hunter alive for ablutions and accoutrements that fetch him again to the snapping fire and strong black coffee and a later leisurely breakfast. Thence to feed setters Billy and Rex. They know the country like ward politicians check their votes. Says John, "Who ever invented that silly business of no breakfast for a bird dog; I'd just as soon go hunting myself. And what's more, for a hard-working, all-day shooting dog, he gets a snack at noon, too, with something sweet thrown in, if possible. I'm no dietary expert but I've come to know conditioning when I see it. Of course, a bird dog's big feed (like ours) comes when work is done and he's rested a bit. If shooting-dog owners give their canine pals half the attention in food and body care they give themselves, it makes an ideal co-operation that helps the life expectancy of both."

So, all hands into the truck again and off to John's farm with thousands of acres of "Government Land" to its north. At the tilling of John's Negro strawboss we find the horses saddled. Day is coming in far too warm and with little squilly winds along the ground. Billy and Rex are in for it.

Billy hightails slashingly to the left across weedy stubble alongside the road. Rex sweeps pasturage toward a thinly sedged postoak ridge and suddenly slows to feather its edges. Just then John calls, "Billy's on point at that tick-grass patch; you can hardly see him in the shadow of the woods—let's go." Dismounting, John has already surveyed the situation. "These birds are scattered feeding and chances are they'll follow form and climb for the timber—every whichaway, too."

We attempt a pincers movement and there's a roar from behind us. All I see are bobs getting themselves lost in dense woods. But John's gun yapped down a straggler. We remount and John sights across the pasture. "Yonder go Rex's birds," he shouts. "They are a tricky bunch, too, and have left the old boy flatfooted." We ascend the ridge and pad along a forest dirt road. The dogs are casting on either side and below us.

"Right yonder," I tell John, pointing on ahead and down into a narrow valley headed by a food patch, "is where we found the first bevy two years ago."

"Correct," rejoins John. "Your memory is definitely still good so now we'll see about your reflexes." Shortly thereafter a third bevy tricks our scouts with a wild flush far ahead. Billy nabs a single farther on and in attempting to dismount I managed to step into a leaf-covered ruthold and take a neck-crunching tumble. But apparently no harm done; in fact later on I'm inclined to think it's done my backbone's piano keys more good than damage. A creek bottom and away go two more bevies; this fussy hot wind is playing the wild with us. But finally the dogs hem up a covey in regal fashion and we take heartening toll. "That's better," laughs John. "We're on our way."

"Today," I reminisce to John, "is a dead ringer for one the great Ariel had to face one morning in his National Field Trial Champion's stake heat. We judges sympathized with both dogs because anything can happen, especially when moving single birds have to be literally rooted out. Handlers cringe from puffy hot winds. But old 'Fred' [Ariel's kennel name] made it that day and is one of our Triple National Champions. On his last try he outlasted the magnificent Tarheelia's Lucky Strike." It's getting too warm for comfort and coats come off when we get down to shoot. But we don them when we ride; there's a hint you'd best remember. Again we score on a woods bevy. Pursuit of the singles yields a bird or two, and John, finding a convenient log, produces our lunches and the good old water bottle. The dogs snug into the warming leaves, toothing burs from their hides and between their toes but alert and expectant eyes open for their cut of Catherine's delicious sandwiches and cake slices. They get 'em, too.

"John," I query, "in your years of farm and wildlife management have you been bothered by the current outcry against beetles and fire ants and an equally fiery opposition's crusading against dieldrin and other poisonous sprays?"

John thought a moment. "On my farms and leases we've been singularly free from pests and controls. I've heard of few wildlife casualties in this immediate sector. But I have heard roars of indignation elsewhere and from men who ought to know. I guess insecticides and pesticides are like any other products fighting for sales; they've got to have selling points like power and speed in cars and I think the danger has simply gotten away from the authorities and that the situation is far worse generally as to wildlife losses than they want it known. I ride my places daily and I keep my eyes open. So far, I'm O.K."

Are there any other shooting preserves in this immediate area?

"There used to be the thirty thousand acre Carrier preserve some thirty miles to the northwest—between Sardis and Batesville. It was under management for years and furnished the Wildlife Service with valuable statistics. Robert Carrier was a wildlife resources benefactor and in later years turned his benefactions toward the University of Mississippi. He said to me once. 'I came to Mississippi a Pennsylvania lumberman's wild son and Mississippi took me in and gave me everything I've ever managed to accumulate—why shouldn't I do all I can for such people?'

"There are still some preserves in the Como area that are well managed. There are some 'natives' who complain, but that type always will resent anything and everything that helps them in the long run." By now Rex and Billy are sound asleep and the ponies doze.

"John," I ask, "nowadays in your vicinity wouldn't it be possible to bag limits of ducks, quails and doves in a single day?"

John thinks a moment over that one. "Well," he concludes, "it shouldn't be too difficult in the latter half of our split dove season; that is, if you got a real early start and had a bit of luck with the ducks. I'm often home with my limit by eight-thirty. Then I drive out here, many times without a gun, just to work the dogs and look after things generally. I go home for lunch and as the dove season opens after noon, I go shoot with some friend who has a good concentration on his picked corn, or popcorn and milo maize. The doves are strongly resurgent due to crop turnovers, farm-pond programs and better sportsmanlike ethics afield. By the way, didn't you start that split-season idea up in Tennessee and finally talk them into it for Mississippi and Arkansas to copy?"

We said we did, but it was hard selling. But by now it's one-thirty and the bobs should be on their afternoon foragin's. Up and at them, Yeomen of the Hunt. Says John, "We're halfway through our limits and the balance shouldn't take too long; this is my favorite valley of all—ahead of us." We soon see Rex and Billy frozen tight as Dick's hatband just ahead of us off the woods road on which we're jogging. It's a scattered bevy and while John tallies a right and left, I manage to scrape down a left-angling bob that doesn't hit the weed too dead. Rex fetches John a bird, and Billy, after considerable flurry, brings in my cripple very gently for John to pouch. Rex retrieves the third victim and John, doing a "rock an' roll" turns to me.

"That crippled bird of yours has crawled out of my sack and is running around all over my bare back up under my shirt—it's the first time in history I've ever had my back scratched by a quail—catch him for me."

John's shirt back is heaving with the struggles of the brave little bird. I gradually work the moving bulge toward John's waistline. "Let it drop into my hand," laughs John. The bob bounces off John's clawing hand and takes wing with Billy in hot pursuit. The last seen of it was a hundred yards across the sedgetops and rising over hedgerill. We search but never pick up quarry scent. "All I hope," says John, "is that the brave little rascal lives to a ripe old age—he's a game bird all right."

By the time we leave John's dream valley we have the limit and cut across hilltops toward the unsaddling barn. But meanwhile Rex and Billy point three extra bevies just to heighten their own batting averages. Horses curried and fed, we truck to the lodge for a bath and a snooze before welcoming Catherine's dinner guests from Greenwood. Old friends Kirby Sabin and Dr. Ira Bright with their lovely wives and Mr. Provine; the last named a Nestor of old-time woods lore. Kirby and I have spent many a pleasant afternoon together after bream and bass, while Dr. Bright, the great heart specialist, writes wondrous tales of the shooting fields and follows pursuits of happiness over bird dogs and retrievers with his Magnums and Purdeys. Platters of smothered quail in gravy for hot biscuits and pone that only a deeper and older generation of Deep South cooks understand. Dove pie, creamed spinach and a dish of eggplant, shrimp, crabmeat, crumbs and cheese in profusion. We've hardly the nerve to mention an ensuing muscadine pudding because very few folks have ever seen or will taste such a dainty. It's as rare as the Wine of Shiraz.

Next morning comes in cloudy, much colder and with a moist underfoot lending scent-sniffers a big hand. At the schoolbus fork of two east-west dirt roads, we find the colored urchins with our horses as instructed yesterday by John.

"Now," says John, handing each a two-bit piece, "when you get home, send someone to drive the truck to your daddy's. Got that? Have it there by two-thirty."

Grins and promissory nods. John and I mount, give Billy and Rex the whistle and start through a woods road—but not for far. Both dogs are pointing just ahead. But they cannot produce and patient relocation is in order. Those birds heard the truck, the ensuing talk and backtracked down through the woods. Sure enough, Billy and Rex soon pick up the scent and follow it two hundred yards down into the hollow and out its far end into the ball-park field. The rise is a bit distant, but two bobs stay behind. It is quite a climb back to the feeding horses.

"Now," says John, back at the forks and taking the left one, "see that old post with the sign tacked to it that's caved into the gulch?" I could see the forlorn landmark all but buried in the red clay. "It says," continued John, " 'Coffeyville four miles.' In my young days I used to leave home right after daylight and hunt sixteen miles westward to the mainline of the Illinois Central. I'd eat lunch sitting on the railroad track and then hunt homeward. When I'd hit here and see that old sign, 'Coffeyville four miles,' I'd feel that I was practically home. I could smell the steak fat and hot biscuits and coffee with gravy cooking for supper. Nothing has ever smelled so good since."

Leaving the road, we rode down through a vast stretch of piney woods and climbed to a hilltop. Ahead of us suddenly stretched a long, bulldozer cut reaching almost to the horizon. "Here," explains John, "is where the great pipeline crosses my property eighty feet wide." It is quite a spectacle of mechanized progress. "And," continues John smiling, "it's about like I figured—see that white spike down yonder, sticking up on the levee? That's Rex's tail—he's already on point."

Billy, emerging from the woods, sights and backs Rex in a trice.

We had a bird apiece and the bevy sprinkles down through the forest. Then the fun started. Uphill and downhill along the pipeway our sure-footed mounts picked their way. The two dogs, working closely along the boulevard picked up four bevies. My timing is sketchy but John is always a Stonewall Jackson. Says John, turning off the pipeline, "We're about halfway through and I have a special spot at which to eat lunch." Billy is soon sighted pointing stanchly about twenty feet inside a tight barbed wire surrounding a climbing pasture. The wires are really tight and both John and I realize that to climb over means flushing the scantily covered birds. We exchange glances, lie down and roll under. It isn't dignified, but it's necessary and works. John eases around to the right. The birds are in sort of a hedgy pocket, and sure enough, try to hoist themselves over a mess of wild grapevines. So I shoot thereabouts and down tumble two bobs. Another cuts back—and tumbles. We roll back under the fence, ride around the wire and John picks up a woods single.

Then, crossing a circus-ring, parklike valley we climb into a cedared hilltop, which, in its heyday must have been a gorgeous home site. Two tall, stone chimneys tower sixty feet or more apart; moss and ivy-grown battlements of a long-gone day. "This," says John, "is where I'm planning to build my new home and use these two chimneys." We eat another delicious, dog-shared lunch, quaff pure water and corn the mounts. And there are questions to be asked John.

"For what distance does that pipeline cross your land?"

"About two miles. Those raised strips across them are called terraces. The quail find them wonderful nesting places."

"Do game commissions or soil-conservation technicians follow your example of planting pipelines for wildlife resources?"

"Probably so, in many instances; if not, they should. The pipeline people themselves sow lespedeza serecia heavily as an erosion control. I add my own assorted quail foods. I've found serecia only fair as a food. I use mostly Kobe. But I also harvest and use a world of field peas, also wild Kobe and peas along ditchbanks. I use perennials heavily. You've noticed, too, that all through our woods and over the cultivated lands there are feed strips. There's stock corn, maize, and, if you like to have doves, try a patch of popcorn. Droughts have taught us lessons; our farm-pond program and withheld waterways are well advanced."

"Isn't the evil and peril of old-time quail bootlegging about over? Thanks to education, undercover enforcement and public indignation at the ruinous practice?"

"Yes, it's about scotched. Sometimes, due to the rising cost of ammunition, local hunters trade merchants birds for shells. Preserve owners watch overkilling very closely. And Mississippi's tough on out-of-state hunters who violate bag limits. Violators nowadays hesitate to tie in with the underground. The problem shows up better by far than in the old days. It just doesn't make sense any more."

"What's your slant on 'burning' to improve quail habitat?"

"Well," John explained, "it must be done in daylight of a windless afternoon. With an assistant or two mounted, I ride about six miles an hour, dropping matches from the saddle and starting a lot of little blazes. This way you don't get a wide line of fire and they burn into one another before attaining volume. This leaves areas that don't burn. It's bound to be a carefully planned operation. If you don't burn at all, sprouts and leaves smother your woods food, and field grasses get so long and heavy a dog can't get through it and quail simply don't fancy or thrive on it. Burn only in late February and early March. And, as you burn, continue scattering wheat or chicken feed or hen-laying mash in the thickets so the birds will have food until grass begins coming up and insects start coming out. Of course, any man with any interest at all in his land's game resources tries to keep some sort of population census in mind and comes to know game range. Indiscriminate burning is senseless and dangerous. Properly done it's indispensable to management."

"Have you any solution as to why, at times, the feeding habits of quail seem to change? Like when two seasons back, they simply took to the woods; lived there and ate acorns almost exclusively?" John thought that one over, too.

"From my observation and studies, until two years ago, at least, I thought quail ate acorns heavily only when their field foods— lespedezas, beggar and ragweeds and pottage 'peas' had not had enough sweetening summer rains to make their foods taste good.

Or that the birds, aside from taste impairment, might have passed them up as impoverished nutritional value. That's the way it was in nineteen thirty, thirty-four, forty-three, forty-seven, fifty-two, fifty-three and fifty-four. A big percentage of our area quail, certainly, fed heavily on acorns those years. All seven summers, according to my records, were extremely dry and abnormally hot. Field seeds were small and not properly rounded out. I think the birds realized their lack of palatability and nutrition. Two years ago, though, we had nice summer rains and not too high temperatures and lespedeza did well. But the quail ate just about acorns *only*. Post oak 95 per cent of my examinations: five per cent, white oak. I still can't solve this mystery. But you have seen the last two days that they are no longer in the woods. So, the foods they're getting in their natural haunts must be suiting them better. I believe the quail's worst enemy is *heat*. And accompanied by real dry winds." All the while, John had been examining crop contents. He spread a handful. "They seem to like the table we are setting—no acorns."

"Now," says John, "the hounds are rested and the mustangs grained. We need five—maybe six—birds. Of all my territory, what we are going to hunt ahead is a prime favorite." We headed through a narrow valley and crossed a deep-green swirling watercourse. Rounding a tall thicket corner, three quail flushed wild from under our horses. John blew in Rex and Billy and put them on the case. Both dogs began feathering. "Symptoms," grins John. "I'll follow Rex and you trust Billy." So completely mutual is the confidence and understanding of John and his dogs that they seemed to instantly understand the situation. Billy and I turned left down the scantily turfed rows of tall bicolor lespedeza, I had to speed up because Billy was trusting his nose for some fancy roading. At the patch's end, he hesitated—and whirled to the right. There he faced a peculiar situation; almost a ballroom floor of matter-down springy hedges. It was like walking a trampoline. Could birds possibly be hiding or moving beneath such a cover? Billy pussyfooted here and there and suddenly almost squatted in a low-headed point—the only one I'd seen him make. Out of the trampoline's floor sprang first one bob—then another. One escaped, and, as I stood desperately trying to reload the

Model 21, birds began spouting in every direction. I heard John shoot twice and heard him calling. Billy meanwhile had been bouncing around on the trampoline and going hog-wild as bobs took flight. This was a newie.

Looking up through the woods I saw Rex, majestic on point. "Come up here and shoot this bird—if there's more than one, I'll take it." I walked in over Rex, now backing Billy, and three bobs departed. It took composure for John not to sack the third member—and—our hunt was done.

"And nearly as I can figure it," says my host, "there must have been a quail convention going on around that corner when we came along and plumped into it." Between there and where we found the truck at the barn, Rex and Billy stood and we moved five more bevies. I had long since lost track of how many bevies we'd raised that short day—it wasn't two-thirty yet.

John takes a high road home atop a sort of divide. Breaking, he looks out across a tremendous scope of country. "Know where you are?" he asks.

"No. I am as lost as the Seven Tribes of Israel."

John's finger points westward. "See that old house away across yonder under the big trees? Well, back in nineteen-thirty-four you and I and Speed Fry ended a wonderful day right there. The limit was twelve birds and you bagged your last one as we came up through the field back of the barn. We're about to come out on Highway Seven where this one is—it was part of our hunting country."

"John," I query, "how far are we from Torrence and the old Bailey lands where I gunned in January, nineteen-eleven?"

"About forty-eight years," he replied. "You didn't think when you moved sixty-one bunches of birds in two days' walking that you'd be shooting nearly fifty years later with the then four-year-old boy in rompers who lived up the dirt road apiece?" He thought a moment and added, "The wonderful thing is that we've both been spared to enjoy it. And we didn't miss our two last shots—did we?"

John eased the truck down to the fork where we met the horses this forenoon. I could see John, a gangling better-than-six-foot stripling, his coat heavy and sagging with a day's kill of quail and rabbits, and, by the signpost, still only four minutes from home. But he was practically there because he could smell the hot biscuits and coffee and steak gravy. Something my old friend Sigurd Olson wrote me recently came surging back:

"Too much materialism these days. Too little the depth of feeling and genuine love of the earth that characterizes the things we like to do. Especially out-of-doors. I have always felt that you cannot divorce emotion and feeling and appreciation of the intangibles from Conservation. Those very intangibles are cleanly the reasons for all the practical things we do. Without them, life has little meaning."

Just then, in the deep gully, the half-buried old signpost flashed past. The one that heartened young John Bailey by reminding him that he was four miles from home. And somehow, I had had some tall hoofing homeward with my old dog running sideways because he was so tired, too. I caught a long-drawn aroma of hot biscuits and coffee and steak gravy from lamplit homes past which I dragged. I'm so glad there are some of John's and my "intangibles." And I'll bet Sig Olson remembers 'em, too.

QUAIL OF THE KALMIAS

Archibald Rutledge

While the majority of his great works portray hunting and wildlife experiences around his great plantation, Hampton, in South Carolina's Santee Delta, Archibald Rutledge wrote often and eloquently of the hunting he enjoyed while serving as professor of English at Mercersburg Academy from 1904 to 1937. There near the Maryland border, under the eastern slopes of the Pennsylvania Alleghenies, he lived the grouse and turkey hunts that he captured so well in his classic stories. This piece from his anthology, An American Hunter, *shows Rutledge on an unusual quail hunt in that area and is the second we're including in* The Bobwhite Quail Book. *Retiring from his teaching chores, Rutledge returned to his beloved Hampton and lived for 36 years, hunting and writing before he passed away at the age of 89 early in the 1970's. On the table where I write these words lies an old, yellowing wild boar tusk Rutledge sent me in 1970, the year I became editor of* Sports Afield. *It and some letters we exchanged are among my prized possessions.*

JUST AS I had found a splendid flight of Wilson snipe where I least expected them, so, too, I have found quail where many good hunters would never dream of looking for them. These birds are said never to migrate; but unquestionably they move considerable distances as the frosts come on and as their autumn cover gets thin. Repeatedly at twilight on an October day I have seen large coveys rise of their own accord, attain unusual height, and head off in a southerly direction; and every quail hunter has had the experience of finding coveys in places where, a short time before, none were known to be.

Wherever bob-white is found, he will have a regular feeding ground and a regular sanctuary. Immediate shelter from danger is as essential to him as food; one preserves his life as essentially as the other. In the deep South quail will take refuge from peril in swamps, along briered ditch-banks, in marshes and even across rivers. In Maryland and Virginia they usually take to friendly patches of woods, to wild ravines and even to dense smothers of wild honeysuckle.

In southern Pennsylvania, about which I am writing—a region that represents, in the East, the northern limit of this fine bird in natural abundance—one of his favorite retreats is into the mountains, where he finds admirable shelter in the great laurel thickets that clothe with eternal greenery the lonely glades of these wild hills. As this type of quail shooting has something different about it and is exceedingly sporty, I believe that my fellow huntsmen may like to hear some account of my experiences with this beloved and wily bird as he is found close to the bases of the picturesque Tuscaroras.

I think it is true that quail develop habits in keeping with their environment. While, in a sense, like people, they are always the same, nevertheless their manner of behavior differs in separate localities. They all have the same heritage, but they vary in character somewhat with their surroundings. In the South, for example, the birds of the cultivated lands have different ways from those of the pine barrens. So these quail, which are bred close to the mountains, vary from the birds of the lowlands and the wide valleys. They are true highlanders, and they have preserved an intensely wild and romantic spirit. Big and strong, they have managed to take on some of the superb speed of the ruffed grouse.

In this part of southern Pennsylvania the Tuscarora Range is only about 800 feet high, but the hills are rugged and slope rather sharply to the pleasant farmlands of the Cumberland Valley, which of old was a happy hunting-ground for the Indians who ranged between the Susquehanna and the Potomac. Now, the whole valley is cultivated, up to the very edges of the mountain-slopes. Within the shadow of these lie long wheatfields, separated from one another by ancient stone walls and briered fencerows. Tiny rivulets trickle down the gullies along the fences from springs high in the hills.

Here, then, we have ideal quail conditions: water, food, good loafing places and a near-by sanctuary in the mountain itself. And here in these stubble fields and in the adjoining thickets I have, for a matter of thirty years, enjoyed as sporty quail shooting as can be had, I think, anywhere in America. These birds are big, they are wise, they fly almost like grouse, and they know more tricks about getting away than a débutante knows about getting her man. Sometimes they lie unbelievably close. They light in trees. They run long distances. And occasionally they take a flight that looks as if it were intended for a world tour. But some real memories of my adventures with them will do more to convince you than general statements.

Except under unusual circumstances, these birds always roost in the fields. I remember going out one misty November morning at daybreak with my old Llewellin setter, Bell. She was at that time old and slow, but she was infallible. She was then seven. From the time she was five years old, I do not recall ever having to tell her what to do. I would just get out of the car in bird country and follow her. A good dog knows the habits of quail and where they are likely to be at certain times of the day.

Almost as soon as we were in the stubble field Bell began to trail. About two hundred yards from the fringes of the mountain, right in the valley-end of the wheatfield, she came to a stand. Experience had taught me that these birds would fly straight for the mountain, regardless of where they were flushed in the field. If I walked ahead into them, I would have a right-hand or a left-hand shot at the covey streaming by, or perhaps they would go straight over my head, which makes the chance an awkward one. If I wanted a straight-away shot, I would have to go round them, so that they would rise between me and the heavy cover which they would surely seek.

When Bell drew to her point in the brown stubble, I thought it would be sporty to walk right in, compelling myself to take the birds at a quartering shot as they passed me to escape into their mountain haunts. What they did always seemed to me about as adroit a maneuver as this crafty little aristocrat ever executes. They arose in two small groups, one led by the old cock and the other by the old hen. There was a difference in intelligence, though not in the size of the birds. Separated by only a few yards, the two groups came hurtling by on either side of me, in strong, low, level flight.

Of course, the thing I did was a foolish one; for when a dog draws to a point on quail, the first thing for a hunter to do is to scrutinize the adjacent country to discover where the flushed birds are likely to go. Depend upon it, they have a sanctuary in mind before they are flushed. It may be a patch of woods, a creek-bank, a briered fencerow, a laurel thicket. Since the direction of your approach will not make them change their minds as to where they are going, the sensible maneuver is to work around behind the covey until the probable refuge lies dead ahead. Then and only then can the hunter be sure of a normal chance at straightaways.

Perhaps one reason why the amateur or the careless quail hunter does not really make good at this exacting game is that he takes too little into account certain standard habits of these fine birds. So many hunters blindly fight their game. But hunting is essentially a matching of wits instead of a physical contest. All the effort and all the endurance in the world will not count if there is a lack of wary intelligence.

With my right I made one of those perfect misses—perhaps the most ordinary of all shots. My second barrel brought a bird down. In a minute the fine covey had crossed the field, topped the fence, risen high above the first fringing thickets of the mountain, and had been lost to sight among a growth of pine and hemlocks.

Whether I follow a covey into such a place depends entirely on how ambitious I am feeling. As the day was young, and as I had not as yet distinguished myself, and as Bell would have it no other way, we entered this difficult fastness. Here are jungles of sassafras and birch, rising out of a low sea of kalmias; here are evergreens and massive oaks and stretches of young locust; here are patches of wild raspberries, blackberries whose canes are big brutes, and smothers of wild grape and honeysuckle. And in a place like this, hunting quail is likely to be a romp of some kind, merry or otherwise.

I had marked the birds down by a towering dead chestnut, but it was nearly a hundred yards farther on that Bell began to get interested. She fell into a stealthy walk, now pausing, then stepping forward like a ghost trailing a ghost. These quail of the kalmias never seem to stay put. They keep moving ahead of dog and man, and they usually move as a covey. After their long fly from the field, they alight almost together, and then proceed to take a swift sneak. If they are followed, they keep on going. And sometimes they flush out of gunshot. In these thickets, with their dense undergrowth of thick evergreens, and the birds as big and as wild as they are, I think the shooting every whit as difficult as that on grouse, perhaps more so, because the hurtling targets are so much smaller.

On the far edge of a little rise the laurels temporarily end. And it is in this green fringe that Bell finally comes to a halt. A man never quite gets used to a big covey's explosion in his face; and under the conditions described, if he can get in both barrels, he is lucky. As I walk forward, making a noise that cannot be helped, the birds run again, chittering; then they are off. And how! This time their flight is eerie and enigmatic. Some slip off on almost noiseless wings, in a low, terrifically fast but unerring flight. Some rocket upward to the tree-tops and drop on set wings toward some far sanctuary.

One bird spiraled upward, making almost as much noise as a grouse. This one I managed to get. But before I could put my gun on a second, they were all out of range. Up the mountain they had gone, into one of my favorite grouse haunts. Here, then, would be a double chance. They would fly, I knew, on the average of about two hundred yards. They don't go so far in the woods as they will from the field into their mountain fastness. As every hunter knows, a covey will have its natural place of safety; and when once in it will be loath to leave. I have seen a quail rise in a little thicket, spin round a corner, and drop again into the cover, not over thirty yards from the rise.

The birds were now scattered, and if old Bell's nose was any-thing better than a decoration, she would find some of them. In such cover, while the bevy will be exceedingly restless and light-footed, single birds, even in the bare woods upon the dead leaves, will lie exceedingly close—in fact, uncomfortably so. There is a psychological distance at which a quail should rise; and anything short of this is likely to be as unfortunate for the hunter as if the quail got away out of range.

These woods have a strange picturesqueness of their own. While they are almost primeval in their wildness, the reminder of a grim calamity, with which man had nothing to do, is constantly evident. All the chestnut trees are dead from the blight—the only disease, so foresters tell me, which ever destroyed a whole species in wide reaches of its range.

By the base of one of these dead patriarchs Bell suddenly hesitated, and then froze. I have often wondered how frequently a bird-dog sees the game it is pointing, and whether sight of it makes for stanchness or otherwise. There seems to be a strange light in the eyes of a standing dog, as if it were in a trance.

In this case Bell was "sleeping" on her point. She was as certain that she had game as if she saw it. I was at the time in an old animal trail that wound easily up the wooded slope. As the leaves were damp, I could step forward almost without sound. The bird must be behind the big chestnut. Before edging nearer, I took a look for the chances for a shot, for in the woods one of these preliminary surveys is often mighty helpful. Directly in the probable line of flight were two big hemlocks, between the dusky intertwining arms of which was a lane of light. The dark trees were only thirty yards off.

"If it were a grouse," I thought, "I know just where he would go."

Hardly had the thought crossed my mind when I heard a slight rustle in the leaves behind a tree, and in an instant a lordly cock grouse was up and away. Straight as a rocket for that aperture between the hemlocks he headed, and instinctively I aimed at the right place. So great was his speed that he fell fully ten yards beyond the point at which he started to fall. Here was luck indeed! And the quail were still ahead of me.

Retrieving my princely bird, I followed Bell into a dogwood thicket, in which, her instinct declared, our birds were. She was right. In ten minutes she had made six points and I had shot three more quail. To be an honest man, I must not forget the detail of missing four, including a double. But if we could kill every one we shot at, where would be the sport, and how many birds would be left at the end of a season?

My old dog and I returned to the stubble fields, which lie parallel to one another below the slope of the mountain and stretch for some three or four miles. In each field there is sure to be one covey; sometimes I have found four in one field. And all these birds act just alike. The minute they are flushed, they head for their home in the hills; and following them there is as I have described.

About noon, when I had almost my limit, I found an old spring in an abandoned orchard, and there Bell and I had a humble lunch together, share and share alike. It had turned out to be a mellow autumn day, with the woods as fragrant as winesap apples, with tawny leaves drifting lazily down, with a golden haze over the world. Far behind me in the mountain I could hear the scattered coveys calling together. These mountain birds use their wings a good deal more than the birds of the open valleys, and fly together at the gathering call. Occasionally, in this way, two coveys get together—which leads me to tell of a remarkable experience I had in the laurels near the top of these same Tuscaroras one winter day.

I had taken out some ears of corn to spike on short bushes for the wild turkeys. There was a little snow on the ground, and in it I noticed a good many quail tracks. As they were fresh, I followed them out of the grapevine-hung dogwood thicket into the kalmias. After a while I saw the birds running on the snow ahead of me. Then what I supposed to be the covey got up. But the getting-up business would not stop. After at least thirty had gone out on the laurel, I began to count; and by the time the flushing ceased, eighty-seven quail had been counted. How is that for a covey?

"Now let me tell one," you say.

But this thing is true, and it serves to disclose a habit of these dwellers in the kalmias that is worth recording. In the dead of winter these coveys from the valley climb the mountain to the shelter of the laurel, and there they naturally come together. Old lumbermen of this region have told me that the birds always congregate in the winter. Moreover, in blizzard weather they seek out an overhanging rock-shelter, where they remain dry and warm until the storm has passed—in this way imitating perfectly what the ancient Indians used to do. Under the same rock-shelter on the shoulders of these wild Tuscarora hills I have found modern quail-roosts and old-time Indian arrowheads!

This congregating of the birds does not take place until after the hunting season has closed; but even if it did, I do not think that the gunner could do much with these birds in a place like that. Immense boulders are grimly strewn, there are many pines and hemlocks, the footing is precarious; and the birds, when they rise, spread out in an immense fan all over the least accessible places. Besides, these birds of the hills develop both a speed of flight and a finesse of dodging that are superior to anything the field birds can show. Hunting such quail in such a place is worse than following the Astor markhor or the Nubian ibex.

As soon as spring comes, these wary mountaineers troop once more into the smiling valley, pair off, and raise their coveys of little patrician hill-billies—if you'll admit the paradox. And after them, when the season opens once again, will come an old quail hunter, with his aging setter Bell, to try to make life a somewhat lively affair for the brown birds.

You may remember that my hunt broke off when Bell and I were drowsing in the old orchard. We did better than drowse. When I woke up, it was nearly three o'clock, and Bell was whining over my prostrate form.

"Old girl," I said, "we have a grouse and eight quail—enough for one day. Going home, I might kill a rabbit for you on the fly, if you don't chase him too hard. But no more birds—until tomorrow."

SHOFFSTALL

FIVE

The Dogs that Make the Hunting

THE OLD MAID

Havilah Babcock

While talking over plans for this book with Gene Hill, he urged me: "Don't forget Havilah Babcock's 'The Old Maid.' It's his best piece." Well, Gene may just be right about that. Certainly, it's always been one of my favorites and is the perfect story to open our bird-dog section of The Bobwhite Quail Book. *Published in* Tales of Quail 'n Such, *the story is one of few to give emphasis to single-bird hunting, that fiendishly difficult business that wears out our hunting pants on briers and our patience on fast, uncontrollable dogs. Somehow, single-bird hunting always reminds me of that old golf expression: "You drive for show but putt for dough." 'Twas thus ever so in quail hunting also. Covey rises are exciting and picturesque, but to really put some birds into our game pockets we've got to pick up a goodly portion of those fugitive singles. And doing just that seems to be growing more difficult over most of bobwhite's range. No-burning laws and reduced grazing practices have resulted in field-side tangles so impenetrable that they provide the perfect refuge for escaping bevies. Shouldering and slugging through those briery, vine-clinging swamps, with dogs usually out of control or out of sight, has become so unprofitable that many hunters prefer to let the singles go and look for another covey. There just aren't enough "Old Maids" left to go around.*

GOOD COVEY DOGS ARE, as Lincoln said of Civil War generals, "as plenty as blackberries." Hardy, spirited rangers that will put up whatever there is to be put up, and give you your money's worth day in and day out. That is, in good bird country.

But if you are ever fortunate enough to get your hands on a real single-bird dog, don't forget to say your prayers regularly. It's the only thing I'd steal without the slightest compunction of conscience—a really good one.

For a covey dog, give me a pointer—stamina, dash, derring-do. For a singles dog, give me a setter—patience, thoroughness, precision. Just one man's experience, and if it doesn't jibe with yours don't sue me for it. All you could get would be covey dogs, anyway. Single-bird dog is in my wife's name.

Also, if you care to, you can give me a setter that has been spayed. And I'll take my setter with a little age on her. Rare old

Ben Franklin advised a young man to pick an old woman to have his affairs with. The same consideration underlies my nomination of an oldish lady for singles hunting.

To carry the specifications a little farther, you can give me a slow dog, one that has plenty of time. There's no such thing as a fast singles dog and a good one.

Funny thing, too, I never saw a good singles dog with a fancy name. A friend of mine has a sedate and aging setter whose name is Bess, but whom we always refer to as the Old Maid, which just suits her mincing delicacy and fastidious thoroughness in the field. The Old Maid is not in the canine *Who's Who*. She has never been in a field trial, nor had her picture in the papers. And you have never heard of her. But I know a couple of hard-headed hunters who wouldn't trade her for a first cousin of the Grand Champion, once removed. Will Carrington is the other fellow. In fact, the Old Maid really belongs to Will, although he always refers to her as "ours." I have mainly a borrowing interest in her.

In golf, you drive for fun and putt for money. In bird shooting, you hunt coveys for excitement and singles for your game. This is truer now than ever before.

Time was when birds were so plentiful that covey hunting would give a man all that he wanted, and more than he was decently entitled to. I reckon such a time once was. If not, the old-timers I've listened to are a raft of unhallowed prevaricators.

I know a whimsical old gentleman who is fond of saying: "I ain't the man I used to be. Never was." Maybe it's that way with birds.

Time was when Bob was a self-contained and chancy fellow who held his ground until properly flushed. But he is not so stable as of old. He has become a bit jumpy here of late, often flushing at the least provocation. In fact, latter-day Bob is fast becoming an ungentlemanly trickster, full of sly ruses and pettifoggin' ways. Or to put it kindlier, Bob has developed a bad case of the d.t.'s. And pray who wouldn't have, what with the "reclamation" of his refuges by a benevolent and misguided Government, the encroachments of a more scientific agriculture, and a highly mobilized Coxey's army a-gunning for him day in and day out?

But for his twentieth-century nerves and growing slipperiness, he would have lost out in the unequal battle. Bob has learned that discretion is the better part of valor. His philosophy is not unlike that of a roguish old darky who "tote de game" for me and always gives as ample reason for running out on a free-for-all-fight: "Cap'n, I'd druther hear 'em say, 'Cain't dat nigger run!' than hear 'em say, 'Don't he look natchul.'"

For good and sufficient reasons, then, the singles dog is coming into his own. And sometimes local weather conditions join other factors to make such a specialist a prime necessity.

For instance, in low-country South Carolina, where I pay a few taxes and shoot a lot of birds, the 1939 hunting season opened in the middle of a drought. There had been no rainfall for more than two months. Fields, woods, even the devilish bays were as dry as tinder. Leaves rattled ominously wherever you stepped. There had been no rain to dissolve the dust from the undergrowth, and our dogs were forever sneezing and coughing. Trailing conditions were next to impossible. As the season advanced, the drought became more pronounced, and the birds more jittery and unstable.

Of the thirty-eight coveys that Will and I raised during the first week, twenty-seven flushed prematurely, slithering away at the first approach of the dogs and holing up in the impenetrable bays, where few bird hunters and *no gentlemen* will follow them. Singles hunting proved equally disastrous. The dogs would either run over the ground-hugging singles in the dusty straw, or flush them in the powder-dry, clattering leaves. It was not the fault of he dogs. Good hunters they were—Jackie, Pedro and High Pocket. Just too fast for dry-weather hunting.

During that unhappy first week, Will and I had one experience that will warm the cockles of any bird hunter's heart, however old and hardened a sinner he might be. A whopping big covey roared up from a pea patch ahead of us and sailed away to a field of golden broomstraw. They didn't clump down in a body, but deployed nicely in two's and three's. As perfect a layout for singles shooting as a body could wish.

"That's the sort of thing that keeps a fellow huntin'," Will grinned. "The sort of thing that don't happen too often in this here modern society."

] 239 [

"Sure looks like the pay-off," I agreed. "And the answer to the bird supper that we've invited all those people to."

"Yes, sir," seconded Will as we strode confidently toward the field; "if a fellow can't fill his pockets with such a layout as that, he'd better quit."

But our hopes were short-lived. While we were still a hundred yards away, birds began to pop out of the dry straw and head for the distant and forbidding bay. We started to shout at the dogs and run—which a good bird hunter seldom does much of. But to no purpose.

Sweeping through the straw, our dogs routed those singles one by one. Even respectable dogs will sometimes lose their heads when things are popping too fast. When we got there, not a blessed bird was left. What can take an unruffled and philosophical spirit and tear it to tatters like that?

"And that's what makes a fellow quit huntin', I reckon." Will slumped forlornly on a log. "Twenty birds in that covey, and we got how many? Nary a one!"

"Pretty thorough job they made of it," I added dismally. "We hunted for that chance a whole week, and had it ruined in two minutes."

"Straw too dry."

"Dogs too fast."

"Birds nervous."

Thus we tersely diagnosed the case, and Will added the clincher: "Ain't goin' to be any better until it rains, and"—he looked toward the discouraged skies—"it ain't gonna rain no more."

"We got to do something about it," I ultimatumed.

"Yeh. Got to," Will dully agreed.

"What you got in mind?"

"Nothing."

I chewed a sassafras twig and wondered if I could put a notion in Will's head without his suspecting my authorship.

"By the way," I said, trying hard to sound honest, "how old is the Old Maid?"

"She's pushin' eleven."

"Too old to hunt, of course."

"Yeh. Too old."

"Fattish, too, I reckon."

"Yeh. Fattish, too."

"We agreed last year not to hunt her any more, besides."

"Sure. Shook hands on it and promised Mary."

"Never do to lie to Mary."

A pretty satisfactory conference, I figured, knowing Will as I do. And when we met the next morning, there was the Old Maid in person, an amiable old blue-ticked Llewellin, squatting like a fat dowager on the front seat of the car. And there was Will, looking happy and sort of sheepish.

"Got her, but had to stand for a lot of kidding from Mary. Said we ought to be ashamed of falling back on an old pensioner, us with our two-hundred-dollar dogs. But my pride is gettin' easy to swallow here lately."

"Of course, we've got to favor her," I conceded, fondling a shaggy ear.

But it was soon apparent that the Old Maid would do her own favoring. Quietly she trotted behind us, contenting herself with an occasional excursion to check up on a likely thicket or a tentative clue that the other dogs had found and abandoned. Nothing could induce her to try her fortunes with the rollicking trio that swept the fields ahead. The Old Maid knew why she had been brought along, and she knew her own limitations, which is about the finest thing either dog or man can learn.

Within half an hour the other dogs had raised a fine covey, the birds flushing wild as usual and sailing off into an overgrown field.

"Now let's call those rambunctious hellions in, tie them to a sapling, and let the Old Main speak her piece," decided Will.

So saying, he produced three lengths of rope and tied up the traveling trio, much to their disgust and the jeopardy of the sapling.

The Old Main had seen the covey and watched it down. As we approached she trotted sedately ahead of us and began to insinuate herself through the undergrowth. Step by step she minced along, sneaking through the dry weeds and straw like a ghost. "Walking on pins and needles," Will called it. And presently she announced a single, which Will brought down and which she retrieved with the same daintiness, carefully retracing her steps on the retrieve to prevent invading untested ground.

"Notice how she came out the same way she went in? Old thing doesn't mean to risk a flush," beamed Will.

"I don't need a guide-book to the Old Maid's virtues, thank you," I answered, and bagged the next bird myself.

Back she went unbidden to her task, tiptoeing tediously about, warily testing every clump of weeds for her high-strung quarry. Once she pointed a single with a bird in her mouth—a heart-warming sight however often you have seen it. And once again she brought in a twosome—not to be dramatic, but because common sense dictated such a procedure when two birds lay side by side.

When her tedious job was done, bless my soul if the Old Maid hadn't pointed and retrieved nine of those singles without a mishap or accidental flush!

One of her traits that had particularly struck me was her quiet self-sufficiency. Not once had she let her anxiety to retrieve betray her into rashness, as might well have happened with a less practiced hand. Not once did she require instructions as to her job. We never talk much when the Old Maid is on a hard case. Matter of fact, she never thinks such a touchy situation appropriate for idle chatter. When a bird was downed, Will simply announced the fact. In him she had complete faith, never requiring reassurance and never relaxing her quest.

That very thoroughness of hers cost us an hour's delay the next day and gave me a side-light on Will's training methods. Will has a way of his own with dogs, and the incident, although a trifle irritating at the time, was highly revealing.

A wing-tipped bird had scurried into a hollow log and baffled the Old Maid's efforts to extricate it. Valiantly she laid siege to that log, prying, scratching and jamming her muzzle into the hollow, but to no avail. Nor did our added efforts help any. I tried to talk her into resigning the case, but no amount of persuasion could induce her to abandon the beleaguered quarry.

"We can't do anything with that derned dog, Will. We've lost fifteen minutes already. Tell her to be reasonable and come on."

"Just against her principles to leave a wounded bird, I reckon," replied Will.

"Heck! Pitch another one near the log and let her retrieve that. Maybe that'll satisfy the fussy old dame."

"That would hardly be honest, would it?" demurred Will. "A dog should be taught not to lie. Best way to teach 'em that is not to lie to them. I taught her that same thoroughness when she was a puppy, and I'm not goin' to fuss with her now. She's right and we're wrong, only she has more time than we have."

With that, Will smiled indulgently and stalked off across the field. A quarter of an hour later he was back with an ax and a wedge, and we fell to splitting that log so that the Old Maid could satisfy her conscience.

"That's what comes of having too good a dog," I chided peevishly. "And damned if you ain't as stubborn as she is."

But in my heart I felt a sneaking admiration for the pair of them.

For the next four weeks, as long as they dry weather lasted, we followed the same procedure: letting the other dogs hunt the coveys and the Old Maid the singles, especially when conditions called for delicate maneuvering. They were altogether the most restful and satisfying hunts I've ever had. And three-fourths of the birds we bagged during that time we owed to the patience and finesse of the old lady.

"That dame is a genius, and nothing else," I conceded after a particularly fine day. "Just as an academic question, Will: what will you take for your half of her?"

"Well, there's my car, my gun and the other dogs. There's the farm, the mules and the kitchen stove. And there's my wife, maybe. But the Old Maid, I reckon she's about the only thing on the place that ain't for sale."

"Think I'll put her in a story," I ventured.

"If you do, be sure to say she ain't for sale."

"No dogs like her nowadays, Will," I insisted, caressing a ragged ear. "Sometimes I think that nothing is as good as it used to be, anyway."

"Oh, you're just getting mellow over your shootin' these last few days. Matter of fact, that puppy I'm workin' on now will be just as good as the old lady in time. It's not hard, if a fellow has the patience, time, the birds—and a dog to start with. But unless a man is cut out by Providence to fool with dogs, I reckon he'd better hire his trainin' done. Best money he ever spent. Or buy one already trained. If he's an important fellow that gets off just now and then, he'd better buy a dog that's set in his ways, an old dog that's got more sense than he has—one he can't ruin. And I don't mean any harm by that. A fellow has got to be out of a job and not worried about it to train a dog right, I reckon."

SHOFFSTALL

THE MYSTERY OF SCENT

Ray Holland

This piece by Ray Holland originally appeared in Field & Stream, *the magazine to which he had dedicated so much of his love and energies as both editor-in-chief and as a writer. Holland retired from the position in 1941 after guiding the magazine into the most prestigious position in the outdoor field. He continued to write and pursue field sports until his death, and this 1952 story results from that period. Holland was unique as an editor because his skills in directing the magazine were backed by a wealth of field experience few could equal. He came from the great American heartland of the Mid-West, growing up in the heyday of game and bird populations. He was tutored in his skills by many old market-hunting professionals. Holland knew how to set a stool of decoys on the best point for any given day, break an unsteady pointer, or walk the ridges for grouse. You name it; he had done it, and excelled! This piece, never before anthologized, gives us plenty to think about on those difficult days when even the best dogs just can't seem to get the job done.*

"LOOK AT HIM, kid! Look at him!" said John Taintor Foote, and he hit me on the shoulder muscle with his fist. "I told you! Jack ain't hunting. He's just romping off across that stubble field to point himself a nice covey of quail."

The big pointer did just that. He didn't cast around searching for scent; he went a hundred and fifty yards straight out into that field and pointed. It was as though he knew those birds were there, and now that we were ready he would go out and show us. Old Decatur Jack was perhaps the greatest meat dog that I ever saw.

Last winter in Cuba I had an experience that definitely settled in my mind one question that pointer and setter men have long argued. Some master dogs do not seem to hunt their birds; they just go to them and point. How do they do it? All dog men of wide experience have seen such dogs, some of them better than others. I have seen three notable dogs of this type, and owned one of them.

My dog, Jingo Ned, discouraged every bracemate that was ever set down with him. Some dogs are quick to suffer from an inferiority complex, and Ned gave them much to worry about. Many dogs when alone or down with a dog of equal ability will hunt well, yet blow up completely when hunting with a dog of superior ability. I have had friends hunt their brag dogs with Ned and have seen the dogs start trailing him after he had found two or three coveys to their none. Ned went to his birds. How did he do it?

I believed it was nose, but he would go so far in a straight line that I didn't dare claim he smelled birds at that distance. I knew when he was heading for a covey by the way he ran. Having heard about Ned, a wealthy field-trial follower sent his kennel man to Will Gladwin's kennels at Brewster, New York, to buy any and all young dogs that Will might have with Ned's blood in their veins.

Old dog trainers contend that this ability to go to game is not nose; that it couldn't be, because some dogs go so much farther than they could possibly smell game. I have heard them say it is a sixth sense. They wish to give the dog some occult power to locate birds. Of course, that is nonsense. A brainy dog will look over his cover and hunt likely spots. He is no good in my book if he doesn't, but that has no bearing on a dog that cuts straight across stubble and goes to a covey of quail.

How far can a dog smell game? I wouldn't know. I gave Ted Trueblood a puppy some years ago, a grandson of old Ned's. Last year Ted wrote me that this dog Joe had caught the scent of a covey of Hungarian partridge a quarter of a mile away and gone straight to them. He said there was a gentle breeze blowing from the covey down a long hill, and the scent must have been carried along close to the earth, where the dog picked it out of the air and raced to the birds. A quarter of a mile is a long piece, but I will believe anything Ted Trueblood tells me, even when he is talking about his dog. I wouldn't like it if anyone else didn't believe it, and neither would Ted. My son Dan hunted over this dog, and when he returned home he asked, "Why do you give away the good ones?"

Summer before last, for something better to do I raised a litter of pups from two dogs I own. The sire goes back to Seaview Rex as the first dog with a national reputation in his pedigree, but Shot is an individual in his own right. As a grouse and woodcock dog he rates. He doesn't go straight to birds, but he covers the cover, and if they are there he holds stanch with high head and tail until you get there, then he goes and finds another bird. I intend to keep him as long as he lives. The dam is a beautiful little bitch sired by Ch. Lucky Strike, and on the other side of the family her grandsire was Jingo Ned. She couldn't help but be good.

There were six in the litter, four dogs and two bitches. I kept the pups and played with them until they were four months old so that I could pick out dogs with certain qualities for certain friends. One of the bitches we called Susie was the best-looking dog in the litter and seemed to have more promise than any of the others as far as brains went, and that is about as far as you can judge a puppy. I gave her to a friend of mine in Cuba, with whom I hunt each winter.

Last year when I reached Cuba my first questions were about Susie.

"She is fine. A beautiful dog. So nice about the house," my friend said, and I sensed something was wrong.

That evening it came out in the open. "I am afraid Suzzie will never make a dog for me," Ernesto told me with a great deal of effort.

"Why not?" I asked.

"She does not hunt like other dogs. I turn her loose, and she dashes off and goes right to quail and drives them into the cane. She does not point. She goes right from one covey to another, and she chases them and will not mind me. She obeys perfectly around the house, but in the field no. I am afraid."

"Will you please repeat that part about her going straight to the birds?" I asked.

"She does," he answered. "You will see. She will find every quail in a field and drive them all out."

All I could answer was, "Well, that's too bad! We must take her out in the morning."

Now, Ernesto has had bird dogs all his life. He had three dogs when Susie arrived. One, a little black-and-white bitch from

France named Tila, could eat regularly in my kennels. Another black-and-white bitch that suffers from fear of doing the wrong thing and a big liver-and-white dog that will point where a quail passed the day before made up his string. In handling these dogs Ernesto never raises his voice. He is soft-spoken naturally, and it is a wonderful way to handle dogs if the dogs will handle. I knew Susie came from a long line of dogs that had been handled by men with loud voices, and I imagined that might be part of his trouble.

The next morning we put Tila down in a pasture near home, and Ernesto kept Susie on a rope. Tila went to work in her businesslike way, but at the end of fifteen minutes she had found no birds.

"Turn Susie loose," I said. "Let's see what she does."

"It will not be good," Ernesto answered. "We wish to shoot the quail. Suzzie will drive them into the cane. I have tried her many times."

I persisted, and finally he gave up and slipped the leash on the nine-months-old pointer puppy. She raced away and without a glance at the older dog, who was near by, she set her sights for the far side of the field. Before I could realize that it could happen so quickly, a covey of birds was in the air and Susie was urging them to greater speed on their way to cover. If she could have lifted just a few feet off the ground, I think she might have caught one of those birds.

Ernesto called to her in Spanish, but she didn't hear him. She was a very busy puppy. "You see," he said. "It is as I say. We will kill no birds if Suzzie is down. I feel badly. I am sorry, but Suzzie is always like that."

I told him I thought she was wonderful, and I talked him into leaving her down. She found another covey and another, and she chased them with malice. Diplomatically I suggested that I might be able to settle her down, and freely Ernesto told me to go ahead and do anything I wished. As he told me he dropped his hands to his sides, palms forward in an eloquent gesture of despair. There I took over the role of dog trainer. It was simple. The first "Whoa!" I loosed on that Cuban countryside awakened memories in Susie. She checked, thought better of it and went on after the covey.

One morning I had her on a string while Tila hunted. During her training I did this for two reasons. First, I wanted to bring her up behind Tila on point. This didn't work. Tila was so infernally jealous that she would jump in on her birds as we came up; furthermore, when she pointed Susie froze and didn't want to go closer. The other reason was to rest the puppy and keep her from running herself to death under a hot sun. It was while on leash that she taught me something.

We were in a great pasture with a long, sloping rise ahead. Susie was straining on the leash. Then she stopped with her head high. For a second it didn't dawn on me that she was pointing. I called Ernesto, and he called Tila. I handled the puppy and she was rigid. Tila came in, paid not the slightest attention to Susie and worked over the cover in front without showing any sign of game. During this procedure Susie relaxed and started to pull ahead again. Just a false point!

We went on up the rise, and again Susie stiffened. Again the old bitch worked the cover without a sign of game. Again Susie pulled forward. I slipped the leash and she raced to the top of the hill and flushed a covey of quail that got up in a wad; I don't believe they had moved from the roost that morning. They were not running ahead, or Tila would have nailed them, for I have always classed her as away above the average gun dog.

My conclusions are that the puppy caught a faint scent of birds on the gentle breeze that was coming down that hill. When the older dog thrashed around in front of her, the scent stream was broken or overpowered by dog scent and she didn't get it. When I turned her loose, she went straight to them, and it was two hundred yards to the top of that hill. And that, for my money, is how some dogs with abnormal noses can go straight to game.

The next morning Susie did it again in a more impressive manner. She stopped in a pasture with good grass cover. She was facing north into a light breeze. Ahead of her about a hundred yards was a deep gulley with brush and brier. I unsnapped the leash and urged her on. She raced in a straight line to this depression and went down in.

When I reached the top of the bank, she was thrashing around, showing no sign of scent. Then she climbed out on the opposite side and again took up her straight-line running. Ahead some hundred and fifty yards was another and larger depression with brush and trees growing in it. When Susie neared it, she started to feather and work here and there in short casts. Then she went over the bank and I saw the birds come out.

It is my guess that this covey had been on top of the bank feeding on the grass seeds and had run into the cover when they saw her coming. She smelled those birds an unbelievable distance, and when I turned her down she headed up the scent stream straight to them. If I hadn't had her on leash, I never would have known that she scented either of those coveys. Or if for some unknown reason she hadn't stiffened when she got this trace of scent while on leash, I wouldn't have known she smelled birds.

The best that man will be able to do is guess when he tries to figure out bird scent and the many things that affect it. We are pretty sure of certain things. Some of us may be too sure of this or that and find we are wrong. I feel certain that high wind, especially a cold wind, will dissipate scent. I have had many a bird hunt ruined by a high wind.

There are other times when bird scent is elusive and man doesn't know why. Several times, while I was judging or watching field trials, scent seemed to develop all of a sudden where there had been no scent before. Three or four braces of dogs would hunt through a bird field where hand-reared birds had been heavily planted and never show the least sign of smelling game. Then the next brace would locate and point stanchly. After that every dog down would find game. Some atmospheric change had taken place and the scent was good. There was no great difference in the quality of the dogs running; they were all class bird dogs, or they wouldn't have been there. The first dogs down didn't have a chance.

I have seen the best of dogs blunder into birds through no fault of theirs. At one trial I saw Mary Blue, shortly after she had won the National Championship, bust bird after bird. She wouldn't have done that if she could smell them. Nor do I believe that a dog's olfactory nerves are good one day and bad the next unless the dog is sick; the ability to smell is the foremost sense that a dog possesses. It would be just as smart to say he doesn't see well today, or he can't hear this morning. When trouble exists, it is lack of scent for the dog to work on. That's my guess.

We are sure that a bird that has made a long flight and been thoroughly air-washed leaves little scent immediately after he has again come to earth. Every hunter of experience has watched a covey of birds scatter in good grass cover and been unable to move more than an occasional bird that he or his dog stumbled into. Coming back sometime later, his dog picked them out one after another. The same is true of a bird killed instantly in the air that does not flutter when it hits the ground. Such a bird is usually hard to retrieve because it leaves no scent.

There is an almost universally accepted belief that during the mating season birds leave no scent, I don't believe that one, either. Kind Nature is supposed to give them this protection in the interest of propagation. It is my guess that when the grass is green and the air is filled with pollen and the odors of many different kinds of vegetation bird dogs as well as foxes and other vermin are badly handicapped. In game-management studies and in bird banding, dogs are used to locate the birds, and they point hen birds on the nest and birds with young broods that are caught with nets and banded. Every hunter knows that after the first freeze knocks down the cover a dog comes into his own.

The ability to scent game varies greatly in pointing dogs. Some have much keener noses than others. One of my pet contentions is that I would much rather have a dog of mediocre nose and a lot of brains than a keen-nosed dog that was shy on think power. The ideal is the dog with a long nose and a head full of brains. I keep thinking back to Dan's remark after hunting with the pup I gave Ted Trueblood, "Why do you give away the good ones?" When I ponder over that remark, I get to thinking about little Susie over in Cuba.

Miss Susie has brains along with that nose of hers. Ernesto was afraid she'd never point. Within a week I walked by her, lifted her by the tail and dropped her back to the ground, then went on and moved her birds. Sure she broke when I shot. She brought back a bobwhite and handed it to me.

That last morning in Cuba, when we put her down, she didn't run; she floated. We were in a pasture between two cane fields.

Susie went away as if she had been cast off in a championship field trial. With her head high and her tail swinging she tore down the right-hand side of that field for two hundred yards. Then she swung to the left and turned left again and raced up the center of that pasture. Her style of running had changed. She was no longer tossing her head. Instead she was running a line with her head held high, as though looking at something far away. I started at an angle to intercept her. I knew. Bang! She hit that body scent and froze in as stylish a point as old Lucky Strike ever made.

Dan called to me to wait, that he wanted to get on the other side of her and take a picture. I waited while he walked around, fooling with his camera as he went. "Walk on up, Dad," he called, "and I'll take one. Then wait until I come closer before you pass her and flush the birds."

"I've got it," Dan said, "but her ear is turned up over her head and it doesn't look too good. Do you suppose you could walk up and turn that ear down?"

I walked up to little Susie and flipped that ear over, and she didn't move a hair. Dan took another picture, and I walked in and kicked out the covey. This nine-months-old pointer, who wouldn't point, stood like a veteran and watched me do it. Susie's got brains. I'd like to own that dog!

JACK

Ray P. Holland

From Ray P. Holland's Seven Grand Gun Dogs (*Thomas Nelson, Sons, New York*), *this story touches on Holland's close relationship with the superb sporting-story writer, John Taintor Foote, and is essentially a celebration of the greatest bird dog they ever saw. One of the problems the average hunter has in training and maintaining the skills in his own dog, I've always felt, is that most shooters have never seen true super-stars of bird-dogdom. The normal standards of performance are loose and tend toward mediocrity. But it's just as well that we never had the chance to hunt over Jack. After that, our own dogs would have never looked the same.*

THREE CARS PULLED UP alongside a forty-acre wheat stubble on the Eastern Shore in Maryland. In each car were men with shotguns and bird dogs. Six hunters piled out, but only one dog was turned down. Six men were going to shoot over one pointer? Unorthodox? Even worse than that, it was inconceivable. Yet under the circumstances, it was excusable. This opening foray was but a prelude to a regular quail hunt. All six men were members of the Honga River Gun Club and four in the party had just come along to see this one dog do his stuff. Lew Borden and Harry Shedd would then go to another bird field and hunt over a pair of Shedd's dogs while Magnus Hopper and Rodney Fiske, the other two spectators, were going back near the clubhouse where they could hunt birds for an hour or two and shoot black ducks later at the close of day.

John Taintor Foote, the greatest sporting-fiction writer this country ever produced, and Ray Holland completed the group. John owned Decatur Jack and we were going to follow him around all afternoon. We had both been talking tall and tactless about Jack, and all members of the club were anxious to see him in action. An old shooting pal of mine used to say that he "wouldn't give a damn for a man who wouldn't lie just a little bit about his bird dog." You didn't have to lie about Jack. He had it.

This Maryland stubble field was almost square and we had stopped at the nearest corner. On two sides it was bordered by pine woods, the edges of which were marked with a heavy growth of honeysuckle. It was quail country—plenty of feed and sanctuary where man and dog could do little with the birds that took cover. Conditions were good, the air was damp and a light breeze was blowing toward us. We all crossed the fence and the parade lined up. Jack took little interest in what was going on. He didn't go in for this dashing around and "let me at 'em" stuff that you expect in a good pointer or setter. Besides, with such a crowd he probably thought we were going on a picnic.

"Now, if you birds are ready," John said, "I'm about to show you something."

With that remark he ordered Jack to go to work. The dog trotted out in front, stretching his head high and drawing in great lungfuls of air. Then he broke into a hobbyhorse gallop that seemed slow, yet which ate up the ground. He didn't cast around to either side but ran a line straight into the field. Two hundred yards from the starting point he stopped. His head was still high and his tail was straight out behind.

"There they are!" John said. "Now, just take your time. Line up when we get there and walk straight on by. When the covey gets up, blast 'em and then you fellows get the hell out of here. Ray and I are going huntin'."

It looked more as if we were advancing on a deadly enemy than on an unsuspecting bevy of bobwhites. I felt a little bit ashamed, but I was going to shoot along with the rest. Just after the scrimmage line passed the dog, a meadow lark sprang from the grass right in front of Jack and went away on its flutter and glide flight. Sighs and grunts of disgust came out of five of the gunners, including John, and someone laughed. But Harry Shedd kept walking straight ahead. To the tune of "Where you going, Harry?"; "The lark went thataway"; and other jibes; he plowed straight into a covey of about twenty birds and grassed two of them. Jack brought them to John with as light a mouth as any dog ever had.

Jack had lived up to his reputation. He wasted no time. If birds were around, he just went to them and pointed. His reputation was not the feelings and boastings of his owner. Georgia is filled with quail-shooting gentlemen and Decatur Jack rated tops with all who saw him in action. John hunted him in other Southern states braced with brag dogs and Jack always delivered. Harry Shedd had thirty or forty shooting dogs and John had visited him in Alabama and Shedd had said, "My dogs weren't feeling good when Jack was down." That was why Shedd had kept on walking when the lark flew. He knew Jack didn't lie.

John Foote once wrote a story about Decatur Jack; it was mostly fiction, enriched with actual performances of the dog. He called it "Lilly Belle Gets the Air." It was a good story, but littered up with characters and plot as it was, it didn't do Jack justice. I don't intend to review any of John's yarn, but to tell the story of how John came by this remarkable dog and the things I saw old Jack do, for he lived at my house and I hunted him while my dogs loafed.

John was writing a play in Atlanta between quail hunts. He met a man who ran a sporting-goods store. They hunted together and John made him this proposition: "You buy all the tiptop dogs you can find in Georgia. I'll pay for them and buy their feed. You kennel them and care for them, and we'll do some serious bird hunting." John said that to watch this man buy a dog was a lesson in advanced economy. Through the grapevine he would hear of a dog some hundred miles away and they would drive down to see the dog at his best. Then if they wanted him, the dickering would start. Usually such a dog would be acquired from the Cracker farmer for $35 or $40, although the asking price had been $75 or $100. As time went on, they gathered a kennel of dogs that could fill a gamebag if the birds were there.

One morning John's friend phoned to say that he would be by and pick him up in ten minutes and to be ready to go away down in the south-east corner of the state to buy the "maaster." Then the man raved over this dog. He had never thought the owner would part with the "maaster," but he had learned that he had put a price on the dog to a friend, and speed was of the essence. They had to have this dog. There had never been another like him and there never would be another. John didn't feel like driving the round trip of three hundred miles or more, so he told his friend to go buy the dog and he'd see him over a gun.

The next day John went to meet Decatur Jack. He didn't get excited over the appearance of this recent purchase. Jack was a big dog, white except for lemon splashes on his face and ears. He had none of the litheness you expect in a good hunter. He wasn't jumping around begging to go. Instead he just stood there and looked John squarely in the eye.

"What did you pay for him?" John asked.

"One thousand dollars!" replied his dog-buying friend. "And I didn't quibble. You can give the rest of your dogs away. This is the master."

John said he had to steady himself against the kennel-yard fence, for in those days $1000 would buy a house and lot. They took the new dog out. After John had been in the field with him, everything was all right. When John came north for the duck shooting at Honga River, he wouldn't talk about anything else. "Boy," he would say, "this baby finds them all. He hunts the cover as he finds it. He will go as wide as your top field-trial dogs and when the birds are in the woods, he keeps you in mind and never goes beyond your vision for longer than a minute or two. He's out of this world, fellows. He can read and write and do higher mathematics."

The next fall John walked into my office at *Field & Stream* in New York City.

"He's here." John grinned. "I brought him up with me."

"Who's here?" I asked.

"Jack, of course. Who else would I be bringing up from Georgia? He's down in the taxi. Get your hat. We'll take him up in Central Park and find a covey or two."

We drove up into the park and John turned the dog loose. That worried me, with cars in solid streams on all the driveways, but Jack turned back at a word and when he had attended to himself after his long train ride, we went back to the office. I hadn't seen anything to get excited about.

"I am leaving him with you," John told me. "You take him home and hunt him on grouse and woodcock and pheasants. He's never seen any of them, but he'll find them and point them and bring them to you when you kill them."

"But John," I objected, "I can't keep him here. I'll be in and out of the office all afternoon, dozens of men and women will be dashing in and out, and it just won't work. Besides, the commuting trains won't carry a dog. They have no baggage car."

"He won't give you a bit of trouble," John insisted. "Just tell him what you want him to do and he'll do it. Besides I've got to hurry to catch my train for home and I don't want him up in the Catskills until after you show him woodcock, grouse, and pheasants. Buy yourself a cab if the train won't carry him."

He handed me the leash, stepped back in the taxi and called, "I'll be seein' ye." I stood there on a crowded New York sidewalk with a big lumbering dog, who wasn't the least bit excited, but instead just stood there looking up at me with as beautiful brown eyes as I have ever seen in a dog, as much as to ask where we were going from there. He rode the elevator as if he had always ridden elevators. He tolerated the heavy petting he got from men and girls as I led him back to my office. He lay down by the file cabinets where I told him and I went back to work. Jack didn't sleep. It was his first trip to New York and he didn't want to miss anything. He watched everyone coming in and out of the office. If a pretty girl knelt down and petted him, that was all right. He didn't get up. The first time I got on my feet and started out, he was up and ready. I told him to go back and lie down and he did. After that I was in and out a half-dozen times and he never moved until I was ready to start for the train and snapped the leash on him.

Going through Grand Central, Jack started to raise a leg at a marble pillar, but I said, "No," and he looked up at me and trotted on. When we got down the ramp to the tracks, I took him clear to the end of the concrete walk, where he found a steel pillar that answered his purpose. Then I started sounding out the trainmen to see if I could get aboard. One after another shook his head. It was against the rules. I had gone back to the part of the train where I rode and where I knew the boys, but they had turned me down. Almost at the front end of the long string of coaches one of the blue-uniform boys started petting Jack and asked if he was good on birds. This fellow belonged. We talked awhile and then I told him I wanted to get the dog to Scarsdale.

"Will he behave?" I was asked, and I assured him Jack was the world's best-behaved dog.

"I'm going to walk down the platform to the next opening," said this new friend who liked dogs and birds and guns. "Get in the end seat and make him lie quiet."

At my home in Scarsdale I had several dogs that by my standard were good. I gave Jack a separate run and the next evening I took Jack and Nip and Tuck over to some cover near home, where I knew there were plenty of pheasants, mainly because no shooting was allowed. I drove out into a field and stopped on the brow of a hill. The land fell away for two hundred yards to where big woods began. The field was covered with broom sedge, goldenrod and other weeds. A swamp grown up with alders lay toward the right and extended down the hill to the timber.

When I turned the dogs down, Nip and Tuck hit with the throttle down. Nip headed for the swamp. Tuck bore to the left and started thrashing the field apart. Jack lifted a leg by the rear wheel of the car and then stood waiting for me to order him away. When I gave him the word, he galloped about forty yards down the slope and pointed. Nip had passed on one side of this spot and Tuck on the other, but neither had winded a bird. I walked down, a little dubious that Jack had a pheasant for he had never seen one or smelled one. When that cock bird left the ground with cackle and clatter, Jack jumped at him and snarled. "Air-minded chicken" was probably what he thought and he didn't approve.

After that we went pheasant hunting together and several times he growled when the birds flushed. When a pheasant ran ahead of him, he went right after it, hell for leather. Of course, some of them flew, for pheasants are like that, but most of them held. The second a bird quit running and squatted, Jack was on point and he thoroughly enjoyed retrieving them. Jack did all right at my house. I would bring him in during the evenings and he would lie quietly and look at whoever was talking. He left the impression that he understood everything that was said and might comment on some of the points at a later date. One of my boys remarked that he wouldn't want to tell any secrets before him. I have always said that I would rather own a bird dog with a mediocre nose and a good brain than a dog with a chokebored nose and a rattle-brain. Jack had both nose and brain.

Next I introduced him to his first woodcock. He pointed when he got the scent. The bird was squatted close to an old woods road that ran through an alder patch. I could see him sitting tight in the leaves. I cast a chunk in and instead of climbing out as I expected, the bird streaked back to the road, turned and gave me an easy straightaway shot. Jack went after him, picked him up and with the same movement dropped him. He stood there looking at that timberdoodle and I kept ordering him to fetch. Finally, he picked the bird up gingerly and brought him to me with a sort of injured air. After that I never asked him to retrieve woodcock. He continued to point them perfectly and I did my own retrieving. He always would find a dead bird and stand there looking at it. He must have thought things had come to a pretty pass, to be housed with a man who shot chickens and birds that smelled like robins.

Now with ruffed grouse it was a different story. He liked that grouse odor. It was like the smell of quail, only probably more so. It was a pleasant, strong scent that made his every action different. He had style and he pointed them stanchly and they lay for him. When one would flush wild, he would look back at me and because I knew he thought he had done wrong, I would yell at him, just to make everything all right.

A man who has owned only a dozen or so bird dogs in his life may feel he has had the best dog in the world. If he thinks that, more power to him. I wouldn't go so far as to advocate that he lie about his dog, as my old friend insists is entirely proper, but I certainly don't disapprove of a little exaggerated appreciation. The only way to tell just how good a bird dog you may own is to hunt him with other good dogs. Then if your dog continues to find more birds than his choice brace mates, you can start boasting. That is the valuable part of field trials, which guarantee the survival of good gun dogs.

Toward the end of the grouse season in New York, John took Jack to his home in the Catskills and he and the men who hunted with him were quick to claim the big pointer was one of the best if not the best grouse dog they had ever shot over. We hunted him with dogs long proven and he always found and handled more than his share of the birds. He did not point in the high-tailed present-day style, but his head was always up. He didn't believe in bouncing his nose on the ground or turning over leaves to hunt for birds. He picked them out of the air.

Jack had no known family tree. In fact he had a most unusual coat for a pointer. It was slick and glossy and lay flat, as approved in the best pointer circles. But strangely his coat was heavy. The hairs were longer than pointer hair and they grew very thick. You could run your hand against the lay of the hair and your fingers would dig down in and almost cover. John always said he must have had a trace of setter in his lineage. My guess? I say foxhound, and a good one, to give him that remarkable nose. A setter cross usually shows a few long hairs in the tail.

Decatur Jack was the best meat dog I ever saw. When I call him a "meat dog," I cast no slur. No disparagement is meant by the term. He had style enough on point, he had endurance enough and he had nose and brains to win any field trial, but he lacked the dash and flash and speed required. I considered him the greatest dog I ever shot over because with his unusual brain and his most remarkable nose he found game for the gun. I never saw him suddenly snap into a point. You got no nerve-tingling thrill when he pointed. He was a beautiful dog on point, but he was too matter-of-fact about it. He knew that it took the man with the gun to get the birds and it was such a simple thing for him to show the man where the birds were.

I placed him at the top because he handled all the species of game birds we hunted over him. He showed that he didn't care for pheasants, but if we wanted them he would find and point them. On quail he was supreme. He found them when scent conditions were poor and other dogs couldn't turn up a bird. His remarkable nose always left the impression that he must have known the birds were where he found them. Times without number we have watched him run a straight line that ended in a covey point. Jack wouldn't hunt down wind; instead, if cast off with the wind he would go to the end of the field and come back to his birds. I never saw a dog use the breeze to better advantage. In hunting small stubblefields he was a wonder. When cast into a cross-wind he would go down the leeward side of the field close to the cover and come back through the center of it with his head turned to the breeze. If he didn't point, he would come back to us and we'd go on to another field.

In John's yarn that mentions Decatur Jack he told of one quail hunt that he and I had on Honga River Gun Club property. It so clearly shows the ability of this dog that I, too, am going to tell of it. We had Jack at the club after the grouse season had closed. John and I had been shooting canvasbacks and redheads all morning and after lunch we wanted to go out with Jack. Our plans were to go back down the club road to the mainland and hunt some of the big fields which were under club lease, but the lunch took unusually long, for everyone there had to tell his story of the morning. Furthermore, the big log fire felt good and before we knew it, time was getting short.

The club superintendent suggested that we hunt on the point of the home property, where he insisted there were seven coveys of quail. I had heard this before. Several times I had hunted that course with Nip and Tuck and five coveys were the most I had ever found. Other club members with good dogs had hunted it with less success. This superintendent was a good man. He lived right there and nursed the game on the place the year round. He swore he knew every covey on the property and that he had watched those seven coveys grow from chicks to mature birds.

We had an hour and three-quarters before dark, so we went at it. Jack found and handled *nine* coveys of birds and there had been no chance of duplication. Furthermore, he worked singles on two of these coveys perfectly and we came back to the clubhouse with two limits. Jack had found two more coveys than were supposed to exist.

"He finds 'em where they ain't!" John said.

John and Jack went back to Georgia late in the season and the next time I saw John I asked first about Jack. John had a peculiar look on his face.

"He's gone," he said and he started to turn away. Then he blurted out, "Don't it beat hell! You find what you have been looking for all your life and you let go because it wouldn't have been the square thing to do to hold on."

CARRY ME BACK

Nash Buckingham

The Chairman of the Board, Nash Buckingham, was never more eloquent or moving than in this look backward upon a turn-of-the-century quail hunt that earned him a new dog, some new friends, and decades of memories. The piece is from the collection Hallowed Years (*Stackpole*).

HAL AND I WERE two worn-down play-boys about caught up with our immediate duck-shooting routines that frosty Monday morning when, in late November's pre-dawn, we debouched sleepily from a Cotton Belt Pullman's all-too-short session of bunk-fatigue to find ourselves back home in Memphis, Tennessee. A hack soon had us and our plunder of guns, bags and sacks of mallards at Luehrmann's fabulous hostelry consuming New Orleans coffee, ham, omelet and French bread. We had camp-hunted three days straight in Bayou Meto's bottoms with a bunch of cronies out of Pine Bluff, Arkansas, and topped off the week-end by squiring a twain of glamorous redheads through mazes of the cotillion, two-step, and the Blue Danube.

So here it was Monday morning, and back on the jobs for both of us. Hal lit a shuck for his embryonic real-estate cubby-hole, while I sought my insurance-office hide-out in the Bank Building, across Main Street. I entered through a side door and stopped at my father's office, where I found Barney, Dad's colored factotum, tidying up the president's sanctum. And there stood my older brother, Miles, tapping his foot and more or less putting the glare on me.

"Where the hell have you been?"

"Why—anything particularly wrong?"

"Wrong!" he yelled. "Dad has been about ready to blow his top. Don't you recall promising him to take Harry Jamerson and two of his visiting Eastern friends on a quail hunt today?"

Chilling inwardly, I muttered rather vague admissions of conversation along such lines, but definitely not as of today.

"Definite or indefinite," bawled Miles, "it's a good thing I worried enough to stick around and get up early this morning to help you out of this jam. You've got to go on through with it. Yonder they all are—in that big red automobile across Madison Street— waiting for you."

I peeked from a window in Dad's office and re-chilled. For, as much as I loved life afield, I was about fed up with shooting for a few days. Sure enough, at the curb lurked an enormous car with gleaming brass baggage-rack laden with wicker luncheon hampers and bedding rolls. A linen-dustered, begoggled chauffeur sat at its straight-up-and-down steering post and wheel.

Miles sketched in details. "It's a French Darracuq, or sump'n like that. The driver can hardly speak English—name's Jacques. They drove all the way here from Philadelphia—it's been in the papers—so get going. Otherwise Dad won't like this delay a bit, and he can bear down on a struggling insurance agent." I didn't like the slightly contemptuous inflection on that "struggling," but this was ominously an order from top-ranking banking brass.

Suppressing a yen to tell Miles off by asking who these guys thought they were, anyway, we started for the great conveyance. A relieved-looking Harry Jamerson greeted me like a long-lost pal and introduced me to two huge, elderly men garbed in expensively tailored moleskin shooting suits. Harry himself was, I knew, no gunner. But he was a right guy otherwise and had a lovely daughter. I noticed that he was packing Dad's cherished bird gun and also wearing my parent's quail jacket.

The visitors looked like sit-heavy, dour-visaged Buddhas, peering stolidly at me though expansive green goggles. Excusing myself, I rushed back into the bank and telephoned my steady bird-shooting partner, Billy Joyner. Thank heaven, he was home and ready to join up. In fact, he became pretty excited that he and Leo, our brawny partnership setter, were to get their initial ride in an automobile.

Back at the Darracuq, a crowd had begun to gather. The chauffeur, a sunny-faced young fellow, tipped his cap, smiled and cranked the monster into gas-fumed, heaving action. Amid a grinding of gears we were off for my house for me to change clothes, grab a gun and some hulls, and fetch pointer Tom Cotton and little setter Lucy from the kennel. That trio—Tom, Lucy and Leo—was notoriously rough on bobwhites. Oddly, the heaving Darracuq proved just another baggage-car or dog-wagon to Lucy and Tom, and into its spacious front cushions with me and Jacques they hopped. That left one of the sedan's back-drop tonneau seats for Billy and Leo.

I had my fingers crossed for what might happen when setter Leo arrived on the scene and spied Tom Cotton in seemingly higher estate than himself. A dog fight amid a mass of fat men wouldn't be so good. But Billy had been ahead of me on that one and had Leo well collared and gripped. Aside from an instantaneous salvo of recriminative snarls, promptly whacked down, order was maintained.

The two visitors scrouged with frightened amazement. Conversation languished. Harry Jamerson did his jovial best to make it a ball-game by explaining that the hunt was being staged to get birds enough for a dinner party and some for his two guests to carry home to Philadelphia. That would mean quite some birds. There were only county game laws in those times, which meant practically none at all, unless some hapless non-resident got caught off first base as legitimate prey for a shake-down in some hamlet J.P.'s court. Quail sales flourished, and country folks, white and black, had "bird-routes" in the cities, along with their chickens, eggs and melons. Restaurants served quail openly. And afield it was just a case of how many bobs one's shooting coat would hold if you could hit 'em.

It struck Billy and me at about the same instant that neither of us had the faintest idea where the hunt was headed; ours were usually quite a piece from the city and via train. We shot everywhere, but no place in particular, territory was that handy and open in three adjoining states. We discussed the happenstance covertly and whispered to Jacques to just keep her headed out the turnpike's rutty gravel. We decided to keep going until a likely-looking vista of quail country opened up, and then dismount and go to it.

Our progress along the Pigeon Roost Road (so named because in times past the myriads of passenger pigeons broke down trees at roosting hours) was a succession of near-runaways by mule teams hauling cotton and as yet unbroken to the impending terrorism of automotive progress. We eyed the rapidly passing coun-

] 269 [

tryside narrowly. Finally, in front of a dilapidated blacksmith shop at a dirt-road corner, we had Jacques bring the Darracuq to a panting halt. Southward opened a vast expanse of as fair and trustworthy-looking quail country as one would want to see. Billy and I exchanged glances, and in a few moments I was standing beside the glowing forge and talking to the smith, a leathery-looking old Joe with a cheek-cud of prodigious bulge.

"Good mawnin', suh, any quails aroun' heah?"

The smith beat a white-hot horseshoe vigorously, sluiced a stream of ham-gravy across infiltrating sunbeams and allowed that there was "more 'n aplenty of 'em mos' anywhurs out yonder way." He tonged the horseshoe into a tub of hissing water and turned on me.

"You wanta see a real bird dawg work, mister? Here, Belle! Here, Belle!"

A whippet-like, lemon-and-white pointer bitch darted through the smithy's rear door and fawned with obvious affection about her master's leather-aproned thighs.

"Is she broke?"

"B-r-o-k-e?"

"Yes, is she steady—will she point, back and retrieve?"

The smith flung down his hammer and cried out that he'd be dod-burned if Belle wouldn't find "mo' birds than any or all of the combined dogs in our party, and handle 'em better, too." I said the only way that could be proved would be for him to bring his bitch and go shooting with our crowd—if he could show us plenty of game. An idea was taking shape in my mind; so I added that if he figured his time would be worth five bucks for a few hours, we'd close the deal on that basis.

The smith, who had by now introduced himself as Mr. Fenley, replied that it would be a deal if we had plenty of shells, because he was plum out of hulls. An escapist pro tem, he was soon back with a rusty-looking hammer double and the bitch, Belle, at heel. Billy Joyner eyed us furtively. Mr. Fenley suggested that the Darracuq be driven into a grove down the side road. When it exploded into life, he was steady to shot, but shook like a highstrung dog too close on his game.

The hunt was broken up into two parties—Mr. Fenley taking

one of the Buddhas and Harry Jamerson behind Belle and Lucy, while Billy and I towed the other hefty with Leo and Tom out ahead. Billy and I had agreed that neither of the big boys would last the hunt's duration; so it was planned to go opposite ways and chart the courses toward reunion at the top of a forested eminence half a mile south. We could then check on how matters went and, if necessary, reorganize the affair.

Mr. Fenley, Harry Jamerson and Mr. A disappeared into birdy-looking country eastward, with the two bitches ranging fairly wide and most industriously. I liked the way Belle moved, too. We let them get out of sight and then swung westward, with Tom and Leo circling to left and right into gradually rising country. It didn't take five minutes for Billy and me to realize that Mr. B didn't know what the hunt was all about. He went to his knees in one shallow gully, and we had to ram clay from his gun muzzles. Billy whispered to me that it wouldn't be long before the guest threw in the towel.

Up ahead a piece, along a shrubbed watercourse, Tom suddenly snagged a bevy out feeding in a low-grassed cove. I knew they were, because Tom whirled and dropped, and he only did that when nose-realization warned him of a tight squeeze. Leo strode in and froze on sight. Those two bullies might fight when off watch, but when on duty every instant was in common cause. They played for the team.

We herded Mr. B in the center shooting position, warned him to keep his gun up and not kill a dog, and to stay level with us on the flush. It was a ball-park rise. Up zoomed a lustrous scatteration of bobs. Billy accounted for a brace; I bowled over a quarterer and then tagged a second swinging still farther around my end. One glance told me that Mr. B hadn't hit the side of a house; so I had Tom fetch me the wide bird first and made out that I thought it was all that fell.

"You got one, didn't you?" I queried. "I thought I saw one fall out yonder way."

Billy chimed in with—"You must have gotten a bird—four went down."

When Leo, well directed, picked up my first dead bird, I

pitched it to Mr. B, who received it with calm assurance. He hadn't touched a feather.

Billy was wise, and it was decided that if Mr. B lasted we would continue to see that he got his share from the rises, but at singles he would have to take the backwash. And he took aplenty. After climbing down and up through several deep and wide washes, Mr. B was about out on his feet. By the time we rejoined Harry Jamerson we had ten birds and our fat boy had bellows to amend. We called in Leo and Tom and awaited developments.

Reunion on the ridge established the fact that our two fat guests, without quite a rest, were just about washed up. It was a gorgeous day for bird-finding: underfoot frost-wet and the day a shade overcast. Harry Jamerson's squad had had up three bevies and accounted for five bobs, all but one of which had fallen to Mr. Fenley's gun. But they had done considerable firing, and Mr. Fenley told me aside that they should have had a dozen sacked. It was just about 10:30 A.M.

Harry Jamerson drew me aside and confided that it would make Messrs. A and B much happier if they rested there awhile and then went on with Mr. Fenley and himself while Billy and I set forth to really accumulate some quail for the dinner party and take-home birds. So while the puffing guests sprawled amid the leaves and sedge Mr. Fenley and Harry Jamerson collared Belle and Lucy. Billy and I cast Tom and Leo southwest. Mr. Fenley pointed out a course of magnificent territory hazing far ahead. The next several hours were to reveal as good virgin bobwhite lands as I've ever seen.

Within three hundred yards Billy and I were in action. It was new country to men and dogs; bevy ranges were totally unknown. What we really did was to walk the higher terrains, spot likely areas and leave the rest to Leo and Tom. By noon our shooting coats had begun to sag a trifle. We stopped for a blow and called in the dogs. We had no snacks, nor the faintest idea of a long trek hunting up the automobile for a whack at those luncheon hampers. Then we sighted a comfortable-looking cabin on a far hillside and made for it. With its roof of overgrown mossy shingles and bricked-up well, it looked comfortable and clean.

The colored goodman (incidentally, he owned the two hundred

acres across which we had been gunning) and his wife were just sitting down to a midday repast of cold hog-jowl, turnip greens, johnny-cake, sweet-potato pie and coffee. There was enough grub on that table to feed a dozen folks; so Billy and I moved in on the full worth of the two dollars we handed our host and hostess. They really enjoyed watching us work on that chuck.

During the next ten years Eben and Ellen Dorsey's cabin became a sort of second home to Billy and me. They were fine, helpful, well-remembered Christian friends. After a brief siesta in front of Eben's hearth, we hit the trail again, with Tom and Leo recharged with johnny-cake and potlicker. Then advised a circular route that would get us back to the Darracuq by four o'clock.

Our dogs found a confusing number of bevies, the singles from one rise often being mistaken as such, only to have another bunch leap from the embrowned coverts. About three-thirty, trudging over a rise, Billy suggested a count-up. We could see a church spire in the village beyond Mr. Fenley's smithy, and realized that we were getting on toward the car.

Billy had thirty-one bobs, and my count was an even thirty. We had turned in the morning's shoot before separating from Harry Jamerson. Nor could we remember a single bevy that had been overgunned; and there were remembered misses. Tom and Leo, untiring searchers, came down on a beautiful cluster of birds within two furlongs of the red automobile. But, much to the amazement of our dogs, we simply flushed and continued on our way.

At the Darracuq the two Buddhas slept with volcanic rumblings. Curled in the front seat, Harry Jamerson echoed their snores. Wrapped in a rug, Jacques was dead to the world under an oak. Billy and I sought out Mr. Fenley, again mighty at his forge. While mashing white-hot horseshoes flat as frog's feet, he opined that "them are fine gent'men, but they couldn't hit nuthin' an' warn't in no shape to hunt birds nohow."

Mr. Fenley further testified that before he started home for lunch at his neat cottage behind his shop they had given him a couple of glasses of fizzy, funny-tasting stuff they called champagne. Fortified by a third glass, he had taken a fourth, and after an interval during which he was unable to accurately account for his whereabouts he came to, beating dents in his anvil. We gave Mr. Fenley his five dollars and said we'd be back in a few days and might want to buy Belle if he was in a mood to part with her. He promised to think it over, but intimated that a bitch of her caliber would cost us a lot of money. She had, he confided, three pups that gave promise of bettering their dam afield.

When Billy and I were unloaded at my home (he was to spend the night with us), the two visitors were still fast asleep, but Harry Jamerson thanked us heartily for a happy day and a heavy sack. Having burred and eyed our dogs and fed them heartily, we dined lightly ourselves, tubbed and retired. We decided that the two Buddhas were complete busts as hunters and just a shade on the snooty side. The least they could have done was to save us a bottle of that champagne.

I was buried under a half week's pile-up of mail next morning when Barney summoned me to Dad's office. And there, immaculately groomed and even more massive, sat the two Buddhas and Harry Jamerson. There were a lot of maps and blueprints scattered over my parent's great glass-topped desk. The Buddhas beamed and Harry Jamerson began a handsome description of Billy's and my efforts of yesterday in their behalf.

"Nash," said Harry, "our two bird-shooting friends here are members of our cottonseed-oil industry, and we are planning a considerable expansion to our local mills. The work is starting immediately—in fact, we've called you in to take charge of the builders' risks and place the entire line through your office later. We figure that you can shoot as straight in our interests as you and Billy did yesterday. The business will run over a million for a starter—how about it?"

Ever since that moment I've known how a bird dog feels that is being steadied to wing and shot. But I made it.

The next night, at a box-party, Harry Jamerson, whose lovely daughter I was squiring, took me aside. "I wonder if, as a special favor, you and Billy can get me a couple dozen birds apiece for Messrs. A and B. They are going to be here longer than anticipated, and I'm about out of quail now—they can eat four or five apiece at every meal."

I said I didn't see how Billy and I could possibly have a go at it until day after tomorrow.

"I'll have that big red car and Jacques to take you out and fetch you home. Don't worry about any lunch. You lads didn't get a break on that wine the other day."

Our household and considerable of the neighborhood turned out to see Billy and me take off. Nowadays a jet-plane attracts less attention.

Mr. Fenley was welding a wheel-rim when we invaded his shop and told him we'd come to try out Belle and that if he thought the pups would be worth looking over for an hour or so we'd leave Tom and Leo and Lucy with Jacques in the car and give the bitch and her rookies a onceover near by. I piloted two of the derbies while Billy and Mr. Fenley used Belle and the other pup. My brace found and handled two bevies with exceptional form. Billy reported that Belle was a corking Lucy all over again, and the pup (a gyp) almost too wide to hunt afoot but holding her game tight and looking like a million meanwhile. Then Billy and I had Jacques drive us a mile or so down the dirt road leading not too far east of Eben Dorsey's cabin and let us out for the serious business of accumulating Harry Jamerson's take-home birds.

By three o'clock, counting the birds we had bagged over Belle and the pups, we had fifty all told, and considered that ample. At the Darracuq, Jacques set out stuffed eggs, turkey sandwiches and an ice-carrier heavy with champagne.

Jacques was sent for Mr. Fenley. After three glasses of very sec Cliquot he decided to part with Belle, the wide-roaming dog pup and his brother, but he'd keep the pert bitch youngster. He could, he said, kill over her all the birds he needed to eat. After a fourth glass or so he became slightly involved while attempting to outline their pedigrees. Jacques, a pretty sunny chap at that, became a bit solicitous that we might perhaps be overdue in the city.

So Billy put the bee on Mr. Fenley—"How much for Belle and the two pups?" Little did we suspect that we were upon the verge of a beautiful friendship that endured through ten years of happy gunning.

Mr. Fenley, lost in abysmal cogitation as he stroked his handlebar mustache, was obviously thinking in astral figures. But, passably oiled with Cliquot and on the verge of a million dollars in insurance headlighting our somewhat unstable finances, what cared we? Then it came. "Boys," said Mr. Fenley, "that bitch oughta be wuth ev'y dime o' twenty-five dollars, an' them two pups'll make good 'uns. How about fifty bucks for them three?"

Billy and I sat stunned. From his look, Jacques, probably figuring the amount in his native francs, was duly impressed.

"Mr. Fenley," I came back firmly, "I positively will not give any such sum as fifty dollars for Belle and two pups."

The old fellow sagged and the suspicion of tears welled into his gander-green eyes. He was crushed by the collapse of his negotiations.

"No, sir," I added, fumbling for my billfold, which, fortunately, held a fair share of my immediate worldly wealth, "I won't give you fifty dollars. Here are seventy-five, and Mr. Joyner here is a top eye-witness to the trade."

Yes, folks, when passing once familiar quail terrains amid which lay the homes and haunts of dear old friends, white and black; and across which race ghostly but beloved bird dog shapes; small wonder that the familiar old refrain about "carry me back" sings from one's heart into life's sundown. I sped past the area recently in a sleek, streamlined limousine that would make the old Darracuq look and move like a mud-turtle, and paused for a check-up on the landscape.

Where Mr. Fenley's lean-to resounded through murk and semi-darkness of hammer-upon-anvil, stands a glistening, modernistic gas-and-service station. Thereabouts is a bustling town. The Fenley family moved there to join a son who wandered west and struck it oil-rich, thank God. Their cottage site is a business block. Many's the night Billy Joyner and I lodged in feather-bed comfort beneath the Fenley roof-tree and heard lulling rain upon its hand-drawn cypress shingles.

A four-lane highway carrying a region's heaviest traffic of wreck-and-ruin mocks the narrow, rutty gravel thread along which Jacques steered the red Darracuq with the same expression on his face of a worried ship's captain clutching his helm amid towering seas. That dirt road southward down which Jacques drove Billy and me to unfurl new bird territory beyond good

Eben Dorsey's land, is now black-top lined with lovely homes and a ranch-house High School on the very eminence up which the tiring Buddhas and Harry Jamerson toiled behind Belle and Lucy. Gaping ditches follow water courses along which Tom Cotton and Leo pointed many a bevy. Up the highway apiece and near where we used to hit the gravel of an evening, is an expansive and expensive Motel. For three bucks you can get a towering T-bone steak but you could not buy a bobwhite for what we paid for Belle and two of her pups.

You might, at that, but conversation and game laws have come to those lands, too late almost. God forbid. All of which you tell yourself with a sigh is irrevocable and immutable. There may be a few pet quail bevies on smallish, closely pastured and manicured farms. But there'll be far more posted signs than birds. If you choose to rate Billy and me as adolescent wildlife delinquents who drove buggies and rode trains and hoofed it endless miles afield long before hordes (with a perfect right to do so) ravaged the nation's game fields as did the Remii, have it your way and make the most of it. Rend us as ye may, but leave us at least, our memories. The last of a golden hoard.

There were six bird dogs in the Darracuq that late, graying November afternoon as it roared along a gloamed turnpike. What a Cinderella start in life for Belle and her two derbies! And they held the pace through long and well-sustained careers afield, too. But the picture that still holds me spellbound is that of the gallant Mr. Fenley when we parted after that magnificent sale he'd made. Arm aloft in stiff salute, he cheered the great Darracuq's carbon-fumed, roaring departure. Then he turned and, with an unopened quart of Cliquot under his other arm, he turned and strutted a slightly weaving way up the shadowed turnpike toward his smithy.

MOLLIE

Paul Hyde Bonner

The late Paul Hyde Bonner's works included several novels and two anthologies of sporting tales of special interest to outdoorsmen, The Glorious Mornings *and* Aged in the Woods. *They were originally published by Scribners, then were re-issued by the Abercrombie & Fitch Library. A Harvard graduate in the class of 1915, Bonner did not begin writing until the thirties, trying his hand at plays first, then magazine articles. After the interruption of World War II, he wrote the bestselling novel* SPQR, *then went on to do other novels and outdoor-orientated pieces in major magazines, including* The New Yorker. *He spent his later years living and writing in South Carolina, with summers in the Rockies, Canada or the British Isles. Bonner's stories are characterized by zest, good humor and the skills displayed by the participants. All of his pieces are extremely readable, but this tale of a mule that wanted to be a bird dog is one of my favorites. It appeared originally in* The Glorious Mornings.

IT WAS NOT until the season had closed on March fifteenth that Purvey began to realize the change that had come over Mollie. The very first day out with the plow he had noticed that she was not pulling her weight. It was on the twenty-acre piece that he had figured on switching from corn to tobacco because it lay in low ground along the branch where there was always good drainage and the soil was a mixture of rich, dark loam and sand. He could tell at once by the way her traces sagged and he had to lean on the right handle to keep the share cutting straight. He had slapped her with the reins for three lengths of the field, then he had cut a nice limber sucker from a sweetgum in the woody copse that followed the course of the branch and given her a good smart lick with it every time her traces were not as taut as Mike's.

When he had bought Mike and Mollie from a dealer up at Andrews three years before, his neighbors had shaken their heads and clucked their tongues. Pretty looking, yes, they had said down at the store, but too small, too neat and fancy for mules that have to be plowing and hauling and doing a day's work. Purvey had not argued. He had known what he was doing. That pair was just what he had been looking for—strong enough to work his land, which was so full of sand it turned soft and easy, and small enough so that the gentleman whose quail leases he looked after could mount into the saddle without him having to give them a leg up. He used to have horses for the gentlemen, horses he rented for the season, but they never worked out right. There would always be one that was skittish and shied at every shoat, or one that was so lazy on its feet that it stumbled into every stump hole. And the gentlemen were always complaining and saying, Purvey, why can't you get us some decent nags to ride? Why, hell, mules would be better than these bucking bronchos.

That had given him the idea, and it had worked out just fine. He had paid Mr. Fletcher, the dealer, two hundred and forty dollars for the pair, which was a bargain because nobody wanted mules that size even though they were perfectly matched, sound as two new-minted dollars, and only four years old. Mr. Jessup had been the first of the gentlemen to shoot that season. He had come down in early December and brought a friend with him. When he had gotten out of the car at the little church for colored folks where they always met to shoot the Rutledge property, he had slapped Purvey on the back and let out a whoop like a schoolboy. That's the slickest pair of mules I ever laid my eyes on, he had said, patting Mollie's shining neck. Don't ever let the Duke of Alba see that pair. He'd give a thousand dollars for them.

Purvey had no idea who the Duke of Alba was, nor why he would fancy mules enough to pay big money for them, but he was pleased by the reception. He had had to admit to Bessie, his wife, when he had ridden off that morning, he on his little gray mare, leading Mollie and Mike, that they looked as pretty as anything in the circus. He had curried and brushed them until their smooth mahogany coats shone like patent leather. Nor had Mr. Jessup's enthusiasm waned after a day in the saddle. They had turned out to be quick, careful walkers who cutely dodged every stump hole and delicately picked their feet over fallen logs. When the dogs had a point, there was no need to tie them up or carry the reins for Purvey to hold. Just dismount and leave them and they would stand there, staunch and immobile.

When, later on in the season, Mr. Dodge and Mr. Weatherby,

the two other members of the syndicate, came down for their shooting, they were prepared to admire, for Mr. Jessup had written them glowing accounts of Mollie and Mike. And it had gone on like that for two seasons, everybody happy about the mules and complaints reduced to the behavior of the dogs, which could not be blamed on Purvey as the gentlemen supplied their own and all he had to do was feed and kennel them from Thanksgiving to March 15th. Of course Purvey also handled them in the field. He was good with dogs, talking to them mostly and never beating them real hard when they jumped a covey. Just a light whack or two on their hind quarters and a real sharp scolding while they lay in the grass and cringed. Dogs knew when they had done wrong, just as well as people, and it often wasn't their fault. Coming down fast on the lea of a covey, they sometimes wouldn't get the scent until they were right on one of the outlying birds, and when he flushed the whole covey was sure to follow.

There were only two out of the six that were what you would call real downright reliable bird dogs. They were Brownie, a small, rangy pointer who was three-quarters covered with liver-colored spots that made it difficult to keep an eye on him in the high broomsedge, and Tess, a big white setter bitch with a black patch over one eye that made her look like Lew Douglas or the Hathaway shirt man. The others were temperamental, sometimes flashy, sometimes messing everything up.

Of course all three of the gentlemen wanted to hunt Tess and Brownie every day. But Purvey was stubborn on that point. Even though it was their leases and their dogs, as long as he was guide and handler all six dogs had to take their half-days in rotation, so they wouldn't get tuckered out and lame and not be able to get through the season. But no matter how often he explained this to them in his soft voice, they would always say to Bessie when they stopped by at the farm to pick up the pair for the morning, what's the matter, Mrs. Gourdine? Why aren't we taking Brownie and Tess? Because Purvey says it's to be Jack and Sunset, Bessie would tell them, because Brownie and Tess was out yesterday and they ain't due to go hunting again until after tomorrow. They grumbled a bit, but they knew that Purvey was right and they respected him for it.

The business with Mollie was all the fault of Mr. Christie. He was the new member who had taken Mr. Weatherby's place in the syndicate when Weatherby had had to give up quail shooting because of a stroke. He had come down for the first time in the early part of February, after Mr. Jessup and Mr. Dodge had had their quota of days in the field and had gone back to Cleveland where they both were something big in the steel industry. This Christie wasn't a Clevelander. He was a New York lawyer, who, according to what he said, handled some legal matter for Jessup and Dodge. He brought his wife down with him, a well-set-up blonde woman he called Gertrude who could ride and shoot as well as any man Purvey had ever guided. They put up at a motel near Georgetown and motored over every day for the two weeks they were down, that is, every day but Sundays.

Purvey took a fancy to the Christies from the start. There was no fuss and feathers about them the way there is about some of the Northerners who come to hunt quail in the Low Country of South Carolina during the winters. They were full of beans and fun, liked to horse around and say silly things, kidding and sassing each other and Purvey. And they were both real smart with a gun—quick and deadly. They used double-barrelled sixteens which they said they had had made to measure in England. With those four barrels they could kill more birds in a day than Jessup and Dodge with their automatics could kill in a week. Maybe there was something to that made-to-measure business. More times than not there were four birds to pick up after a covey rise.

It was because he liked Christie that Purvey felt so mean about Mollie. For it was Mr. Christie who had ruined her, made a trollop out of a good steady mule. If he hadn't given her to Christie on that very first day, all might have been well. He had given Mike to Mrs. Christie because Mike's saddle holster was newer and nicer looking. Well, that was the big mistake. He had not known then that Christie was one of those city fellows who just can't help spoiling animals. Anything with four legs made him go soft. He just couldn't bring himself to cross that mule on one little thing. If Mollie wanted to go around a tree to the right, he let her go to the right. If Mollie wanted to stop near a pond and eat cane, Mollie stopped and ate cane. If Mollie looked longingly at a streamer of Florida moss that was hanging out of her reach, Mr. Christie would reach it for her and lean over in the saddle so that she could take it in her dainty, gunmetal lips. He brought a pocketful of sugar every day to feed her, and gave her half his lunch. No Duke of Alba was ever more stuck on a mule than Mr. Christie was on Mollie. It got to be so that Mrs. Christie would look disgusted and say, why Dan, anyone would think you were in love with that mule, and Christie would whoop and shout, love her? I adore her. Don't I, my sweet little Mollie?

By the time March first had come around and the Christies had said good-bye and Christie had kissed Mollie on the nose, she was the most ornery, stuck-up mule in Williamsburg County. She wouldn't work. She wouldn't eat unless there was some cane in the hay, and she treated Mike like she'd never been in harness with him. Let him swing his nose over towards her and her ears would go back and one of those little black hooves on her back feet would flash out so fast you couldn't follow it with your eye.

"Look, Bessie," Purvey Gourdine said to his wife one evening in late April when the tobacco was all set out and he was resting up to plant the cotton. "There ain't nothin' to it, I jes got to get rid of Mollie. She's ruint, plum ruint. She won't work. She's ornery. Kicks Mike or any other animal gets near her. It's all right havin' a mule that the gentlemen likes to ride huntin', but I didn't buy that pair jes for saddle. From March to November they got to do their share of the work around the farm. I ain't in no position like Jake Ferrier over to the Longleaf Plantation who ain't got nothin' to do the year round but plantin' lespedeza and shootin' hawks when he ain't takin' the gentlemen out huntin'. I ain't paid on that basis. I got my farm to run if you and me and the kids ain't goin' to starve. Jake's got horses in the barn that never carries nothin' but a saddle, but my mules has got to work when there's work to be done."

"Mebbe you could trade her with Mr. Fletcher for another the same size," Bessie suggested as she cut a piece of denim from a pair of old overalls which was going to patch another, less old pair.

"Yeah, well mebbe I could," Purvey said, with doubt in his voice.

"Mollie's a right pretty lookin' mule," Bessie commented, having noted her husband's hesitancy.

"But she ain't got a good reputation," Purvey said.

Bessie Gourdine looked up from her sewing and smiled at Purvey. "I do believe you're carryin' on like Mr. Christie, talkin' about Mollie havin' a reputation jest as if she were some slut of a girl."

"Things like that gets around," Purvey said, moodily.

"Shucks, Purvey," Bessie said impatiently, "who-all knows about Mollie not workin' right except you and me and our kids and old Jim?"

"They're laughin' about it down to the store," Purvey said sorrowfully. "I heerd 'em. They was sayin' how Mr. Christie has ruint her for work."

"Tst, tst," Bessie clucked. "You reckon the story's got as far as Andrews?"

"I reckon it has. Seems like it's some kind of big joke on me. Mr. Fletcher's likely to be laughin' fit to burst his collar."

There was a long silence while Purvey sucked on his pipe and Bessie sewed on the patch.

"Mebbe Jake Ferrier might use her over to Longleaf Plantation," Bessie said finally.

"I done speak to him a'ready. He says his gentlemen ain't ridin' no mules."

"My, oh my!" Bessie murmured and sighed.

That summer seemed the longest that Purvey Gourdine could remember. Though his son Harry, a strapping boy of eighteen, and old Jim, the colored hand, were willing, they could be of little help except to work Mike alone or run the pick-up truck. Mollie would not work for them at all, and if neither of them came near her, she just kept turning her rear artillery in their direction. Purvey was the only one who could get her to move, and to do that he had to keep after her every minute with a stout, limber switch. You might have thought she would come out of it, forget about Mr. Christie and his sugar and his patting, but not Mollie. She had a long memory and she knew well that, come the first frost of November, she'd have that saddle on again and would be lazing her way across the savannahs, through the longleaf saplings, snipping dainty bits here and there when the fancy took her, and smelling the sweet scent of warm dead partridge in her saddle bag. Those were the days she waited for in her pettish, ornery, feminine way.

Sure enough, the day Purvey and his son came back from Monks Corner with the six crates of bird dogs in the pick-up and set them loose in the kennels, Mollie trotted across the small field where she and Mike and the gray mare were pastured with her big ears up and forward like twin bayonets. She stuck her head over the wire fence and started a song that was half bray and half whinny. From that moment she was a redeemed animal, sweet and gentle as a kitten. Anyone, Harry or old Jim, could walk up to her in the field and toss a halter over her head. And she took to nuzzling Mike again, something she hadn't done since March. But Purvey was not fooled. He knew that the change of heart would only last as long as the bird season, that next spring she would be worse than ever.

When Mr. Dodge and Mr. Jessup came down together in early December, Purvey could hardly wait to tell them his sad tale. They met at the Simons farm on the first day. Because Purvey knew that there were at least ten coveys using there, he started them off with Brownie and Tess. The day was bright and sunny, with a scattering of fleecy clouds blowing high from the west, and the night dew had been heavy enough to leave a good scent. Everything was perfect for a good day of sport except the state of Purvey's mind.

As they rode out through the back gate of the farm into a broad savannah, Purvey turned in his saddle and spoke to Mr. Jessup who was behind him on Mollie. "That mule you're ridin' like to ruin my summer," he said with feeling.

Mr. Jessup chuckled. "Mollie? Why, what's she been up to?"

"She won't do a lick of work no more, and she's got so ornery she'll kick anyone gets in range of her."

"She was as gentle as a lamb when I mounted her," Mr. Jessup said, patting Mollie's neck reassuringly.

"Sure, she's all right now, now that the huntin' season's on. She likes you gentlemen right fine, and following the dogs suits her.

But she's got it into her mind she's too good to pull a wagon or a plow."

Mr. Jessup roared with laughter and turned in his saddle to Mr. Dodge who was following on Mike. "Did you hear that, Jerry?" he said. "Purvey says that Mollie has delusions of grandeur. She only likes to go shooting with us. Won't work anymore."

"I always said that was a damn smart mule," Mr. Dodge said, and they both laughed loud and long.

"Next year she'll be wanting to spend the summer at Newport," Mr. Jessup said, wiping the tears from his eyes.

Purvey was disturbed. No one wanted to take his problem seriously. It was just a big joke, and he was the butt of it. "With me it ain't so funny as it sounds, Mr. Jessup," he said earnestly. "I've got me a farm to run. I can't afford to feed no mule as thinks she's too good to work. If she cuts up next spring the way she did last, I'm goin' to find me another mule."

Mollie stopped to pluck a bunch of laurel leaves. Mr. Jessup jerked her head up and kicked her with his heels, but she did not move until the branch was secure in her mouth. "Come on, Mollie," Mr. Jessup commanded, "no feminine temperament. You're out hunting now."

Purvey shook his head. "You see what I mean, Mr. Jessup."

But they never really did believe the story of her wickedness. How could they, when she was always so docile, so clever on her feet, so stanch when the guns were firing and she was left alone? They put it down to Purvey's natural pessimism, the pessimism of a man who spends his life in a struggle with Nature. It delighted them that Mollie had the instincts of a lady and preferred the sporting life to the drudgery of the farm. It was a story they would tell and retell back home on Shaker Heights.

Purvey's gloom persisted in spite of fine days with many coveys found. The gentlemen were happy even though they fired four shells for every bird killed. It was the pines against the blue and the dogs racing back and forth in the wind-billowed broomsedge that thrilled them as much as the shot fired. But poor Purvey knew that in another two weeks Mr. and Mrs. Christie would arrive and that would be the end of any chance to retrieve Mollie from her path of glory.

How right he was! The morning the Christies arrived, as they stepped out of their station wagon at the colored church, Mollie, who was tethered to the fence under the chinaberry tree, lifted her head, her ears forward, and gave forth with her combination bray-whinny.

"Mollie, sweet Mollie!" Mr. Christie called, and forgetting his wife and the yelping dogs in the back of the car, rushed across the yard and flung his arms around Mollie's neck. The mule pushed at his pocket with her nose. "Oh, it's sugar you want, my Mollie-O." He pulled out a lump and she picked it daintily from his palm. "What a mule! What a memory! Did you see that, Gertrude? Did you hear her call to me? She knew me the minute I stepped out of the car. Oh, Mollie, if you could only talk." Mollie let out a low snort. "By God, Purvey, she understands me. She tried to answer."

Purvey Gourdine, who was slipping the guns into the saddle holsters, grunted. "I reckon she knows what you're sayin' aw right. That's the trouble with that mule, she knows more'n is good for her."

Mrs. Christie laughed. "Now don't tell me she gossips, Purvey."

Purvey walked over to the station wagon, opened the rear window and let the dogs out. They were Flotsam and Blitz, a pair of fast, unreliable pointers. He was saving Brownie and Tess for the next day when they would be shooting the paper company lease where there were at least twelve coveys using. Purvey watched the dogs race around the church yard. He was worried. He liked the Christies. They were nice, kindly folk, and they shot like masters. Yet they, that is, he, was the cause of all the trouble. He hated to disappoint him after that greeting with Mollie, but it was no use, he had to tell him sooner or later, and it might as well be now.

"Ma'am," he said to Mrs. Christie, "that mule is doin' the last bit of huntin' she's ever goin' to do on my property. She's so spoilt she won't do a lick of work outside of ridin' gentlemen after birds. When the season's over, I'm gettin' rid of her. I jes can't afford to own a mule that won't do her share."

"What's that? What's that?" Christie asked in astonishment. "You're going to get rid of Mollie?"

"Yes, sir, Mr. Christie," Purvey said firmly. "She's gettin' too smart for her own good."

"Now listen, Purvey," Christie said genially. "Let's not talk about this now. Gertrude and I have come down for a pleasant two weeks of sport and we don't want any sorrows hanging over it. Just give Mollie another chance for the moment. Let me talk to her. Then if she doesn't behave, you can have a second look at the problem."

"Jest as you say, Mr. Christie," Purvey said skeptically. "Only I'm warnin' you, and—" he nodded toward Mollie—"her too, that she's got to pull that plow and keep her hind feet on the ground or else."

As usual Flotsam and Blitz ranged so wide that they were out of sight half of the time. Purvey did not worry so much about Blitz, who he knew would hold stanch if he did find a covey, which was not too often as he preferred to range the cotton fields and corn stubble where quail are seldom found. It was Flotsam he was not sure of. He had a suspicion that this dog liked to get out of sight for the express purpose of flushing coveys. More than once he had seen birds flying from a direction where Flotsam had been heading. He told the Christies to keep an eye on Blitz while he trotted off to see what Flotsam was up to.

Christie and his wife had ridden on a hundred yards or so, whistling for Blitz whom they could see far off on the right, racing across a plowed field as if he were a sweepstake greyhound, when Mollie lifted her head, shot her ears forward, and gave a little rattling snort with her nostrils.

"She's worried about Purvey and the gray mare leaving us," Gertrude Christie said.

Christie patted Mollie's neck. "Never mind, old girl," he said, "they'll be back in a minute."

Mollie stopped, her head still high, her nostrils still fluttering. Christie paid no attention. He was intent on getting Blitz out of the plow and back to the feed patch of lespedeza which was just ahead. He put the whistle betwen his lips again and blew two long, sharp blasts. Blitz must have heeded finally, for they could see him turn sharply, bound the low hedge that bordered the plow, and come racing towards them.

"Come on, Mollie," Christie said, giving her a gentle tap with his heels.

Gertrude Christie reined in Mike and turned in her saddle. "What's got into Mollie?" she asked. "What's she looking at?"

"I can't imagine," her husband replied. "She seems to be watching Blitz."

When Blitz was about fifty yards from them, bowling along, he suddenly jammed on his brakes and froze. The point was a solid one. Every muscle of the dog was petrified into the final attitude of stopping, his front feet thrust forward, his head down, his tail as rigid as a bent stick.

"Down we get," Christie said to his wife, excited. "This is it. No stink bird this time."

They both slid out of the saddles, pulled the guns out of the holsters and loaded.

"I think we had better lead the mules around behind Blitz so they won't be facing us when the birds get up," Mrs. Christie said.

Christie pulled on Mollie's bridle. "Come, girl," he urged. But she did not move. Her head was still high, her ears still forward. She was as frozen as Blitz. Christie gave the bridle a yank. "Come on! What are you frightend of?" It was useless. He might as well have tried to move a bronze statue. "She's not going to move," he said to his wife.

"Well, leave her, then," Gertrude Christie said impatiently. "If she gets a pellet in her hide, it's her own stubborn fault. I'm beginning to see what Purvey was talking about."

The Christies took a wide circle and came up behind Blitz, who had never moved a muscle. Christie came well forward on the left side of the dog in the hope of making the birds break away from the direction of the mules. When a lone cock quail rose at Gertrude's feet, she nailed it. Then the whole covey exploded and Gertrude dropped another, while Christie missed with his first shot and killed one with his left barrel. They both stood where they had fired, intently watching to mark where the birds would settle.

Christie tried to call in Blitz to retrieve the dead birds, but he found it hopeless. The over-excited dog was racing in circles like a chicken with its head cut off. So he and Gertrude did their own picking up, which was not too difficult on the sparse ground.

Mollie was eating grass when Christie came up to her, carrying the three dead birds. "You know, Gertrude," he said, "I wonder if Mollie was pointing that covey."

"Don't be an idiot," Mrs. Christie said crossly.

Christie dangled the birds in front of Mollie. She lifted her head and sniffed them deeply, then ruffled their feathers with her prehensile lips. "Did you smell 'em, Mollie?" he asked. "Did you get that point? Was Blitz only backing you up?"

Purvey came riding up with Flotsam running behind him. "I seen where some of your birds lit," he said. "I got 'em marked good. How many did you get?"

"The little lady got two, but I muffed my right barrel. Too excited," Christie said, and mounted into the saddle. "Okay, let's go. I want to get that bird I missed."

They rode over to a spot where the pines grew closer together, Purvey keeping the dogs in at heel. Finally Purvey halted and told them to dismount. "They're right in there by them saplin's," he said, pointing to a cluster of young longleaf pines that looked like green brooms up-ended. Purvey dismounted too, walking between them, talking to the dogs, cautioning them to take it easy and hunt close. Christie and his wife went forward cautiously, guns ready, as the dogs worked back and forth in front of them, noses to the ground. Flotsam was the first to get a point and Christie took it. A single bird rose up, curled, and flew back over their heads. Christie wheeled and killed it high and far out. He was surprised to see that it dropped near Mollie. Then he realized that she had moved, that she had left Mike and the grey mare and had wandered fifty yards to the right. That was unlike her. Never before had she budged from the spot where he had left her. He walked over to pick up the dead bird and Blitz followed him.

He was about to scold Mollie when he saw that she had again assumed that rigid, watching posture, with her head high and her ears forward. Blitz galloped up beside her and froze to a point. Christie turned to Purvey and his wife. "Look at that!" he called excitedly. "Mollie's pointing a single and Blitz is backing her up again."

"More'n like she smells a snake," Purvey said.

"Do be careful," Gertrude warned.

"Blitz he's pointin' your dead birds," Purvey said.

"No, he isn't," Christie said, walking forward. "That bird of mine is right here." He stooped down and picked it up. "Blitz ran right over it." Stuffing the bird quickly into his pocket, he moved forward cautiously, edging between Mollie and Blitz, his eyes on the ground, fearing it might be a snake after all.

When the quail flushed, Christie took his time and killed it neatly, then he turned and came up to Mollie whose ears were drooping mulewise now. He put his cheek on her soft nose. "Mollie, my lass, you're the wonder of the age," he crooned. "You found a covey and you found a single. And those dumb people wouldn't believe you. They thought you were just ornery. They thought you were seeing snakes. Well, we'll show 'em who's the best damn quail hound in South Carolina. Come on, Mollie."

He walked in the direction of the dead bird, Mollie coming along behind him, nuzzling the pocket where he kept the sugar. Stopping a few yards from the spot where the quail had fallen, he pointed. "Now fetch it, Mollie" he said. "Fetch dead and you get your lump of sugar."

Mollie looked at him, then punched her nose hard against his pocket.

Christie shook his head. "No, Mollie, not until you fetch that bird."

Mollie hesitated, then out of the corner of her eyes she saw Flotsam running over to the spot where the dead bird lay. With a spring she jumped forward, pushed the dog away with her head and picked up the quail in her lips. Tossing her head as if in triumph and snorting through her nostrils, she brought it back to Christie. He took it with his left hand and offered her a lump with his right.

"Nobody's going to sell you down the river," he whispered to her, stroking her sleek neck.

Mrs. Christie and Purvey had come up, looking bewildered.

"This is weird," Mrs. Christie said. "It's fantastic!" She turned to Purvey. "Tell me, did you ever hear of a mule pointing birds?"

Purvey shook his head. "No, ma'am, I can't rightly say as I have. It don't look to me as it's quite natural."

"You saw it, didn't you?" Christie asked.

"Yes, sir, I saw what looked like it," Purvey admitted.

"And, Gertrude, you saw her point the covey, didn't you?" Christie asked his wife.

"I suppose I did, but I still think I dreamt it," Gertrude said.

"What did you pay for Mollie, Purvey?" Christie asked.

"I give Mr. Fletcher two hundred and forty for the pair," Purvey replied.

"Well, you can keep Mike. I'm giving you three hundred dollars for Mollie this very day," Christie said, with the smile of a man who has acquired a masterpiece. "And what's more, I'm paying you for her feed and keep." He turned to Mollie. "No more bloody plowing for you, my Mollie-O."

"It's sure kind of you, Mr. Christie," Purvey said, embarrassed, "but I don't reckon there's a mule on earth is worth . . ."

"Says you!" Christie shouted with a whoop at the end. "Wait till the Duke of Alba hears about Mollie. He'll pay anything to get her for his partridge shoot in Andalusia."

"Yeah?" Purvey said skeptically, taking off his cap and scratching his head. "Mr. Jessup was speakin' about that Dook. He must be powerful fond of mules."

GOOD-TIME CHARLIE

Horace Lytle

Horace Lytle became gun dog editor of Field & Stream *in 1927 when Ray P. Holland was beginning to build his strong editorship. The two left the magazine at the same time, in 1941. Lytle produced several "how-to" gun dog books and two anthologies of stories,* Point! *published by Stackpole in 1954 with an introduction by his close friend, Nash Buckingham; and* Gun Dogs Afield, *published in 1942 by Putnam, with an introduction by Ray P. Holland. Lytle had a particular affinity toward setters. Development of the breed, training and performance in the field dominate much of his writings, of which Ray Holland said: "When you read this book, you hunt with Horace Lytle. You will pick your favorite dog. You may choose Sam Illsley, or Mary, or that grand red dog, Smada Byrd. Or you may pick one of the many others that race through the broom straw and across the stubble in this sportsman's book. You can't help but enjoy each chapter. And, as you finish each chapter, clear to the very end, you will realize that Horace Lytle knows his bird dogs and that he knows the game of the men who love bird dogs." Well, that's high praise for* Gun Dogs Afield *and is exactly the reason we have two pieces from the book in* The Bobwhite Quail Book. *The first is about a little setter that was one of Lytle's favorites. He'll become one of yours, too.*

MY SHOOTING TRIP to Mississippi in February of 1942 was memorable for many reasons. A year earlier the doctors would not let me go for fear a horse might fall while hunting and ruin forever an ankle with a badly ruptured Achilles tendon. The same ankle was still far from mended a year later—but I went anyhow to the land that I love. You get that way after such long starvation from dogs and days afield—if hunting is bred in your bone. That foot, if caught in a stirrup, would have been fully as serious as twelve months earlier. But what of it! Yet I admit to being careful—and lucky.

It was memorable because so very many things were different than in any of the many years before Pearl Harbor. It was the first year in which I did not have a single dog of my own along. One was with a friend in South Carolina. One was with a trainer—and not yet finished. Another was with a handler who wanted to start her in a field trial and begged me not to take her shooting. His pleading finally melted my resistance. And it was the first year in which I've ever gone later than January. Which in itself shows that being able to get away at all was a close call. Not too strange—with the world at war!

And it was memorable, too, for still many more reasons: for several fast new friendships formed; for more birds than I've seen raised since the—to me—famous last day of the 1929 season, in Huston Bottoms; and it was memorable because of "Charlie."

Now a Kipling might call that Huston Bottoms reference "another story," which, indeed, it really is. But not being a Kipling, more's the pity, I think I'll tell you quickly of it—because it may have certain meaning from the angle of birds.

Confirming the date as 1929 is both easy and certain. All you have to do is subtract one year from 1930, which no hunter can ever forget because a nation-wide drought swept away America's game birds to an extent that has defied natural breeding replacement to date. Up till 1930, where I hunt in Mississippi, from eighteen to twenty coveys a day was just normal—and thirty coveys not too extreme a possibility. Which was the condition the day I closed out the 1929 season in Huston Bottoms.

The dogs were my field-trial-winning Irish setter bitch, Smada Byrd, and my English setter, Betty Buckeye. And because it was so simple to kill the then-limit of fifteen birds, we didn't even bother to saddle horses and make that serious a hunt of it. We just left the house about nine o'clock in the morning and sogged along in a car through the mud for six miles to Huston Bottoms. There we drove across the vast cotton fields to park the car not far from the thicket that completely borders these fascinating Bottoms. The edge of this long thicket line is indented every few rods by sedgy pockets.

Heading for the nearest such pocket, the dogs were soon on birds. Came the flush and a shooting score, the birds pitching straight into the thicket. Following for a chance at singles, we came to the next pocket—and there another covey! Repeating the same performance, we came to the third pocket and the third covey in a matter of minutes!

There is no use in prolonging the details. Every single, solitary pocket that day yielded a new covey. I'd never seen anything quite to match it before in my life—and regret to say I know I never shall again. A very few singles were raised—but not many. Almost all of the shooting was on new coveys. And, so it seemed, before we'd got more than fairly well started the hunting coat began to feel bulgy. Better count 'em up, I thought. But there were the dogs on point again. I flushed the birds, and the memory is still clear how funny I felt at missing. So I then took time out to count the birds already in my coat. There were exactly fifteen!

We quit right there and then, to start slushing back through the mud. On the way, we stopped at Whit's store for mail, to gossip a bit, and to bid all friends good-by. It marked the end of another glorious season. Reaching home, at Lucius's house, the job of packing was tackled with the inevitable regret—and no small task, either, with stuff strewn about for a month. Then a leisurely lunch—and the parting for another year. As I waved the final good-by to Lucius and Mrs. Morgan, I glanced at my watch. It was exactly one o'clock! The time element alone tells the story more eloquently than words. And that quickly tells the story of the greatest single day's shooting this writer has ever known. Small wonder, then, that I have ever since carried a mighty warm spot in my heart for Huston Bottoms—and always will.

But anything approaching that day's shooting has never been repeated. The drought of 1930 took care of that. I have, of course, gone back to those Bottoms many times. And always with pleasure—though never with much success. Nor have I ever elsewhere found anything even remotely to compare with it. What's more, the reports for the 1941–42 season were unanimously the very worst yet. So that, when Rowan and I went down, we weren't even counting on much hunting. Just thought we'd maybe try it for a day or two, more for old time's sake than anything else; also visit friends, and ride the several field trials which were in full swing at that time. In fact, it was the latter that we banked on for pleasant days afield in the saddle.

And then came Monday, February 16, with just five more days of the season to go. It was raining so hard that the running of the Amateur Championships had to be postponed. So we drove into town to call on Major Short and his partner, Mr. McCraw. And that's when it happened!

"Well, Mr. Lytle," the Major said, "we've been having some pretty nice shooting." I almost fell off my chair—but steadied myself and held on. Then I looked squarely at him to see if he might be joking. He wasn't.

"We haven't found it so," I told him, "and haven't even expected it. For months the reports have all been of the poorest season in years. But I'd sure like to have just one good hunt."

"What're you doing tomorrow?" the Major asked.

"Meeting you here in the morning," I answered quickly—and smiled.

"No, not till noon—no use hunting all day," he said. I knew then that his bird supply must be good. I could hardly wait for the next day to dawn. But that was still a long ways off. So we stayed on, just visiting, for the rest of the day—while the rain continued to pour down outside. I felt a burst of good feeling inside—I don't mean inside the store, but inside of *me*.

"I'm going to show you a good little setter you'll like," the Major said. "We call him Charlie—Good-Time Charlie."

"Good," I said—politely, but not warming up. Every fellow who ever owned a dog of any kind always wants to show you one. An Old Timer gets pretty fed up on it. The average of what you're called to see doesn't justify enthusiasm. In the Major's case, I knew we'd see something well above average. But I frankly wasn't looking for what we did see, nor what Charlie showed us, next day.

Sid Harris dropped in during the afternoon—and any visit with Sid is always a tonic. He's the best storyteller I've ever heard, bar none. I believe he could make even a poor one sound funny. But I don't know—I've never heard him tell any but a masterpiece. It takes Sid himself to tell 'em though, with just the right sauce and spice.

Even so, here's one of them. Sid had given a dog to an old man, who named the dog "Sid" in honor of the gift. And Sid's description of hunting with that old man and his dog was side-splitting—I just wish you could hear Sid tell it! Every time the dog's new owner would call out, "Careful, Sid"—though the dog paid not too much attention—Sid Harris would quickly look to his gun to see if he might be holding it wrong. And all day long, each time the old gentleman would say "Sid" to the dog—Sid himself would promptly answer "Sir?"

Rowan and I were both too itchy to wait for noon next day, so we put in an appearance some three hours early and sheepishly announced ourselves. I think the Major must have understood how it was with us, for he graciously drove us right out to the Plantation and delegated Archie to take care of us as guide and general factotum. The Major himself still insisted he could not join us before noon.

There were exactly one hundred mules loose in a great pasture, and three darkies, each with a bridle, went forth to round up three of them for us to ride. Watching that performance was just about as fascinating as hunting. Capturing the first mount was fairly easy and accomplished rather quickly. But the next two— they were something. The boy on the captured mule dashed bareback hither and yon. The two still on foot were artists in getting into the right positions at the right time. Sometimes by slow, almost creeping maneuvers—at other times dashing for some strategic position—they finally rounded up and bridled a second mule.

Even with two boys now mounted, however, I began to doubt if that third would ever be bridled. He just didn't intend that he should be! The combination of mule and darkies put on a performance worth paying money to see. Once the loose mule went galloping headlong down a ditch bank, closely pursued by one of the riders. All of a sudden the ridden mule—as if deliberately to aid his pal's escape—turned at direct right angle toward the ditch and slammed on all four brakes at once. I expected to see that black rider catapulted clear across that ditch. Instead, he grabbed a mule ear in each hand as he went over his head, and eased himself to earth as prettily as a gymnast. About that time black boys began to spring up in that pasture from out of nowhere. Soon they seemed to be about a fourth as numerous as mules—and I guess they actually were. And when they delicately inched up, a slow step at a time, on that cornered mule—he was a goner, at long last.

There was no further delay. We mounted and were off. The white mule fell to my lot, and he was slow but certain. Rowan turned his good Nick dog loose, and he went away with a rush. Archie said we couldn't hunt the best country and get back in time to meet the Major at noon—but he allowed as how he hoped we might find a few birds. I noticed a medium-sized white and orange setter starting to follow us about that time.

Archie said: "Come on, dog."

"What's he?" I asked.

"That's Charlie," Archie told me.

"He the one Major was telling me about?" I casually inquired.

Archie simply said: "I reckon so."

The prediction of not finding many birds before lunch proved correct. We encountered but two coveys, to be exact. And Charlie scored first. It was one of those merited finds "way out on the end of a limb," as we say in field trials. He was pointed headed into a gulley a good quarter mile to our left, making a rather long ride to reach him. But he never wavered, and his white stood out boldly from the red of the sedge. It was the kind of a find that always thrills me—I want a dog that dares to dig on out and find his birds. The close-ranging putterer never appeals—not to me. Not in quail country, anyhow. As we drew up to that point, however, I began to lose faith—for Charlie's tail, though somewhat arched, was gently waving. I figured, at least, that the birds had started to run.

But in reply to my question, Archie said: "No, that just means it's a covey—he's *got 'em.*"

So Rowan and I both dismounted, kicked out the birds directly in front of Charlie's nose—and we scored. Getting back on our mules, we rode down the ravine toward where we thought some singles had dropped. Pretty soon Charlie was on point again. But this time his tail was up higher than before—too, it was stiff as a ramrod.

"Now he's got a single," Archie said, and so it proved—and one of us killed it.

"D'you know that's funny," I told Archie as we rode on, "most dogs would style up more on coveys, and less on singles—but

Charlie is just the opposite. Does he always signal coveys and singles that way?"

"Yas, suh," Archie said. "Charlie ain't like most other dogs no way at all. He's differ'nt."

Nick scored the second and last covey as we headed for the house; and I don't blame Rowan for his pride in an even division of dog honors for the morning. In fact, you'd have to grant Nick some edge—for it was all new country to him, while Charlie was hunting at home. And that can make a whale of a difference. On the other hand, I guess maybe Charlie simply hadn't yet started to roll into high gear. Or, could it have been canine courtesy!

The Major and Bos were already there and waiting for us as we rode up; and they had brought sandwiches plus a big thermos of good hot coffee. As we sat enjoying these, the afternoon plans were changed.

"We'll all go together this afternoon," the Major proposed—"but I won't shoot at all. That way there won't be too many guns. Don't care a thing in the world about it, anyhow—an' I want to be free to use the 'covey finder,' so's surely to beat Bos. That'll be the most fun for me."

It seems these two had made a bet of ten coveys before sundown. I think Bos must secretly have hoped he'd lose—for we lingered too long for lunch, and it was he who urged to get going, instead of wasting any more time. So we mounted and were off: the Major, Bos, Rowan, and me—with Archie riding in second position. The Major sure rode a traveling mule. No one ever got ahead of him—not always the dogs! Mention of the dogs reminds me to say that there were four: two pointers and a setter belonging to Bos, and Good-Time Charlie. We'd been riding for a while when Bos, who's never seen a field trial, said to Rowan:

"I expect your dogs are wider than these, aren't they, Rowan?"

Rowan's answer was a honey. "I doubt if any dog would look very wide in front of the Major on that mule," he said. But there wasn't much time for conversation. It kept us all too busy kicking away at our mules to keep the Major in sight. Thus I still hadn't found out what the Major had meant when he had referred to a "covey finder." Perhaps he was referring to Charlie, I thought, and that was a good name for what I had begun to realize was a

truly great little dog. The Bos pointers had nice style on game—
and the setter an unique mannerism. If at all uncertain—whether
on his own points, or backing—he would stand. But if the birds
were there, he'd just *sit down*. Several times the Major had us wait
for this setter to sit, before going in ahead of the other dogs to
flush the birds. I will say this—that every time that setter sat the
birds were there. It tended to stimulate confidence.

As if confidence needed stimulating behind that Charlie dog!
On, on and out he'd go, hour after hour. And he'd score—and
he'd tell you in advance what he had. This warning of what to
expect was a nice aid to shooting. The arched waving tail meant a
covey; the stiff ramrod said single. And the score of covies stood at
nine, and the Major was ribbing Bos hard, when I discovered the
"covey finder."

As he topped a rise, the Major ahead was seen to rein in his
mule—a welcome relief to me, for prodding my slower white mule
was wearing me down.

"Archie!" the Major commanded, in stentorian tone and austere brevity—"bring the *covey finder.*"

Archie produced from his saddlebags; and, as the Major finished a good swig and smacked his lips, he said: "I never insist on
anyone joining me, but it's there—an' you're welcome." But we
who were shooting decided to wait until later—well, two of us
did.

"Now, Archie, head us toward the tenth and winning covey"—
and the Major's ground-covering mule was again leading us on.

"Go on you, dog," Archie commanded. And Charlie went on.
Not only to the tenth—but to the fifteenth covey before sunset.
The Major quit counting after the eleventh—"One extra for good
measure," he said—but I counted right on up to the last. I don't
know whether Charlie was tired—I don't know if Charlie ever
gets tired—but the cast he made to dig up that last find was
beautiful to behold. To me, there is nothing more magnificent
than a game dog reaching ever onward and outward for birds and
showing the judgment to explore only the right places with no
waste motions. Fifteen coveys in one afternoon! The joy of it
thrilled me to my boots. I hadn't known anything to compare
with it for thirteen years, since that last day of which I've told you

in Huston Bottoms. The stars were indeed shining—in more ways than one—as we later tucked ourselves in for the night.

The next day we hunted some of my old haunts and over two grand pointers—as good as they come. They were faster and flashier than Charlie; and they were bird dogs, every inch of the way. Rowan remarked on liking them better than Charlie—and I could well understand what he meant. But these pointers were fresh, and we didn't hunt them to exceed two hours—I doubt if even that long. Whereas we had seen Charlie go *all day*. He'd probably been at it thus many days. And that makes a mighty difference.

Friday, February 20, 1942, was the last day of the Mississippi season, and again we went to the Major's. He had two other guests. But he turned Charlie over to Rowan and me—with Archie as handler and guide. And it is based on his work for us that day that makes me rate Good-Time Charlie in the very top bracket with the few really great bird dogs I have known. For true greatness in a dog, as in a man, must be measured and carefully weighed before the pronouncement. I have seen a few dogs—very few—who might have matched Charlie as a covey finder; a rare few more who might—possibly—have equaled his endurance; a few, perhaps, that might even have surpassed his work on singles. But I believe I have never seen any dog do so many things well, nor with such satisfying smoothness.

One requisite for greatness in a dog is *adaptability*. The late eminent authority, A. F. Hochwalt, would never rate a dog among the immortals if his exploits were all limited to one locality or one type of familiar territory. He claimed that a truly great dog must prove both the willingness and the wisdom to adjust himself to the conditions as he finds them—whether it be in the quail country of the South, or the vast open spaces of the Saskatchewan prairies.

Now Charlie has, perhaps, never hunted anywhere except in northern Mississippi. However, the character of the territory on different parts of the Major's plantation varies about as greatly as Texas differs from Ohio. And it is of Charlie's adaptability in meeting these conditions as they changed, that I would speak. Our start was made straight across the middle of great open cotton fields, and Charlie's range "reached to the horizon." He starts off at an easy lope—and that's the same gait at which he finishes, no matter how long nor how hard the going may be. I truly believe he'd not come down to a trot if hunted every day, all day, for a week. A very large part of any dog's endurance comes from physical stamina to stand the strain. But I shall always believe that *heart* has as much to do with it as stamina. And that's what I believe of Charlie—though, of course, he has both assets to a remarkable degree.

A feature of Charlie's range that I especially admire is its definiteness—he never wavers from a selected objective. I can't tolerate a dog that can't make up his mind—and then stick to the decision, come what may. That's a fetish with me—perhaps my most extreme one. I almost despise to see a dog dash about, this way and that, but to no place in particular and with no sense of reason or judgment behind his movements. And worst of all is the dog that casts out somewhere—and then comes casting back to you, retracing his footsteps to no purpose, except needlessly to tire himself out.

There's no such uselessness in any move Charlie makes. His every cast is onward and outward—from one likely-looking objective to another. Yet his every aim and object is service to the gun. I loved the way he'd turn now and then—way out—just to check up on us and be sure we were coming. But I loved even more the quick promptness with which he'd turn back and dig on the very instant the check-up showed him what he wanted to know. Most dogs might make such a stop an excuse to loaf a little. Not Charlie! His starting-on jumps seemed just a bit faster, as if to gain back time lost in the pause. Not a loafing bone in his body nor a lazy hair in his hide.

But I've seen a number of dogs that would go fully as wide as Charlie, though I've never seen one do it with better judgment in selecting *where* to go, nor with less lost motion in the process. So now I'm going to tell of what I saw Charlie do that I consider especially amazing. We came to a great, wide ditch that ran the entire length of the Major's six thousand acres. And Archie knew that several coveys used that ditch at various places. Charlie was off ahead on a prodigious cast—almost, it seemed, beyond whistle range. Yet when Archie blew the come-in signal, Charlie heard it—looked for an instant—then came loping straight to us. It was the only "back cast" I saw him make in two full days! It showed a responsiveness I may never see equaled—certainly never surpassed. For, be it ever remembered, there always is—and must be—a strong independence and initiative in any really great hunting dog. Such a dog may be taught to "bend" to a handler's commands, but is apt, on occasion, to try to evade prompt obedience. Which is what made Charlie's quick and cheerful willingness so impressive. Yet even more evidence was in store for us, when Archie said, on Charlie's arrival:

"Dog, git down in that ditch an' fin' us some birds." And—believe it or not—Charlie never came out of the ditch until after he had found the next covey! Those of you who know anything about the general characteristics of wide dogs will realize that seeing one so completely biddable was like having a ring-side seat at the performance of a miracle. Of course, though, you just can't beat a darky with a dog—or a mule! Which is not said to take one whit of credit from Charlie.

Good-Time Charlie! Long may you live to roam and comb both the flat lands and the sedgy hillsides of Mississippi. And for a dog like you or a guy like me—I hope and pray it's not sacrilegious to say it, I don't mean it to be—I often really wonder what we can possibly find, some day beyond the Pearly Gates, to take its place.

SHOFFSTALL

THE BISCUIT EATER

James Street

This long piece of fiction has knocked around considerably since novelist and short-story writer James Street first wrote it back in the thirties. It appeared originally in The Saturday Evening Post, *was the basis of a widely acclaimed feature motion picture, and has appeared in several anthologies, including Street's own* Short Stories, *published by Dial Press in New York in 1945. The tale was the forerunner of a Street bird-dog novel,* Goodbye, My Lady, *published by Lippincott in 1954, and also made into a feature film. Some authorities have reported that the expression "biscuit eater" (meaning a worthless dog) has become a part of our daily language. Street confesses: "I made up that title with my tongue in my cheek. When I was a boy, the expression "biscuit eater" didn't mean a worthless dog and never was used in polite company. In those days, the epithet "son-of-a-bitch" meant a spanking from your father (if he heard about it) and a black-eye from the other fellow. It was the first blow of any fight. So to avoid the danger and punishment and still get over the idea we had a way of saying, 'son of a biscuit eater'."*

LONNIE POKED OUT his lower lip and blew as hard as he could, trying to blow back the tousled brown hair that flopped over his forehead and got in his eyes. He couldn't use his hands to brush back his hair, for his hands were full of puppies. He held the puppies up, careful to protect their eyes from the sun, and examined them.

Then he cocked his head as his father often did and said solemnly, as though he were an expert on such matters, "Yes siree bob-tail. Fine litter of puppies. Pure D scutters, sure as my name is Lonnie McNeil"

"Think so, Son?" Harve McNeil glanced up at his only son. He wanted to laugh at Lonnie's solemn expression, but he wouldn't. Never treat a child as a child, treat him as an equal. That's what Harve McNeil believed. The boy was serious, so the father must be serious too. "Mighty glad you think so. You're an A No. 1 bird dog man and I have a heap of respect for your judgment."

Lonnie's heart swelled until it filled his chest and lapped over into his throat. He stuck out his chest and swaggered a bit. Then he put the puppies back into the big box where he and his father were working.

They were Bonnie Blue's pups, seven squirming, yelping little fellows that tumbled over themselves in greedy attempts to reach their mother, lying in a corner of the box and watching her litter proudly. They were nine days old and their eyes were open.

The boy sat on his feet next to his father in the crowded box and helped him doctor the puppies. Now that their eyes were open they must be prepared to face a blinding sun. Soon they must have shots to ward off diseases, but first their eyes and ears must be cleaned. A bird dog with defective sight and hearing is no 'count.

This was the first time Lonnie had ever been allowed to help his father with a new litter. Harve held a puppy in his big hand, wiped each eye with a clean piece of cotton, then bathed the pup's ears.

"Hand me another, Son," he said. "But handle him gently. Ol' Bonnie's got her eye on you and if you hurt one of them she'll jump you like a jay jumps a June bug."

Lonnie picked up a puppy and cuddled it. "Hi, puppy dog. How you doing, ol' puppy dog? Know me now that you got your eyes open?" The pup flicked out his tongue and ran it across Lonnie's face. Then he caught Lonnie's ear and began sucking it. The boy laughed and handed the puppy to his father.

Harve looked the dog over carefully. "He's a beaut all right." He ran his finger over a small knot on the pup's head. "Ummhh. Little knot there. But it'll go away. Then he'll be perfect. Ought to be. Good blood line in this litter. Hey, Bonnie Blue, ol' girl. I'm bragging on your pups."

Bonnie Blue perked up her ears and rubbed her nose against Harve. She was a champion. She was almost as good a dog as Silver Belle, the pride of the place. Bonnie had won more than her share of field trials, and once she had run in the Grand National up at Grand Junction, Tennessee, the world series for bird dogs.

But the puppies had a doubtful strain in them, inherited from their father, a fair to middlin' bird dog until he killed one of Farmer Eben's sheep, and was shot, according to the code of the piney woods. Farmer Eben lived across the hollow from the McNeils.

Mr. Eben warned Harve that any puppies that had the sheep killer's blood in them were bound to be no 'count by the law of heritage. Bonnie's litter was on the way when the father was killed and Harve believed he could cure the pups of any bad habits. The father had had a lot of courage, a strong heart and a good nose. Maybe the pups would be all right.

Harve scratched the pup on the belly, then passed him back to a huge grinning Negro, black as a swamp at midnight. The Negro was First-and-Second-Thessalonians, the handyman around the place. Everybody called him Thes.

"Yas suh, Mistah Harve," Thes said as he put the pup into another box. "Me and you and Mistah Lon and ol' Bonnie Blue got us a good litter this go-round. And ol' Mistah Lon handles 'em just like he was born with a pup in each hand. Just like a natchel bird dawg man."

It was too much for Lonnie. He was so happy he wanted to cry. Everybody bragging on him. His father beamed and resumed his work. It was good working there in the shade, with his son at his side and good dogs to work with. Harve McNeil was very proud of his boy and his dogs and his job. He trained dogs for Mr. Ames, the Philadelphia sportsman, and Ames' dogs, handled by McNeil, were known at every important field trial from Virginia to Texas. The Ames plantation, almost hidden in the piney woods of South Mississippi, was Lonnie's home. There were many bird dogs in the kennel, pointers and setters, and some were as valuable as race horses. Mr. Ames could have named his own price for Bonnie Blue and Silver Belle, but money couldn't buy them.

Cicadas sang in the water oaks as Harve worked. Humming birds darted around the red cannas and the mellow cape jasmine. June bugs buzzed around the fig trees. Jay birds scolded in a pecan tree and mocking birds warbled. In a field near by, a Bob White whistled and Bonnie Blue lifted her ears. Yes, Harve McNeil thought, it was good, working there with his boy in such a beautiful peaceful land. So he began humming:

"Went to the river and couldn't get across,
Singing polly-wolly-doodle all day—"

Lonnie took up the melody:

"Paid five dollars for an old gray hoss,
Singing polly-wolly-doodle all day."

Thes doubled up with laughter. "Listen to ol' Mistah Lon sing that gray hoss song. Just like a natchel man. Know this 'un, Mistah Lon?"

The big Negro tilted his head, shuffled his feet and chanted:

"Peckerwood a 'sittin' on a swingin' limb,
Bluejay a 'struttin' in the garden—"

Lonnie joined in:

"Ol' gray goose a 'settin' in the lane,
She'll hatch on the other side of Jordan."

Thes slapped his thigh. "Hot ziggity-dog. How 'bout this 'un: 'Thought I heard somebody say—'"

"Soda pop, soda pop, take it away." Lonnie sang so loudly that the pups quit yelping and looked up at him.

They doctored six pups and as Harve finished the last one he told his son, "Run in the house and tell Mama we'll be in for dinner in a minute."

Lonnie jumped up and started away. Then he stopped suddenly. "But we got another puppy, Papa. We only done six. There's seven in the litter."

Harve looked over at Thes and the big Negro turned his head. The father reached down and lifted the seventh pup. "We won't fix him, Son."

"How come?" asked Lonnie. He stared at the pup, a scrawny little fellow with spots that looked like freckles, a stringy tail and watery brown eyes. He was the most forlorn looking pup Lonnie had ever seen.

"He's no 'count, Son," Harve said sadly. "He's the runt of the litter. Thes will get rid of him."

"You mean kill him?" Lonnie said.

"Now don't look at me that way," Harve said. "He'll go easy. You're a bird dog man, Son. You know there's a bad 'un in most every litter. All these dogs got one strike on them 'cause their papa was a sheep killer. But this one has got two strikes on him."

All the blood drained from Lonnie's face and his heart went to the pit of his stomach. "I was a runt," he said. "And I got freckles. Why didn't you drown me?"

"Don't talk that away, Mistah Lon," Thes said. "It's hard 'nuff to kill him without you carryin' on so."

Harve McNeil looked at his boy a long time, then at the runt. Slowly he began cleaning the puppy's ears. "We'll keep him, Thes," he said. "If my boy wants to keep this dog, we'll keep him."

Lonnie's heart climbed from his stomach back to his chest and he choked up again. "Is he mine, Papa?"

"He's yours." Harve got up and put his hand on his boy's shoulder. "He's your dog, Son. But don't feel bad if he's no good. I'll help you train him, but he looks like a biscuit eater."

"He sho' do," said Thes.

"He don't neither," said Lon. It was his dog now and nobody could defame him. "He ain't no biscuit eater. Are you, puppy dog?"

He held the dog close to him and began running toward the branch, beyond which lived his friend, Text. Text as Thes's little brother and was just as black.

Harve and Thes watched the boy out of sight. "How come Mistah Lon want that li'l ol' pup, you reckon?" Thes scratched his head.

"Nobody, Thes," Harve said, "has ever understood the way of a boy with a dog. I reckon the boy wanted him because nobody else did."

"Reckon he's a biscuit eater?" Thes asked.

"It sticks out all over him," Harve said. "He ain't worth a shuck. But he's Lonnie's dog and heaven help the boy who calls him a biscuit eater."

A biscuit eater is an ornery dog. He won't hunt anything except his own biscuits. And he'll suck eggs and steal chickens and run coons and jump rabbits. To a bird dog man, a biscuit eater is the lowest form of animal life. Strangers in Mississippi often are puzzled by the expression until natives, who usually eat biscuits instead of light bread, explain that a biscuit eater is a no 'count hound that isn't good for anything except to hunt his meat and biscuits.

Lonnie found Text down at the branch, fishing for shiners, long silver minnows that thrived near the bank. Text was the youngest of Aunt Charity's brood. A shouting, sanctified, foot-washing Baptist, Aunt Charity lived close to God and had given her children names that should be fitting in the eyes of the Lord. She had heard her preacher take text from this and text from that, so she reckoned Text was a superfine name.

The white boy held the puppy in his arms so Text couldn't see him and said, "Guess what I got."

"A gopher," Text suggested.

Lonnie sat on the ground and opened his arms. The puppy tumbled out and Text's eyes popped open. "A puppy dawg. Be John dogged, Lon. And he's ours!"

"Mine," said Lonnie.

Text took the dog in his arms and ignored Lonnie's claim of complete possession. "We finally got us a dawg. Heah, pup."

The pup's tail drooped, but his big eyes watched Text. He was awkward, scrawny and wobbly-legged. "Ain't he a beaut, Lon?" Text said. "Boy, we got us a dawg."

There was no denying Text a claim to the pup so Lonnie said, "You tell 'um. We got us a dog."

The pup whimpered and licked Lonnie's hand. "Knows me already. Better get him back to his mama."

Text went with him, but before they put the pup in the kennel, the little Negro turned him over, placed his hand over the pup's heart and muttered:

"Possum up a sweetgum stump, raccoon in the holler
Wake, snake! June bug done stole yo' half-a-dollar."

Lonnie said, "What's that for?"

"Luck," said Text. "I put the ol' charm on him. I got better charms than that, but I'm savin' 'em."

The boys hung around Bonnie Blue's kennel all day, watching their dog. They called him Pup for lack of a better name and in the weeks that followed they worked hard at his training. The dog developed fast. The freckles grew into big spots. His chest filled out and the muscles rippled in his legs. The boys saw only love and loyalty in his eyes, but Harve and Thes saw meanness there, and stubbornness. He was slow to learn, but the boys were patient.

A bird dog must know many things. How to carry an egg in his mouth without breaking it. How to get bird scents from the air and how to stand motionless for an hour if necessary, pointing birds, showing the master where the covey is. A bird dog knows instinctively that quail live in flocks, or coveys, usually a brood. They feed on the ground and fly in coveys until scattered. A bird dog must know all the habits of quail and never try to round them up, or crawl and putter around them. Only a biscuit eater who can't catch air scents rounds up birds in an effort to sight-point them. A quail's only protection is his color and when a dog sight-points him, the bird knows he's been seen and will take off. Good dogs must know how to keep their heads up and hold birds on the ground until the master is ready to flush the covey by frightening the quail. Then, when the birds take wing fast as feathered lightning, bird dogs must stand still until the hunter shoots the birds and orders his dog to fetch the kill.

He must know how to cover every likely looking spot, passing up bare ground where quail can't hide. He should have a merry tail that whips back and forth. And he must cast with wisdom and range wide.

He must know to honor the other dog's point by backing him up and standing still while the other dog holds the birds. A good dog knows that if he moves while another dog is on a point, he might flush the birds. Such behavior is instinct with good dogs and not really a sense of honor.

Harve tried to help the boys train the pup, but was not able to get close to his affections. There was no feeling between him and the pup, no understanding. The pup cowed at Lonnie's feet when Harve ordered him into the fields to hunt. And then one night Harve caught him in the hen house, sucking eggs.

An egg sucking dog simply is not tolerated. It hurt Harve to get rid of the dog, but there was nothing else to do. He walked with Lonnie out to the barn and they sat down. Harve told his son, "You're a bird dog man, Son. A hunter. It's in your blood."

Lonnie sensed what was coming and asked, "What's my dog done now?"

"Sucked eggs. I caught him last night."

"No, Papa. Not that. He ain't no suck-egger."

"Yes, he is, Son, and remember his father was a sheep killer. The bad streak's coming out. He's a biscuit eater, and there's no cure for a biscuit eater. We've got to get rid of him. He'll teach my good dogs bad habits. He's got to go."

Lonnie didn't say anything. He compressed his lips, knowing that if he opened them he would cry. He walked out of the barn and down to the branch where he could think over his problem. Text could keep the dog. That was the solution. They could keep him away from Harve's fine dogs. Lonnie ran to tell Text the plan, but while he was away Harve took the dog across the ridge and gave him to a Negro. He didn't have the heart to kill him or let Thes kill him.

Harve shoved the dog toward the Negro and said, "He's yours, if you want him. He'll run rabbits. But I warn you, he's no good. He's a suck-egg biscuit eater."

The Negro accepted the dog because he knew he could swap him. That very night, however, the dog stole eggs from the Negro's hen house and the Negro tied a block and rope around his neck and beat him and called him a low-life biscuit eater. The dog immediately associated the block and rope and the beating with the term biscuit eater and he was sorely afraid and hurt. He was hurt because the man was displeased with him and he didn't know why. So when the Negro called him biscuit eater, he ran under the cabin and sulked.

When Lonnie learned what his father had done with the outcast, he went to Text, and together they went over the ridge to bargain for the dog. On the way, Text paused, crossed his fingers and muttered:

> "Green corn, sweet corn
> Mister, fetch a demijohn,
> Fat meat, fat meat
> That's what the Injuns eat."

Lonnie said, "Puttin' on a good luck spell?"

"Uh huh. That's one of my best charms. We going to need luck to make this swap."

The Negro man was wily. He sensed a good bargain and was trader enough to know that if he low-rated the dog, the boys would want him more than ever. The dog had a cotton rope around his neck and the rope was fastened to a block, and when the dog walked, his head pulled sideways as he tugged the block. The dog walked to Lonnie and rubbed against his legs. The boy ignored him. He mustn't let the Negro man know how badly he wanted the dog. The man grabbed the rope and jerked the dog away.

"He's a biscuit eater!" The Negro nudged the dog with his foot. The animal looked sideways at his master and slunk away. "He ain't worth much."

"He's a suck-egg biscuit eater, ain't he?" Lonnie asked. The dog watched him, and when the boy said "biscuit eater," the dog ran under the cabin, pulling the block behind him. "He's scared," Lonnie said. "You been beating him. And ever' time you jump him, you call him 'biscuit eater.' That's how come he's scared. Whatcha take for him?"

The man said, "Whatcha gimme?"

"I'll give you my frog-sticker." Lonnie showed his knife. "And I got a pretty good automobile tire. Ain't but one patch on it. It'd make a prime superfine swing for your young'uns."

The Negro asked Text, "What'll you chip in to boot?"

Text said, "You done cussed out the dawg so much I don't want no share of him. You done low-rated him too much. If he sucks eggs at my house, my Maw'll bust me in two halves. Whatcha want to boot?"

"Whatcha got?"

"Nothin'," said Text, "cep'n two big hands what can tote a heap of wood. Tote your shed full of light'r knots for boot."

"What else?"

Text thought for a minute, weighing the deal. "Lon wants that dawg. I know where there's a pas'l of May haws and a honeybee tree."

The Negro man said, "It's a deal, boys, if'n you pick me a lard bucket full of May haws and show me the bee tree."

Lonnie took the block from the dog and led him across the field. Then Text led him awhile. Out of sight of the Negro's shack, the boys stopped and examined their possession.

Text ran his hand over the dog, smoothing the fur. "He's good dawg, ain't he, Lon? Look at them big ol' eyes, and them big ol' feet, and that big ol' short tail. Bet he can point birds from here to yonder. Betcha if he tries, he can point partridge on light bread." He looked down at the big, brooding dog. "We got to give him a name. We can't keep on calling him Pup. He's a big dawg and if'n you call a big dawg Pup it's like calling a growed up man young'un. What we going to name him, Lon?"

Lonnie said, "Dunno, Text. But listen, don't ever call him—" He looked at the dog, then at Text. "You know." He held his fingers in the shape of a biscuit and pantomimed as though he were eating. The dog didn't understand. Neither did Text. So Lonnie whispered, "You know, 'biscuit eater.' Don't ever call him that. That's what's the matter with him. He expects a beating when he hears it."

"It's a go," Text whispered. "Let's name him Moreover. It's in the Bible."

"Where 'bouts?"

"I heard the preacher say so. He said, 'Moreover, the dog,' and he was reading from the Bible."

Lonnie held the dog's chin with one hand and stroked his chest with the other. "If Moreover is good enough for the Bible, then it's good enough for us. He's Moreover then. He's a good dog, Text. And he's ours. You keep him and I'll furnish the rations. I can snitch 'em from Papa. Will Aunt Charity raise Cain if you keep him?"

"Naw," said Text. "I 'member the time that big ol' brother of mine, ol' First-and-Second-Thessalonians, fetched a goat home, and Maw didn't low-rate him. She just said she had so many young'uns, she didn't mind a goat. I 'spects she feels the same way 'bout a dawg, if'n he's got a Bible name."

"I reckon so, too," said Lonnie and ran home and told his father about the deal.

Harve told his son, "It's all right for you and Text to keep the dog, but keep him away from over here. I don't want him running around my good dogs. You know why."

Lonnie said, "He's a good dog, Papa. He just ain't had no chance."

Harve looked at his son. The boy was growing, and the man was proud.

He noticed his son collecting table scraps the next morning, but didn't mention it. "I'm going to work Silver Belle today. Want to come along?"

Lonnie shook his head. Harve knew then how much the boy loved Moreover for, ordinarily, Lonnie would have surrendered any pleasure to accompany his father when he worked Silver Belle. She was the finest pointer in the Ames kennels and Harve had trained her since puppyhood. Already, she had won the Grand National twice. A third win would give his employer permanent possession of the Grand National trophy, and Harve wanted to win the prize for Mr. Ames more than he wanted anything in the world. He pampered Silver Belle. She was a magnificent pointer, trim and beautiful. There were no characteristics of a biscuit eater in Silver Belle. She was everything that Moreover was not and when hunting she ranged so far and so fast that she had to wear a bell so the hunters could keep track of her. She had seen Moreover only once and that was from a distance. The aristocrat had sniffed and Moreover had turned his big head and stared at her, awe and admiration in his eyes. And then he had tucked his head and run away. He knew his place.

Lonnie set the greasy bag of table scraps on a hummock of wire grass and leaned over the branch, burying his face in the cool water.

A lone ant poked its head from around a clover leaf, surveyed the scene and scurried boldly to the scraps. The adventurer scrambled about the sack and then turned away. Soon the ant reappeared with a string of fellow workers and they circled the bag, seeking an opening. But the boy didn't notice the ants. He lifted his head out of the water, took a deep breath and plunged it in again.

A beetle lumbered from behind a clod and stumbled toward the scraps. One of the working ants spied it, signaled the others and the little army retreated into the grass to get reënforcements. The beetle went to the scraps and was preparing for a feast when the ants attacked.

Lonnie paid no mind to the drama of life. He wiped his mouth with the back of his hand. Hundreds of black, frisky water bugs, aroused at his invasion of their playground, scooted to the middle of the stream, swerved as though playing follow-the-leader, and scooted back to the bank.

The boy laughed at their capers. Slowly, he stooped over the water. His hand darted as a cotton-mouth strikes and he snatched one of the bugs and smelled it. There was a sharp, sugary odor on the bug.

"A sweet stinker, sure as I'm born," the boy muttered. If you caught a sweet stinker among water bugs, it meant good luck, maybe. Lonnie mumbled slowly:

> "Eerie, oarie, eekerie, Nan,
> Fillison, follison, Nicholas, Buck,
> Queavy, quavy, English navy,
> Sticklum, stacklum, come good luck."

That should help the charm. Everybody knew that. Lonnie held the mellow bug behind him, closed his eyes, tilted his head and whispered to the pine trees, the branch, the wire grass and anything else in the silence that wanted to hear him and would never tell his wish: "I hope Moreover is always a good dog."

Then Lonnie put the bug back in the branch. It darted in circles for a second and skedaddled across the creek, making a beeline for the other bugs. There were tiny ripples in its wake. The boy grinned. He was in for some good luck. If the sweet stinker had changed its course, it would have broken the charm.

He picked up his bag of scraps and brushed off the beetle and ants, crushing some of the ants. The beetle landed on its back and a blue jay swooped down and snatched it. Lonnie watched the bird fly away. Then he studied the earth near the stream. No telling what a fellow would find if he looked around. Maybe he would find a doodlebug hole and catch one on a straw. That was good luck, too; better luck than finding a ladybug and telling her, "Ladybug, ladybug, fly away home; your house is on fire and your children are alone." He found no doodlebug hole but there was a crawdad castle, a house of mud that a crawfish had built. There was no luck in a crawdad, but Lonnie marked the place. Crawdads are good fish bait. He crossed the branch on a log and moseyed to the edge of the woods where the cleared land began. The land was choked with grass and stumps. Lonnie pursed his lower lip and whistled the call of the catbird, watching the cabin in the field where Text lived.

Lonnie saw Text run to the rickety front gallery of the cabin and listen. He whistled again. Text answered and ran around the house, and a minute later he was racing across the field with Moreover at his heels. The white boy opened his arms and the dog ran to him and tried to lick his face. The dog almost bowled the boy over. Lonnie jerked off his cap and his long, brown uncombed hair fell over his face. He put his face very close to the dog's right ear and muttered to him the things that boys always mutter to dogs. The dog's tail wagged and his big eyes looked quizzically at the boy. He rubbed against the boy's legs and Lonnie scratched him.

Text waited until Lonnie and the dog had greeted each other properly and then he said, "Hydee, Lon. Ol' Moreover is glad to see you. Me and him bof'."

Lonnie said, "Hi, Text. He looks slick as el-lem sap, don't he? Been working him?"

"A heap and whole lot," said Text. "Turned him loose in the wire grass yestiddy and he pointed two coveys 'fore I could say, 'Lawd 'a' mercy.' He's a prime superfine bird dawg, Lon. He ain't no no'count biscuit eater."

Lonnie put his arm around his friend. "You mighty come a'right he ain't no biscuit eater."

The dog had wiped away all class and race barriers between Lonnie and Text, and they were friends in a way that grown-ups never understand. They didn't brag about their friendship or impose upon it, but each knew he could count upon the other.

They worked hard and patiently trying to train the dog and sometimes the task seemed hopeless. Once he pointed a flock of chickens, a disgraceful performance. Again he ran a rabbit and once he left a point to dash across a field and bark at Mr. Eben who was ploughing a mule. Mr. Eben threw a clod at him.

The boys couldn't teach the dog to carry an egg in his mouth for he always broke the egg and ate it. Once when he sucked an egg, Lon put his arms around the dog and cried, not in anger but in anguish.

Cotton hung loosely in the bolls and dog days passed. Indian summer came and the forest smelled woodsy and smoky. Sumac turned to yellow and gold and the haze of autumn hugged the earth.

Moreover improved slowly, but the boys still were not satisfied. "Let's work him across the ridge today," Lon said. "Papa's got Silver Belle in the south forty and he won't want us and Moreover around."

Text said, "It's a go, Lon. I'll snitch ol' Thes' shotgun and meet you 'cross the ridge. But that there lan' over there is pow'ful close to Mister Eben's place. I don't want no truck with that man."

"I ain't afraid of Mr. Eben," said Lonnie.

"Well, I am. And so are you! And so is your Paw!"

Lonnie's face flushed and he clenched his fists. It was the first time he had ever clenched his fists at Text, but nobody could talk about his papa. "Papa's not afraid of anything and I'll bust you in two halves if you say so." He jerked off his cap and hurled it to the ground.

Text rolled his eyes until the whites showed. He had never seen Lon angry before, but he wasn't afraid. "Then how come your Paw didn't whup Mister Eben when Mister Eben kicked his dawg about two years ago?"

Negroes heard everything and forgot nothing. Everybody in the county had wondered why Harve McNeil hadn't thrashed Eben when the farmer kicked one of McNeil's dogs without cause. The code of the county was, "Love me, love my dog." And one of the favorite sayings was, "It makes no difference if he is a hound, don't you kick my dog around."

But Harve had done nothing when Eben kicked his dog. Harve didn't believe in settling disputes with his fists. As a young man he had fought often for many reasons, but now that he was a father he tried to set a good example for his son. So he had taken the Eben insult although it was hard to do.

Lonnie often had wondered why his father didn't beat up Mr. Eben. His mother tried to explain and had said, "Gentlemen don't go around fighting. Your father is a gentleman and he wants you to be one."

Lonnie was ashamed and embarrassed because some of the other boys had said Harve was afraid of Eben. And now, Text said the same thing. "Papa didn't whip Mr. Eben 'cause Mother asked him not to, that's why," Lonnie said defiantly.

Text realized that his friend was hurt and he 'lowed that Mr. McNeil was the best bird-dog man in the county. The flattery might help to offset the charge of cowardice that the little Negro had made against his friend's father. Text couldn't stand to see Lonnie hurt. He jammed his hands in his overall pockets and grinned at Lonnie. "Lady folks sho' are buttinskies," Text said. "All time trying to keep men folks from whupping each other. Lady folks sho' are scutters. All 'cept your maw and my maw, huh, Lon?"

Lonnie said, "Mr. Eben is just a crotchety man. Mother said so. He don't mean no harm."

"That's what you say," Text said. "But he's a scutter from 'way back. Maw says when he kills beeves he drinks the blood, and I'se popeyed scared of him. His lan' say, 'Posted. Keep off. Law.' And I ain't messin' around over there."

They turned Moreover loose near a field of stubble and watched him range. Lonnie often had worked dogs with his father and had seen the best run at field trials. He trained Moreover by inspiring confidence in him. The first time Text shot over him, Moreover cowed, but now he no longer was gun shy and worked for the sheer joy of working. Lonnie never upbraided him. When Moreover showed a streak of good traits, the boys patted him, when he erred, they simply ignored him. The dog had a marvelous range and moved through the saw grass at an easy gait, never tiring.

He had a strange point. He cocked his long head in the air, then turned slowing toward Lonnie as he froze to his point. But having caught Lonnie's eye, he always turned his head back and pointed his nose toward the birds, his head high, his tail as stiff as a ramrod. He was not spectacular, but constant. He ran at a sort of awkward lope, twisting his head as though he still were tugging a block. But he certainly covered ground.

"He sho' is a good dawg," Text said.

They were working him near Eben's farm and Moreover, catching wind of a huge covey, raced through the stubble and disappeared in the sage. When the boys found him he was frozen on a point far inside farmer Eben's posted land. And watching Moreover from a pine thicket was Eben, a shotgun held loosely in the crook of his arm.

Text was terror-stricken and gaped at Eben as though the stubble-faced man were an ogre. Lonnie took one look at his dog, then at the man, and walked to the thicket. Text was in his shadow. "Please don't shoot him Mr. Eben," Lonnie said.

The farmer said, "Huh?"

"Naw, suh, please don't shoot him." Text found his courage. "He couldn't read yo' posted sign."

Eben scowled. "I don't aim to shoot him. That is, less'n he gets 'round my sheep. I was watching his point. Right pretty, ain't it?"

Lonnie said. "Mighty pretty. He's a good dog, Mr. Eben. If ever you want a mess of birds, I'll give you the loan of him."

"Nothin' shaking," Eben said. "He's that biscuit eater your paw gave that niggah over the ridge."

Moreover still was on the point and when Lon heard the dreaded word he turned quickly to his dog. The dog's eyes blinked, but he didn't break his point. Text protested, "Don't go callin' him that, please, suh. He don't like it."

"He can't read my posted sign, but he can understand English, huh?" Eben laughed. He admired the dog's point again and then flushed the birds by rustling the grass. The quail got up and Eben shot one. Moreover didn't flinch. Eben ordered him to fetch but the big, brooding dog turned his head toward Lonnie and just stood there. He wouldn't obey Mr. Eben and the farmer was furious. He picked up a stick and started toward the dog, but Lon and Text jumped beside Moreover.

The dog showed his fangs.

"I'll teach that biscuit eater to fetch dead birds," Eben snarled.

"If you touch my dog, I'll tell Papa," Lon said, slowly.

"I'm not afraid of your papa. And get that dog off'n my land or I'll sprinkle him with bird shot." He glared at Moreover and the dog crouched to spring. "I believe that dog would jump me," Eben said.

"He will if'n you bother me or Lon," said Text. "He won't 'low nobody to bother us."

Lonnie patted his dog and whistled and Moreover followed him and Text.

Lonnie was moody at supper and his mother reckoned he needed a tonic or something. He didn't eat but one helping of chicken pie, corn on the cob, string beans, light bread, molasses, butter and sweet potato pie. Usually he had two helpings and at least two glasses of buttermilk. His mother was worried about him, but his father knew that something was bothering the boy and kept his peace.

Finally, Lon took a deep breath and asked his father, "How come you didn't whip Mr. Eben that time he kicked your dog?"

Harve looked quickly at his wife and swallowed. "What made you think of that question?"

"Nothin'," said Lon. "I was just wondering. If a man kicked my dog, I'd bust him open."

"Well, I tell you, Son. I've had my share of fighting. It never proves anything. Anything can fight. Dogs, cats, skunks, and such things. But a man is supposed to be different. He's supposed to have some sense. I don't mind a good fight if there's something to fight for. I'd fight for you and your mother and our country, but I won't fight for foolishness." He knew his wife was pleased with his words, but he wasn't pleased with himself. He wished there was some way he could meet Eben without everybody knowing about it. He was a peace-loving man, but not too peace loving.

Harve knew his son wasn't satisfied with the explanation. He frowned and glanced at his wife. He hadn't punished Eben simply because he didn't think the crime of kicking a dog justified a beating. There had been a time when he thought differently. But he was older now, and respected. He wondered if Lonnie thought he was afraid of Eben, and the thought bothered him.

"I wish we had the papers on Moreover," Lonnie changed the subject. "I want to register him."

Harve said, "I got the papers, Son. You can have 'em. What you gonna do, run your dog against my Belle in the county-seat trials?" He was joshing the boy. Ordinarily, Harve wouldn't enter Silver Belle in such two-bit trials as the county meets. She was a national champion and no dogs in the little meet would be in her class. But Harve wanted to get her in perfect shape for the big meet and the county trials would help.

Lonnie looked at his father. "That's what I aim to do," he said. "Run my dog against yours."

The father laughed loudly, and his laughter trailed off into a chuckle. Lonnie enjoyed hearing his father laugh that way. "It's a great idea, Son. So you have trained that biscuit eater for the trials! Where are you going to get your entry fee?"

"He ain't no biscuit eater!" Lonnie said defiantly.

His mother was startled at his impudence to his father. But Harve shook his head at his wife and said, " 'Course he ain't, Son. I'm sorry. And just to show that me and Belle ain't scared of you and Moreover, I'll give you and Text the job of painting around the kennels. You can earn your entry fee. Is it a go?"

"Yes siree bob," Lonnie stuffed food in his mouth and hurried through his meal. "I'm going to high-tail it over and tell Text and Moreover."

Harve walked down the front path with his son. It was nice to walk down the path with his son. The father said simply and in man's talk, "Maybe I'm batty to stake you and your dog to your entry fee. You might whip me and Belle, and Mr. Ames might give you my job of training his dogs."

Lonnie didn't reply. But at the gate he paused and faced his father. "Papa, you ain't scared of Mr. Eben, are you?"

The trainer leaned against the gate and lit his pipe. "Son," he said. "I ain't scared of nothing but God. But don't tell your mother." He put his hand on his boy's shoulder. "You're getting to be a big boy, Lonnie. Before long you'll be a man. I'm mighty proud of you."

"I'm proud of you, too, Papa, even if you didn't whip Mr. Eben."

"You and Text have done a mighty fine job with your dog. It takes a good man to handle a dog like yours. He ain't had much chance in life. He really ain't much 'count. But you boys have shown patience and courage with him. So I'll tell you what I'll do. If you fellows make a good showing at the trials, I'll let you bring that dog back to the kennels."

"Is it a deal, Papa? If we do good, can I bring my li'l ol' dog back home?"

"It's a deal," said Harve, and they shook hands.

Lonnie ran down to the branch and whistled for Text and told him the good news.

"Gee m'netty," Text said. "But who's going to handle him, me or you? Can't but one of us work him."

"Count out," said Lonnie. "That'll make it fair and square."

Text began counting out, pointing his finger at Lon then at himself as he recited slowly:

> "William come Trimble-toe,
> He is a good fisherman.
> Catches hens, puts 'em in pens,
> Some lay eggs, some lay none.
> Wire, brier, Limberlock,
> Three geese in a flock,
> One flew east, one flew west,
> One flew over the cuckoo's nest.
> O-U-T spells out and out you go,
> You dirty old dish rag you."

Text was pointing at himself when he said the last word, so he was out. "You're it, Lon," he said. "You work him and I'll help."

Mr. Ames sat on the steps of the gun-club lodge and laughed when he saw his truck coming up the driveway. His cronies, who had come to the county seat for the trials—a sort of minor-league series—laughed, too. Harve was driving. Silver Belle was beside him. Lonnie and Text were on the truck bed with dogs all around them, and behind the truck, tied with cotton rope, loped Moreover. Mr. Ames shook hands with his trainer and met the boys.

"We got competition," Harve said, and nodded toward Moreover.

Ames studied the big dog. "By Joe, Harve! That used to be my dog. Is that the old bis—"

"Sh-h-h!" Harve commanded. "Don't say it. It hurts the dog's feelings. Or so the boys say."

Ames understood. He had a son at home. He walked around Moreover and looked at him. "Mighty fine dog, boys. . . . If he beats Belle, I might hire you, Lonnie, and fire your father." He winked at Harve, but the boys didn't see him.

They took Moreover to the kennels. They didn't have any money to buy rations, so Text ran to the kitchen of the lodge and soon had a job doing chores. Moreover's food was assured, for it was easy for Text to slip liver and bits of good beef for the dog.

Lonnie bedded his dog down carefully and combed him and tried to make him look spruce. But Moreover would not be spruce. There was a quizzical look in his eyes. The other dogs took attention as though they expected it, but Moreover rubbed his head along the ground and scratched his ears against the kennel box and mussed himself up as fast as Lonnie cleaned him. But he seemed to know that Lonnie expected something of him. All the other dogs were yelping and were nervous. But Moreover just flopped on his side and licked Lonnie's hands.

Inside the lodge, Ames asked Harve, "How's Belle?"

"Tiptop," said Harve. "She'll win hands down here, and I'm laying that she'll take the Grand National later. I'm gonna keep my boy with me, Mr. Ames. Text can stay with the help."

"What do those kids expect to do with that biscuit eater?" Ames laughed.

"You know how boys are. I'll bet this is the first time in history a colored boy and a white boy ever had a joint entry in a field trial. They get riled if anybody calls him a biscuit eater."

"Can't blame them, Harve," Ames said. "I get mad if anybody makes fun of my dogs. We are all alike, men and boys."

"You said it. Since the first, I reckon, boys have got mad if a fellow said anything against their mothers or dogs."

"Or fathers?" Ames suggested.

"Depends on the father," said Harve. "Wish Lonnie's dog could make a good showing. Do the boy a heap of good."

They were standing by the fireplace and Ames said, "I hope that big brute is not in a brace with Belle. She's a sensitive dog."

Then he laughed. "Be funny, Harve, if that dog whipped us. I'd run you bow-legged."

All the men laughed, but when a waiter told the pantry maid the story, he neglected to say that the threat was a jest. The pantry maid told the barkeeper. The barkeeper told the cook, and by the time the story was circulated around the kitchen, the servants were shispering that rich Mr. Ames had threatened to fire poor Mr. Harve because his son had fetched a biscuit eater to the field trials.

The morning of the first heat, Text met Lonnie at the kennels, and together they fed Moreover. "Let's put some good ol' gunpowder in his vittles," Text said. "Make him hunt better."

"Aw, that's superstition," said Lonnie.

"I don't care what it is, it helps," said Text.

Lonnie didn't believe in tempting luck, so Moreover was fed a sprinkling of gunpowder.

Text said, "I got my lucky buckeye along. We bound to have luck, Lon."

Lonnie was getting too big for such foolishness, but then he remembered. "I caught a sweet stinker not so long ago," he whispered, "and he swum the right way."

"A good ol' sweet-stinking mellow bug?" asked Text eagerly. "Lon, good luck gonna bust us in two halves."

Harve took Silver Belle out in an early brace and the pointer completely outclassed her rival. Her trainer sent her back to her kennel and went into the fields with Ames to watch Moreover in his first race. He was braced with a rangy setter. Even the judges smiled at the two boys and their dog. Text, in keeping with the rules of the sport, gave no orders.

The spectators and judges were mounted, but the handlers were on foot. Lonnie put his dog down on the edge of a clover field and the judges instructed that the dogs be set to work. Moreover's competitor leaped away and began hunting, but Moreover just rolled over, then jumped up and loped around the boy, leaping on him and licking his face. The judges scowled. It was bad behavior for a bird dog. Lonnie and Text walked into the field and Moreover followed. Lonnie leaned over his dog and whispered in his ear. The big dog jerked up his head, cocked it, and began casting. He ranged to the edge of the field and worked in. He loped past a patch of saw grass, slowed suddenly, wheeled and pointed, his head high, his right leg poised and his tail stiff as a poker.

Lonnie kept his dog on the point until the judges nodded approval and then the boy threw a stick among the birds and flushed them. Moreover didn't blink an eye when the birds whirred away and Lonnie shot over him. Then the boy called his dog to the far edge of a field and set him ranging again. He was on a point in a flash.

Ames looked at Harve. "That's a good dog, McNeil. He's trained beautifully. He'll give us a run for our money sure as shooting. If that dog beats Belle, it'll make us look bad."

Harve was beaming with pride. "It proves what I've always preached. A bird dog will work for a man, if the man understands him. I couldn't do anything with that dog, but he'll work his heart out for my boy and Text. But don't worry, Mr. Ames, he can't beat Belle."

To the utter amazement of everybody, except Lonnie and Text, Moreover swept through to the final series, or heat, and was pitted against Silver Belle, for the championship. Harve regretted then that he had entered Belle. He wasn't worried about his dog winning. He had confidence in Silver Belle, but the mere fact that a grand champion was running against a biscuit eater was bad. And, too, Harve hated to best his own son in the contest. News that father and son were matched, with the famous Belle against a biscuit eater, brought sportsmen and sportswriters swarming to the county seat. Harve and Lonnie slept and ate together, but the man didn't discuss the contest with his son. He didn't want to make him nervous. He treated Lonnie as he would treat any other trainer.

Neither Harve nor Lonnie had much to say that morning at breakfast. Once the father, his mouth full of batter cakes, looked over at his son and winked. Lonnie winked back. But the boy didn't eat much. He was too excited. The excitement, however, didn't interfere with Text's eating. The other sportsmen kidded Harve and joshed him about the possibility of a biscuit eater beating Silver Belle.

The spectators and judges rode to the edge of a field of stubble and Harve snapped a bell on his dog's collar. It was the first time he had used the bell during the trials and Lonnie knew what it meant. His father was going to give Silver Belle her head, let her show all that was in her, let her range far and wide. Lonnie's heart sank and Text rolled his eyes. Silver Belle stood there beautifully, but Moreover tucked his head and flopped his ears. The judges gave the signal and Harve said, "Go get 'em, girl."

The champion dashed into the stubble and soon was out of sight. Moreover didn't leap away as he should have, but rubbed against Lonnie's legs and watched Silver Belle for a minute, then began running along her trail. There was no order between Lonnie and his dog, only understanding. Moreover looked like a biscuit eater all right. He didn't race as most bird dogs do, but he sort of trotted away, taking his time. The judges smiled.

The men heard the tinkling of the bell on Silver Belle and knew that the champion was still casting. The dog had ranged far beyond a ridge and Harve did his best to keep her in sight. Suddenly, the bell was silent and Harve ran to his dog. Belle was on a point and was rigid. Her trim body was thrown forward a bit, her nose, perfectly tilted, was aimed toward a clump of sage. She didn't flex a muscle. She might have been made of marble.

"Point!" Harve shouted, and the judges came.

Moreover crept behind Silver Belle and stopped, honoring her point. Harve smiled at his son and Lonnie's heart beat faster. It was a beautiful point. The judges nodded approval and Harve flushed the birds and shot over his dog, and Belle took it as a champion should.

When the echo of the shot died away, Belle walked to her master and he patted her. Lonnie took Moreover by the collar and the judges gave the signal that the dogs be released again. Belle raced into the stubble, but Moreover swung along at an easy gait. He cast a bit to the right, sniffed and found the trail that Belle had just made. He never depended on ground scents but on body scents and kept his nose high enough to catch any smells the wind blew his way.

He got the odor of birds and the muscles of his legs suddenly bunched. He leaped away, easing his nose higher in the air and raced back up the trail Belle had made. Suddenly, he crouched. Slowly, noiselessly, he took two steps, then three and froze to a point. His right leg came up slowly, deliberately. He cocked his head in that strange fashion, and the quizzical, comical look came into his eyes. Moreover was a still hunter and never waited for orders. Lonnie clicked the safety off his gun and watched his dog. Text was beside him. The judges and spectators were far away.

"Look at that li'l ol' dawg," said Text. "He's got himself a mess of birds."

Lonnie cupped his hands and shouted to the judges, "Point!"

"Point!" Text whooped.

Moreover held his point as Lonnie shot over him. Belle honored his point and as soon as the gun sounded and Moreover got a nod from Lonnie, the big dog dashed to the right and flashed to another point.

The judges whistled softly. "Most beautiful work I ever saw," whispered one. Ames' face took on a worried look. So did Harve's. The big dog had picked up a covey almost under Belle's nose.

Belle settled down to hunt. She seemed everywhere. She dashed to a point on the fringe of a cornfield and got a big covey. She raced over the ridge, her nose picking up scents in almost impossible places. Moreover sort of ambled along, never wasting energy, but every time Belle got a covey he honored her and then cast for a few minutes, pointed and held. He waited for her to set the pace and it was a killing pace.

Belle held a covey for ten minutes near a rabbit's den. The smell of rabbit was strong in her nose, but she knew birds were there and she handled them.

It was then that Moreover pulled his downwind point. He was running with the wind and didn't get the odor of the covey until he had passed it. But when the hot odor of birds filled his nose, he leaped, reversed himself in mid air and landed on a point, his front feet braced, his choke-bore nose held high.

It was the most beautiful performance of the morning. Belle

tried to match it, but couldn't. She was hunting because she was bred to hunt. Moreover was hunting from habit and because Lonnie expected him to.

It was exasperating. Belle tried every trick of her training, but her skill was no match for his stamina. Her heart was pumping rapidly and she was tired when the crowd passed near the club house and the judges suggested refreshments. Harve and Lon rubbed their dogs while they waited. Belle's tongue was hanging out, but Moreover just sat on his haunches and watched his master. Text ran into the lodge to help fetch food and drink to the crowd. He strutted into the kitchen and told the servants that Moreover was running Silver Belle ragged.

The servants shook their heads and one told him that Mr. Ames would fire Harve if Moreover beat Belle. Text couldn't swallow his food. He ran out of the lodge and called Lonnie aside. Lonnie's throat hurt when he heard the story that Moreover's victory would cost his father the job of training Mr. Ames' dogs. He stared at Moreover and then at Text.

"That Mr. Ames sho' is a scutter," said Text. "A frazzlin' scutter. He's worse'n Mr. Eben. What we gonna do, Lon?"

Lonnie said sadly, "He's half your dog, Text. What you say?"

The little Negro put his hand on his friend's arm. "We can't let yo' paw get in no trouble on account of us. He got to have a job. He got to eat, ain't he?"

Lonnie nodded and bit his lip. He noticed that his father's face was drawn as the contest was renewed. Ames was nervous. The two men had worked for years to get Belle to perfection, and win the Grand National for the third time. And here an outcast dog was hunting her heart out at a minor meet. Lonnie thought his father was worried about his job and that Ames was angry.

His mind was made up. He watched Moreover leap across a branch, then race toward a rail fence. He and Text were right behind him.

The big dog held his head high for a split second, than sprang. He balanced himself perfectly on the rail fence, turned his face to Lonnie and seemed to smile. The he tilted his nose and pointed a covey just beyond the fence.

Lonnie and Text just stood there for a minute, their mouths

wide open. Pointing quail from a rail fence! Lonnie choked up with pride, but he didn't shout "point." He didn't want the judges to know, but the judges saw Moreover.

The stopped their horses and gaped. One judge said in a whisper, "That's the best dog I ever saw."

Harve said, "Pointing from a fence. I'm looking right at him but I can't believe it. No dog's that good. That beats Belle."

A judge told Lonnie to flush the birds and shoot over his dog. The boy didn't move, however. His tongue was frozen to the roof of his mouth. Then he cupped his hands and said, hoarsely, "Hep!" It was an order Moreover had never heard. Lonnie thought the strange order would startle his dog and cause him to break his point, but Moreover stood rigid.

Again Lon called, "Hep!" The dog didn't budge. The judges couldn't understand the action of the boy and Harve was puzzled.

Lonnie tried again and Moreover turned his head and faced his master, amazement in his eyes.

Ames whispered, "He's breaking. That good-for-nothing streak is cropping out."

Moreover didn't break, however. He settled to the point and in desperation Lonnie walked close to him and hissed, "Biscuit eater! Low-life, no'count, egg-sucking biscuit eater."

Text cringed when he heard the words. Moreover faced the boy again and blinked his eyes. Slowly his tail dropped. Then his head. Lonnie repeated it. "Biscuit eater." There were tears in his eyes and his voice quivered.

Moreover tucked his tail between his legs and leaped from the fence, flushing the birds. Then he turned his big, sad eyes toward Lonnie. He couldn't believe his ears and must see for himself that his master had thrown him down. Lonnie stood there by the fence, his fists clenched and tears rolling down his face. Moreover ran to the lodge and hid under it. He wanted to be alone, away from the sight and smell of men.

Lonnie and Text ran after him. They couldn't face the crowd. The judges didn't know what to make of it and the spectators muttered at the strange performance.

Ames looked at Harve for an explanation, and Harve said, "I

don't get it. My son called his dog off. He quit. He threw his dog down."

The judges awarded the trophy to Mr. Ames, but the sportsman wouldn't touch it. "We didn't earn it. Those kids and their dog beat us. I won't have it. You take it, Harve."

Harve shook his head slowly. "It's not mine. I don't want the thing. I can't understand my son. I can't understand why he quit. That dog worked hard for those boys and they double-crossed him. I heard my boy call his dog a biscuit eater. He would fight anybody else who called him a biscuit eater. My boy broke his dog's heart. . . ."

It took Lonnie and Text a long time to coax Moreover from under the lodge. The dog crawled to Lonnie's feet and rolled over. Lonnie patted him, but Moreover didn't lick his face. "He's mad at us," Text said. "He don't like us no more."

"His feelings are hurt," Lonnie said, as Moreover lay down and thumped his tail. . . . "I'm sorry I said it Moreover, I had to."

Text said, "We sorry, puppy dawg. We didn't mean it. But us had to say it, huh, Lon? Aw, don't cry, Lon. Ol' Moreover knows you didn't mean it. Please don't cry. Don't let ol' Moreover see us bawlin'."

Harve didn't speak to the boys as they loaded the truck. Mr. Ames wanted to tell the boys good-bye, but they walked away from him. Harve had his boy sit on the front seat by him. They said good-bye to the crowd and rolled away.

Finally, Harve asked Lonnie, "How come you did that, Son?"

Lonnie didn't reply and the father didn't press the point. "Don't ever quit, Son, if you're winning or losing. It ain't fair to the dog."

"My dog is mad at me," Lonnie said.

"We'll give him a beef heart when we get home. His feelings are hurt because you threw him down. But he'll be all right. Dogs are not like folks. They'll forgive a fellow." He knew then that Lonnie had a reason for what he had done, and he knew that if his son wanted him to know the reason, he would tell him.

Back home, Lonnie cooked a beef heart and took the plate to

the back gallery where the dog was tied. Moreover slunk into the shadows and Harve said, "Untie him, Son. You can let him run free over here. I made a deal with you and I'll stick to it. You can keep your dog right here. He needn't go back to Text's house."

The boy hugged his father gratefully and untied his dog. Moreover sniffed the food and toyed with it. He never had had such good food before. Lonnie and his father went back into the house.

After supper, Lonnie went to see about his dog. The meat hadn't been eaten and Moreover was gone.

"He's still mad at me," Lon said. "He don't like me no more. He's gone off and I'm going after him."

"I'll go with you," said Harve, and got a lantern.

Text hadn't seen the dog. He joined the search and the three hunted through the woods for an hour or so, Lonnie whistling for Moreover, and Text calling him, "Heah heah, fellow. Heah."

Harve sat on a stump, put the lantern down and called the boys to him. He had seen only a few dogs that would refuse to eat beef heart as Moreover had done.

"Text," he said sharply, "did Moreover ever suck eggs at your place?"

Text rolled his eyes and looked at Lonnie. "Yas, suh." He was afraid to lie to Harve. "But I didn't tell Lon. I didn't want to hurt his feelings. Moreover was a suck-egger, good and proper."

Harve said, "Go on, tell us about it."

"Maw put hot pepper in a raw egg, but it didn't break him. My ol' brother, ol' First-and-Second Thessalonians, reckoned he'd kill Moreover less'n he quit suck-egging. So I got to snitching two eggs ever' night and feeding them to him. He sho' did like eggs."

Lonnie said sharply. "You hadn't ought to have done that, Text."

Harve said, "Did you feed him eggs tonight?"

"Naw, suh," said Text. "I reckoned he had vittles at yo' house. We had done gathered all the eggs and Maw had counted them by nightfall."

Harve got up. "I'm worried. Let's walk up the branch. . . . Text, you take the left side . . . Lonnie, you take the right side. I'll walk up the bank."

Lonnie found Moreover's body, still warm, only a few feet from the water. He stooped over his dog, put the lantern by his head and opened his mouth. The dog had been poisoned. Lonnie straightened. He didn't cry. His emotions welled up within him, and having no outlet, hurt him.

He knelt beside his dog and stroked Moreover's head. Then he pulled the dog's body into his lap and whispered, "My li'l ol' dog, my li'l ol' dog. . . ."

He looked up at his father and said simply, "I'm sorry I called him a biscuit eater."

Harve was too choked up to speak and Text sat down by Lonnie and stroked the dog, too. "He was trying to get to water. I sho' hate to think of him dying, wanting just one swallow of good ol' water."

"Who killed him, Papa?" Lonnie got to his feet and faced his father.

"That's what I'm aiming to find out." The man picked up the lantern and walked away, the boys at his heels. They walked over the ridge to Eben's house, and Harve pounded on the front gallery until the farmer appeared.

"My boy's dog is dead," Harve said. "Reckoned you might know something about it."

Eben said, "If he was poisoned, I do. He's a suck-egg dog. I put poison in some eggs and left them in the field. Seems he mout' have committed suicide, McNeil."

"Seems you made it powerful easy for him to get those poisoned eggs," Harve said.

"Ain't no room round here for suck-egg dogs. His daddy was a sheep killer, too. It's good riddance. You ain't got no cause to jump me, Harve McNeil."

Harve said, "He's right, boys. A man's got a right to poison eggs on his own land, and if a dog sucks 'em and dies, the dog's to blame."

Eben said, "Reckon you young'uns want to bury that dog. Buzzards will be thick tomorrow. You can have the loan of my shovel."

Lonnie looked at the man a long time. He bit his lip so he couldn't cry. "Me and Text will dig a hole with a stick," he said, and turned away.

"You boys go bury him," Harve said. "I'll be home in a few minutes."

Lonnie and Text walked silently into the woods. Text said, "He sho' was a good dawg, huh, Lon? You ain't mad at me 'cause I fed him eggs, are you, Lon?"

"No, Text. Ain't no use in being mad at you. Getting mad at you won't bring ol' Moreover back. Let's wait up here and watch Papa. He can't see us."

Back at Eben's gallery, Harve propped against a post and spoke slowly, "I would have paid you for all the eggs the dog took. My boy loved that dog, Eben."

"Looka heah!" Eben said. "I know my rights."

"I know mine," Harve said. "I always pay my debts, Eben. And I always collect them. I ain't got no cause to get riled because that dog stole poisoned eggs. But I ain't got no use for a man who will poison a dog. If a dog is mad, shoot him. It's low-life to plant poisoned eggs where a dog can find them. But you were within your rights. I ain't forgot another little thing, however. Two years ago you kicked one of my dogs . . ."

"He barked at me and scared my team on the road," Eben said.

"A dog has got a right on the road, and he's got a right to bark." Harve straightened slowly. A look of fear came into Eben's eyes and he backed away. Harve said softly, "You're a bully. I don't like bullies. I don't like folks who go around causing trouble, picking on their neighbors and keeping everything upset. I'm a peace loving man, but even peace loving folks get fed up sometimes." He reached out and grabbed Eben by the collar.

"I'll law you!" Eben shouted.

Harve didn't reply. He slapped the man with his open palm, and when Eben squared off to fight, Harve knocked him down.

In the shadows of the woods, Lonnie whispered to Text, "What did I tell you? Papa ain't scared of nothing, cep'n God."

They buried their dog near the branch. Text poured water in the grave. "I can't stand to think of him wanting water when there's aheap of water so close. Reckon if he could have got to the ol' branch he could have washed out that poison? Reckon, Lon?"

"Maybe so."

They were walking to Lonnie's house. "My ol'buckeye and

your sweet-stinking mellow bug ain't helped us much, eh, Lon? Luck is plum' mad at us, ain't it, Lon?"

Lonnie waited at the gate until his father arrived. "Me and Text saw the fight," he said. "I won't tell Mother. Women are scutters, ain't they, Papa? Always trying to keep men folks from fighting."

Harve smiled and kept his right hand in his pocket. He didn't offer the boys another dog. He could have easily, but he was too wise. Lonnie and Text would have other dogs, but there would never be another dog like their first dog. And Harve knew it would be crude to suggest another dog might replace More-over.

He peered into the darkness and saw a car parked behind the house, then hurried inside. Mr. Ames was warming himself by the fire and talking with Mrs. McNeil. She went to the kitchen to brew coffee, and left the men alone, after calling for Lonnie and Text to follow her.

Ames said, "I heard why your boy called his dog off. Call him and that little colored boy in here. I can't go back East with those boys thinking what they do of me."

Lonnie and Text stood by the fire and Ames said, "That story you heard about me isn't true. I wouldn't have fired this man if your dog had won. We were joking about it and the servants got the story all wrong. I just wanted you boys to know that."

Harve said, "Yes. But even if Mr. Ames would have fired me, it wouldn't have made any difference. You did what you thought was right, but you were wrong. Don't ever quit a race once you start it."

Lonnie told Mr. Ames, "My dog is dead. I'm sorry I called him a biscuit eater. He wasn't. I just want you to know that."

Ames lit his pipe and passed his tobacco pouch to Harve. He saw Harve's bloody hand as the trainer accepted the tobacco.

"Ran into some briars," Harve said.

"Lots of them around here." Ames' eyes twinkled. "Just been thinking, Harve. We got some fine pups coming along. You need help down here. Better hire a couple of good men."

"Good men are sort of scarce," Harve said.

"The kind I want are mighty scarce," said Ames. "They've got to be men with a lot of courage, who can lose without grumbling and win without crowing."

"Believe I know where I can get hold of a couple to fill the bill." Harve put his hand on Lon's shoulder and smiled at his son and at Text.

"Well, I'll trust your judgment," Ames said. He shook hands all around. "I've got to be going. Good night, men."

THE HUNTING COAT

Paul Annixter

This warm and moving story, told through the eyes of a setter, is one of my all-time favorites. Paul Annixter was an extremely prolific magazine writer, producing over 400 stories published in nearly every magazine in the United States, Canada and England. His novel, Swiftwater, *was widely praised, as was his collection of tales of outdoor action and adventure,* Brought to Cover, *published by A. A. Wyn, Inc., New York, in 1945.* The Hunting Coat *originally appeared in the Canadian magazine,* MacLean's, *in 1947, and was later included in* Brought to Cover. *I promise that you'll find this eloquent tale the perfect last chapter for the dog section of* The Bobwhite Quail Book. *If your eyes aren't misty when you read the last paragraph, you're a better man than me, McGee!*

IT BEGAN to look as if he had another young hunter to initiate in the niceties of the game. The very thought of that tired him. He had been so tired anyway, just doing nothing. All summer he had drowsed and dreamed the days away at the great kennels, only going out for his short daily exercise. He had thought it might go on like that. But fall was coming on. Birds were beginning to band in restless flocks. Morning and evening the tang of hunting weather was in the air. That stirred him. As long as he lived he would always answer to that. Of course, you had to have a man with a shotgun when fall came on, or die.

As the days sharpened, more and more men came to look at him and stand talking before his runway—gun-dog, championship talk—while he looked away pretending not to hear what they said. So many masters he had had to train since Cam Royster died. Four of them during those eight years and now this Bryanston, the fifth, the youngest of them all. He was too famous; there had been too much potential money in him, as Champion Maidstone Hi-Pockets, winner of the Continental, for them to let him stay on with the mistress when Cam's small estate was broken up. So he had gone with the rest of the things, sold to the highest bidder; he whose code and life had been to serve one, to obey one, and to love one master only.

Four times passed from hand to hand. And each of the four owners had thought himself a hunter and slowly Hi-Pockets had had to undo their many faults and teach them the punctilios of the hunt, as well as discipline their callow young dogs. Even before he had won the Continental he had been a stickler on form. One of the four had lacked even respect for the laws of the game and had shot a sitting bird when no one was looking. Hi-Pockets had stood looking at him witheringly and the man had shouted orders and cursed him when he refused to bring the dead bird in. Hi had picked it up at last, as if it were something dirty, but he refused to bring it to hand, simply dropped it on the ground and looked away, lip lifted from his teeth in his twisted sneer of disgust. Only an Englishman could have taken the man down half so effectively. His integrity, his sheer consecration to the game had gotten under the hide of even that callow hunter and during the year and a half Hi remained with him he had changed the man over from a high-handed tyro to a regular hunter, one of the cult.

He who was the most faultless quail dog in the South had been used for duck all one year and another year he had been taken north to Minnesota to hunt the wily partridge. That was a breach of taste as well as etiquette, but within an hour he had mastered both techniques. In quail hunting you could show your flashing form, you went as fast as you could and you saw the country for miles and miles and it was glorious! Duck and partridge were interesting, but you must go very quietly and at the first faint scent slow to a creep, and never, never flush your bird, never overrun it. He had flushed both duck and grouse on his first try and had been reprimanded until he grinned in an agony of contrition. After that no more birds were flushed. He had just crept about finding birds in every direction, but there was no excitement in it, no way of showing the marvelous field technique for which you had worked for years. He disliked it because it was strange. He disliked strange things that interfered with well-learned habits.

At first he had thought that Bryanston might be the callowest of all his owners, but he began to have certain reservations on that even before the transaction was over. Bryanston stood talking with the kennelman in the runway, and the smell of him and the sound of his voice were all to the good. That counted most. Something had made Hi rest his shoulder against Bryanston's strong leg as a traveler might rest against a tree, and the man's hand had come down to his head. The feel was right too.

". . . but a thousand dollars! It's a frightful price for a dog of his age."

"He's getting old; we're not hiding the fact," said the kennelman. "But he's a champion, man; as famous in the sporting world as Sarah Bernhardt was on the stage. It's worth the money just to associate with such a dog in the field."

"But he may not last more than a season; two at most."

"Perhaps not. His speed's gone. But he's got all the brains and all the nose in the world. And while he lasts you'll have sweet and faultless hunting. You'll see and learn things you'll never forget. If he flushes a single bird on you, sir, we'll be ready to pay your money back. . . . But of course, if you'd rather try one of these young dogs . . ."

Bryanston had looked up and down the line of kennels, but his eye came back to Hi. He knelt for a minute, his hand with cunningly moving fingers running down Hi's neck and back. The old Champion was a Llewellyn setter, with the vivid black and white coat that makes the ideal gun dog, black and white constituting the apex of visibility in fog or dense cover. This had been a high point in his favor on that long-ago day of rain and blow when he had won the Continental. Two prominent body spots like pockets, high on each white shoulder, had given him his name. He was deep-chested and big-boned for endurance, his seamed phlegmatic face scarred by briars, his worn and broken nails testifying to the countless trails he had followed. There was a world of wisdom and dignity in the splendid dome of his head, craft to solve the riddles of the woods and field, soul quality to probe to the core of a man's heart.

"I'll take him," Bryanston said, rising, and Hi, who knew many English words and could catch the very sense of a man's thought, knew the matter was settled.

"One thing, sir," said the kennelman, pulling something out of the kennel door. "This old hunting coat must go with him. It belonged to Cam Royster, his original trainer. He's slept on it for years and I fancy you'd have some trouble with him if you left it behind."

"I see," smiled Bryanston. "One-man fixation. A good dog always has it."

Things began with a bit of a boner on Bryanston's part. "Come on, old boy," he had called as they reached the car, and patted the front seat cushion. Hi had come and heaved himself onto it courteously, but he hadn't stayed. After a minute or two he climbed laboriously over the seat back, his legs for some reason stiffer than ever that day, and dropped into the rear seat. No dog belonged in the front seat as everyone ought to know. The back of the car was for dogs. The front seat was for another hunter or two who might be picked up along the way. So it had always been.

But Bryanston didn't seem aware of his blunder. He was young, but he had dignity and a certain containment. Hi studied him intently as they drove away, muzzle lifted high in air like an aerial to get the subtler story that eyes and ears didn't tell. So intent was his scrutiny that Bryanston turned. Hi's mouth snapped shut and he blinked at the man down the length of his jowl.

"It's all right, old snoozer," chuckled Bryanston. "Do it your way; your idea's as good as mine."

The voice reminded Hi of something. "Snoozer"—The word echoed down the years from those all-conquering days when Cam Royster was the core and soul of his existence. Strange. Cam had called him that.

They drove a long way through gorgeous country filled with streams and wonderful bird cover, but they did not pick up any more hunters. Hi had expected a kennel full of young dogs, but there were no other dogs at Bryanston's home. He could scarcely believe it. It was like those days of his young prime when Cam had brought him home and they'd gone out to work—just the two of them—in the golden Virginia woods.

There were splendid kennels at the Bryanston place, but apparently he was not going to live a kennel life. He was taken at once into the house, where he gravely made friends with Bryanston's wife and small daughter. He sniffed loudly over the silly names they called him and kept his head high in dignity. He had always disapproved of this hugging business and women in general. But he approved of the deep wide leather chair Bryanston led him to. It stood near the fireplace and he guessed it was going to be his chair when he saw Bryanston spread Cam's leather coat in it. Years before there had been a chair like that, an open fire, and the Coat.

He put his forefeet into the chair and heaved himself up, his toes scratching and slipping on the leather. He was so big that his hind legs trailed over the edge. Later Bryanston slid a hassock up in front of the chair. The hassock held up his legs and it was like a step by which he could walk easily into his chair. Hi saw what it was for, but threw his head high, blinking into space, to simulate that he had no idea why it was there and had no earthly use for it. He was going to be a long time approving of it, he decided.

But somehow he couldn't help approving somewhat of the mistress and the little girl. The touch of the mistress' hand, some caressing quality in her voice, got into his blood and ran along all his nerves in a soothing tide, in spite of the ridiculous things she said. He was Champion Hi-Pockets of Maidstone, attending to vital business, not a precious lamb or an old dear. But her ways were new and different and wonderful. His eyes would follow her with a searching questioning scrutiny as she walked away, but if she turned and caught his look his head would snap high, his haughty gaze losing itself in space.

"Heavens, what dignity—what integration!" Maude Bryanston said. "He makes one utterly self-conscious."

"Everything's strange to him. He'll adjust his life to us in a few days."

"You mean we'll adjust ours to his. Why, you can feel him and his thoughts in the house more than the average person."

He had his dinner in the kitchen, much more than he wanted. Nowadays he was never very hungry. He had to leave two pieces of meat in the dish and it mortified him.

In the evening some of Bryanston's friends came in. Hi-Pockets thumped the chair with his tail two or three times in the hospitable courtesy demanded of such occasions. Everyone gathered around him and a real dog man scratched him expertly back of the ears. It was all utterly familiar. His soft setter eyes went from face to face and presently he closed them with a long sigh, thrusting his nose into a fold of the hunting coat. Long ago the scent of Cam Royster had gone from it; it was thin and worn from many cleanings, but it was a link to hold to—like holding one's bird while the master was gone. It was beyond any understanding of his where Cam had gone, but someday, somehow, he would find him again. All the generations of dogs' confidence in man had kept faith burning within him.

The voices and the snapping of the fire grew fainter and fainter. And presently he was eating his dinner again, but it wasn't Bryanston who stood beside him, it was Cam Royster. And again he had to leave two pieces of meat. He, a young and powerful dog, turning down the fine food the master had given him. It was horrible. He twitched and mumbled in his sleep.

While he slept the people talked.

"You're a lucky beggar, Bryanston," one man was saying. "This is as close as I've ever been to a real champion—much less *the* champion—"

"Yes, this is really something," said the eldest man of the company. "You'd realize it better if you'd been in at the making of him as I was. I can see that stormy, blowy day now as clearly as the details of this room—visibility cut off every now and then by gusts of rain and sleet—most of the dogs quit long since—but Hi-Pockets running, running, a mere white speck sweeping the distant thickets, smashing into his bevy finds, one after the other, and holding, holding his birds, like a statue—then on again, while hundreds of seasoned hunters shouted and cursed him lovingly and galloped after. Never anything like it, I give you my word."

"You're not going to hog him all to yourself, I hope," said the first man. "I'd practically barter my wife and child for a day behind this fellow."

"Hi and I have to get used to each other first," Bryanston said. "We're starting out tomorrow. There'll be some kinks to iron out. He can't forget his original owner, they tell me—"

"Cam Royster. Greatest dog trainer the South ever had. Why, old Ira Eddy, the millionaire sportsman from Philadelphia, and another man in New York used to ship their young dogs across country for Cam to smooth them out."

Next day he and Bryanston went forth together in the October woods. They started at midafternoon, but it was early enough for Hi. No more hunting for him from a pink dawn to a violet dusk. Those days were gone forever. He knew it and hoped it was his secret alone. Bryanston knew it and hid the fact from him.

This year he didn't even feel like moving, though it vaguely shamed him, and perfect gentleman that he was, he simulated eagerness when Bryanston got out his gun. But as soon as they got away from the house he really did feel all the old thrills and did all the old things. When they came to "The Place," he heard the thousand ancient voices in the ancient wind and all the olden scents and meanings were there. It was fall. And you collaborated with a man and a gun in the fall, or you died trying.

He was glad there were no other dogs. He caught Bryanston's glance, put spring into his old legs, and ran to a thicket, skirting it with care to show that he was ready. Bryanston didn't need to speak. Slowly they advanced and almost immediately, he was on a point with high proud head and level tail, moveless as stone. Somewhere within a hundred feet ahead poised a breathless bevy of gold-brown birds with close-held wings. A sharp "quit-quit" and a roar of wings and they were up and Bryanston brought one neatly down.

Hi brought it in without ruffling a feather. They went on and in three minutes he did it again. But Bryanston made a rank miss. Hi turned a rolled-up eye on him and sneezed with disgust. There was a look on his face that Bryanston would never forget—a grin blent with a twisted sneer of pain that wrinkled his black lip. The grin was because he was a gentleman, the sneer was the acute torment of an impresario over an ineptitude. Bryanston stood reprimanded, yet he could scarcely refrain from a shout of laughter.

Sheer self-consciousness had caused the thing. From the outset he had been working against odds. The dog had been touted to him from every quarter as faultless. In him was a youthful sense of diffidence at working with a Champion; then there was the sense of Hi's drill-master perfectionism, and something else—a shadow or a memory—the memory of Cam Royster, who had been as faultless as Hi himself.

They went on and Bryanston took hold of himself, determined

to rub out his error. It was a memorable afternoon. For the first time in his life he was shooting over a dog who looked upon his calling as a consecration. It kept the man on his toes. Only Hi-Pockets' physical powers had flagged, he saw. His form was faultless; his nose, which was his soul, was still the nose of a champion. And bird-sense—Bryanston had never seen anything like it. Hi could tell for hundreds of yards around whether a stretch of woods would be empty or not.

They had two hours of sweet hunting. And shortly before dusk Bryanston partially rubbed out his blunder by making a brilliant double, one of them a cross shot. Not long after that Hi, as if in competition, pointed some more birds, a long way off, with a dead bird still in his mouth, a feat which only the coldest-nosed dog might ever achieve. He brought in the downed bird, so proud, earnest, and intent that it wrung the heart. Bryanston pummeled him on the back quite as he might another hunter. Then they sat resting while a new rapport grew between them. No nuzzling or lying with his muzzle in Bryanston's lap; none of that stuff. Hi simply lay looking up into the strength and shelter of the man's face while wonderful memories that he wouldn't quite admit as yet stirred within him.

They went home in full darkness and Hi sought the Coat and chair, leaving it only long enough to eat. Next morning they tried it again, but Hi's legs were stiff and tired; he moved with heavy feet. He'd have gone on till he fell, but Bryanston took him home before noon. After that it became plain how age was taking its toll on him and Bryanston took him out only on alternate days, with a day of rest between.

They came to dovetail perfectly in the mechanics of the hunt. All the small niceties of the game that Bryanston usually disregarded were carried out to their uttermost convention and the man began to see the deeper reason for them all. It stayed warm and they had a long run of good days. Sometimes Maude Bryanston accompanied them and sometimes a friend of Bryanston's, but it never made any difference to Hi's form or attitude.

Through it all Bryanston never had the usual sense of owning the dog. Between them was a man's understanding of mutual restraint and respect, something to be felt, not seen. A single word of commendation, a touch on the head, was all that passed between them, but it sufficed. To Hi it was all so like those old days with Cam Royster that memory often wavered, scenes overlapped; an old world was being slowly forgotten; another world remembered, come true.

Bryanston sensed the gradual transformation, the slowly strengthening bond of the spirit, and pride filled him. He was fulfilling a great picture of a great hunter and dog-man, or Hi would not have accepted him thus. It was like an accolade, but it was not an ordinary transference. Hi was being faithful not only to Cam Royster, but to a nobler thing, the faithfulness which was in himself.

All too soon the season was over. In December winter set in, the brisk open winter of the South, with bright frosty days and nights. For Hi-Pockets hunting was over, but he and Bryanston often took long tramps together through the leafless woods. Sometimes Bryanston shot squirrels, rabbits, or possum. Hi gravely approved of this, but did not co-operate. Birds were his sole province.

But indoors his Gibraltar had quite broken down. Grudgingly he had allowed his aloofness to melt away under Maude Bryanston's constant affection and still more grudgingly he accepted the love of Bryanston's seven-year-old daughter, Fran. But by midwinter he was shamelessly allowing himself to be petted and hugged by both. Once his love was aroused he was constant as the pole star. This strange new thing, this woman-love—he had never known it before, but it gripped in a way that nothing had ever done, for in it there was need for all his high and knightly courtesy, his gentleness and protection. Each morning he accompanied Fran to school and by afternoon he was waiting for sight of her return.

When summer came he was removed to the kennels for coolness. He lapsed into the apathy of all gun dogs between seasons, lazing the hot weather away until the time came round again to follow gun and trail, the prime reason for a bird dog's existence.

Then another October, another opening day, and once more he and Bryanston roamed the fall woods together. For a month they had halcyon weather and hunting such as Bryanston had never known before. Then in mid-November the years seemed suddenly to whelm the old dog. His eyes had been going bad and it had gotten so he couldn't hold still on a point. He'd tremble with slow vibrations as of palsy and sometimes his hind legs would give out and he'd go down on one hip, his head and tail still holding, holding the point. Long ago, as a tiny pup, before he had been taught anything, it had been like that. He had stood point on the blackbirds and linnets that alighted in his kennel runway. He would hold them, hold them, until his puppy legs trembled and gave under him, though no one ever came to flush the birds for him.

It got so his breathing became raucous at the slightest exertion. His heart was giving out, said the vet who was called in. And there was nothing that could be done about it.

But hunting still meant the breath of life to him. And he wasn't able to forget it, for quail nested just over the ridge back of Bryanston's house. So each day Bryanston tried to take him out—sometimes in the car—for a short swing of twenty minutes or a half hour. On the days when he went forth alone, Hi would watch from the living-room window, mumbling and rumbling in a humility of shame and misery. And he'd wait as if on point for the moment of Bryanston's return. When he saw his figure, when he caught his voice or whistle approaching, he would lie for another few moments, head raised, eyes glowing with intensity, little whines escaping him as though the intensity was too much for him. But before Bryanston would arrive he would return to the Coat and the chair to preserve what little dignity remained to him.

The final day was altogether strange. Even the movements of the wild things weren't altogether according to Hoyle that day, though Bryanston was never sure just how much of it was true and how much due to the hypped-up state he had been in. Fran had been sent away to her aunt's that morning, for it was plain that the end was near.

It was a golden day toward the end of the month, a hunter's hey-day, bright and warm and still, the woods aflame with the first frost fires. Nature seemed putting on a show. The faint smell of wood smoke was in the air and one could catch the pungent breath of nitro powder, too, for some hunters had passed by at midday. Cock quail called on the ridge; wedges of water-fowl were winging southward; squirrels grunted from their knothole doorways.

All afternoon Hi had watched from the open window, taking it all in as if he could never get enough, at times panting and gasping for air, the thudding of his heart quite audible in the room. Toward sunset he lapsed into a doze. Bryanston was sitting by the window when abruptly Hi's old tail went thump, thump, thump on the floor. Bryanston listened, but no one was coming, the house and grounds were utterly quiet.

Hi got stiffly to his feet and came toward him. His tail whirled blissfully; his gaze fixed on Bryanston, yet beyond, in a way that made the hair stir across the man's scalp. An adoring love and devotion filled the steady brown eyes.

He moved over to the chair and the Coat, but his eyes were fixed above, as if awaiting orders, and to Bryanston the whole room was warmed with a glow of union and love. He himself had known enough of death to have had a glimpse through certain veils between the worlds. He always maintained that Cam Royster had come to get his dog that night. Later it was there to be seen in Hi's still open eyes. Glorious in reunion, his spirit was sweeping new hunting grounds, flashing into point after brilliant point, and holding, holding his birds.

Some Fireside Quail Stories

PLAY HOUSE

Nash Buckingham

This gem of a Nash Buckingham story will probably always be indentified as part of "sporting literature" genre. While that distinction will certainly not taint its fame and appeal, the piece seems to me to be good enough to be included in any *anthology of great American short stories. The marvelous quail hunting scenes are but part of a larger tapestry, which Nash weaves with all the story-telling skill of the great masters. The story was first published in* Field & Stream *in January, 1929, and was later reprinted in all editions of* De Shootinest Gent'man. *George Bird Evans, who has become the leading authority on Nash's work and who did the most detailed biographical pieces on Nash and his stories in* The Best of Nash Buckingham (*Winchester Press*), *tells us: "In* Play House, *most of the characters bore fictitious names, excepting Nash's family and the dogs. Nash's daughter knows of no Cousin Charley Johnson. The setter Leo belonged to Nash's long-time friend Bill Joyner (who also appears in* Carry Me Back —Ed.*); 'double nosed' Tom Cotton, with a cleft nose like the Papes strain, was Nash's white-and-liver pointer. That line in the first paragraph about the point 'just where a curlycue broom's end of weeds plaited in among thinning stalks' would speak to a bobwhite hunter if he never read another book, and a hundred years from now those cornstalks will rustle in the wind and those dogs will stand pop-eyed on point because of Nash's words. Mr. Pomp Eddins may not have been in the flesh under that name, but I have known that exceptional type of old gentlemen who lived among coveys of bobwhites on their land without having taken a shot at them for years. Irma Buckingham's family—'Yo' wife's folks . . . th' ol' Cap'n Joneses'—owned Cedar Grove, purchased from them by Hobart Ames to become home grounds of the National Field Trial Championship. Irma's great-uncle John Jarratt—'with Forrest'—was a keen-eyed lean man, as his photo in* Blood Lines *indicates. Nash gave me the original photograph, inscribed in Nash's hand, 'he "fit thru" the whole war, a gentleman and bird hunter to his fingertips.'*

"The description of the Manton makes you smell and feel it: '. . . muzzles paper thin, locks that sang like harp strings; stock fit and balance that made

shoulder spot and eye all in one.' When, on occasion and in lesser stories, Nash's writing slips into journalese and adjectives begin to pile up like too much paint on canvas, it is well to recall passages like that. Now and then a bit of writing comes along that should, in all fairness, be read by anti-hunters, not, perhaps, to dissuade them, but to give them insight into what they seek to eliminate. The scene with the old Pomp Eddins and his grandson's first kill on quail is such a bit."

Amen, to that, Brother!

"Oh! happy Boy; you have not lost your years,
　You lived them through and through in those brief days
When you stood facing Death! They are not lost!
They rushed together as the waters rush
From many sources! You had All in One!
Why should we mourn
Your happiness? You burned clear flame, while he
Who treads the endless march of dusty years
Grows blind and choked with dust before he dies.
And dying, goes back to the primal dust
And has not lived so 'long' in those long years
As you in your few, vibrant, golden months,
When, like a spendthrift, you gave all you were."

Anonymous.

COUSIN CHARLEY AND I had figured to turn the hunt homeward. Quite a piece it was, too, across those hardwood ridges, pine domes and sedge hollows that made a skyline for Big Hatchie basin. Leo and Tom Cotton were off on cast. We trudged across the furrowed aisles of a rustling corn patch, and found them both stanchly on birds, just where a curlycue broom's end of weeds plaited in among thinning stalks.

Leo was strictly in character, head and plume aloft, dog aristocracy posed and poised. Brawny, lumbering pointer Tom, having evidently swung off-hill a trifle late, was bowed into an upstanding study in rigid, pop-eyed liver and white. Since that good day, almost a quarter of a century ago, the memories of those two valiant comrades and that particular happening have never left me.

Their like comes about once in a lifetime, and perhaps rightly so.

Leo belonged to Billy Joyner, and Tom Cotton to me. But in those brave days shooting interests were so unselfishly interlocked that dog sharing was an indissolubly companionate affair. Leo had handled chickens from the Texas Panhandle to the wild-rose hedges of Saskatchewan. Many a time he had stopped to stare at the dust trails of antelope. And fight? He and Tom met in many a sanguinary set-to at catch-weights. But their issue, whatever it was, was never definitely settled. Sometimes Tom took the count and limped pitifully for days. Again, it was Leo who licked gaping gashes in his burr-curdled hide. From kennel to bird field in baggage car or buckboard, the air was electric with intoned mutters and snarled dares. Once thrown down on the job, however, and stretched out for a day's business, no more friendly or loyal brace of comradely co-operators ever spoored an upland or fought tooth and toenail in common cause.

Many a mob of snipe-snouted, shaggy mongrels have I seen surge forth and wolf down upon Leo and Tom. And just as often their frenzied yowls of impending mutilation would suddenly crescendo into notes of dismay as "our boys" met them more than halfway and filled the impromptu arena with whirling casualties. They had a way, too, of traveling meekly past some rural danger zone; one in front as a skirmishing decoy, the other lagging warily in support behind our horses. Out would bluster some chunky, coarse-pelted bully, fat, meaty tail awhirl and ruff abristle, cocked and primed to swarm all over the apparently shrinking and submissive stranger. Camouflage and ambush! Apparently from thin air, a very devil incarnate in dog hair would suddenly fasten upon Shep's unprotected flanks, nosing for a rib-smashing roll-over and the deadly paw hold. And sometimes it required apologies and peace offerings of cash after such flurries. But, their day's hunting done, Leo and Tom immediately resumed their private feud.

Well, that's how we came on them that particular afternoon. I was on the left, with left-handed Cousin Charley beside me. A segment of tumble-down rail fence 'twixt us and the birds. And a sign "NO HUNTING" tacked to a near-by persimmon tree. Funny how one remembers such things, but that was the setting. It had been an altogether gorgeous day. Lunch time almost before we realized it. We found a sunny spot just off Fish Trap Dam and lazed on the pine needles, while we munched well-browned soda biscuits and lardy spare-ribs. The Big Hatchie is a rare sight from the eminence of Fish Trap. It comes curving and slushing past an arrow-headed island, above where the darksome Sally Hole Swamp juts its fist of cypress into the river bottoms among the hardwoods. Then it fans into a sheet of greenish black enamel with a habit of switching to lumpy amber when heavy thunderstorms scour the seamed faces of the basin's red headlands.

But up and on our way again! It was ideal bird finding time when we broke out atop that hogback and slanted down in search of our dogs. Our shooting coats were bulging toward completed quotas—larger then. Another find or two meant finis. We paused in disturbed contemplation of the "NO HUNTING" sign.

Cousin Charley grunted. "Got 'em sure as shootin', but that's jus' exactly what we kain't do—shoot."

"Why," I questioned, balancing gingerly on a rotting rail and peering past him at Tom and Leo, sculptured against the dun swale, "how come we can't shoot?"

"Ol' man Pomp Eddins' place—tha's 'how come'—see that sign, don't you—well, he means it."

"Who th'—who is Pomp Eddins—mus' be hard boiled." Cousin Charley clucked tongue and cheek mournfully. The situation was ruinous. "Ol' man Pomp Eddins," he explained gravely, "is one o' them kind o' ol' gent'mans h'it don' do no good t' fool with—tha's all."

"Bad actor?"

"Well, naw, not 'zactly a bad actor, but if he gits in behin' you f' good cause, he'll jes' natcherly run you right on t' degradation—an' we're a long ways from home t' start runnin'—too."

"Can't we ease around an' drive those birds off his land?"

"Might, but I guess we better not—ou'h folks an' Mister Pomp has always bin ve'y fren'ly—but I ain' presumin' nuthin'—they tell me folks that does don' have no luck."

To the infinite consternation of Leo and Tom, Cousin Charley quietly flushed a bevy that scattered enticingly on a hillside not far away. Cousin Charley, as shooter and host, was using his wits. "Now then," he grinned, "le's go to th' house an' as't his permis-

sion to shoot a few birds on his place—I know him well enough t'
do that—an' we ought to, anyhow."

We struck off up a winding road. "I know right where them
birds lit," remarked Charley. I said I did, too. "I ain' seen Mister
Pomp in quite a spell," he went on; "him an' papa wuz in th'
Confed'rate Army t'gether—but th' ol' gent'man is mighty
queer." Leo and Tom, sensing, as dogs have a way of doing, that
the hunt had taken an odd turn, were in at heel. Charley told me
more of Mister Eddins. Retired now, he used to keep store in
town—president of the bank once upon a time. Knew some of
Billy's and my kinfolks in the city. "If he lets us shoot we can git
cleaned up all-fired quick," concluded Charley.

The twists and turns of our way mounted higher among conif-
erous knobs. "Great folks, them Eddinses," puffed Charley; "th'
Civil War 'bout cleaned them up—clan seeded down t' ol' man
Pomp; but he kep' things t'gether—don't owe no man—an' had a
sight o' cash money an' sev'ul hundred acres—yep—daughter-in-
law an' grandson—always been 'folks' an' still are, them Eddinses." We walked out into a clearing. Deeply set amid holly and
cedars squatted an antebellum, white brick cottage, its wide
chimneys giving off squills of wood smoke into the keen sunshine.

It was young Mrs. Eddins who ushered us cordially into the
cozy vastness of a low-ceilinged chamber, filled with crowded
bookshelves, hair sofas, armchairs and a grandfather clock that
would have made a collector's acquisitive hair stand on end. She
spoke gently to a tall, gray-haired, angular old gentleman who
unwound from a deep rocker. "Daddy, here's some company
come t' see you." Cousin Charley stepped forward: "Mister
Eddins, this is Charley Johnson; good afternoon, suh!"

"Yes," he acknowledged gravely, his eyes meanwhile measuring
us both in rapid appraisal, "I know you well, Charley; h'its bin
som' time sence we met, howsomever. Yo' folks all comin' 'long all
right I hope?"

"Yes, suh, Mister Pomp—uh—Mister Pomp—this is—uh—
Mister Buckin'ham—from down in th' city—comes out bird
shootin' onc't in awhile. Ou'h dawgs got into a covey down yonder on th' brushy side o' yo' place, but we seen yo' posted sign an'
come on up t' ast if you'd mind us ashootin' a little if we run into

another bunch on ou'h way home—we're meanin' t' head that away."

Mister Pomp's keen eyes, deeply recessed 'neath shaggy brows, swept me from head to foot. He slowly extended a leathery, man's sized hand. "Buckingham—is it?"

"Yes, suh."

"Gran'son o' ol' man Henry?"

I nodded.

"He wuz frum th' Nawth—an' sided that way."

"Yes, suh."

"But his brother—yo' great Uncle Fred—he went out fu'st with Walker an' got set with th' Federals—crossed under a flag o' truce at midnight when his term expired second day o' th' battle o' Fredericksburg, an' re-enlisted under Lee—transferr'd later to th' Louisiana Wildcats—they blowed him up on th' *Queen o' th' West.*" I listened in amazement. We had quickly gotten down to rock bottom on party platforms.

A moment of hesitant recapitulation by Mister Pomp.

"Which one o' ol' man Henry's boys is yo' Daddy?"

"Miles."

"Ummm—in th' bank?"

"Yes, suh."

"Th' two younger boys—Gunn an' Hugh—in th' dry goods business—they yo' uncles, o' co'se?"

"Yes, suh."

"Well, I didn't hav' no better fren's than them boys—all o' them—back in th' hard times panic o' '93—they carried me— took care o' me an' mine." His brilliant eyes turned from piercing scrutiny of me off through the window toward the Basin's distant rim. A resurgent sun poured over it. He quidded rapidly. Another line of evidence must be established. He said: "Yo' wife's folks wuz th' ol' Cap'n Joneses, warn't they?"

"Yes, suh."

"Ummnn—tho't I heard tell—Jones wuz my Cap'n—fought all over his own lan', too—Yankees, rich 'uns f'um up Nawth own it now an' fine folks they are, too, I'm told." He spat explosively into the fireplace.

"If I rec'llect rightly, yo' wife's a gran' niece o' ol' man John Jarratt's, ain't she?"

"Yes, suh." No use to elaborate; best to stand hitched and come clean.

"John an' me done some tall ridin' an' shootin' t'gether—we wuz with Forrest. On'ct in awhile we had t' do some all-fired runnin', too." An aquiline nose twisted into a grim snicker at the recollection. Half reverie apparently swept us from his thoughts. Then, "You boys take chairs, git warm—you're welcome t' shoot on my lan' whenever you choose—I'll jes' go 'long with you a piece t'day—I ain't shot at a bird in fifteen yea'hs—John—John Yancey—aw—John Yancey!"

A rough and tumble specimen of shaver hardihood, with clear gray eyes and mop of tousled red hair, darted in from the hallway. The grandfather's eyes blazed with pride. "Say 'howdy' to th' gent'men—say 'howdy,' John Yancey—then run an' fetch Grandpa's gun."

With a whoop of joy the little fellow sprang away and soon returned lugging an old but beautiful muzzle-loading shotgun. It was in superb condition—muzzles paper thin, locks that sang like harp strings; stock fit and balance that made shoulder spot and eye all one. With it was handed up belt, powder horn and shot pouch. A genuine Manton!

"Git yo' hat, John Yancey—you an' Grandpa's goin' bird huntin'—I want you t' watch these good shots an' learn how t' hit 'em, boy—you'll be needin' some such knowledge one o' these days." There was a method in Charley's madness as we retraced that quarter of a mile to the vicinity of our scattered birds. They had moved around an orchard's rim just outside some splash pine. Tom nailed them tightly. I believe to this good day both he and Leo had an idea what was up.

How I wish more of today's "sports" with magazine guns could have watched that old gentleman hustle his percussion Manton into action. In my own boyhood I had, of necessity, performed a like manual, but with nothing remotely comparable to his exhibition of rapid and orderly precision. Nipples capped, he stepped forward and to the left. Charley spun one victim from the rise.

But old man Pomp Eddins laid down a bang-up right and left that served notice how he played the game. Congratulations over, we followed the singles across a gully and into a patch of low broom hedge, where we found both Tom and Leo on point.

"Do you boys mind," queried our host, "if I let this little chap try t' see kin' he hit a quail on th' wing—he's shot a few rabbits an' some squirrels, settin'—but this'll be his firs' chance flyin'— an' over a dawg?" He turned and smiled at the grandson— "Come on—boy." The Manton, recapped and hammers drawn, was thrust into the lad's eager hands. All must go well with Grandpa there to see it done. Gun below the elbow, keen for contact with a long-awaited moment, he braced for the rise. In every gunner's life, in every father's heart, there should be, at least, one such undying memory.

"Walk on in—walk right on pas' th' dawg—when th' bird gits up—take yo' time." Step by step the child obeyed leadership. "Both eyes open, John Yancey, pick yo' bird an' keep both eyes jes' on him."

Singles took leave on every hand. I can still see that broth of a boy, stockinged calves and butternut knee breeches spraddled into a resolute stance among the sedge stems. Determined arms slamming the burled stock—a long pause as the child leveled and swung. B-o-o-m—b-o-o-m. A boy on his knees peering beneath a smoke screen, an old man's shrill cry, "You got him, son, you got him!" A race through the grass as youth and old age broke shot for the retrieve! Oh! the radiance on their faces! Pomp's aglow with pride; the boy's alight with the greatest thrill any possessor of game heritage treasures as no other in life.

For the next half hour neither Charley nor I fired a shot. Then, borrowing the Manton, we took turns at finishing our limits with the tool of a vanished field gentility.

Gulch bottoms were beginning to darken. Shadows thrust claws across the Basin. The crest of a steep ridge split away cleanly, dropping almost a hundred sheer feet to the railway gash. Behind Mister Pomp, we followed a well-defined trail across the hump. It ended in a spacious alcove, swung like a dirt dauber's nest above the brink. I looked about me in wonder! Some grim business hereabouts! Pomp Eddins slackened pace and motioned about him. "I tho't mebbe you'd like t' see h'it." He placed the Manton care-fully aside and seated himself on a lichened boulder. "There wuz big doin's went on he'ah—big doin's back in Shiloh times." Mis-ter Pomp smiled reflectively. "I'll bet Charley ain't ever bin in this spot befo' in his life—y'see—from he'ah this height com-mands th' railroad plumb across t' th' Basin—from whur' th' ol' M. & C. comes outa th' far gap." Somehow he seemed to kindle, take fresh grip on himself. He lapsed into the speech of ancient ac-tion; words of almost broad patois leaped from him—"This he'ah wuz an ol' fo'te—I hepp'd build h'it—look yonder at them tim-bered bastions stickin' outa th' groun'."

He glanced ruminatively at worn, angled earthworks and crumbling casemate. Lethargic burrows in their aged blanket of peaceful silt and grasses. "We wuz dismounted an' order'd on de-tail t' mount two pieces—told t' hold this position at any an' all cost. H'it warn't no easy job, young men, gittin' them guns so high—but h'it wuz wuth th' labor."

His eyes snapped fire; he was at work again. "We come in from behin'—aroun' yonderways—lak we come while ago—with an in-fantry company in suppote fuh ambush."

I visualized that scene. Gaunt, dog-tired gunners in ragged gray. Slobbery, lathered horses, sputtery whip lashes, straining traces, laborious heaving through steamy morass and unaxed swamp. What a beehive of slap-dash, slaughterous activity and toxic hate. A steady voice continued: "I 'member how we stopped 'em th' fust time—a supply train with guard—we wuz hid out an' ready when their locomotive come th'u th' gap and pulled jus' onto that trussle y' see down yonder. We had it blocked with logs; they seen 'em jus' in time as they run outa th' curve. We let 'em git out an' start unloadin'—then we cut that injin' t' ribbons—blowed h'it t' Hell-an'-Gone." He leaped to his feet and almost swarmed to a counterattack—"Ou'h boys swung ovah th' hill an' flanked 'em—some tried t' make h'it away th'u yon' valley," he chuckled, "but h'it warn't no use—we—we—had 'em—them hillsides yonder wuz strew'd with dead." He was telling it to High Heaven! "We sho' raised Cain in these parts fo' mo'n two months—but fin'lly th' Yanks come in fo'ce with heavy guns an' shell'd th' livin' hide offn us—we—we—had t' abandon th' position and fall back—damn it."

I looked about me more carefully. Through worn embrasures grinned two dummy cannon, fashioned from pine logs painted black and mounted upon hewn wooden gun carriages. About them, in orderly stacks, were piles of round shot—mud balls! As I half grasped all their significance, the flaming realism of this old man's passion and adoration gripped me. I saw sweating, unshaven half-mad men lashing back on lanyards; blistering hands fumbling at red hot gun muzzles; hell-and-damnation curses turning peaceful quail country into a sudden shambles of thudding smooth bores. Mister Pomp caught my look and smiled grimly. "This he'ah," he injected half fancifully, "is whuṭ me an' John Yancey calls ou'h 'Play House.' " He dropped a comradely arm about his grandchild's shoulder. The child cuddled lovingly against him.

"Y'see," he went on, a proud sort of wistfulness creeping into his tone, "y'see, I had t' raise this chile—me an' his Ma—that is—we come t' this ol' fo'te when he wuz jes' a babe—in m' arms—h'it come t' me one day t' fix things up lak you see 'em—I jus' built it all in mem'ry o' them times—an'—an' as John Yancey growed up, we jus' kep' comin' an' addin' t' things." His jaw suddenly tightened—he spoke proudly: "Anyhow, this he'ah ain't no bad Play House t' bring a boy up in." John Yancey spoke up, softly: "Gran'pa, we hav' a lot o' fun he'ah, don't we?" The old man turned to me. "I fought—we all o' us fought," he cried passionately, "f' ou'h conception o' home an' rights jus' as t' other side seen theirn—my father fought in Mexico, I fought with Forrest— an'—an'—this chile's Daddy—th' only son God Himself could ever give me—wuz killed at San Juan Hill—he couldn't no mo' stayed at home when th' call come than John Jarratt coulda' he'ped ridin' off with us boys."

We shook hands and exchanged "good-bys" and "come agains." He said simply: "Tell all yo' folks y' met ol' man Pomp Eddins—yo' Daddy'll 'member me—sen' me a bird dawg puppy some time—I'll train him an' John Yancey t'gether—John's gittin' too big f' th' Play House anyhow." So, leaving them to turn back across their darkening trail through the hills, Charley and I slid down a precipitous path to the railroad ties and a starlit trek to home.

Fifteen or twenty years is a long, long time! Again, however, Cousin Charley and I munched soda biscuits and hog meat at Fish Trap Dam. The bottomlands still challenged change, but it was there, however furtive. The drone of an airplane might impeach the years, or some raucous motor change the face of things.

"Charley," I asked, "whatever became of the old gentleman way back over yonder across the Tubba—Mister Eddins, who knew my folks an' let us hunt on his land an' showed us his old Rebel's 'Play House'?"

"Daid," responded Charley, laconically. "He lived t' be pas' eighty—but he passed away aroun' Christmas time—didn't las' long after th' Worl' War."

"And the boy," I went on. "I suppose he turned out to be a bum bird hunter, like we are, and runs the old home place now?"

"Yep," replied Charley, and something in the way he spoke made me look up. "There was sho' one mighty fine, honest-t'-Gawd boy, too."

"He's—"

"Yep!" Cousin Charley was a direct narrator. "They hadn' no sooner started talkin' war with Mexico, back in '16, but what John Yancey an' his Gran'pa showed up in town with John's gripsack all packed. That kid signed up an' went on with th' National Guard—an' I mean he lef' out right now." I might have guessed as much. Cousin Charley loosened a rib's end and kept on with his story. "Then, y' know, come sho' nuff war—with Germany. By that time John Yancey had turned out t' be a natcherl born soldier—his Grandad darn near passed out, he was so proud when th' boy went to an officer's training school an' come out with a commission. I never seen no one quite as happy. Why—why—there wuz times he'd talk about h'it an' tears'd come to his eyes. John Yancey's wuz a first unit overseas, too."

Charley paused. Tossed a welcome shred of fat meat to a dog. "Ol' man Pomp Eddins come t' town a lot in them days—wanted news 'bout th' war, an' that boy, mebbe. He'd sit aroun' in a big swivet 'till he got his mawnin' paper off th' 'Cannonball'—talked about how he wish'd he coulda bin along with John Yancey. That ol' man meant ev'y word he said, whut's mo'. He'd say: 'This he'ah makes fo' wars f' us Eddins—fo' wars an' th' Lawd only knows how many mo'. John Yancey—he'll be comin' home befo' long—an'—an'—marryin' off.' "

A flock of ducks suddenly dipped through the chute and whizzed across the spillway. Cousin Charley grabbed his gun and sorrowfully watched them dwindle into specks. He loved to sneak mallards and jump them around bends. He went back to his story.

"I happ'n'd t' be at th' sto' th' night th' tel'graf operator brought up th' message 'bout John Yancey. Somebody jus' had t' ride out an' git th' news to his folks. So I run out in m' car—they'd done gone t' bed long ago. But ol' man Pomp he come to th' do'h with a lamp in one han' an' that ol' muzzle loader o' hisn in t' other. He seen h'it wuz me an' says, 'Why—come in, Charles," says, 'glad t' see you—my daugher'l be right he'ah. Whut you got—a message fo' us 'bout John Yancey winnin' another medal o' honor,' says, 'how many Germans is that boy done kilt this time?'

" 'Bout that time, his Ma, Mrs. Eddins, come into th' room—I guess I musta looked kinda funny—maybe h'it wuz whut they call 'mother's intuition'—I don't know—guess she jus' sorter suspicioned—you know? All I could do wuz jus' han' her th' War Department's telegram—you 'member how they wuz worded?" Charley looked at me, and remembering, turned quickly away. He hadn't meant to put it that way, good old scout!

He clucked softly and sorrowfully. "Never s' long as I live, Buck, will I evah fergit th' look that come over his Ma's face. She handed Mister Pomp th' wire—but he didn' hav' his specs, so she had t' read it to him—an'—man—her voice wuz as steady—" Again Charley clucked into his cheek. "Seemed at firs' lak Mister Pomp couldn't understand—then—all of a sudden, seemed lak, h'it come to him. I wuz lookin' t' see th' ol' fellow bust out—but not a single tear com' hoppin' down his face—he warn't th' cryin' kind. Naw—he jus' sorter clutched out f' Mrs. Eddins—clasped her in his arms—sorter like he had done 'come to attention'—an' wuz listenin' f' sumpthin'. They both jus' stood there an' shivered. I tried t' say sumpthin' comfortin' like—but th' old man interrupted me: 'I'm obliged t' you, Charles,' he sayd, 'f' bringin' th' word—hit's sho' bad news,' he says, 'but,' he says, 'on th' other han',' he says, 'John Yancey Eddins has won th' highes' an' mos' distinguished honor that can befall a gallant soldier of our country.' " Charley wiped his greasy fingers on his hunting coat and turned to me reflectively again. "Do you 'member whut an' unreconstructed Confed'rate ol' man Pomp wuz? But in th' end he wuz sold jus' as strong on Uncle Sam." Charley had the thread of things toward the knot. "But about that time," he concluded, "ol' man Pomp raised his face t'odes th' ceilin', an his whole heart jus' seem'd t' break out in one great cry—'Aw Gawd'—he says—'You know,' he says—'h'it ain't right!' Mrs. Eddins seen he wuz fixin' t' giv' down. She held him tighter in her arms an' says, soothing like, 'There—there—Daddy,' she says, 'th' Lawd giveth an' th' Lawd taketh away, blessed be th' name o' th' Lawd.' Buck, there warn't one single tear ev'ah com' t' ol' man Pomp's eyes. 'I know,' he wailed; 'I take it all back—Gawd—but, oh,' he says, 'John Yancey's th' las' one o' us—no mo' John Yancey—Oh! Christ,' he says, 'no mo' Eddinses fo' th' wars—no mo' Eddinses fo' th' wars!' "

BOBWHITE BLUE, BOBWHITE GRAY!

Nash Buckingham

Once again, I will prevail upon Nash Buckingham's expert biographer, George Bird Evans, to share his thoughts on the background of this vintage Buckingham classic. His words are excerpted from his introduction to the story upon its publication in The Upland Gunner's Book, *which George edited for Amwell Press in 1979:*

"It is impossible to know how many men of my vintage had read and loved Nash Buckingham's stories long before my book, The Best of Nash Buckingham, *was published. But after it appeared, what amounted to an entire new generation of young shooters has been in touch to thank me for revealing a rich world that, to lift words from one of Nash's transcriptions in one of his books, 'lay just beyond our door.'*

"With 'Bobwhite Blue, Bobwhite Gray!' I think I am serving them another choice Buckingham morsel they will not have savored, unless they have delved deep. For this story appeared only in his book De Shootinest Gent'man, *published by Derrydale in 1934, and by Putnam in another edition nine years later. Written in Nash's early period, his words have flamboyance and the full flavor of a fine Havana cigar.*

"I recall first reading this story with the hot blood of eagerness, impatient to get through the first pages about the Christmas Ball in the old courthouse and on to shooting bobwhites. But while the years have not dulled my love of gunning, mileage has mellowed me to a degree that Nash's memories of those places and times mean more and more. There has never been a time when the charm of the setting has not enhanced my shooting, but I now take a special pleasure in the mood of the places I have gunned, and in the more colorful sense, the character of the people I have known there. I think it is this extra quality about 'Bobwhite Blue, Bobwhite Gray!' that impelled me to have it in these pages.*

"I get (in research—Ed.) no clue as to when 'Bobwhite Blue, Bobwhite Gray!' took place. Hugh Buckingham's letter does not bracket the period he leased Brick House, but Nash's story obviously was laid during that time. That Colonel Harold Sheldon was in the party dates it somewhere after 1926, when Sheldon went to Washington to serve with the Bureau of Biological Survey and where he undoubtedly met Nash, who lived there at that* *time, and before 1936, when Sheldon's Derrydale* Tranquillity *was published, containing the stories of Sheldon's shooting visit to 'Mister Nash.'*

" *'Hal' in this story is Hal Bowen Howard, Nash's shooting friend from boyhood, who died in 1933. This reduces the span of our estimate to 1926–33.*

"Nash's love for the vastness of this great quail land—'remote valleys where another season may pass ere human eyes again peer into such sequestered haunts'—is almost mystic. We don't write like that today, and it wouldn't do, if we did. But it did beautifully for Mr. Buck, and he clasped that country and its birds and dogs and people with emotional zeal."

EVELYN'S RESPONSE WAS characteristic. "Entirely all right and welcome to include the Colonel. The right hand of fellowship to his Yankee breeding. If he's a good shot (and he must be or you wouldn't be playing around with him) and don't mind 'cawn toddies,' okay to his passport. Plenty of birds and my dogs in such high fettle I'd better be knocking on wood. I'll meet you in town. It'll be New Year's eve so we'll simply have to stay awhile for the Court House ball. Hal will put us up for dinner at the old home place. If the road is as bad as I suspect it will be, we'll load the plunder into Jack's wagon and drive on out to Brick House."

So, in abundant glow of anticipation that brooked no dwindling of enthusiasm, Hal and I and the Colonel from "Vermawnt" came to Brick House to gun bobwhite with Evelyn. Perhaps I ought to say "came back," for to Hal and me it is almost "home." True to Ev's prediction there had been heavy rains. Our trek to the "old home place" led through stately old Aberdeen. Past the huge court house, crumbly with its struggle against the years; reminiscent of impassioned oratory and bitter but courtly legal battles. At intervals, we glimpsed through spacious boundaries of wintry cedar hedges, towering, leafless oaks. And resting amid winding rose walks and arborous gardens, old-fashioned homes of singular and comforting beauty. Some with their broad porches and superb lines of colonial paneling drooping into an almost sagging dilapidation of Civil War impoverishment. Others bespeaking an eloquent survival of defiance of time.

I am firm in the belief that nowhere on earth is the real pleasure of friendship and Christmas value so well preserved or deeply cognizant of its own tender ties as at the Yuletide ball in an old aristocratic southern community. These festive gatherings are held each year, just as were predecessors of like step and fancy, in either the town hall or court house. In our particular happy instance the assembly room of the municipal building, waxed as to floor and festooned with crimson-berried holly and inviting mistletoe past any semblance to the austere forum of political and legal strife, was thronged with gay couples. The music, changed only through the encroachment of hitherday step and tune, never really in personnel of players or true substance of melody, "swayed valiant summons to the dance." From beyond home circles came guests from smaller towns and regional cities. Beautiful visiting misses armed with charming darts aimed directly at unshrinking home stalwarts! College lads in newly acquired dignity, and amazingly adept in the latest flights and fancies of Terpsichore. Everywhere one encountered well-set-up men and lovely girls, radiant together in a warmth of genuine and cordial reunion and jovial familiarity of life-long association. In some cases appeared unmistakably perceptible symptoms of far deeper interest.

Along the high-windowed walls, beneath portraits of distinguished legal kin and departed but not forgotten courtiers of the bench or bar, sat grave old gentlemen whose dress suits, for the most part, bespoke a vintage of remote years, and gave off, upon the occasion of an affectionate slap upon the shoulder, a subtle yet nevertheless convincing odor of camphor. Beside them sat sweet little silver-haired ladies, very, very dear to the hearts of all concerned. These gravely smiling old gentlemen in their camphorated tails and their little old ladies in queenly silks had danced here in their own bright long agos—just as their sons and daughters and grandchildren were doing now. It was good to realize, too, that yonder, come all the way home for the holidays, sat President J., of the great B. & L. system; that sitting proudly beside one of the dear old sweet ladies, in place of his father, the Colonel, was Doctor E., famous surgeon the world over. The beaus and belles were there to uphold the right of modernity; those who had gone forth and returned laden with success were present because to them, this with all its loved memories was home. There were no harsh words or uncomely thoughts for those who had fared away so bravely only to return rebuffed and downhearted. For them, as for everyone, the level eye of kindliness and a hand of heart-meant good cheer. There was brave, sad fortitude and greening memory for those who could never return. Hands sometimes clasp hands at these dances where the garden of years had grown rank with weeds of bitterness and cold restraint. Land suits and petty fallings-out of the neighborhood are perchance settled out of court across the punch bowl; indictments of love argued and dismissed. The blood and bone and sinew of a clan come together in a blending of "peace on earth, good will toward men" at the Christmas dance in their Old Home Town.

We have lent ear to good music and foot to the dance. Now for the long, long road to Brick House. Thank goodness for an honest "hack" with spring seat and mettlesome "hay-burners." I'm sick of gasoline and upholstered leather on shooting trips. "Watch that off-mule, Jack, he's fixing to load us all skyward." Coat collars up and a jolt into the dark. Now to navigate through the out of town in the mule manner and like it.

They built the Brick House, so Aunt Dora's crone of a Black Mammy told me in her cabin one night years ago, "long 'bout som'time befo' ol' Cunn'l hisse'f clamb up on he big white hawss an' rid off t' fight wid d' Mexicums!" In so definitely affirming this relevantly important reminiscence, Granny Captola inhaled three sucky draws upon the sparky dregs of her usually overstuffed corncob pipe and solemnly knotholed two highly accurate sluicings of "ham gravy dip" into the sputtery ashes of her cavernous chimney hollow. She could almost remember, she said, "seein' de stars fall, an' know'd all 'bout how ol' Satan riz up same as saleratus raises in de biscuits an' shuk all de lan' t'well h'it reel an' rock an' de ground sunk an' de big ribber runned back'uds!" You figure it out, if you've a mind to, how long ago that cosmic upheaval took place.

They called it the Brick House then, and the name has stuck right down to this day. "They" means a pitiful remnant such as Granny Captola herself, for example, and a few remote others bedded about in hutches and crossroads burying grounds, mostly with one or both feet in the grave. And pretty much all the rest are descendants of those who "toted" and sawed and broad-axed to help clear it. Brick House is citadel and community center! How naturally, hopefully and sometimes with almost wistful respect the black folks look to it for advice and aid. And rarely in vain—God be praised! To its front door for solution of those perplexing things they know they must do, but with castdown eyes to its back door for absolution from those things they know they ought not to have done.

Go a long piece off across Big Sandy bottoms, where the "humpty-dumpty" road to town tumbles into a deep, shady gash that brings teams or automobiles out panting and puffing high above the Great Marsh and from there you first glimpse Brick House, looming castle-like on its bench at the shoulder of McClellan's Grove. Off to the northeast fifteen or twenty miles is where for many and many a year, over much the same lovely quail country of swale, thicket and wastrel gully land as surrounds Brick House, field trial contenders have matched stride and sagacity for national hunting supremacy of the upland. And not so very far to the southeast, the upper reaches of another famous old field trial course peters out on the slope of Persimmon Ridge. It, too, knew the stifled ambitions, the joyous heart throbs and questings of a race of upstanding pioneer sportsmen and brainy, wide-going, iron-lunged bird dogs. It is a land of engaging and cordial hospitalities fully in keeping with its legends of largess. It is a land of innate sporting lore handed down from father to son, of fox hound strains and blue blood in setters and pointers. But above and best of all, it is a land of unabashed, level-eyed yeomanry, of frugality and toil well repaid in nourishing and self-respecting yield!

Well, then, you rattle and bump and squeak across one after another of Big Sandy's runs, spoored with bird and rabbit and "varmint" paddings; drag gradually uphill again for a couple of country miles, and pop out all of a sudden right in front of Brick House! There you are! A formal front yard, palisaded with hand-drawn white oak staves; a limpety-crackety gate and a shrub and flower-bordered walk of curiously cobbled squares. An alleyway, overhung by stately oaks and fringed sweepingly with interliners of gnomelike, berried cedars. In summertime long-bladed grasses are sacheted with locust and honeysuckle crumblings, and flirty south winds strew the lawn with muslin mull from dogwood and peach orchard. The lovable homestead is a babel of chortling bird life. Nests are woven or swung aloft in a charming profusion of unvigilant domesticity. From fields and woods lot come the mingled low-noted plaint and quavering "Cheerio" of dove and bobwhite. But in winter, layer upon layer of leafy mold carpets, jonquil and hyacinth. Tender bulbs and cuttings are hooded in loam for their long, warm sleep. And Brick House, shorn of its joyous camaraderie of song and cloying sweetness, bares its seamed, weather-wrought old face to the challenge of storms and stresses it has never feared.

Clump into its austere but welcoming center hall! Never mind the mud on your boots and leave the dogs be! "Here with the bootjack—you with the poached-egg eyes—do some yanking and scraping or find yourself in the middle of a tough something!" Pile your bird hunter's plunder in Captain Ev's bedroom—over yonder—it used to be the parlor, when crinoline waltzed to the "Mocking Bird"! Now look about you.

Rare old furniture everywhere and more of it sheathed in storage in the vast attic. Thump those paneled doors and toe those hewn floor boards—wide as your forearm is long. What massive sills and beams, and such plaster. Not a sag or a crack! Here and there, though, you'll notice bogs of brick and mortar gouged from side walls, and some of the windows have splintery holes drilled through the panes and ugly slug cavities in the shutters. Aunt Dora grinningly tells "outside folks": "Dem wuz done du'in' war times, yaas suh—when us fit wid d' Yankees—ol' Cap'n ain' nuvvr 'lowed nobody t' put in no new glass—says he want 'em t' stay jes' lak dey wuz made—an' ef' nobody don't lak de wind whistlin' thu dem bullet holes—den dey kin' jes' buil' up de fiah an' git closer to h'it." And Aunt Dora dies off in a gale of suppressed merriment that agitates each and every one of her amplifications!

Then, if you like, come along and we'll ramble down around the moss-roofed, saggy old barn, with its blended odors of oat crunchings, currycombings and sweaty leather. What a litter of trace chains, mule collars, plow points, axle grease and rusty junk!

Grunty porkers nose about and soft-eyed Moo-Cows moo, turn bovine scrutiny after us.

Lacing of red pepper strings and pottle gourds, bundles of warping fish canes, bowlegged urchins and huge iron wash pots are jumbled about the "Quarters." And the same oft-tolling plantation bell, tottery on its aged stilts, still "rings in and rings out," just as it began calling along about the time Granny Captola claims she almost saw the stars fall!

Brick House smiles a rare and all-embracing welcome the full width of its classic facings. It seems to say: "Come along with you, young folks—I've minded generations of you through sunshine and shadow—all of us Old Timers have—light down and hitch, for fox hunters and bird shooters—I know every one of you— sweethearts and wives and good old dogs and jumpers—aye—and your Daddies and Gran'daddies, too—hurry up—come on in he'ah—I miss you and I'm getting along—I'm yo' *home!*"

So, look affectionately if not reverently upon Brick House. Go close to it. Feel of its oddly shaped, time-dulled red bricks patted into shape and burned by slave hands that were such in loyalty only. Do this as I am not ashamed to confess having done, with a comforting sense of pride in heritage.

And, if I am not very much mistaken and disappointed, something will whisper to you as it did to me: "All such stalwart and noble homes, faithful tenantry and toilsome lands about them must endure as most representative and worthy in the preservation of American ideals—swear to it—deep down in your hearts—that all they have stood for shall never stand for contamination." Whether they drowse in the land of cotton, beaten biscuits and beautiful women, or cling, by the sign of the sacred codfish and sap of the maple sugar bucket, to the rock-ribbed true blue hills of Old New England!

Brick House, though the hour is midnight. Wood fires snapping. Welcoming lamplight. Ministering black hands. Innumerable silhouettes in reserve. Evelyn speaking—"You bed in that corner, Colonel—yonder for you all, Buck and Hal—and I'll bunk in this corner (four "four-posters" in one chamber, think of it)—shake a leg. Will, quick with the sugar and water—you're slipping."

Jack bustles in, doubling from hostler to bus boy— the fastest passer of hot biscuits on earth. A timid emissary from Aunt Dora's culinary domain: "A l'il bite t'eat raidy." A vast dining room; cheerful hearth spotted with plates warming—great brand of service Jack puts out. Lofty china closets and wainscoted silver vaults. Considerable clatteration from the kitchen. Aunt Dora's strident voice demanding less fuss and inviting several sitters-below-the-salt, to "git outa he'ah now—git on outa he'ah I says—naw—I ain' gwin' giv' you much ez er mouf'ful—git on out fo' I busts you side de haid wid dis skillet."

Did I say a "snack"? Fluffy omelet, Sally Lunn, country butter, native honey. "Which do you crave, Colonel?" asks Ev, spooning discerningly into the smoky eruption of a pot pie's dome— "chicken bosom, rabbit thigh, spare parts, or just considerable of evy'thing?" The Colonel requisitions full company rations. Jack, meanwhile, stages a whirlwind campaign, reporting to the kitchen that "Mistah Nash had done et a lot befo' hit seem lak his appetite done really come to him." Deaf to his entreaties, we stagger to the east room profoundly burthened.

Enter Gus. For all the world a Weller senior, in low chocolate. Tightish pantaloons tucked into gaitered bootees, sleek embonpoint sheltered in a sheep-lined surtout and a gay scarf at his throat to polish off effects sartorial. He has prodded his favorite mule a long way for this important conference and its invariably delectable aftermath! An influential and faithful henchman, Gus! Owner of fat kine, full barn, an unmortgaged tilling and lengthy stair-stepping of cotton-pickin' chilluns. No mean hand at repartee, Gus! The examination gets under way—

"You been well, Gus?"

"Well—that is—er—I bin tol'able—thankee, suh, Cap'n."

"No chest pains, chilblains, falling arches or flaming youth?" Gus registers searching personal diagnosis and denies any symptoms relative to this four out of five perspective.

"Your mule all right, too, Gus?"

"Yaas, suh, him an' me 'bout alike."

Will Joy, grinning Master of the Kennel, is next in line and steps one pace forward! Will admits to me later that "he wouldn' swap jobs wid nobody—I got de bes' Boss Man in de whole worl'—if I dooes wrong an' he fiah me—which lak he'll sho' do, too—I gwi' crawl back abeggin' on my han's an' knees—when Cap'n says, '*Do dis*'—I know he means '*Do dis*'—an' das de way hits gwi' git dooed!"

A sound philosophy and farsighted policy, William! Jack and Aunt Dora, their dishes done, are now standing in the delegation.

"What dogs do we take tomorrow, Will?"

"Us better take de Ol' Man—Joe—an' maybe Nellie—an' Seymour—an' sho'ly les' us take da' puppy o' mine, da Jim dawg—Cap'n, he gwi' be a sho' nuff dawg. You all gwi' walk or ride—Cap'n?"

"We'll walk tomorrow—be here at eight o'clock sharp, Will." Will becomes a file closer. Gus recaptures the spotlight. The Captain's tone becomes grave. "Gus, how is the Coaster?" At mention of the Coaster the entire group is mantled in concern. Gus straightens and "a-h-e-m-m-s" throatily, several times.

"He dooes ve'y well, Cap'n—leas' ways he wuz so doin' de las' time I had bizness wid 'im!"

"His choir been practicin' regularly an' improving right along?"

"Yaas, suh, Cap'n, dey dooes putty well now, suh, considerin'—"

"Considerin' what?"

"Well, suh-uh-uh, considerin'—considerin'—de consideration he bin able to giv' 'em—y'know, Cap'n, deys mos' done bin twins com' t' de Coaster's house!" Gus beams! Chorus of "Sho' is bin!" from the ensemble.

"Who sings soprano now?" Deep meditation. Aunt Dora comes to the rescue. "Cap'n, de reg'lar s'prano done bin had er turble col'—misery all up in his ches'—bin had de doctor wid 'im—nuther young nigger bin spellin' him in de choir—but he 'bout all right again now—de herb practor bin lately radicatin' him wid possum grease salve."

"Suppose you can persuade the Coaster to bring his choir over tomorrow night and sing for the Colonel—you and Will and Jack are elders in the Household of the Loyal Order, ain't you?" Thus severally and individually identified as accomplices to prominence, a special whispered Board Meeting is held, the caucus ren-

] 377 [

dering a pronouncement committing the Coaster's choir sight unseen and song unsung. There being apparently no further business to come before the meeting, "excusin' " as Aunt Dora would say, the most important matter of all—the company fidgets. Sensing this, Captain relieves the situation by dispensing a liberal nightcap. Acknowledgment of hearty wishes for joint safekeeping throughout the night—and we are alone.

Colonel and Captain are soon hard at it again—in France! Under cover of a barrage of apparently desultory but effective minor preparations, Ye Chronicler, betaking himself to a deep and downy billet, lies listening—snatches of trench talk fend off raids of overmastering drowsiness—"Do you remember—uuuummm—around by Nantillois—that bridge head at Bethancourt—direct fire—hell, wasn't it—Verdun—we went over on the fourteenth—it was up by Chemin des Dames—coal scuttles—took cover like rabbits—shrapnel—more blood and guts than you ever saw—Heinies—Frogs—rain—barbed wire—more rain—guns oriented—kilometers—cognac—Paris—wine—the damned M. P.'s!"

A black shape at my bedside—Jack, with a cheery "Good mawnin', Boss," and an aromatic cedar bucket from which he ladles an eye-opener of icy cistern water. He sets a dazzling pace at breakfast—broiled pork steaks with creamy gravy, matched sets of eggs and biscuits and joyful Java! Dogs barking outside and Will Joy bows in, accoutered for the chase. "Why the rabbit sack, Will?" "Well, suh, you knows I allus did favor *them* boys!"

Mr. Porter rides up to acknowledge introductions and pass salutations. Mr. Porter is a gentleman of some seventy-odd years of intimate contact with the policies and "grapevines" of the county. The Captain's carryings-on are Mr. Porter's for delivery, and in such course he has an M.A. degree. He promptly suspsects and challenges the Colonel's being a "Vermawnter." Judgment therefore is suspended until further facts are developed. We assemble outside. A gray morning—squalls lulled, but a sullen, leaden jumble on the horizon, liable to start anything. But the ground is in great shape for dog work! Mr. Porter stands to horse, throwing a deft leg over his skittish pinto colt. We branch off at the lane bars—"You boys be sho' now an' stop off by my house for a snack aroun' about noon time," he admonishes. A parting shot from the young Captain—"Don't let that pin ear sling you off, Mr. Porter," elicits a curled lip from the old gentleman—"I'Gad if he does it'll be th' fust one evuh done it!'"

The dogs have scattered to work. We round off onto a high point, magnificent vistas of quail country rolling to the skyline through open piney clumps. Flashing spots off across the valley— the dogs! On a distant hillside Will Joy wigwags. "Joe's gone that way," codes, Ev, and we swing to the southeast. You'll doubt what I'm telling you now about Joe, a great rangy, black and white ticked pointer of the old school—a throwback to days of real bone and sinew and minds, twelve-year-old Joe! One of those really magnificent bird-finders of all time—unsung, perhaps, but not unhonored! His original blinding speed has slackened a trifle, but not his space-devouring lope, uncanny nose and supreme bird sense. Foot-hunting behind Joe is a cross-country chase with Will Joy as liaison officer. More wigwagging from Will—Joe has located his first bevy!

By the time we get up, the three setters are backing here and there on the outskirts of a briar-bordered plum thicket with puppy Jim watching Will Joy for orders. The Colonel circles a devious route toward where Will points out Joe, up ahead and a taut symbol of real pointer form. We edge in a trifle. The Colonel's new twenty-gauge is going up for its baptism of fire. The thicket explodes and takes wing—a single whisks my way and is tumbled. "What about the gun? How'd the Owen go?" "Oh, fine," he stammers with delighted excitement. "Think I made a double!"

This proves to be the case, and never minding singles, we climb the ravine. Will Joy is already far ahead on the route—Joe has cast that way and can be seen when we reach the crest—a speck of blurred white lashing a hillside. An hour later, with several finds behind us, we are in the deep woods. Only puppy Jim has done a solo stunt on birds to keep pace with the Old Master; but it was a stanch reward for industry, and Will's pride knows no bounds. A shout from Will, for Joe is at it again up there in the open woods. But nothing happens when we close in. Something wrong here! No telling how long he's been standing there—they've run off—

give him a little time—get on, Old Head! The other dogs back trail, cold trail, and "some tall inquestin'," as Will puts it, goes forward. But the Old Master, cutting a slashing half circle, suddenly whips to the right, high headed—no foolishness with him! He's nailed them this time. "Cock your musket, Colonel, we'll defend the Manor House with our lives!"

"Zooks," he mutters, when the uproar has subsided—"if only the little beggars wouldn't fluster the living daylights out of me when they beat it,"—Will Joy is pointing on ahead—"Dey drapped 'long side da' l'll dreen." The dogs had three singles spotted but we passed them up and six more that we flushed, watching the spat-throated cocks and mottled hens whip swirling back to wood's haven for another season. "Good luck to you, you gallant little rascals!" The dogs have all disappeared and we separate, searching for a bevy point. A brooding, gray stillness pressing about, with a few wisping crumbs of snow—surely it won't last. But suddenly big, wet flakes come tumbling, faster and faster. "Head for Mr. Porter's across the hollow yonder," calls Ev through the blizzard.

We put our best feet forward—the downfall is beginning to stick, and the dogs are worried—even old Joe comes in. Just before we angle uphill he suddenly wheels to one side and points into a fallen tree top. We catch a glimpse of hovering birds afoot—and then they are away through the brush, and the Colonel being handy scores a right barrel. "Where my experience as an old New England pah'tridge shooter stood me in good stead," he explains. Mr. Porter's comfortable home dispenses dyed-in-the-wool good cheer. Takes women folks to make matters just right. Jack meets us with the wagon. "Take Joe home," instructs Ev, "give him a possum salve rub and bed him down soft. Fetch back Dan and Ned. If it clears we'll go on; if it doesn't we'll make a red day for the rabbits—how about it, Mr. Porter?" Mr. Porter, field trial impresario emeritus, sniffs disdainfully—"like a passel o' boys—runnin' rabbits in th' snow—I might go 'long tho'!"

Too bounteous a board, Mr. Porter's, for an impending hard afternoon of it. "If you see me bog down on some low ground," mouths the Colonel, shifting gears in a wedge of meringued sweet potato pie, "leave me, I entreat thee, I'll only be putting on my chains and going into second." The Mason and Dixon's line issue is touched upon lightly but none-the-less positively, Mr. Porter, as host, assuming a most chivalrous bearing. "I ain't sayin' it o' co'se, 'caus' you come from V'mont, Colonel, but back in '82, I think it wuz—two Yank—er—two No'the'n boys settled in he'ahbouts, an' when 'lection time rolled 'round, two-three o' th' Vig'lance committee come t' me a' say—s'i'—'Them fellers ain't fixin' t' try t' vote, is they?'—right then an' there s'i—'right is right—if you all votes—they votes—whut good is it goin' t' do them, nohow'!" The Colonel, not to be outdone in any exchange of generosities, pays high tribute to the fighting qualities of some Southern boys with whom he soldiered. "Fight?" avers Mr. Porter grumblingly. "Fight?—o' co'se th' Hell they'll fight!"

But time has flown, brilliant sunshine has cut away the storm and Jack is on hand with a relay of fresh dogs. We bid good-by to Mr. Porter and strike off east through the rapidly disappearing slush. "Fourteen bevies this forenoon," counts up Ev; "twelve of them for Joe." Dan, a hard-going young setter, proves the afternoon's hero. What a ramble we take, into territory that even Ev hasn't penetrated all season, clear around the headwaters of the Great Marsh, picking a cautious, mucky way across an arm of it trying to locate some crafty singles.

"Pretty much anything in here you want," remarks Hal, "duck, woodcock, snipe." We find the largest of six bevies just before we climb the backbone of a ridge that slopes from Brick House and almost divides the Marsh. Brick House again—bulking huge against a serried sunset of plum and gold. Frost in the offing, cows plodding up from the pasture, a darky chunking clods and yodeling. Jack is the mainstay from then on—Jack with his fires going, hot water and towels and cold water and sugar; Jack with the slippers and easy chairs. Jack hot footing it about another table laden to nourish the inner man—good, faithful Jack!

We retire for coffee, and preparations for the Coaster's visit go forward. Rumbling wagons unload a considerable gathering, with whispered doings-about for the ceremony. We are finally summoned to the west room. Two long, highbacked pews have been arranged before the fireplace. We are introduced and given seats to the rear. The Coaster stands aloof, a tall, solemn personage of almost monastic mien, a Savonarola in *café au lait!* He holds a glistening peeled hickory baton. His choristers arrange themselves along the pews. Jack, it develops, handles basso profundo. Aunt Dora, Will and sundry other pot-wallopers are grouped as congregation to the service. The Coaster raises an impressive arm. Silence. Pointed fire darts lick high into pilastered moldings; the chamber is in half darkness.

"We'll firs' reques' Brother Lovingood t' lead us in prayer." A grizzled and heavy-lidded Elder rises and in all reverence speaks a worthy plea for souls such as ours—God forbid that I speak in levity here in the presence of an engaging and simple strength of Faith—"Lord our Christ," he entreats, his countenance alight with zeal and his sonorous exhortation deepening into fervid texture, "look down upon us, we beseech Thee, as strivin' in ouh 'umble way t' show 'preciation o' Thy power an' Glory—mek us thankful, O Lord! that all Yo' Chillun's voices be raised in Thy glo'fication an' that You may rejoice, too, O Lord! that we can have come with us into Thy Presence this evenin'—the hearts of our white friends whose kindnesses to us th'u the years—in health an' sickness—in happiness an' sorrow—is known to us as bounty in Thy Sight an' o' Thy Providin'—Amen!"

A rustling of hymnals—a whisper. "Number twenty-fo'!" The Coaster's baton rises, tenses and falls, and an exactly pitched, mellow harmony swells out in sweetly blended rhythm. "Come 'long t' Glory, on th' far side th' mountains, whar' th' burden o' my sins rolls away, rolls away—" a remarkable tenor, the Coaster's—and Jack's bass, deeper and deeper and truer as the refrain dies away! Spirituals follow, choir and company working itself into the full passion of religious fervor. "An' now, my brethren, sisters, all o' you, lif' up yo' eyes an' hearts t' Him—t' Him—a-hangin' up dar on de Cross. Le's us follow d' Marster, follow him th'u de Ritual o' Jesus at de Well!" The baton is aloft—a volume of "Amens." The Coaster's tenor in solo—he is on his knees now—his perspiring face tense and drawn, his clutching fingers groping into space. "An' dar—he—hung—an'—uh—He—uh—looked down—an' says—uh—somebody—please take my po' ol' Mother—home." He is on his feet now, darting to right and left, beseeching, exhorting. The gathering swells toward him and the awaited chorus goes throbbing forth. "Yaas—My Lawd—Jesus gwi' mek up—my—dyin'—bed—Jesus gwi' mek up—my dyin' bed!" Aunt Dora's shrill treble has joined the outpouring. The assemblage is racked with turmoil—on and on—verse after verse of the Coaster's own creation—the Last Supper, the Betrayal, the Bloody Sweat, the Tomb That Opened—the Coaster sinks into an exhausted heap!

Again the yearning to slumber, but somehow the Coaster's ritual comes ringing back; a homely recital that challenges and summons in the very strength of its purity. Jesus will indeed make up many a dying bed in token of such faith. Would that my own—

Jack again with the cedar bucket. Jack with his hot Java. Jack puzzled when the Captain bids him fetch the Kodak—the Kodak, you know, Jack. The black box in the leather case—Jack's face brightens—picture-making strikes but one sense with Jack—Art. He beams. Identification is complete. "Aw, Cap'n, you means bring you do 'Artry'!" Thus does second nature and native instinct exert a true sixth sense of appropriate designation far beyond expensively coined phrases.

Today we are a cavalcade. Will Joy and his special saddling mule are hard put to it to spy on old Joe. Spruced by his massage and rest, the Old Master cut a dizzy pace. But Nellie slips in with the first find. We miss and locate her behind us in a deep ravine, backbone deep in the wintry sedge, and stanch as the Ark. Hal and Ev descend with satisfactory results when a huge covey roars down the chute and into the dense woods.

Then off on a long and wandering route of Joe's coursing— around hillsides, into remote valleys where another season may pass ere human eyes again peer into such sequestered haunts. Forests, briar-guarded post oak patches, rocky defiles, wafted scents of juniper and sassafras. Open fields, cabin homesteads, the blur of drifting wood smoke—always the outrider, Will, searching for the gaunt pointer! The crack of guns spitting through barriers of boughs and grasses—over and over and over again one's poignant gratitude for the given grace of such moments.

But look yonder by the wood's edge. Young puppy Jim, pointing as though his life depends upon it. "Dar he!" yells Will. "I couldn't luv' da l'il ol' dawg no mo' 'n ef he wuz mah own son. Ef he ain't got birds yu gent'men jes go on an' shoot me down. But ef h'its er rabbit—jes' 'member Jim's youth—an' th' size o' mah fambly!" But Jim comes into his own! "Thirty-two bevies since yesterday morning!" counts Ev, who has done little if any shooting himself. "Twenty-three or four for the Old Master—fine work, Old Timer!" And Joe, sensing his work as done, heads over the fields toward Brick House.

Across the windless sheen of approaching noon comes the summons of a bell, from Life Boat Chapel on the hill off yonder, Will tells us. Riders and wagons are heading that way. "De Coaster gwi' preach a sermon dis mawnin' on Gen'ul George Washin'ton, d' Father o' our Country, an' tell all de chilluns dey mus' grow up trufeful." As we swing up through a fence gap and out into a sandy road, a horseman, cantering past, draws rein to bow us a respectful and dignified "Good Mawnin' "—a grave and reverend Coaster, riding into the zentih hour of God's own sunshine, on the mission of Him who makes up *all* our dying beds.

Again Jack and the hay-burners. At the gate of Brick House came parting of the way for the Colonel and Ev. Blue eyes met gray eyes and two strong hands clasped across the Mason and Dixon line of true sportsmanship in a grip that said as plainly as did words of hearty farewell: "We like you, Yank; you're a good shot and a right man, come back to see us—do!"

"Same to you, Johnny Reb, and more of it. You've treated me white. Long life to you and yours."

"Well," questioned Hal, when our horses' heads were set toward home, "how does the Minute Man from up Boston Way like an everyday, Down-in-Dixie bird hunt, with a little Rebel Yell stuff on the side?"

The Gentleman from Vermont sighed a sigh of rich content and stretched wearily in his seat.

"You are now speaking," said he, with the methodical diction typifying a delineation of accurate verbal juxtaposition characteristic of the ultra-grammatical New Englander, "of the very best thing in the Universe."

"D'm'f 'taint," I echoed softly.

And Hal triple-plated this confirmation in the tongue of our Fatherland.

"Sho is."

THE HOME COVEY

Tom Kelly

My friend, Grits Gresham, shooting editor of Sports Afield *magazine, tipped me off on a talented newcomer to the outdoor writing field. His name was Tom Kelly, he lived in Alabama and worked in the timber and logging industry, and he had just written a book on turkey hunting. Well, by the time I got a copy of the book, called* Tenth Legion *(published by Spur Enterprises, 33 Northgate Drive, Monroe, Louisiana 71201), I had moved over to* Outdoor Life. *It didn't take turning many pages of the book to see that Grits was dead right: Tom Kelly wrote with style, wit and originality. I phoned Tom to obtain permission to excerpt a portion of the book in* Outdoor Life *(which was subsequently run), and I asked him if he did any quail hunting. He said, "Lamar, I haven't shot a dog over a quail in five years." After I managed to stop laughing Tom told me he was only kidding and that he would be happy to do a quail piece for* Outdoor Life. *"The Home Covey" was the result, and it ran in the August, 1978, issue. I guess as pressures on the availability of hunting land keep increasing, so will our sense of loss at the thought of other hunters* blam-blaming *into the coveys we thought belonged to us exclusively. Tom knows that feeling, and he shares it unsparingly.*

IT'S MEAN TO HAVE to work at 2:30 in the afternoon in November. And if you have to do it on one of those golden days when it has rained half the morning and cleared by noon, and the dogs are restless in the pen behind the house, it nearly constitutes peonage.

If the house and the office are both in the woods, so that you can look out the window and see the sun among the trees and smell the air, and if you are convinced that the work you are doing is useless anyway, then the peonage approaches slavery.

And if, furthermore, you have to sit and work and send somebody else hunting and listen to them shoot after they go, then the whole miserable business turns into slavery under cruel and unusual circumstances.

I was right in the middle of the workup of the field tallies of the latest Johnson timber cruise on just such an afternoon. Then a car turned off the highway and into the office drive.

Ashley Johnson is a member of one of the old families in the county. In fact, he is the patriarch of one of these families. He is no more going to sell his timber than he is going to sell one of his grandsons. But every two or three years he sends out invitations to bid, invitations handwritten in Mrs. Johnson's delicate Spencerian script, to his regular trapline of prospects. Since he owns a half-section of prime longleaf, and since all timber buyers are incurable optimists anyway, everybody digs out the Johnson cruise from last time, exclaims over the volume per acre, and sends the cruisers out again.

All of us work up the new cruise carefully, add the extra dollar a thousand we think is finally going to buy it, and attend the bid opening for what we swear is positively the last time. Ashley opens the bids one by one in the Johnson living room, reads the figures, thanks the bidders, and calmly rejects them all.

There are dozens of loggers in south Alabama who have no idea who John Keats was, unless he was that guy wo played third base for Booklyn in 1938. But the emotion that Keats ascribes to the boy chasing the nymph on the Grecian Urn, the line that says, "Though thou has not thy bliss, forever wilt thou love and she be fair," is familiar to them all. For Ashley Johnson's timber, like Keats's nymph, has been dancing before the saws of Covington County loggers for nearly 20 years.

I temporarily abandoned my hopeless pursuit of naked Greek virgins when the car stopped in the office yard.

Three men came up the steps, through the screen door, and said good afternoon. They wanted hunting permits, which was expected, but what was unexpected was that they frankly and openly proposed to use them at once and said so.

I would not care to guess how many hunting permits I have written. Thousands for sure, maybe millions. But almost invariably the individual who asks for and accepts the permit disclaims any intention of using it.

He will say, for example, "I probably won't ever go, but I just happened to be passing by and I thought I would drop in and get one while I was thinking about it." Or they will say, "I don't know why I bother to do this. I still have the ones for the past five years in my top dresser drawer."

I have had individuals disavow any intention of ever hunting, when I was writing the permits, and while they were talking, the car parked in the office yard had the trunk propped open so the dogs could breathe, and there were men in hunting clothes waiting in the front and back seats.

It can only be described as astonishing.

My state requires that the hunter have written permission from the landowner in order to hunt, and everybody knows it. The state sells 200,000 licenses a year as well, so it is palpably impossible for all these people to be able to hunt on their own lands. Most of the corporate landowners cheerfully and willingly write hunting permits, some free, some for a modest charge, and everybody knows that. I think that everybody knows that the purpose of getting a hunting permit is to be able to have a place to hunt, but what I don't know is why they are unwilling to admit it.

At any rate, the three of them came in, and were honest. When I had written the permits, I explained that we didn't have a big map they could have. But I said I had one they could look at. They looked, thanked me, and left.

This map business is another stunner for the semi-professional permit writer. The U.S. Coast and Geodetic Survey prints maps for sale to the public that are nothing short of marvelous. They are printed in colors, are accurate enough to find section corners with or to shoot artillery from, and are on a scale of an inch to the mile. The general hunting public appears to be astonished at the news of their existence.

Knowing this, most corporate landowners print maps that they distribute along with the hunting permits. The maps welcome the hunter, are printed in two or three colors, and are usually on a scale of about three inches to the county. The maps are adequate for finding out if the land on which you are going to hunt is east or west of the Mississippi River. You sure aren't going to be able to hunt from them. But they are free, everyone wants one, and they go out the door holding it as if it showed the locations of sunken Spanish galleons.

I stood by the window and watched the car go back out of the drive to the highway. It crossed the highway and the railroad and started east down the county road that leads away from the office.

I saw the car pull abruptly to the side of the county road and stop, and saw both front doors fly open. I knew what had happened. They had run into the home covey.

The home covey was one of two that lived on the same 40 acres as the house and the office, and both coveys were pearls of great price. I used them to work the puppies on, and I shot them as carefully as diamond cutters split stones. Every once in a while I would shoot one bird—either working with a dog on his steadiness or his retrieve—but never otherwise. I never let either covey go to the end of the season with less than 10 birds. These coveys were not left there to hunt, they were left as training aids. It was obvious that whether I liked it or not, one of them, the home covey itself, was about to get hunted. The home covey crossed the county road going south at about the same time every afternoon, and it had undoubtedly been at the point of crossing when my visitors had seen the birds from the car.

Cursing all the hunters in the world but myself, I left the window and went back to the desk and sat down. I wished I knew enough about my visitors and their business so that I'd be able to run across the road with the news that the stock market had just fallen sharply, and that they had better come over to the phone and work with their brokers to salvage what they could.

I wished I knew the Governor personally, and was so rich and powerful and he owed me so many favors that I could call and get him to close the bird season in south Covington County instantly.

I couldn't do any of those things. So I had to sit helpless and wait for the shooting to start. It started soon enough.

The first volley had six shots in it. There was a distinct pause between the first and longer element and the final three shots. I knew what had happened. They were shooting two men up and one man back, and the covey had gotten up in two waves. The second wave had been late enough for the third man to step around the front two and contribute his three rounds from a plugged gun. And I knew what was going to happen next, especially what was going to happen with people who shot nine times on the covey rise.

The land across the road, where the home covey ranged, was perfectly flat. It had a tendency to be wet anyway, and years ago when the railroad had been built, the fill thrown up under the track had served as a natural dam for three or four miles and made it even wetter. There was not a creek in it. The drainage, what little there was, went into a sprinkling of small ponds none of which was bigger than an acre or two. These ponds had a thin screen of scrubby water oak around their rims and a few scattered mayhaw trees near the center. None was big enough to grow cypress. What was worse, none of them had enough cover to make the singles sufficiently difficult to find after the covey had been flushed.

A man with a good singles dog, and no scruples, could find every single after the covey rise and could, if he wanted to, eliminate the entire covey.

From the shooting that was now coming from across the road, it sounded as if a program of covey elimination was well under way.

They were shooting the singles two up and one back just as they had shot the rise. At just about the right timing for the dog to find yet another single at the edge of another pond, there was another and another volley.

I paced the office from the window to the desk and back to the window. In my rage and frustration, I doubled up three of the tally sheets and made a 200,000 board-foot error in the Johnson cruise. Damned near bought the timber on the strength of it too. At the next bid opening, Ashley turned down all the bids again as usual, but he dropped his coffee cup when he opened my envelope and read my bid, and he broke the handle off one of Mrs. Johnson's Lowestoft cups.

The miserable afternoon finally dragged itself to its conclusion, and at quitting time I locked the office and walked across the yard to my house, convinced I was exactly one covey short. I refused to play with my little girl, told my wife I thought she was gaining weight, and complained about the supper. There was, take it all around, little joy in Mudville that evening.

The next afternoon I went to the pen and let Lady out and walked her across the road to see if maybe they had missed a single bird. I took a gun, since Lady did not consider the situation to be serious unless a gun was present, but I did not load it.

Lady was old and rheumatic and slow, and she had to warm up

like an ancient ballplayer. But her deficiencies were all in wind and leg and not in nose. She had more sense about puppies than any dog trainer I ever met, and I believe she would have retrieved a dead ostrich. But she had one fault.

She would not retrieve woodcock.

For the benefit of those who are not members of the true faith, we have woodcock in south Alabama. They come in flights, late in the year and for a day or two after one of the flights the ponds across the road would be full of them. Lady pointed them with a sheepish expression. I do not think any power on earth could have made her put her mouth on one. I shot a few from time to time, partly out of curiosity and partly out of respect for the memory of Burton L. Spiller, and she would invariably go to the downed bird and sit. The bird would be there on the ground in front of her but she would neither touch it nor look at it. She would turn her head away with the same frozen expression seen on the faces of old ladies of good family who have just been accosted by drunks.

About 150 yards across the railroad and south of the county road by about that much, Lady slowed and turned her head. She took a dozen slow, stiff-legged steps in the direction she was looking, and locked into a point. Woodcock, I thought, since I knew the quail was dead. I walked past her nose with the gun still unloaded and broken over my left arm and stood in open-mouthed astonishment as the whole home covey got up with a roar. As best I could judge, the last time I had flushed this covey it had 15 birds in it. I counted 16, and I still don't know what happened.

It doesn't seem possible for people to shoot that poorly over as long a period of time as the shooting had lasted the day before. It seems that the percentages would have to even out eventually. I supposed it was theoretically possible for them to have found another covey, but I considered that to be almost out of the question. The place was right for this one, and the time, and it did not seem possible that there could be another covey. It was just as improbable that this covey should not have been decimated. But here they were.

I stood in front of Lady and watched them go while she gave me the look she reserved for the mentally defective—people who either wouldn't or couldn't kill birds she had been generous enough to find for them. I called her in, snapped the lead on her collar, and we started back across the road. I wouldn't have popped a cap at that covey that afternoon for $1,000. After what they had been through yesterday, they had to be suffering from a combination of ruptured eardrums and battle fatigue. They certainly didn't need any more shooting. What they probably needed was a long period of peace and quiet, and maybe a series of sessions with a top-notch psychiatrist.

Lady and I crossed the highway and got into the car in the office yard and drove down the woods road that parallels Flat Creek after it makes up behind the house. We followed this road to its end.

She found a brand-new covey, one not even in my covey book, 20 minutes after I let her out of the car.

I doubled on the rise, as snappily as I have ever done in my life. Both birds were dead in the air, 15 feet apart, and Lady retrieved them one at a time and reared up to put them in my hand when she brought them back. The singles flew south, downhill a little bit, toward the other branch of the creek. We waited 10 minutes for them to settle down, and then we walked down that way.

The first single she pointed was a double, not a single, and when they got up the birds crossed in the air just as I pulled the right-hand trigger. They fell together just beyond a little clump of gallberry.

For the first and only time in my life a dog retrieved two birds for me simultaneously. Lady fumbled around out there on the ground for a minute; I could not see her head. When she came in she had a bird, held by the head, hanging from either side of her mouth.

We quit right then. There is no way for you to improve on perfection, so there is no real reason to try.

We got back into the car and drove up the little road to the house. I went out in the yard and played with my charming and delightful daughter. Then I went inside and made admiring comments about the slim and youthful beauty of my lovely wife.

Supper was delicious.

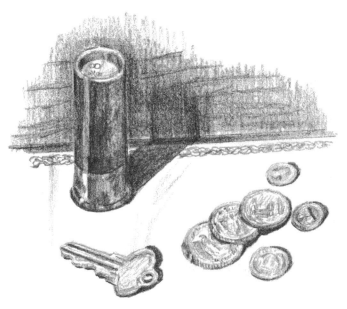

SHOFFSTALL

THE SHELL

William Humphrey

When I was fortunate enough to become editor of Sports Afield *in 1970, I was determined to bring more writers with national reputations outside the outdoor field into the magazine. I knew William Humphrey to be the talented author of short stories and novels, including* Home from the Hill *and* The Ordways. *I also knew that he was from Texas, loved hunting and fishing and had written a fastastic short story based on quail hunting. It had originally been published in a small literary magazine and had later been included in his collection of short stories* The Last Husband and Other Stories (*Lippincott*). *Bill was kind enough to grant me permission to use the story in* Sports Afield, *where it was an enormous hit with the readers in the September, 1970, issue. What follows is a powerful, emotional piece of writing. It is a story that belongs in any treasury of the all-time greats.*

THIS WOULD BE the season, the year when he would have the reach of arm to snap the big gun easily to his shoulder. This fall his shoulder would not be bruised black from the recoil. The hunting coat would fit him this season. This would be the season—the season when he would have to shoot the shell.

It was a twelve gauge shotgun shell. The brass was green with verdigris, the cardboard, once red, was faded to a pale and mottled brown, the color of old dried blood. He knew it intimately. On top, the firing cap was circled by the loop of a letter *P.* Around the rim, circling the *P,* were the two words of the trade name, *Peters Victor;* the gauge number, 12; and the words *Made in USA.* The wad inside the crimp of the firing end read, *Smokeless;* 3¼; 1⅛-8. This meant 3¼ drams of smokeless powder, 1⅛ ounces of number 8 shot—birdshot, the size for quail. It was the one shell he had found afterwards that had belonged to his father, one that his father had not lived to shoot. So he had thought at first to keep the shell unfired. But he knew his father would have said that a shotgun shell was meant to be fired, and he, Joe, had added that any shotgun shell which had belonged to him was meant to hit what it was fired at. For four years now it had been out of Joe's pocket, and out of his hand fingering it inside his pocket, only to stand upon the table by his bed at night. For four years now he had been going to shoot it when he was good enough, but the better he became the further away that seemed to get, because good enough meant, though he did not dare put it to himself in quite that way, as good as his father had been.

He had been in no great rush about it during those first two seasons afterwards, then there had been time—though now it seemed that even then there had been less time than he admitted. But on opening day of the third, last year's season, he had suddenly found himself sixteen years old—for though his birthday came in May, it was in November, on opening day of quail season, that he really began another year—time was suddenly short, and then overnight gone completely, after that day when he returned with the best bag he had ever taken and, in his cockiness, had told his mother about the shell, what he had saved it for and what he meant to do with it.

He had not allowed himself to forget that at that moment he could hear his father saying, "Do it and then talk about it." He had argued weakly in reply that he was telling only his mother, and then it was not his father but the voice of his own conscience which had cried, "Only!" Because whom alone did he want to tell, to boast to, and because already he knew that that was not what his father would have said, but rather, "Do it and don't talk about it afterwards either."

She had seemed hardly surprised to learn about the shell. She seemed almost to have known about it, expected it. But she handled it reverently because she could see that he did.

"Aren't you good enough now?" she said.

"Hah!" he said.

She was turning the shell in her fingers. "I always knew nothing would ever happen to him while hunting," she said. "I never worried when he was out with a gun . . . Well," she brought herself up, "but I worry about you. Oh, I know you're good with a gun. I'm not afraid you'll hurt yourself."

"Not with the training I've had," he said.

"No," she said. "What I worry about is the amount of time and thought you give it. Are you keeping up in school? The way you go at it, Joe! It hardly even seems to be a pleasure to you."

Pleasure? No, it was not a pleasure, he thought. That was the name he had always given it, but he was older now and no longer had to give the name pleasure to it. Sometimes—often times when he enjoyed it most—it was the opposite of pleasure. What was the proper name for it? He did not know. It was just what he did, the thing he would have been unable to stop doing if he had wanted to; it was what he was.

"I see other boys and girls your age going out to picnics and parties, Joe. I'm sure it's not that you're never invited."

"You know that kind of thing don't interest me," he said impatiently.

She was serious for a moment and said, "You're so old for your age, Joe. Losing your father so young." Then she altered, forced her tone. "Well, of course, you probably know exactly what you're up to," she said. "It's the hunters the girls really go for, isn't it? Us girls—us Southern girls—like a hunting man! I did. I'll bet all the little girls just—"

He hated it when she talked like that. She knew that girls meant nothing to him. He liked it when she let him know that she was glad they didn't. He liked to think that when she teased him this way, it was to get him to reaffirm how little he cared for girls; and yet she should know that his feeling for her was, like the feeling he had for hunting, too deep a thing for him to be teased into declaring.

He took the shell away from her.

"You're good enough now," she said.

"No," he said sullenly. "I'm not."

"He would think so."

"I don't think so. I don't think he would."

"I think so. You're good enough for me," she said.

"No. No, I'm not. Don't say that," he said.

He was in the field at daybreak on opening day with Mac, the speckled setter, the only one of his father's dogs left now, the one who in the three seasons he had hunted him had grown to be his father's favorite, whom he had broken that season that he had trained, broken, him, Joe, too, so that between him and the dog, since, a bond had existed less like that of master to beast, more like that of brother to brother, and consequently, he knew, he had never had the dog's final respect and did not have it now, though the coat did fit now.

He had not unleashed the dog yet, but stood with him among the bare alders at the edge of the broom grass meadow that had the blackened pile of sawdust in the middle—the color of fresh cornmeal the first time he ever saw it—to which he, and the big covey of quail, went first each season, the covey which he had certainly not depleted much but which instead had grown since his father's death.

The coat fit now, all right, but he wore it still without presumption, if anything with greater dread and with even less sense of possession than when it came halfway down to his knees and the sleeves hung down to the mid-joints of his fingers and the armpits looped nearly to his waist and made it absolutely impossible to get the gun stock to his shoulder, even if he could have lifted the big gun there in that split second when the feathered balls exploded at his feet and streaked into the air. He had not worn the coat then because he believed he was ready to wear it nor hunted with the big gun because he believed he was the man to. He had not been ready for a lot of things. He'd had to learn to drive, and drive those first two years seated on a cushion to see over the hood; he had not been ready to sit at the head of the table, to carve the meat, to be the comforter and protector, the man of the house. He had had to wear the coat and shoot the gun and rock on his heels and just grit his teeth at the kick, the recoil.

Maybe there had been moments later—the day he threw away the car cushion was one—when he was pleased to think that he was growing into the coat, but now, as he stood with Mac, hunching and dropping his shoulders and expanding his chest inside it, it seemed to have come to fit him before he was at all prepared for it to. He heard the loose shells rattle in the shell pockets and he smelled the smell of his father, which now, four years later, still clung to it, or else what he smelled was the never-fading, peppery smell of game blood and the clinging smell of gun-powder, the smell of gun oil and the smell of the dog, all mixed on the base of damp, heavy, chill November air, the air of a quail-shooting day, the smells which had gone to make up the smell his father had had for him. Reaching his hand into the shell pocket he felt something clinging in the seam. It was a faded, tangled and blood-stiffened pinfeather of a quail. It was from a bird his father had shot. He himself had never killed so many that the game pockets would not hold them all and he had had to put them in the shell pockets.

He took from among the bright other ones the shell and slipped it into the magazine and pumped it into the breech. He would have to make good his boast to his mother, though he knew now that it was a boast made no more out of cockiness than cowardice and the determination born of that cowardice to fix something he could not go back on. He would have to fire the shell today. He had known so all the days as opening day approached. He had known it at breakfast in the lighted kitchen with his mother, re-membering the times when she and himself had sat in the lighted kitchen over breakfast on opening day with his father, both in the years when he himself had stayed behind and watched his father drive away into the just-breaking dawn, not even daring yet to yearn for his own time to come, and later when he began to be taken; he had seen it in the dog. Mac's eyes as he put him into the cage, the dog cage his father had had built into the car trunk though it was the family car, the only one they had to go visiting in as well, that he would have to fire the shell today, and he had known it most as he backed out of the drive and waved good-by to his mother, remembering the times when his father had been in the driver's seat and she had stood waving to the two of them.

Now he felt the leash strain against his belt loop and heard the dog whimpering, and out in the field, rising liquid and clear into the liquid air, he heard the first bobwhite and immediately heard a second call in answer from across the field and the first answer back, and then, as though they had tuned up to each other, the two of them fell into a beat, set up a round-song of alternate call and response: bob bob white white, bob bob white white, and then others tuned in until there were five, eight separate and dis-tinctly timed voices, and Joe shivered, not ashamed of his emotion and not trying to tell himself it was the cold, but owning that it was the thrill which nothing else, not even other kinds of hunting, could ever give him and which not even his dread that it was the day when he would have to shoot the shell could take away from him, and knowing for just that one moment that this was the real, the right feeling to have, that it was the coming and trying that mattered, the beginning, not the end of the day, the empty, not the full game pockets, feeling for just that moment in deep accord with his father's spirit, feeling him there with him, beside him, listening, loading up, unleashing the dog.

As soon as the dog was unleashed his whimpering ceased. Joe filled the magazine of the gun with the two ordinary shells and stood rubbing the breech of the gun, watching the dog enter the field. He veered instantly and began systematically quartering the field, his nose high and loose, on no fresh scent yet, but quickening, ranging faster already. They claimed—and of most dogs it was true—that setters forgot their training between seasons, but not Mac, not the dog his father had trained, not even after three seasons, even with no better master than him to keep him in training. He watched him now in the field lower his muzzle slightly as the scent freshened and marveled at the style the dog had, yet remembered paradoxically that first day, his and Mac's, when each of them, the raw, noisy, unpromising-looking pup and the raw, unpromising-looking but anything but noisy boy, had flushed birds, the pup a single but he a whole covey—two of which his father had bagged nonetheless—for which the pup had received a beating and he only a look, not even a scolding look, but a disappointed look worse than any beating he had ever had.

The dog set: broke stride, lowered his muzzle, then planted all four feet as though on the last half-inch of a sudden and unexpected cliff-edge, raised his muzzle and leaned forward into the scent streaming hot and fresh into his nostrils, leaned his whole body so far forward that the raised, rigid, feathered tail seemed necessary as a ballast to keep him from falling on his face. You could tell from his manner that it was the whole big covey.

He called as he set out down the field. "Steady, boy. Toho," he called, and on the dead misty air his voice did not seem his voice at all but his father's voice, calling as he had heard him call, and he was struck afresh and more powerfully than ever before with the sense of his own unworthiness, his unpreparedness, which seemed now all the more glaringly shown forth by the very nearness he had attained to being prepared; he felt himself a pretender, a callow and clownish usurper.

Now the birds were moving, running in the cover, still banded together, and Mac moved up his stand, so cautiously that he seemed jointless with rigidity. Stock-still, trembling with controlled excitement, his eyes glazed and the hair along his spine bristling, you could have fired an artillery piece an inch above his head and still he would have stood unflinching for an hour, until told to break his stand, and so Joe let him stand, to enjoy the sight, as well as to give his pounding heart a moment's calm, before going in to kick them up. He held the gun half-raised, and the shell in the barrel seemed to have increased its weight tenfold. Alongside the dog he said again, "Steady, boy," knowing that this time he spoke not to the dog but to himself.

It was as if he had kicked the detonator of a land mine. There was a roaring whir as the birds, twenty of them at least, burst from the grass at his feet like hurtling fragments of shell and gouts of exploding earth, flung up and out and rapidly diminishing in a flat trajectory, sailing earthward almost instantly, as if, though small, deceptively heavy and traveling with incredible velocity.

The gun went automatically to his shoulder, snapped up there more quickly and gracefully than ever before. He had a bird in his eye down the barrel and knew that he had got it there quickly enough to get a second shot easily. But his breath left him as though knocked out by the burst and pounding rush of wings. Fear that he might miss, miss with the shell, paralyzed him. He lowered the gun unfired. Turning to the still-rigid dog, he saw— as one in such case is always liable to see on the face of a good bird dog—his look of bewildered disappointment. In that instant it seemed to Joe that the fear of finding just that look was what had unnerved him, and though he was ashamed of the impulse, all his own disappointment and self-contempt centered in hatred for the dog.

As soon as he was given leave, Mac went after the singles. He set on one instantly.

Joe kicked up this single and again the anxiety that he might miss, such that sweat filled his armpits and he felt his mouth go dry, overcame him, and with trembling hands he had to lower the hammer and lower the gun unfired, and was unable to face the dog.

He tried on three more singles. It got worse. He knew then without looking at him that Mac had given him up and would refuse to hunt any more today. He did not even have to put him on the leash. The dog led the way out of the field. Joe found him lying at the rear of the car, and he did not need even to be told, much less dragged, as usual with him on any shooting day but especially on opening day, to get into the cage to go home.

The lemon pie was in the refrigerator, the marshmallow-topped whipped yams in the oven and the biscuits cut and in the pan and on the cabinet waiting to go into the oven the moment the birds were plucked—all as it always was when his father returned in the evening of a quail-shooting day when he and his father, and still later when he came home alone and laid the dead birds in her lap, as he had laid the first dollar he ever earned.

She said cheerfully, that it was a lucky thing she happened to have some chops in the house. She added that she had learned that long ago. A woman learned, she said, never to trust to a hunter's luck—not even the best hunter. He was both grateful and resentful of those words. He knew she had never bought meat at the store against his father's coming home from a hunt empty-handed.

He rested a day, went to school a week, and practiced, shooting turnips tossed into the air and hitting five out of seven, then he went back. The quail were there, you could hear them, but when he looked at Mac as he as about to loose him and felt himself quaking already, he snapped the leash on again and went back to the car and home.

And so what it turned into, this season for which he finally had the reach and the size, the endurance, in a word the manliness, was the one in which he fired no shell at all.

The Thanksgiving holidays came and he spent every day in the field with the shell in the barrel of the gun—a few bright brass nicks in the dull green now where the ejector had gripped pumping it in and out of the breech—and the magazine full behind it of his own waiting shells and with Mac. He hardly spoke to the dog now, gave him no commands and no encouragements, nor did the dog give tongue or whimper or even frisk, a kind of wordless and even gestureless rapport between them, the two of them hunting now in a grim, cold fury of impotence.

The dog had gone past disappointment, past disgust, past even bewilderment, and seemed now to have divined the reason or else the irresistible lack of all reason behind the coveys kicked up, the boy—almost the man now—raising and cocking his gun, but shaking his head even as he raised it, holding it erect and steady on his mark, then lowering it slowly and soundlessly and releasing him from stand and hunting on. His mother gave up trying to keep him at home, and seemed to have sensed the desperate urgency in him.

And now as the days passed and closing day of the season neared he could feel the whole town watching him, awaiting the climax of his single-minded pursuit, their curiosity first aroused by what they would have been most certain to observe: the lack of interest which they would think he should have begun to show in girls. The boys had noticed, had taken to gathering in a body on his shift at the Greek's confectionery at night, ordering him to make sodas for them and their dates, and ribbing him.

"Haven't seen much of you lately, Joe. Where you been?"

"Around."

"Yeah, but around who?"

Guffaws.

"I've been busy."

"I'll bet you have, old Joe."

Titters.

"Busy. Yeah."

Then he would blush. "I've been hunting," he said.

"I'll bet you have!"

He blushed again and said—he could never learn to avoid that kind of double meaning—"Quail."

They roared. "Getting many?" they said, and "Aren't we all?" and "Watch out for those San Quentin quail," they said.

Everybody knew everybody else's business in town anyhow, and moreover he was a kind of public figure in his way—they could not have helped but watch the coming-of-age of the son of the greatest wing shot the town ever had—so that he felt now that the ear of the whole town was cupped to hear the report of the shell, a sound which to him it had come to seem would have no resemblance whatever to the noise of any other shotgun shot ever heard.

At nights he studied the shell, trying to discover the source of its charm. He had come to fear it, almost to hate it, certainly to live by and for it.

How can you, he asked himself—no, he could make the question general, for he asked it not self-ironically but just incredulously—how can a boy want to be better than his father? Not better. It was not that. Not even as good as. That was not what he wanted at all. What was it? It was that you wanted to be your father, wasn't it? Yes, that was it. That was more what it was. And you weren't.

But wasn't there just a little bit of wanting to be better than, mixed in with it? Wasn't there, in fact, just a little bit of thinking you were better than, mixed with it? All right, yes. Yes, there was. Why? It was because you believed that being half him you had all he was, and being half your mother you had that much again that he wasn't, that he did not have. And you knew that he would have agreed with this, which did not make you believe it entirely, or stop believing it.

Then it was closing day. The big covey was long gone from the broom grass meadow now, ranging from the swamps and brier patches to the uplands and the loblolly pines at the thicket edges. You had to work to find them now and any shot you got was likely to be a snap shot, through branches or brush. But this was how he wanted it. Let it get hard enough and it would be the shot and he would take it.

There were no waiting shells in the magazine of the gun today. He wanted no second shot, at least not on the same flush.

It was about eight in the morning when Mac got a warm scent. Did he know it was closing day? You would think so from the way he had suddenly taken cheer—or hysteria—determination, certainly. He spirits were not dampened even by the lowering of the unfired gun at the first single he found. He seemed in agreement that this one had been too easy.

They were hunting in uplands, in blackened stover bent to the ground and frozen, so that it snapped against Joe's boots. Then Mac headed down out of the cornfield, crossed a fencerow and was in a swamp, in sedge, tall and dead and bent. Joe could follow Mac, as 'way ahead of him the tall stiffened grass parted and closed heavily behind the dog's passage. Then he could not follow him any more and he whistled, and when he got no answer he knew that the dog had set and could not give tongue.

He began to rush, though he knew that Mac would hold or follow the birds. Feeding time for the birds was almost over. They would be drifting toward the thickets now and in another hour would go deep into the pines and then the dog could not hunt them, no dog. Then the hunting would not be good again until nightfall and that was the very last chance. It had better be now.

The dog continued for as far as he could see in the milky mist and he stood for a moment wishing the dog would give tongue just once, knowing that he was too well trained, and then he decided to go left, south. The land soon began to rise and the sedge got shorter and soon he could see where the swamp gave out at a fencerow and beyond that he soon could see a clearing rising out of the fog and rising up into pine woods. He could see no sign of the dog, but that was where he was sure to be.

He climbed over the barbwire, still looking ahead up into the clearing, and bent to get through the briers and came out with his head still raised looking up and almost stepped on the rigid, unbreathing dog, his nose in the wind, pointed as stiff as a weathervane.

He cocked the gun and stepped into the brush and kicked. They roared out toward the pines. He swung on his heel, holding the gun half-raised, picking his bird. He swiveled a half-circle, twisted at the waist, and saw the big cock, big as a barnyard rooster, streaking for the pines. He shot. The sound seemed to go beyond sound, one of those the hearer does not hear because the percussion has instantly deafened him, and he felt himself stagger from the recoil. But down the barrel of the gun he saw the bird, pitching for the ground at the thicket edge, winging along untouched, without a feather ruffled, and he knew that he had missed. From old habit he was already pumping the gun, and it was when he saw the big shell flick out and spin heavily into the brush that he realized he had heard no sound but a light dry click. The shell had not gone off. The shell was a dud. He had kept it too long; it had gone dead.

He said it aloud. "I have kept it too long. It's a dud."

Then he felt himself soaring as though in a burst of wings like the cock bird, as though he had been shot at himself and gone unscathed, free.

He dropped the shell into his pocket. It would rest permanently on his bureau now, he had time to tell himself. Then he was fumbling for fresh shells, his own shells, and dropping them all over the ground at his feet and getting one into the chamber backwards and saying to Mac in a voice he could just recognize as his own, "All right, don't stand there! Go get 'em! Go get 'em, boy! Go get 'em!" And he could tell that Mac knew it was his master's voice speaking now, a hunter's voice.

A PRIVATE AFFAIR

Harold P. Sheldon

This piece will come as a pleasant surprise to the many readers who perhaps thought that Colonel Harold P. Sheldon's byline appeared only on grouse or woodcock pieces. Well, as you'll soon see, he could hold his own in quail country too. The story is from his famous "Tranquillity" series. Sheldon wrote Tranquillity *for Derrydale in 1936. Countryman Press printed three volumes in 1945:* Tranquillity, Tranquillity Regained *and* Tranquillity Revisited. *In 1973, Winchester Press published all three combined in one book. Some of the richest writing in the outdoors can be found in Sheldon's tales. This one is from* Tranquillity Revisited.

As IT SANK behind the gentle Virginia hills the sun threw a final suffusion of amber light across the Campus. It was the quiet hour before supper. Undergraduates coming from the tennis courts and the athletic field strolled along the winding brick walks swinging racquets and clubs and chattering of the important affairs and matters that engage the interests of the young. Somone at the Old Dormitory struck a few soft precise chords from a guitar, and voices took up the merry wistful melody of "Oh! Susannah."

The Dean shoved a sleek pair of brown riding boots under his desk and thought that probably "Hooter" Gordon's gang had gotten hold of a bottle of sherry. Well, it wouldn't hurt them. He hummed a bar or two of the old familiar song:

> "I'll be comin' back from Oregon
> With my gold dust on my knee."

"Marse Robert" looked gravely down at him from a panel over the fireplace where hung a long Remington Dragoon revolver in a black leather holster with the letters C.S.A. embossed on the worn flap, and beside it a heavy cavalry saber with more than a full yard of steel projecting beyond the dented guard. The weapons were there because a man in a dusty, disheveled blue uniform had said: "Officers may retain their side arms."

At last the sunlight lifted reluctantly from the crimson crown of

] 409 [

the gum tree outside the Dean's window, and then someone knocked gently upon a panel of the old door.

"Come in, Esau."

A fat old Negro in a white mess coat eased himself into the room.

"Cunnel, suh! He done come," he announced. Then he closed the door and advanced to the desk for a confidential report on the matter.

"Cunnel, suh! He is dest de spit an' image ob de Ol' Cap'n! I declar', suh, he sholy is! An' he got his dawg too. Lawd A'mighty! Big long'haided ol' setter wid eggzackly de same sassy patch on de right eye!"

"All right, Esau. Show 'em in. And then find my grandson, Mister John, and ask him to come here, please. Tell him that Mister William has arrived."

A lean stripling of eighteen or thereabouts entered, paused for a moment and then came forward as the Dean rose and put out his hand.

Colonel Bristol, sir," said the boy with diffidence, "I'm William Stovall. I hope I find you well, sir."

"Of co'se, of co'se! William, I'm glad to see you, and if I didn't know for a certainty that your Grandad is as old and as gray and generally decrepit as I am this minute, I'd swear you were that man! Ten or fifteen pounds lighter, possibly, than I remember him, but that's all. And this must be Soldier."

At the sound of his name the big setter came up, his great plume waving, sniffed gently with a broad muzzle at the brown boots and lifted approving hazel eyes to the gray ones above him.

The Dean chuckled: "I declare, son, I never saw a man and his dog look more like another man and *his* dog." His hand dropped to the broad arch of the dog's skull. "I hope you'll let me shoot over him sometimes."

"Why, sir, Soldier and I would be completely paralyzed—I mean we'd be awfully glad if you would, sir! Grandad said he thought you might. Soldier hasn't had much experience with quail, but I 'spect he'll learn 'em."

"I expect he will," said the Dean. "His grandsire did."

"Yes, sir," said the boy with a quick, shy smile. "Grandad told me about that time."

Another youngster came in then, and the Dean made introductions.

"Son, this is William and this other gentleman is Soldier. Will you take them home, please? Tell Miss Annie that I'll be there in time for supper."

He turned again to William: "And we'll talk about your studies tomorrow, if you please. Right now you'll want a bath and some of Rachel's fried chicken—and I want to do a little thinking."

The two went out, and the Dean watching them thought how alike they were with their lean, loose-limbed bodies, straight backs and gentle manners. He sat down and lighted a cigarette.

In a weather-beaten tent in a wood on the north bank of a narrow river, young Captain William Stovall awoke, yawned and shoved his long legs over the edge of his cot. The morning rays of the sun were in the feathery tops of the pin oaks outside and there was frost in the air. A golden reflection illuminated the rough fabric over his head. A big setter with a dissolute bluish patch over his right eye rose from a blue blanket in a corner, came over to inquire formally as to the state of the young officer's health and then turned his gaze hopefully on the entrance.

The Captain reached for boots and breeches. He spoke to the setter.

"Hi, Soldier. Think you can find 'em today? Let's try 'em, eh?"

At the sound of the voice a fat soldier with a disordered mop of red hair scratched perfunctorily at the tent flap, then stepped inside and came to a rigid "Attention!"

"Mornin', Chauncey. Stand easy. Fetch me a bucket of fresh water and bring up my breakfast."

"I already got the Cap'n's washin' water an' his breakfast, too."

"And see if you can snake out six raw eggs for Soldier."

"Got the aigs, too," remarked Chauncey stolidly.

"All right, Perfect! Now let's see you convey my compliments to Lieutenant Hines and tell him he's in command today—that I'm goin' out on a reconnaissance. Tell the cook to put up three lunches—two big ones for me and Soldier and a little teeny-weeny one for you. You're gettin' too fat. You're ridin' with us, too."

"Yes, sir, Cap'n, I got the grub already. But does the Cap'n reelize this ain't no time to go shootin' 'round after them leetle insignificant birds? Take about four of 'em to make one reel pa'tridge, anyhow! And what's to prevent us gittin' picked up by a Secesh patrol, I wanter know? Nothin'! The Cap'n may like the idee o' Andersonville Prison, but, by Judas Priest, the Cap'n's orderly don't!"

"Shut up—you'll go where I say to go! Get out my shotgun and look to the ammunition pouches, understand? Get started, and don't let me hear anything more from you but silence—an' damned little o' that!"

"I already 'tended to that," said Chauncey reproachfully.

A half-hour later they splashed through the shallows of a ford and climbed the red earth bank to the uneven and weed-smothered fields on the opposite side. Chauncey wore an air of badly concealed trepidation, and a service revolver, fresh caps glinting on the nipples, was strapped to his plump unsoldierly waist. His apprehensive gaze scrutinized every inequality of terrain and sought to penetrate the thickets of cat brier and wild plum. It was so quiet that the sudden raucous yelping of a swamp woodpecker made Chauncey flinch visibly.

The Captain laughed:

"Don't be so damned jumpy! There ain't a gray jacket within ten miles according to our patrols."

"Yessir. I guess that's right—only our patrols ain't never yit seemed to be able to git their permanent address, Cap'n. Those jaspers jest don't seem to want to cooperate with our patrols."

"Well, they ain't going to bother us today," said the officer. With a wave of his hand he sent the setter forward.

The dog moved out eagerly, plume flying, nose straight, but from the restrained manner in which he covered his ground a "shooting-dog man" would have known that he had learned his trade in the grouse and woodcock thickets of New England rather than among the sedge levels, gullies and pea fields of Dixie. His action was sure and bold, but the racing, distance-covering swoop of the quail dog was not his. It mattered not at all, for the bottom land was full of birds and Soldier could scarcely move a hundred yards without freezing fast on a fresh covey. This land was part of a great plantation, but its wide fields were empty now of workers; no mules plodded behind the untrimmed hedges, and no sound either of human joy or woe came to the ears. A blackened chimney stood in an irregular rectangle of live oaks on a hill, a mournful witness of the pointless waste and useless destruction of war.

Whenever Soldier stood, the young officer dismounted, drew a burnished double-barreled gun from the saddle scabbard and walked up to the immobile dog. He shot well, and by midmorning Chauncey had counted a score of birds into a gunny sack and was thinking longingly of the generous lunch in the saddlebags. His earlier apprehensions had not diminished—on the contrary they had mounted steadily as their course led imperceptibly toward the wooded hilly ground south of the stream. Somewhere, he knew, beyond that sunny barrier lay the Army of Northern Virginia, and from past experience with that crowd he wasn't anxious for further contact.

"Either you got to fight like Hell or run like Hell, an' I fer one ain't partial to neither," muttered the fat trooper.

Soldier crossed a weed-grown field and disappeared in a gully where bare red earth showed through the yellow sedge.

"He's probably on point," said the Captain. "I'll take this one, and then we'll find water and unsaddle for lunch."

The dog was standing rigid when they saw him, but the find, they perceived, was not his own. He was honoring another dog, a lean, hard-muscled pointer, posed in rigid style with his snakelike head turned to catch the scent that drifted to him from a tangle of frost-killed vines.

The Captain spoke in wonder. "Where'd that dog come from? Look at him! He's no tramp! That feller is a bird dog, and somebody takes good care of that animal!"

They rode nearer, and the Captain had already dismounted when an exclamation from his soldier servant directed his attention toward the top of the draw. There a man in faded gray with a shotgun across the saddle came riding on a big bay hunter. He was followed by a slender Negro swathed in a wondrous assortment of garments and mounted on a gaunt mule.

The newcomer hesitated for the briefest instant when he saw the strange setter honoring his dog's point and caught sight of the two blue-shirted men standing by. Then he came quietly on.

Suddenly Chauncey swore and clawed at his holster flap.

"Let that pistol be!" his officer told him sharply. "Don't be a damned fool! That Johnny ain't going to hurt you. He's birdin', too."

"He's probably got him a hull troop hid out in them pines," muttered Chauncey, who snuffed in his nostrils the stench of Andersonville and felt in his belly the gripe of its starvation rations.

"If so, they'll not feel any more friendly to us if we murder the Troop Commander," advised the Captain.

The stranger was a man of his own age, lean and brown. The insignia on his jacket gave him the rank of Captain, and there was an indefinable suggestion of alert and easy confidence about him that marked him as a veteran, an active man and a cool man, one likely to be quick and violent in a fuss. As he pulled up his horse, his gray eyes glanced carelessly at the unbuttoned flap of the orderly's pistol holster. Then he dismounted easily, and there was a perfunctory exchange of salutes.

"Looks like they got 'em," he remarked, and his teeth shone in a brief smile.

Stovall grinned, too, and there was a perceptible relaxation of tension.

The Confederate looked at the dogs and appeared to cogitate.

"Cap'n, suh," said he, "may I inquire if yo' carry yo' views opposin' the rights of the States to secede from the Union into the spo'tin' field?"

"No," replied Stovall, "and even if I did I'd lay 'em aside on a day like this with two dogs fast on a covey and more of 'em in the fields. Since your dog has found this lot, I may even go so far as to say that I'd accept an invitation to shoot with you, sir."

"You have it, and right cordially, suh," was the response. "Shall we flush 'em?"

So they did, and the dogs went forward and retrieved four birds neatly picked from the opposite flanks of the bursting covey.

"My name is Bristol, suh, commanding C Troop, 1st Virginia Cavalry."

"I'm Stovall, Commanding A Troop, 1st Vermont Cavalry," responded the other, and they shook hands. It was on Stovall's tongue to say that they had met before in the yard of a certain tavern in Northern Virginia, but he checked the impulse. "I was about to knock off for a couple of hours, find some water and have lunch. Would you join me, Captain? We can rest the dogs and go on later."

The Southerner agreed, and presently the two officers were seated companionably on a log on the shady bank of the creek. Bristol's Negro, whose name was Esau, brought out a paper package containing a flat cake of corn bread and a few scraps of bacon, which meager fare Stovall sought unostentatiously to supplement from his own ample rations. There was no concealing the eagerness with which the newcomer's teeth bit into the slab of white bread and beef.

"Yo' General Grant has been keepin' us shuckin' 'round so fast lately that we don't seem to find time to gather up a good bait of grub," he explained. "Yo' people ain't so careless with yo' supply trains as you used to be, either, an' I want you to know that some of our ridin's boys are right peeved about yo' attitude on that subject."

"Well," said Stovall, defensively, "it's mostly their own fault. They've got a kind of boisterous way about 'em when they come to draw their rations."

They ate and chatted companionably, each feeling the pull of an instinctive liking for the other that was unhindered by wartime animosities.

Stovall found himself thinking how difficult it was to support a high fine rage against a good man who wore another sort of uniform but who liked the same things that he liked. Three years of fighting had somewhat dulled the indignation he had earlier felt against these people. Of course, they oughtn't for their own good try to split themselves off from the rest of the family and they ought also to have sense enough to see that they couldn't keep to their old romantic way of living in the face of what was happening to the rest of the country. The principle of slavery was wrong, too, but as these people managed it it wasn't so bad, after all. Not the least bit like they did things in that show he'd gone to see in

Rutland City once. "Uncle Tom's Cabin or Life Among the Lowly" was the name of the play, he recalled. The bonds upon the black folk, he personally observed, were the opposite of harsh—just firm enough to keep them in ways that were good for them. Deprived of their white folks he knew that these poor souls were at once lost and pitifully demoralized. Lots of them had come into the lines, men, women and children, pathetic in their helplessness and asking only that someone feed them, give them clothes to wear and tell them what to do.

Thinking wasn't a soldier's business, that was for others to do, but nevertheless he had for some time suspected that these Southerners, the good ones, at least, had ideas fundamentally not so very different from his own.

Reflections of somewhat similar nature must have been in the Southerner's mind.

"I don't see any horns on you, suh," he remarked after a bit, "an' I conclude that my kinsman, Uncle Wally Beaufort, was maybe right about the matter. He spent much time in Boston befo' the war an' he always claimed there were *some* nice folks up No'th. But if you'll kindly allow me to observe you don't look yo' best when you come a-shootin' an' whoopin' an' raisin' Hell."

"And neither do you," said Stovall with conviction, and both knew that some sort of a pledge had been passed between them.

Once during the afternoon the Yankee unostentatiously steered the shooting party away from a wooded promontory that overlooked the wide expanse of fields. If the Confederate noticed the maneuver or attached any significance to it he said nothing. Once, a little later, he, too, mildly suggested a slight change of direction to bear away from another distant woodland.

"There might be some folks oveh in that way this evenin' who wouldn't rightly undehstan' the nature of our expedition," he remarked casually.

Never again did either of the two experience such shooting as they enjoyed that afternoon between the lines of the Army of the Potomac and the Army of Northern Virginia, as these lay licking their fresh wounds and alert for the next opportunity to grapple in a continuation of the bloody struggle that was to bring them to the gates of Richmond and from there even unto the Confederacy's Garden of Gethsemane at Appomattox. In those sunlit fields where the delicate haze of Autumn hung there was nothing to indicate that it was a stage upon which a long and bitter tragedy was moving toward the final curtain. The birds, long unmolested in the abandoned fields grown up to sedge and pea vines, had multiplied beyond description. Rabbits bounced from underfoot, and once a flock of wild turkeys rose from an old orchard in grand turmoil before the two dogs and at such close range that even the light quail charges brought down two to appease Chauncey's yearning for game "that had more'n two mouthfuls of meat on it."

He even forgot, momentarily, his perturbation as he fastened a big bronze gobbler to his saddle.

When Bristol's powder flask ran empty he called up Esau, who fished a double handful of paper rifle cartridges from the pockets of his numerous jackets, broke them open one by one and spilled the black powder into the brass spout of the canister. The packages were marked with the label of the United States Government.

"Not very good powder, either," the Southerner complained slyly.

"Judas Priest," Chauncey muttered, "ain't these boys got *nothin'* that they ain't stole?"

Before they knew it the sun was down behind the rim of the woods and it was time to part.

"Captain, suh, it has been a great day and I have enjoyed shootin' with you an' over yo' dog. He's a grand animal. I would surely love to see him work on grouse." He touched his game bag. "You'll be pleased to know that a portion of these pa'tridges will grace the General's breakfast table. He's powerful fond of fried pa'tridge."

A gleam came into Stovall's eye, and he began hauling birds out of Chauncey's sack.

"I was going to send a dozen of mine up to General Grant's mess," said he. "Let's trade. You take *my* birds to Marse Robert and I'll take yours to our General. Maybe we'll do well not to say who sent 'em."

The exchange was made, and the two rode away.

"Hope to see you again, Yank," said Bristol. "Keep yo' head down and yo' shirt tail tucked in."

"The same to you, Reb," replied Stovall.

It was a hot day in early Spring some months later, and at a ford on another quiet creek a little way to the west of Richmond men were assembling to take part in one of those small, violent and bloody affairs that were so common that they have been generally ignored by the historians of the great conflict between the North and the South. References to them are mostly buried in faded casualty lists and in field messages hastily scrawled and stained with the sweat of horse and man. The rear of a weary, desperate column of Confederate troops moved painfully along a road that paralleled the stream. A small detachment of their cavalry rode down to the ford and dismounted, and while some of the men led the animals into the concealment of the woods the others flung themselves down behind trees and stumps and drawn carbines and pistols, intent to cover the crossing until the dragging column of the infantry and guns had cleared the defile. They had not long to wait. There was presently a muffled trampling sound of horses and men beyond the creek, and blue uniforms showed briefly amid the soft green of the Spring foliage.

"Fire at will! Commence firing!" said a quiet voice.

It was followed instantly by the sharp crackle of the carbines. There was momentary confusion across the ford, and then the white puffs from the southern bank were being answered by irregular spurts from the opposite side. These thickened and increased as fresh Union troopers came up to support their advance party. Bullets splashed in the water, throwing up sudden jets of spray; others cut white gouges in the bark of the trees. A horse screamed somewhere in the woods, and a man yelled and cursed. The firing from the north bank deepened in volume as the Union line was strengthened, and soon every battle-wise veteran in ragged butternut knew that under cover of the musketry the Yankees were forming and braced himself for yet another of the annihilating blue charges that could still be met but no longer stopped. Not that it mattered much anyway. The jig was up. Marse Robert, cornered at last, was trying without hope to draw his limping, starving columns from the jaws of a trap already nearly closed, and the world that had been the Old South was shattering about their ears. Then from the road sounded the blast of a whistle blowing "All clear!" and a swarm of men leaping from cover ran to their mounts and scurried off through the bullet-whipped woods.

The last to leave, as is entirely proper on such occasions, was the officer in command of the detachment. When his rearmost man had mounted and was away amid a shower of slugs, this one came gallantly out of the woods at a gallop, pistol in hand, and set his horse at the ditch bank. What was left of a grand bay hunter made a brave effort at a barrier that would have been no barrier at all three years before, a mere ridge of old earth not three feet high it was, but the poor brute failed at it and in its stumbling plunge threw the rider headlong and helpless into the trail in full view of his enemies a scant forty paces distant across the ford. Two or three of these ran out from cover and raised their carbines for the shot—after all war is war, and a good combat captain is worth fifty good fighting men any day—but an officer yelled suddenly:

"Don't shoot that man!"

Then he added somewhat inadequately and lamely and as if he felt it to be necessary to excuse his saving action, "I know that Johnny! He's a hell of a good bird shot!"

Across the creek the Confederate heard the order and the explanation of it.

He gathered himself, his reins and his mount and went into the saddle like an eel over a wet stone. With his long pistol at high present and his face splitting into a quick familiar grin of recognition, he called:

"Thank you, Cap'n! And so are you, suh!"

Then he wheeled his poor old crowbait—the same that once romped away from the best of 'em in the Blue Grass—and rode away after his men.

The Dean stirred in his chair. It was nearly dark outside, and "Hooter" Gordon's guitar had been silent for a long time. The Dean thought maybe he had better go along home. Miss Annie would be waiting for him.

SHOFFSTALL

THE SUNDOWN COVEY

Lamar Underwood

Back in 1973, before he founded Amwell Press and was still associated with Winchester, Jim Rikhoff asked me to do an original hunting piece for a new Winchester Press anthology he was editing, to be called Hunting Moments of Truth. *I gave the project my best shot, and the result was "The Sundown Covey," which Jim still likes so much he wanted me to include it in* The Bobwhite Quail Book. *The piece grew out of my actual experiences in the area where I did most of my early quail hunting, in and around Bulloch County, Georgia.*

NOBODY EVER USED that name, really. But it was the covey of bobwhite quail that we always looked for almost with longing, as we turned our hunt homeward in the afternoon. By the time we came to that last stretch of ragged corn and soybean fields where this covey lived, the pines and moss-draped oaks would be looming darkly in the face of the dying sun. The other events of the afternoon never seemed to matter then. Tired pointer dogs bore ahead with new drive; we would watch carefully as they checked out each birdy objective, sure that we were headed for a significant encounter before we reached the small lane that led to the Georgia farmhouse. I always chose to think of those birds as "the sundown covey," although my grandfather or uncle usually would say something like "Let's look in on that bunch at the end of the lane." And then, more times than not, the evening stillness would be broken by my elder's announcement, "Yonder they are!" and we would move toward the dogs on point—small stark-white figures that always seemed to be chiseled out of the shadowy backdrop against the evening swamp.

There's always something special about hunting a covey of quail that you know like an old friend. One covey's pattern of movements between fields and swampy sanctuaries can be an intriguing and baffling problem. Another may be remarkably easy to find, and yet always manage to rocket away through such a thick tangle that you've mentally colored them *gone*, even before your finger touches the trigger. Another might usually present a good covey shot, while the singles tear away to . . . the backside of the moon, as far as you've been able to tell. My best hunts on more distant but greener pastures somehow have never seemed as inwardly satisfying as a day when a good dog and I can spend some time on familiar problems like these. Give me a covey I know, one that has tricked me, baffled me, eluded me—and by doing so brought me back to its corner of the woods for years.

In this sense, the covey we always hunted at sundown was even more special. As the nearest bunch of birds to the house, it was the most familiar. Here, trembling puppies got onto their first points. A lad learned that two quick shots into the brownish blur of the covey rise would put nothing into his stiff new hunting coat. A man returning from a war saw the birds running quick-footed across the lane and knew that he really was home again. The generations rolled on through times of kerosene lamps and cheap cotton to Ed Sullivan and soil-bank subsidies. And that same covey of bobwhites that had always seemed a part of the landscape still whistled in the long summer afternoons and hurtled across dead cornstalks that rattled in the winter breezes.

The hunters who looked for that covey and others in the fields nearby disciplined themselves never to shoot a covey below six birds. That number left plenty of seed for replenishment, so that every fall the coveys would again number fifteen to thirty birds, depending on how they had fared against predators.

Eventually, all that acreage moved out of our family. My visits to those coveys became less frequent as I necessarily turned toward education and then fields of commerce that were far away. But even during some marvelous quail-hunting days in other places, I often longed for return hunts to those intriguing coveys of the past. Would the swamp covey by the old pond still be up to their usual trick of flying into the field in the afternoon? Where would the singles from the peafield covey go now? Would the sundown covey still be there?

Finally, not long ago, the opportunity came for me to knock about a bit down in the home county. Several hunts with friends seemed as mere preludes to the long-awaited day when I got a chance to slip away alone to the old home grounds.

A soft rain had fallen during the night, but when I parked the truck by a thicket of pines just after sunrise, a stiff breeze had started tearing the overcast apart, and patches of blue were showing through the dullness. Shrugging into my bird vest, I ignored the shufflings and impatient whines that sounded from the dog box and stood a moment looking across a long soybean field that stretched toward a distant line of pines. I was mentally planning a route that would take me in a big circle to a dozen or so familiar coveys, then bring me to the sundown covey in the late evening. I unlatched the dog box, and the pointer, Mack, exploded from the truck and went through a routine of nervous preliminaries. I did the same, checking my bulging coat for shells, lunch and coffee. Then I clicked the double shut and stepped into the sedge alongside the field, calling: "All right, Mack. Look around!"

The pointer loped away in that deceptive, ground-eating gait that was his way of going. At age four, he had not exactly developed into the close worker I had been wanting. His predecessors who had run these fields in decades before were big-going speedsters suited to those times. Controlled burning and wide-roaming livestock kept the woodlands open then. Now most of the forests were so choked with brush and vines that wide-working dogs brought a legacy of frustration. Mack was easy to handle but tended to bend out too far from the gun unless checked back frequently. I really hated hearing myself say "Hunt close!" so often, but I hated even worse those agonizing slogging searches when he went on point in some dark corner of the swamp a quarter-mile from where I thought he'd been working.

The sun was bright on the sedge and pines now, and the air winy-crisp after the rain. Mack was a bouncing flash of white as he worked through the sedge and low pines. Once he started over the fence into the field, but I called him back. I wanted him to keep working down the edge. While the bean field seemed a tempting place to catch a breakfasting bevy, the cover bordering it offered much better chances—at least three to one, according to the quail-hunting education I had received here as a youngster. I could still imagine the sound of my grandfather's voice as he preached:

"Never mind all them picturebook covey rises in those magazines you read. It's only now and then you'll catch these old woods coveys in the open. Birds once had to range wide and root hard for their keep. Now all the work's done for 'em. Combines and cornpickers leave so much feed scattered in the field the birds can feed in a few minutes, then leg it back into the cover. That's where you want to work. First, if they haven't gone to feed, you're likely to find 'em. If they've walked into the field, the dog'll trail 'em out. If they've already been into the field and fed, you'll still find 'em. Only time you'll miss is when they've flown into the field and are still there."

I had seen this simple philosophy pay increasing dividends as the years wore on. As the cover became thicker and the coveys smarter, the clear covey shot had become a rare, treasured experience. To spend a lot of time working through the fields was to be a dreamer of the highest order.

Still in the cover, we rounded the end of the small field and headed up the other side. I was beginning to feel the bite of the day's first disappointment; Mack had picked up no scent at all. Where were they? This covey had always been easy to find. Maybe they had been shot out, I thought. Maybe the whole place has been shot out.

I decided to play out a hunch. I pulled down a rusty strand of fence and stepped out into the field. Mack leaped the wire and raced away at full gallop. Far downfield he turned into the wind and suddenly froze in one of the most dramatic points I've ever seen. I knew he was right on top of those birds, his body curved tautly, his tail arching. "Oh ho!" I said aloud. "So you beggars *did* fly to the field."

My strides lengthened and became hurried. I snapped the gun open and checked the shells in an unnecessary gesture of nervousness. Normally steady hands seemed to tremble a little and felt very thick and uncertain. My heartbeat was a thunderous throb at the base of my throat.

My tangled nerves and wire-taut reflexes scarcely felt the nudge of a thought that said, "Relax. You've done this before." The case of shakes I undergo every time I step up to a point makes it difficult to attach any importance to that idea. Covey-rise jitters are known to have only one cure: action.

On my next step, the earth seemed to explode. The air was

suddenly filled with blurry bits and pieces of speeding fragments, all boring toward the pines that loomed ahead. I found myself looking at one particular whirring form, and when the stock smacked against my face, the gun bucked angrily. The brown missile was unimpressed. He faded into the swamp, along with a skyful of surviving kinsmen. My loosely poked second shot failed to drop a tail-ender.

Mighty sorry gathering up of partridges, I thought, using the expression that was my uncle's favorite on the occasions when we struck out on a covey rise. "Sorry, boy," I called to Mack, who was busy vacuuming the grass in a futile search for downed birds.

My elders would have thought that bevy's maneuver of flying out to the field was the lowest trick in the book. But now the practice had become so typical among smart southern Bobs that it was hardly worth lamenting.

I called Mack away from his unrewarding retrieve and headed after those singles. The woods ahead looked clear enough for some choice shooting if I could keep Mack close.

Thirty minutes later I emerged from those woods a frustrated, angry man. My estimate that the birds had landed in the grassy, open pinelands was about two hundred yards wrong. Instead they had sailed on into one of the thickest, darkest sweet-gum swamps I've ever cursed a bird dog in. It took Mack all of fifteen seconds to get lost, and when I found him on point after ten minutes of searching I proceeded to put the first barrel into a gum tree and the second into a screen of titi bushes. Then the heebie-geebies really took over as I walked over two separate singles that jumped unannounced. Finally, Mack pointed again, but as I fought through the tearing clutches of briers and vines to get to him, I bumped another single, which I shot at without a glimmer of hope. That action caused Mack to take matters into his own hands and send the bird he was pointing vaulting away through the trees. Then followed a lot of unnecessary yelling, and we headed for the clear.

I should have known better. Single-bird hunting in that part of Georgia had become a sad business. Now I was discovering that my old hunting grounds were in the same shape as the rest of the county. If you were going to mess with singles, you had to wait for the right type of open woods. Most were just too thick to see a dog, much less a six-ounce bird. The day's shooting was certainly not going to follow the patterns of the past when it came to singles. I would have to wait until I got a bevy scattered in a better place.

We cut away from the field into a section of low moss-draped oak trees. Mack ranged ahead, working smartly. My frustrations of the first covey slipped away as I began considering the coming encounter with the next set of old friends. This covey, if they were still in business, would be composed of dark swamp birds that lived in the edge of the creek swamp but used this oak ridge to feed on acorns during early mornings and late afternoons. They were extremely hard to catch in the open, sometimes running for hundreds of yards in front of a dog on point. But what a sight they always made as they hurtled up among the moss-draped oaks on the lucky occasions when we did get them pinned nicely.

This oak ridge was fairly open, so I let Mack move on out a little bit. When he cut through one thickish cluster of trees and did not come out right away, I knew he had 'em.

Incredible I thought. *The first two coveys are still here, and we've worked 'em both.* Then the words turned into brass in my mouth as I eased up to the dog and past him. The thunderous rise I had been expecting failed to occur. I let Mack move on ahead to relocate. Catlike, he crept through the low grass for a few yards, then froze again. I moved out in front once more, and still nothing happened.

Then, suddenly I heard them. Several yards out front the dry leaves rustled under the flow of quick-moving feet. The covey was up to its old trick of legging it for the sanctuary of the swamp.

I hurried forward, crashing through the briers. Just ahead, the low cover gave way to a wall of sweetgum and cypress that marked the beginning of the swamp. Too late! I caught the sound of wings whirring. The birds had made the edge and were roaring off through the trees. They seemed to get up in groups of two and three. I caught an occasional glimpse of dim blurs through the screen of limbs and snapped a shot at one. Leaves and sticks showered down as Mack raced forward. Seconds later he emerged from the brush carrying a plump rooster bobwhite.

Had you seen me grinning over that bird, you might have thought I hadn't scored in five years. But the shot seemed mighty satisfying under the conditions. A few moments like this could make the day a lot more glorious than a coatful of birds ever could.

Now we followed an old lane that led down across the swamp and out beside a tremendous cornfield surrounded by pine and gallberry flats. I expected to find a couple of coveys here—and did, too, as the morning wore on in a succession of encounters with my old friends. A heart-warming double from a bevy Mack pinned along a fence row was followed by a succession of bewildering misses when we followed the singles into an open gallberry flat where I should have been able to score. Then we had the fun of unraveling a particularly difficult relocation problem when Mack picked up some hot scent in the corn but could not trail out to the birds. The edge of the field sloped down a grassy flat to an old pond with pine timber on the far side. I just knew those birds had flown across that pond to the woods to hole up for the day. When I took Mack over he made a beautiful point, standing just inside the woods. I wish I could always dope out a covey like that.

We spent the middle of the day stretched out on the grass on the pond dam. The sandwiches and coffee couldn't have tasted better. The sun was warm, and crows and doves flew against the blue sky. I thought about old hunts and old friends and couldn't have felt better.

In the afternoon we had a couple of interesting pieces of action, but failed to find some of my old neighbor coveys at home. My thoughts kept reaching ahead to the late-afternoon time when I would near the old now-deserted house by the lane and see the sundown covey again. Surely they would still be there. After all, we had been finding most of the old coveys. Who says you can't go home again? Who's afraid of you, Tom Wolfe?

The sun was dipping toward the pines and a sharp chill had come on when I skirted the last field and entered a stretch of open pine woods where I was counting on finding the covey of birds that I had carried in my mind all my life. Before I had gone fifty yards I came on something that shocked me as though I'd walked up on a ten-foot rattlesnake. A newly cut stake had been driven in the ground, and a red ribbon tied to the top of it. Farther on there was another, then another.

I had known that the new Savannah-Atlanta-Super-High-Speed-Interstate-Get-You-There-Quick-Highway was to pass through this general area. But surely, a couple of miles away. Not here. Not right here.

Gradually, my disbelief turned into anger. I felt like heading for the car right then and getting the hell out of there. Then suddenly three-shots boomed in the woods some distance ahead.

Well, it was apparent that the sundown covey was still around. But an intruder had found them. I decided to go on up and talk to whoever it was. Actually, he probably had as much right to be here as I did now. I couldn't believe he was a regular hunter on this land, though. The coveys I had been finding all day were too populous with birds to be gunned heavily.

I walked slowly through the pines for a few minutes without spotting the other hunter. Then his gun thudded again, this time from farther down in the swamp. He's after the singles now, I thought. I called in Mack and waited there opposite the swamp. The other fellow would have to come out this way.

During the next few minutes two more separate shots sounded. The sun sank lower, and the breeze blew harder in the pines. Finally, I heard the bushes shaking and a man came out of the cover. When Mack started barking he spotted me and headed my way. As he came up I saw that he was young, carried an automatic and wore no hunting coat. He had some quail by the legs in his left hand.

"Looks like you did some good," I said.

"Yea, I got six."

"Where's your dog?" I asked.

"Oh, I don't have a dog. I spotted a covey crossing the road down there by the lane. I had the gun in the truck, so I went after 'em. Got three when I flushed 'em and three more down in the branch. Tiny little covey, though. I don't think there were more than six when I first flushed 'em. I imagine people been framin' into this bunch all the time." My heart sank when he said that. I didn't know what to say. He paused a minute, looking at Mack. "That's a nice dog. He any good?"

"Fair," I said. "Maybe you shouldn't have done that."

"What?"

"Shoot a small covey on down that way."

"Don't mean nothing. There's always a covey of birds along here. Every year. But there won't be for long. Interstate's coming through."

"Yea," I said slowly. "I see it is."

"Well, I gotta run. That's sure a nice-looking dog, Mister. See you around."

I watched him walk away. Then I leaned back against a pine, listening to the swamp noises. The wings of a pair of roost-bound ducks whispered overhead. An owl tuned up down in the swamp. Somehow I kept thinking that I would hear some birds calling each other back into a covey. Perhaps two or three had slipped away unseen from the roadside.

The night pressed down. Trembling in the cold, I started for the truck. Orion wheeled overhead. I started thinking about some new places I wanted to try. But never again did I hear that flute-like call that had sounded for me from that swamp so many times before.

SHOFFSTALL

THE END OF A PERFECT DAY

Horace Lytle

Well, friend, the scattered singles are calling where-r-ye, where-r-ye, the dogs have come in to trot easily beside us in the gathering dusk, and it's time to turn the hunt homeward. I can't think of a better way to do it than with Horace Lytle's "The End of a Perfect Day." He had an eye for all the little things that make a simple hunt into one of big memories, and he never wrote better of those feelings than in this piece from Gun Dogs Afield.

Good luck to you, friend. Thanks for spending some time with my quail-hunting buddies. I trust you've enjoyed the pleasure of their company and will call upon them again many times over the years.

Your obedient servant,
LAMAR UNDERWOOD
Amwell, New Jersey
January, 1980

IT TAKES a heap o' things to make a hunt—just as Eddie Guest has said, "It takes a heap o' livin' to make a home." Good bird work by the dogs may be marred by poor shooting; just as good shooting may be marred by poor bird work on the part of the dogs. A hunt in territory that proves alive with game can be spoiled by an uncongenial companion; while the best partner in the world cannot, alone, make up for an almost total absence of birds. Anticipation itself plays an important part in any adventure—and so, as we said at the start, it takes a heap o' things to make a hunt.

Red-letter days are those that contain these "heap o' things" in abundance—or at least in such nice balance as to have produced a perfect picture on the whole—a picture that is destined to endure, being painted on memory's canvas in colors that cannot fade. It is of such a long-ago day that I am writing now. The artist's hand was firm and true—there being not even the slightest slip of the brush to mar the picture that is still painted in my mind. Perhaps, therefore, it may bear telling—although I warn you now to be prepared for nothing but a very simple story, in which a succession of big little things stand out in bold relief.

The invitation had been given me a month earlier, when I had met John Gregersen at a field trial. It was our first introduction, but immediately we had something in common. That is how it came about that the hunt was planned and the date set. This, then, marked the beginning of a period of pleasant anticipation, for some sixth sense told me that my new-found friend would know where to take us to those Indiana birds. Thus were the first preliminary strokes applied to the canvas, the background sketched in.

Then came the day before; and I could scarcely wait to leave the office and pack up the car for the drive of one hundred and thirty miles that night, to be ready for an early start next day. What a thrill, just to get ready for such a trip! But I was much younger then, and the thrills came more easily. For me they can never be lost—but would that some of youth's wild exuberance could be recaptured.

First the guns, shells, and duffel bag go into the car—then the dogs. I've always loved especially to take hunting trips with my dogs. No business clothes to bother about spoiling, and you can enjoy *such* intimacy. I've never been lonesome when the dogs are with me. The very minute we started at dusk that night to roll toward Indiana, the first touch of color for the picture was added to the canvas.

Driving at night can be two separate and distinct propositions. I detest it when one is constantly passing a stream of headlights. But on a lonely river road, with only a strip of water separating you from the hills of Kentucky, I dearly love the lure of it. A fascinating mystery was being painted into the picture with swift, sure strokes. With that winding river road I had long been familiar; but it never failed to prove ghostly at night. Many landmarks are then lost entirely. Others seem simply trying to deceive. The green eyes of a prowling cat by the roadside attract your attention just before you come to the big white bridge—and suddenly, as you lift your eyes, the faithful old structure itself seems as strange as a foreign land. You wouldn't trade such a ride at night for a hundred just like it in daylight! You are gripped by the spell of it and you dream as you drift along.

Finally, with a quickening pulse I saw ahead the lights of the little river town with its half as many people as used to live there in the "days when the river was king." The same old darky shuffled down the hotel steps to take my duffel bag, while I first fed the dogs and made them comfortable for the night. Then I went inside and engaged my room. But who can ever sleep the night before a hunt! Some can, I know—but I was not one of them then, so it was midnight when I quit reading and pulled down the sheets. And still I was up bright and early next morning, for this was the day when the truly vivid and lasting colors—the colors that would really make the picture—were to be applied to the canvas.

The minute I shook hands with John that day I just knew he would do. You know what I mean. I don't have to explain it. And we hadn't been in the field very long before my intuition was proved. My little red bitch threw her nose in the air, as she was running an old snake fence that bordered a woods, and merrily signaled with her tail that something was about to happen soon. With one spring she cleared the rapidly rotting rails, cast into the depth of heavy brush at the edge of the timber—and locked up her birds. It was the first bevy find of the day—and it came within ten minutes—and it was a peach. It was one of those finds that are earned—not merely "lucked into." You just knew she *had 'em*, even if you didn't know her. In the latter case, you'd bank your last dollar bill against a note for a cent for a year without interest. Head up—tail up—paw up—style—class! That's the kind of a point it was. And then it was that Gregersen said something that clinched forever my first impression of him.

"You step in an' shoot," he said. "I'd rather just watch her this time."

And so I did it, knowing he meant what he said. The birds got out at a bad angle, and the brush intervened, but I killed with the first barrel, missing with my second.

As the little red lady laid the bird in my hand, Gregersen said: "Well, that already makes a day of it for me, even if we don't find another bird. I've never seen an Irish setter handle game like that before, and I never expect to again. My hunt's a success if we quit right now."

And yet he hadn't pulled a trigger! That, gentlemen, is the kind of sportsman of which America could stand a good many more.

It was a great big bevy that might well be thinned out some, so we decided to see what we could do in the way of finding some singles. But even at the time of this story singles weren't what they used to be. No more dropping off in plain sight. They fly farther. More than that, they turn corners and double back these days. They're just as likely as not to be behind you while you are look-ing for them on ahead. They always make for cover; but the nearest cover is almost invariably used as merely a screen to hide the line of their flight from there. I am convinced that all this is very deliberate; and not at all accidental. It used to be merely a question of a quick, frantic getaway; now it seems to be a nicely planned program of *staying* away, as well. The birds are using their brains. All of which makes the plot of finding them more fas-cinating, even though it cuts down the kills. Which, perhaps, is just as well also. What we are—or should be—out for is a good time; not merely so many dead birds. No dead bird will ever fur-nish sport a second time to anyone.

Well, the birds of that first bevy took a line of flight straight through the woods, but angling to the right, as far as we could judge. As it later turned out, I am convinced that this angling to the right was simply to throw us off the track—and that they cut back sharp to the left after they had put a sufficient screen of trees between us and them. Anyhow, we picked up no singles on our first line of march. This line of march, however, carried us to our second bevy, which was found by King. It was in the deepest kind of a tangle, and one bird to each gun was the best we could do.

Again we started out, bent in pursuit of this new crop of singles. The cover was still heavy and dense, but finally King stopped short with his head high. He was always so high-headed that I was not prepared for what transpired in this instance. When I walked in ahead to put up the bird, it was not there—at least not on the ground. As I brushed by a bush, however, a quail left the limb on which it was perched, and I did not even get a shot. I think we put to flight all the singles of that second bevy, but we bagged nary a one. They kept getting out of the trees all around us. Not one bird was flushed from the ground. And neither of us was in position to shoot as the birds decided to leave their respective limbs. Which again only serves to prove that there is nothing monotonous in quail shooting, provided you're finding birds at all, for you'll be treated to an interesting variation of performance all day long. If variety is the spice of life, so also is it the spice of a hunt. You may bag fewer birds, but you'll have more fun—and you will more truly earn those you do get, which has a lot to do with inward satisfaction. For it is always true, I think, that the more nearly any sport approaches a fifty-fifty proposition, the keener the thrills it produces. The birds have taken matters into their own hands, so to speak, and are giving themselves a more even chance than formerly against their pursuers. That's only fair, and no sportsman will ever quarrel with fairness. A hunt with no evidence of game is a grave disappointment; but it is a rare good hunt indeed when there is something doing all the time, even though the game itself is doing its full share of it.

How King did hunt that day! It would have earned him a place in most field trials. But he was always a funny scamp. He would never strut his stuff just for a gallery; though he never failed for the gun. It was his mother, however, who found the third bevy. And this one was a little more kind to us, two birds falling to *each* gun on the rise. We worked them out a bit, when I saw a farmhouse in the distance and began to feel the pangs of hunger. I think John had planned to hunt right on through without eating, but the sincerity of my selling arguments won out, and we headed in the direction that my stomach urged. I think it was a wise measure, too, for the dollar each that we insisted on paying for a couple of eggs, bread, and coffee apiece simply carried the good farmer folk fairly off their feet. We were not merely asked to come again—but it was insisted upon until we promised, not a hard promise to extract from us.

One thing that added many beautiful shades of deep meaning to the picture of a perfect hunt that was being painted for us that day was the character of the country in which we were hunting. It was away from all beaten paths. I love to roam hidden fields well off the highways. A paved road which may parallel even a good quail field subtracts a subtle something from the keenness of one's satisfaction. There was nothing of that kind to detract on the occasion of which I write. The farmhouse at which we ate lunch was the only one we saw all day that was occupied. We worked cover adjacent to a couple of others that were deserted and appeared to have been in this state for quite some time. Such weed-grown spots make the best kind of cover for quail; and it was, in fact, in one of these that King found our fourth bevy. Again we each scored a *double* on the rise. The bag now wasn't so bad—although well below the legal limit—and I hated having to consult my watch, for I had decided to make the long drive back home that night.

"Let's find at least one more bevy, though, before we call it a day," was John's proposal—and you know the answer. There was no telling what this decision might do to the plans for getting home; but there is never a bit of use crossing your bridges before you come to them.

You know how it is in such cases. You may never find that last bevy that you've set as the final goal. If you've decided to stop at the sixth, the fifth find may not elude you; but when the fifth is to be the final—well, that's different again. Each dog had found two bevies, an even score. So, just to add a bit of spice, I suggested that we make a little wager as to which would find the fifth bevy—and I gave John his pick of the dogs. He chose King, so I laid my money on Smada Byrd. The stake was only a dollar a dog, but it keyed up our anticipation like the very mischief.

There was a dandy framework for the final setting of the picture. To the west was an angling woodsline, bordered by an old snake fence, as far as the eye could see. To the east stretched wide-open fields of ragweed, sedge grass, and little borders of broom corn. And we were heading into a pocket that pierced the woods. We could see King cutting up his cover swiftly ahead of us; but after a bit it dawned on me that I had not seen his mother for quite some time. Whenever that occurred, it was well to look her up—and she was always pretty sure to be there somewhere with her birds. So I began to swing back and toward the right, while John kept on in the opposite direction.

Pretty soon I heard him call "Point over here—King's got 'em!" And I hurried over.

Coming in from a different angle, I noticed the waning sunlight brightening a spot of red that was foreign to the cover, and some twenty feet ahead of where I saw King standing. I called John over and pointed it out to him. Without comment, he took a dollar from his pocket and handed it to me, saying:

"Our bet's on the bevy, an' this may be a single—so you take the shot, an' if it's a bevy you're already paid."

But I just knew it was a bevy and prepared to shoot accordingly. It was a nasty place to make a double—you'd have to beat two birds to the woods, and we were right at the very edge of it. A bevy it was—and they sure did duck for cover quickly! It was awfully hard to get on a bird, and it's foolish to shoot unless you do. Yet the first barrel produced no apparent effect. I kept this bird covered, giving up all thought of the much coveted double. The second barrel produced a cloud of feathers, but I still felt sure the bird had kept on going—which fact John confirmed, yet I knew it had been hard hit.

We climbed over the rotting rails and into the woods. I was bound to find that bird and needed it to make the even number I had sort of pledged myself to take home. Besides, I conceive it to be every hunter's solemn duty to seek until he shall find every possible piece of game that is known to be hard hit. Suddenly we heard one of the dogs plunge into a pile of brush. It sounded as though a bird had been flushed—and John so expressed his fears and his regret. But I mighty well knew better, for those dogs never did that. I felt I knew what had occurred.

"The little bitch has the bird!" I said, "and she'll be here with it in a minute."

Just then we saw her coming, and it proved as I had spoken. She handed it to me very carefully, for the bird was still alive, but I quickly pulled its head and gave it to her as a well-earned reward.

"That's the first false move she's made all day," said my companion, "but she oughtn't to have done that, even though she did catch the bird."

"Ought not to have done what?" I asked.

"Jump in on her point an' catch it."

"You're all wrong," I told him. "That's the bird I hit a minute ago—and she knew it. She'll never jump in on an unhit bird, but she knows the difference between such and a cripple. That's one of the things that make her such an excellent retriever."

"Let me see that bird," said John.

I gave it to him and watched him begin to pull back the feathers. "You're right, by Golly!" he said. "Here's the marks." And, as he handed that last bird back to me, the expression on his face told me, without words being necessary, that for him, too, it marked the end of a perfect day.

For me, there still lay ahead the long night drive back home. At times I had to pinch myself to keep awake—but even this added to the eeriness of it all and helped to shroud otherwise familiar landmarks in a fascinating sort of mystery and give them an interesting strangeness. Through this framework, the picture of the hunt itself still stands out clearly and in bold relief. And it is just such pleasing pictures that it is a hunter's happiness to carry around with him in memory down through the years.

John Gregersen wasn't the only person who picked King to beat his more famous mother. Among many such others, Ted Cottrell once had the same idea in Alabama. And I'm only happily proud to admit that I saw King do just that more than once in the course of a hunt. But she'd lay it all over him—as she did also to many others—when it came to competition. Just as she won me John's dollar when I backed her to make our last find that day. And as she won Ted over, down in Alabama, when we ran her against the Triple National Champion, Feagin's Mohawk Pal—on his own home training grounds. She was always at her best when the chips were down—and she seemed to know when that was! But if King had had that same sixth sense—and had he responded to its messages as she did—then I must admit Smada Byrd might have met her match in her own son. Perhaps, even her master.

Yes, dogs are as individual in their traits as we mere humans ever are in ours.

One Saturday afternoon not long ago, I was faced with the task—not unpleasant, of course—of getting out my Gun Dog copy for *Field & Stream*. But thoughts of what to write about just wouldn't come. And the harder I tried to think of something worth saying, the further away I seemed to be drifting. With my mind a blank—perhaps as usual!—there was nothing to do but give up. So I drove over to watch a young friend play tennis.

But his doubles partner was late, so we talked till he came. And the conversation soon drifted to the profits from successful newspaper syndicating. This subject was prompted by the fact that his uncle had recently become a syndicated columnist.

"Yes, and think what a snap Will Rogers had of it," Rowan said. "Why he only wrote just a few words—and look what he got for it!"

"But it would be still easier to be in Grantland Rice's shoes," I told him. "It isn't the number of words—they're not hard after you get started. It's the start that's so tough—*what* to write the words *about*. The calendar of sports keeps Rice constantly supplied. Oversupplied, most likely. But I'll bet Rogers was perpetually worried and wondering what to write—and what about—in his few words. And, once you get going, it's harder to say much in a few words, than to say less in many."

"Well, I don't know 'bout that." Rowan was doubtful.

"Take me right now," I said. "I ought to be home writing something about dogs—but I swear I can't think what to say about what."

Rowan thought a moment. Then he said: "Well, I'll tell you what you might tell *me*. It's pretty generally agreed that the best way to stanch a dog is to handle and 'work with him' on point. But no one's ever told me yet how to reach him, before he's stanched, so as to get your hands on him. How about answering that one for me?"

"Thanks!" I said. "Now run on to your tennis. I'll go back home and write you the best answer I can. You've given me a lift on the job—but you've spoiled my fun watching your game."

And because the point raised calls for an answer worth passing on, this seems both a good time and place to do just that. But first let me again remind one and all that there can be no set rule to fit all cases.

Years ago I had a pointer bitch that proved one kind of exception to the rule. We need but to mention her. She pointed stanchly, at ten months of age, the first covey of quail I ever knew of her smelling. Furthermore—wonder of wonders!—she was even steady at flush. She never really needed any training. Merely a case of practice making perfect. And we gave her plenty of practice. No problem here of getting up to her to "handle." You may never have one just like this—I probably won't ever again—but this reference to Spot does serve to show the possible individuality of type. Thus she gives us one example. Miss Illsley pointed her first birds stanchly, but she wasn't otherwise as steady as Spot—until trained.

Mention of Spot does remind me, though, that the first bird dog I ever owned was a Gordon setter that was also stanch to the first birds I ever knew of him handling. But that was almost fifty years ago, when dogs may have had somewhat more point and less run in their make-up. So this example means less today, since it's not modern. I think Rowan had reference to dogs with more run, and less natural pointing desire—so we'll come to that kind. It's worth while first, however, to realize that there still are dogs you can get to on point without problem. So *one* answer to Rowan's question may be simply to get hold of that kind.

The first dog I ever fully finished myself was a young setter bitch. I almost got to thinking she never would point. In fact, I even came to believe she might not—and was pretty discouraged. But an experienced old hunter kept urging me on. "Don't you give up," he'd say. "Just keep on working her an' some day, I don't know when—but sure as the sun sets—she'll lock up that first point. An' when she does, you'll agree it's been worth the waiting."

And one day she did! It was a single, and she had it pinned tight. As we were "in singles" at the time, I was close to her. Her attitude was such that I believe she'd have held it a long while, even if I hadn't been close. And had she happened to have made this same find way off where I might not have seen and got to her, it is my firm conviction that it would have started her on the idea of pointing—so that, in any case, it would not have been very long before she would have found and pointed another when the chance for me to reach and stanch her might have been good.

On the other hand, though, the dog you're trying to teach to point stanchly may be of that fortunately rarer type—brimful of eagerness to run and hunt, but little to point. This type may prove a tartar—and don't I know! I know because I had and worried about such a one for the better part of five years before she finally "came down to it." But she did that of her own accord—after I'd given up hope. Which at least shows that most of them will—if you'll wait. She was one of the best, while she lasted. But it had taken her so long to *start* pointing that happy days were naturally fewer than I wish they'd been. Especially as hers was too short a life anyhow.

Now, of course, there are many things that might be said in answer to the question before us, pertaining to this type. In the first place, you can keep the dog with you on a long lead and let a trained dog hunt for and find birds. Then you can let the pupil go up to back—but keep hold of the lead for control. Thus you can get to the dog to soothe and work with him to your heart's content and the dog's great benefit. A professional trainer would either do it this way, or else have an assistant to help round up a truant pupil and bring him up to work with when an old trained dog finds game. That's about the whole story. It nets down to this: if training a dog that will cock up on point, given time, there's not much to it but to give him the time that it takes. But, if you have a "problem child," you've got to be governed accordingly.

You can't turn such a dog loose time after time and just hope for the best. Such mere hope isn't a good enough gamble. And you can't successfully work such a dog with two or three others. He should be worked either alone, or with just one other steady old dog, to find game and serve as sort of assistant teacher. And, no matter how much he might welcome a run, or even need it, I can conceive of a certain type of problem child that should never be trusted with freedom in the field until either stanched—or discarded.

There's something else that might be suggested—just the opposite of what I've been preaching. What's been said so far applies to half-hour or hour training periods out of season. If it's the open season—and if you can be free to hunt every day—and if you think enough of "reaching" the dog not to mind too much if some of your hunting is spoiled—and *if* you're in country with plenty of game, try this plan: Hunt the dog all day, every day, till he's really hunted down. You can get to him then! And a tired dog will often point where a fresh dog wouldn't. The tired dog welcomes the rest. In many ways this is your very best bet. But it's important that the tired dog finds game and sees you bag it *because* he has found, pointed, and held it. Thus he associates the connection between his proper performance and your accomplishment. But this plan depends on plenty of game. Merely tiring the dog to no purpose gets you nowwhere.

Dogs that don't take kindly or quickly to pointing may be too long delayed in getting the idea of it all. They don't understand either what's wanted—or why. The tired dog that points and sees his work consummated by your kill is thus given the idea. And you'd be surprised how often that's all it takes! I set a great deal of store by a dog *wanting* to do the right thing. But he can't—unless or until he *knows what right is.* Therefore, your job is somehow to make understanding of his job clear to him. And, when that's done, if he willfully still doesn't respond, you don't want advice—you want another dog.

Finally, in training and stanching a dog—and getting to him—you need to be favored by fortune. In training, as in golf or on the football field, there's a lot in "getting the breaks." If a young wide dog never finds and points close enough for you to get to him, you're unlucky. If he finds close to you and holds, under command, long enough for you to get your hands on him, you're favored by fortune. So wish yourself luck.

And may you, too, have many fine endings of many perfect days afield with your gun and dogs.